# The Vulgate of Mark with the Synoptic Parallels

DALE A. GROTE

Bolchazy-Carducci Publishers, Inc.
Mundelein, Illinois USA

*Editor:* Laurel Draper
*Contributing Editor:* Bridget Dean, Connor Hart
*Design & Layout:* Adam Phillip Velez
*Maps:* Mapping Specialists
*Cover Graphic:* Portraits of Mark, Matthew, and Luke from Byazntine Gospel Book, The J. Paul Getty Museum, Ms. 65 (Getty Museum) (Public Domain)

**The Vulgate of Mark with the Synoptic Parallels**

Dale A. Grote



**Bolchazy-Carducci Publishers, Inc.**
1570 Baskin Road
Mundelein, Illinois 60060
www.bolchazy.com

Printed in the United States of America
**2016**
by United Graphics

ISBN 978-0-86516-835-0

---

Library of Congress Cataloging-in-Publication Data

Names: Grote, Dale A., editor.
Title: The vulgate of Mark with the Synoptic parallels / Dale A. Grote.
Other titles: Bible. Mark. | Bible. Luke. 2016. | Bible. Matthew. 2016.
Description: Mundelein, Illinois, USA : Bolchazy-Carducci Publishers, Inc., 2016. | Includes bibliographical references. | Latin text of Mark with parallel passages from Matthew and Luke. The Latin text of each letter is accompanied by vocabulary and notes.
Identifiers: LCCN 2016021080 | ISBN 9780865168350 (pbk. : alk. paper)
Subjects: LCSH: Bible. Mark.
Classification: LCC BS2582 .G76 2016 | DDC 226.3/047--dc23 LC record available at https://lccn.loc.gov/2016021080

# Contents



## The Vulgate of Mark

# Preface

The book you're holding isn't the product of a carefully thought-out plan that was methodically implemented over the years. Instead it's the outcome of the diverse influences, accidental experiences, and various objectives that typically characterize a long career in academia.

As a newly minted PhD in Classical Languages with a specialty in Sophocles, I found myself assigned to teach large survey courses in Western religious thought, something I was wholly unqualified to do. The extent of my training in the area was a slap on the back and the exhortation, "You'll do fine." It was the paradigmatic nightmare all teachers have, where you suddenly find yourself at a podium in front of a large audience with no idea what you're supposed to say or even what the class is about. (In my version of the nightmare I'm not wearing shoes for some reason.) But this was no dream. It was real life.

I approached my problem with a classicist's bias for primary documents and made the sacred texts the only assigned readings on the syllabus. The agenda for the classes was to read from the Old Testament, the New Testament, and the Koran with fresh eyes, make our own observations, and draw our own conclusions. It was in the two years of teaching this class that I discovered the complexity and historical layers of the Old Testament and the Gospel accounts in the New Testament. We studied the Wellhausen hypothesis that tries to untangle the sources that were blended into the first books of the Old Testament. We learned about the area of study known as the Synoptic Problem that originates in the undeniable literary interdependence of the first three Gospels. In our class discussion we found ourselves practicing Redaction Criticism, which tries to deduce consistent editorial policies that underlie both the similarities and differences in the three Synoptic Gospels. I'll come back to all this later because at this point in the story, I became a tenure-track, tenure-bound classics professor.

The institution where I've spent my career prides itself on providing top-quality, preprofessional training. As a consequence, the humanities in general fit in the mix of requirements as service classes, and language study in particular is largely justified as a résumé enhancer. The language requirement varied over the years from four semesters for all to none for anyone, and finally stabilizing as none for some, two semesters for many, and three for a few. It's a long and interesting story, but the practical outcome is easy to summarize: I had become in the eyes of my students a fussy old pedant. Here's why.

By training, we classicists treat elementary language training as the foundation for more advanced reading in real authors, who are worthy of our time and respect. We force-march our students through grammar and essential vocabulary in the first several semesters with the promise that their suffering will eventually be rewarded. But what happens when only a vanishing fraction of our students, if any at all, go beyond the first two or three semesters?

To me, the answer came in a sudden cold shiver about ten years ago in the middle of a third-semester class. After I had filled two boards with an exquisitely engineered presentation of the sequence of moods, I had an epiphany. In a terrifying instant I saw in my students' faces that they couldn't care less. They'd had it up to here with grammar and syntax, and I saw myself as they must have seen me. I was nothing more than a pitiable, harmless old drudge. They were kind enough to tolerate me until the end of the term, but I was a goofy old uncle, who chatters at length about things that no one's interested in over Thanksgiving dinner. They knew they weren't going on to study more, and they just wanted to find a polite way out of a one-sided conversation.

After wasting several self-absorbed months cursing modernity for making the world unsafe for ancient Greek and Latin, I eventually hit upon a more useful line of thought. If I had only a limited time with my students, I had to get something into their hands they'd find interesting and would give them a sense of accomplishment after their two semesters of Latin or Greek. This brings us back to the Gospels.

Everyone acknowledges that the Greek and Latin of the New Testament are comparatively easy to read. The message may be complex, but beginning and intermediate students won't be researching forms and looking up every other word to get through a sentence. We can also stipulate that every student will have an opinion one way or another about the Jesus story, even if their opinions may not be especially well informed. But no one in the room will fail to have something to say about it. This can't be said of Xenophon, Caesar, Cicero, even Plato or any of the other canonical third-semester authors in the standard (i.e., mid-twentieth century) curriculum. Rare indeed is the student who begins Greek with a passionate desire to prove that Sophocles is a better dramaturge than Euripides (he is, by the way), or submits to the rigor of Latin because she wants to be able to defend the reputation of Cato the Elder. So to this degree, the Gospels fit nicely into the modern language curriculum on two counts: The language is accessible, a suitable payoff for two semesters of study (or two years at the high school level), and the subject is of inherent interest and will inspire (or incite) classroom discussion. But there were challenges.

When I first began adding biblical texts to the third-semester curriculum, there was some pushback. One above-average Latin student dropped third-semester Latin when she saw the syllabus; she didn't want to read "Bible stories" and claimed she knew "all that stuff already." I tried to explain the difference between the historical/textual approach we'd be using and the pastoral/doxological approach she might have been thinking about, but to no avail. Other students as well were suspicious of my motives and didn't respond well at first. But I plowed ahead undaunted. It seemed to me that the choice was between boring my students or provoking them. I didn't have to think very hard about that one. If inspiring a student isn't an option, irritating him is a good stand-in. I chose provocation over boredom.

Even students from religious backgrounds found the approach challenging at times. Most of them were surprised at how much the Gospel of Mark *didn't* square with their expectations. They were also unaware of the subtle differences in the Synoptics even when narrating the same event. I hoped that these students would come away from the experience with an appreciation of the rich and fascinating complexities of the texts that underlie their faith.

I found, however, that there was nothing on the market on the Vulgate of Mark designed for classroom use. I resorted to handouts and printouts for the first several years, starting with the text of Mark and gradually matching it with the parallels from Matthew and Luke and adding historical and supplemental grammatical notes and a running vocabulary. The body of material grew and eventually stabilized into a book-length manuscript. That in a nutshell is the natural history of the book you're now holding. The text assumes, if not the validity, then at least the usefulness of the priority of Mark as the structural basis of the readings. All this is more fully explained in the book's introduction.

Before I let you go, there are some people I need to acquaint you with who've inspired me over the years to pursue this project and finish it. First to the students at Berea College in Berea, Kentucky, where I was fortunate enough to start my career as a two-year visiting assistant professor of classics, and where I first formulated the idea of using the Gospel of Mark as the first "real" author in their language curriculum. Thence to the Harvey Center for Family Learning, an online homeschooling network that graciously allowed me to try out the text with its exceptionally talented students in a semeter-long third-semester Latin class. From there the text passed to a private group of friends I've been tutoring in both Greek and Latin online for many years now. They not only encouraged me along the way but also proofed the final draft for me, purgining it of a not insignificant number of errors that might have slipped into the book. I hope they won't mind if I cite them by name: Tony Bell in Alaska, Michael Hopkins in North Carolina, and Jenny and Elizabeth Vo-Phamhi in California. And finally to my father, who has recently developed an active interest in all things classical and has accumulated an impressive video library from the Teaching Company. This has given me the invaluable opportunity to have my own ideas leavened by his extraordinary mind.

Finally, my heartfelt thanks to Laurel Draper of Bolchazy-Carducci, who, with unimaginable talent and skill, turned a box of files into a book, and to Bridget Dean, also at Bolchazy-Carducci, who encouraged me to keep at it, even when the complexity of the project seemed impossibly overwhelming.

Dale Grote
1 April 2016

# Introduction

## *Mark and His Gospel*

What we "know" about the Gospel of Mark in the strict sense of the word is interesting but limited, and well short of what we wish we knew. Mark is the name attached to the second of the four canonical Gospels of the New Testament. It's the shortest and lacks much of the material contained in the other three. We could go on and count words, tally up the types of grammatical constructions that appear in the text, and tabulate the textual variations of key passages. These are the kinds of things we can say we "know" about the Gospel of Mark. Everything else beyond these straightforward facts and others like them is alloyed with some amount conjecture. We don't know, for example, when Mark was first written, where it was composed, by whom, for what reason, or from what materials. We can't even say with certainty who the "Mark" in the title is supposed to be.

There is no Mark ever mentioned in any of the four Gospels. That shouldn't come as much of a surprise. There's no Luke in the Gospels either. Even Matthew (a.k.a. Levi), who's the supposed author of the first Gospel, is a minor figure among Jesus's disciples and drops out of the story nearly altogether after Jesus's death. It may be that this Mark is the John Mark mentioned in Acts, where he's a companion of Paul for a brief time, but that's far from certain.

A very important ancient source, however, from the third century CE gives us some tantalizing information about Mark and how the Gospel of Mark was composed. The historian Eusebius wrote, among other things, a history of the early church, and he has this to say:

> Concerning Mark, who wrote the gospel, Papias [circa 70–163 CE] put it this way: "And the Elder also said this: 'Mark was the interpreter [*hermēneutēs*] of Peter and he wrote down accurately, but not in order, the things which were spoken or done by our Lord, as much as he remembered. For he neither heard the Lord nor followed him. But later, as I said, he followed Peter, who provided instruction according to what was needed, but so not as to make an orderly account of the Lord's sayings. So Mark did not err in anything in writing some things this way, that is, as he remembered them. For he was attentive to one thing: not to leave out anything that he heard or to make any false statements in them." So this is what Papias said about Mark. (*Ecclesiastical History*, 3.39.14–16)

Eusebius is quoting from an earlier source, Papias, who we have reason to believe lived in the first half of the second century CE (70–168). Papias, in turn, is quoting someone he calls the "Elder," a figure about whom we know very little. If we assume, however, that the "Elder" was older than Papias—which seems to be a reasonable conjecture—then this puts the Elder in the generation before Papias. That takes us to the time when some of the first disciples were still alive. What we potentially have, then, is a very early source of information about the Gospel of Mark, perhaps one that was contemporary with the author himself. This merits serious attention.

This "Elder" informed Papias that Mark never met Jesus but was a companion of the disciple Peter, one of the three leaders of the early church and one of the original twelve disciples of Jesus. Mark followed him on his missionary journeys and served as his *hermēneutēs*, a Greek word that often means "translator." Did Peter need a translator? From what we know about Peter, it's entirely likely, indeed probable, that he spoke only Aramaic, the local language of his homeland in Galilee. He would have been unable, consequently, to preach in his own words to his intended Greek-speaking audiences when he took his message outside of the province of Palestine. He would have needed a translator.

If Peter is the source for Mark's Gospel, we need to imagine what Peter was trying to communicate about Jesus and how he would have gone about it. As a preacher, he wouldn't have been teaching history classes on the life and times of Jesus, any more than a modern preacher does. He was preaching the essence of Jesus's life and mission, and the essence of this news is easy to summarize: Jesus came to announce that the end of time as promised by the Old Testament prophets was at hand and that everyone hoping for everlasting life in the coming Kingdom of God should repent and be baptized. There's more to it than that, obviously, but reduced to its barest outline this is his message, or *kerygma* in Greek.

None of this was entirely new to anyone. There had been many prophets before, during and even after Jesus's life who'd been saying pretty much the same thing. What's so special about Jesus? What made this call different in the minds of his followers was that Jesus performed many miracles that were witnessed by hundreds of people: He healed people of various afflictions, cast out demons, brought a young girl back from the dead, walked on water, feed thousands of people from virtually nothing, and more. At one time he was even physically transfigured in the presence of three of his closest followers. He courageously revealed that he was in fact the Messiah (in Mark, at least), when he knew that it would lead to his suffering and death. Most importantly of all, his followers say that he was physically resurrected from the dead after his crucifixion at the hands of the Romans. So in addition to communicating the essential meaning of Jesus's teachings, Peter would surely have wanted to confirm the uniqueness of Jesus by recalling the miraculous events that were a part of his life. So Peter's sermons would have been party theological and, of necessity, partly historical. Let's return to Eusebius and the testimony of the Elder.

The Elder says that Peter never tried to give an orderly and comprehensive account of Jesus's life and his teachings, and that makes perfect sense. No modern-day preacher ever does that either. Instead, Peter no doubt would have used incidents in Jesus's life to illustrate the general point he was making in the course of his sermon. We can imagine that none of the sermons Peter gave was ever repeated verbatim on other occasions. Peter probably approached an audience or a setting with a general outline of what he wanted to say, but he never memorized a set speech that he delivered again and again, and he never told everything he knew about Jesus in one sitting.

This means that over the years Mark would have heard Peter's different sermons many times. He would have gotten to know very well the story of Jesus's trial, crucifixion, and resurrection, which probably made up the bulk of any of Peter's addresses. Mark would have heard scattered references to Jesus's life and his times with the disciples as well as the many miracles he performed. But never once would Mark have hear the story told from the beginning to the end, with all the events precisely in order, at any one time. When the time came for him to write his Gospel, he would have had to sort through this mass of material and organize it in some way. The Elder gives

Mark a high grade for getting the content of each episode correct, though he's not so generous with how Mark arranged them. To be fair, we don't know what the Elder's objections are and what he meant by "in order." It's possible that he meant some kind of thematic organization and not a chronological one, for Mark's Gospel does follow Jesus's life in a way that is temporally and geographically consistent. Jesus begins modestly in and around the region of Galilee, gradually expanding outward until he arrives at Jerusalem where he is crucified. Aside from a few minor glitches here and there, Mark's account of Jesus's travels are easy to plot out on a map and they make sense geographically.

The Elder's criticism notwithstanding, the Gospel of Mark exhibits precisely the characteristics we'd expect to see based on Mark's source in Peter's sermons.

Anyone reading several contiguous passages from Mark will notice that the first nine chapters or so are made up of short scenes with Jesus as the central figure. Jesus confronts the religious authorities, performs a miracle, cures a sick person, casts out demons, delivers a parable, and so on. These little scenes are strung together with transitional expressions, such as "and then," "straightway," as well as brief editorial comments from Mark to move the setting from one location to another. These little vignettes have all the appearance of having being been written down on scraps of paper—a notecard, if you will—and then pasted together to make a longer narrative. Scholars call these short scenes "pericopes" (peh RI koh pees), or a "pericope" in the singular. The word is Greek for "excerpt" and literally means "cut around" or "a cutout." We can imagine that over the years Mark had assembled a collection of several slips of paper with different short episodes on each one. When he sat down to write his account, he would have sorted through these pericopes and organized a chronology of Jesus's life as best he could. Mark perhaps was indifferent as to the question whether the miracle of walking on water preceded or came after the miracle of the fish and loafs; whether Jesus's parable about the sower came before the parable of the mustard seed or after it; and so on. He was primarily concerned, as the Elder said, of getting each episode right, regardless of where it actually fit into the true chronology.

To sum up, the evidence that Eusebius has from Papias, who in turn is relying on the Elder, is consistent with the text of the Gospel as we now have it. Mark got the material for his Gospel from the preaching of Peter and sorted it out as best he could. What then becomes of Mark's Gospel once it's a written document?

## *The Interconnectedness of the First Three Gospels*

Reading at length from the first three Gospels (Matthew, Mark, and Luke) produces a repeated experience of déjà vu. In many places, they are strikingly similar, almost identical. We'll look at just one example. Mark records the calling of Levi at 2:13–17, an episode that is repeated by Matthew at 9:9–13 and Luke 5:27–32. The similarities are visually obvious when the three accounts are set next to each other in parallel columns and read horizontally (my translations):

| **Mark (2:13–17)** | **Matthew (9:9–13)** | **Luke (5:27–32)** |
|---|---|---|
| **13** Jesus went out again toward the sea. The whole crowd gathered around him, and he preached to them. | | |
| **14** And while he was passing by, he saw Levi, the son of Alphaeus, sitting at a tax table, and he said to him, "Follow me." And standing up, he followed him. | **9** And when he was passing through there, he saw a man sitting at a tax table, Matthew by name, and he said to him, "Follow me." And standing up, he followed him. | **27** And after this he left and saw a publican, Levi by name, sitting at a tax table, and he said to him, "Follow me." **28** And leaving everything behind, standing up he followed him. |
| **15** And it happened when he was sitting at dinner at that man's house, many publicans and sinners were sitting together with Jesus and his students. For there were many people and they followed him. | **10** And it happened when he was sitting at dinner at home, behold: many publicans and sinners, coming in, were sitting together with Jesus and his students. | **29** And it happened that Levi had a big feast for him at his home. And there was a big crowd of publicans and others, who were sitting at the table with them. |

| | | |
|---|---|---|
| **16** And the scribes of [some] Pharisees, seeing that he was eating with sinners and publicans, said to his students, "Why does he eat with publicans and sinners?" | **11** And [some] Pharisees, looking on, said to his students, "Why does your teacher eat with publicans and sinners?" | **30** And [some] Pharisees and their scribes were complaining to his students, saying, "Why do you eat and drink with the publicans and sinners?" |
| **17** And Jesus, this being heard, said to them, "It is not necessary that the healthy have a doctor, but those who are doing poorly. I haven't come to call the righteous but sinners." | **12** But hearing, he said, "There is no need for a doctor for the healthy, but for those doing poorly. **13** Go on and know what this is: 'I want compassion and not sacrifice.' For I haven't come to call the righteous but sinners." | **31** And responding, Jesus said to them, "Those who are well don't need a doctor but those who are doing poorly. **32** I haven't come to call the righteous to repent but sinners." |

An overview like this is called a "synopsis," from the Greek word that means "seeing together." This is why these three Gospels are referred to as the "Synoptic Gospels," or just the "Synoptics."

The questions associated with this undeniable interconnectedness of the Synoptics make up what is known as the "Synoptic Problem." How did it come about? An easy answer to the question is that since they're all talking about the same events, it's only natural that Synoptics would be very similar. But this doesn't take into account why the Synoptics aren't even more similar. For example, Mark's Gospel lacks the famous nativity accounts and the complex genealogies that begin the other two Synoptics. It has only a fraction of the Old Testament references. Even more surprisingly it doesn't report the famed "Beatitudes" and ends before Jesus's visits with his disciples after the resurrection.

After 150 years of research and careful study, a consensus view has emerged that Mark was the first Gospel to be written, sometime between 60 and 70 CE. It was available to the authors of Matthew and Luke, who used it about twenty years later as the historical framework—the "first draft," so to speak—of their Gospels. To the stock of material they got from Mark, Matthew and Luke added other texts that were not available to Mark, including, among other things, a collection of Jesus's sayings, which is called "Q" (an abbreviation for the German word for "source," *Quelle*). Finally, Matthew and Luke supplemented all this—Mark and Q—with information each of them had independently of one another. This can get to be extremely complicated fast, but the basic flow of narratives and texts into the three Synoptics can be mapped out like this:

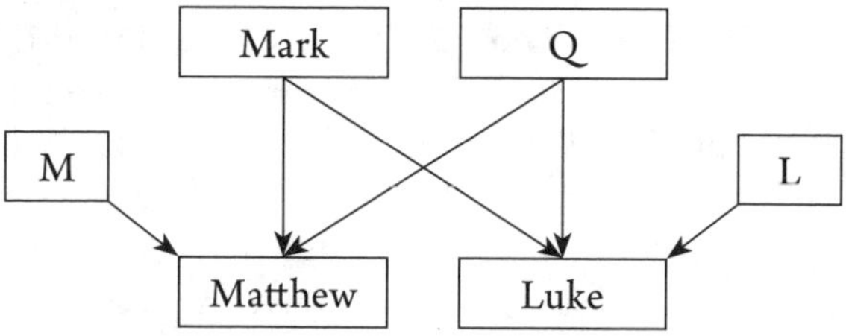


Starting at the top, Mark and Q both flowed independently into Matthew and Luke. (Remember, Mark did not have Q.) Then Matthew added some material only he had, which is represented by the letter "M" off to the left. Similarly, material exclusive to Luke is represented by the letter "L" off to the right. This thesis is known as the "Four Document Hypothesis," inasmuch as Matthew and Luke demonstrate the existence of four documentary sources:

1. Mark (used by both Matthew and Luke)
2. Q (used by both Matthew and Luke)
3. M (used only by Matthew)
4. L (used only by Luke)

So much for why the three Synoptics have so much in common. A closer inspection, however, shows that neither Matthew nor Luke reproduced the material they got from Mark verbatim. They change an expression here, add an editorial comment there, and even cut out entirely material that was in Mark. Some of the changes can be explained simply as an effort to rephrase or recast Mark's rough style. For example, in one scene Jesus tells Simon and Andrew that if they follow him, he will make them fishermen of men. Literally, this is what Mark wrote (1:17): "Come after me, and I will make it that you become fishermen of men." We can understand what he means, but it's a somewhat clumsy way of putting it. Matthew smooths the original over at 4:19 in his Gospel: "Come after me, and I will make you fisherman of men." Finally Luke writes simply at 5:10: "From this time on you will be catching men." It doesn't seem that there is much more going on in Matthew and Luke than a straightforward effort to make the language more readable.

The majority of the pericopes in Mark have parallels in both Matthew and Luke. In some instances there is a parallel in Matthew but not in Luke, or vice versa, and in other instances the pericope is unique to Mark. From Mark 6:45 to 8:27, there are no parallel passages in Luke. This is called Luke's Great Omission. One explanation for this silence is that he was working from a copy of Mark that didn't include this section. Scholars speak of an Ur-Mark, a hypothetical earlier version of the Mark we now have. To this text more material was added at different times and in different places until finally the Mark we now have was stabalized in the tradition. It's possible, if an Ur-Mark existed, that Matthew and Luke had different versions of the text. This would explain why Matthew includes parallels to Mark 6:45–8:27 and Luke does not. But this is all very contentious, and theoretically there may have been many Ur-Marks. Whatever we make of the theory of Ur-Marks, Luke's Great Omission is one of the great mysteries in the Synoptic Problem.

Sometimes, however, the changes reveal substantive interpretative departures from the original. For instance, in one episode in Mark, Jesus returns to his hometown, where the local people, including his family, think he's gone mad. Because of their disbelief, Jesus is incapable of performing any major miracles: Mark 6:5: "And he could not make any miracles there, except for curing a few sick people by putting his hands on them." That's what Mark says. Jesus *could not* perform miracles. Matthew reworks this line as follows (13:58): "And he didn't perform many miracles there because of their disbelief." He changes Mark's "could not" to "did not." This eliminates the suggestion that Jesus's power was limited in any way by the people around him. It's not that he couldn't perform miracles; he simply chose not to. Luke goes further by leaving out Mark's comment altogether.

Collecting the parallel accounts in the Synoptics and taking note of how they differ are the first steps to asking an even more interesting question. Is there a detectable pattern to this interpretive editing? Can we uncover a consistent rationale that explains why Matthew makes the changes he does? Why Luke makes the changes he does?

The kind of inquiry—the search for an editorial policy, so to speak—is called "Redaction Criticism." "Redaction" comes from the French word *redaction,* which simply means "editing." So "Redaction Criticism" means making judgments based on the editing process we see in Matthew and Luke. It forms a major part of all academic and pastoral training in New Testament studies, and it also underlies the structure, nature, and pedagogy of this book.

## *Redaction Criticism as Used in This Book*

The main section of this book is the pericopes that make up the Gospel of Mark, each followed directly by the parallel passages from Matthew and Luke. On the one hand, this builds into the daily classroom routine the process of review. After translating the passage from Mark, the parallel accounts in Matthew and Luke will be so similar that they will nearly function as a review of Mark. Luke may rewrite an ablative absolute in Mark as a subordinate clause and Matthew may change a relative clause into a participial expression. It should be interesting for students to see how real authors find ways to express similar ideas in different ways. In addition to providing more insight into the structure and different styles of Latin, having the opportunity to read parallel passages also invites students into the discipline of redaction criticism and to start thinking like scholars. What's the effect of the changes Luke and Matthew make to the material they got from Mark? Is there a discernible reason? Are the changes merely stylistic or do they reveal something deeper?

I have provided grammatical and historical notes on each of the pericopes, but their purpose is rather narrow. It's not to encourage a particular understanding. It's to clear the way of grammatical questions likely to consume unacceptable amounts of classroom time and to suggest lines of inquiry. They are historical and textual only, and not pastoral.

## *The Vulgate*

Mark and the two other Synoptics were originally written in Greek, and various Latin translations had begun circulating in North Africa and Italy in the second century CE for those who couldn't read Greek. Over time errors had begun to creep into these early Latin translations, and significant variations started showing up. Something needed to be done to stabilize the tradition. In 382, the polyglot scholar Jerome was commissioned to produce a definitive Latin version of the four Gospels by Pope Damasus. He did more than just the Gospels over time, and eventually the work of other translators of different books of the Bible were collected together with his work. This new Latin Bible replaced other existing Latin translations and became more than just a translation of the Bible; for the West it was the Bible itself. Medieval theologians did their work based on this Latin translation, since the Greek language and the Greek Bible had been lost to the West.

By the thirteenth century, the Latin Bible could be referred to as the *versio vulgata* ("common version"). Nowadays, the adjective "vulgate" is capitalized and used to refer to the text as a whole. So we can talk about "The Vulgate" and mean the Latin Bible. But the root of the word is *vulgus,* meaning "the common people." "Vulgate Latin," therefore, strictly means the nonliterary Latin that common people spoke. This is why we can say that the Vulgate was written in vulgate Latin and not be guilty of a tautology.

## *Vulgate and Classical Latin*

The majority of first-year Latin curricula tend to focus on classical, that is, literary Latin, as opposed to vulgate Latin. There isn't enough difference between the two to warrant an extensive introduction, and the most common divergences likely to surprise the intermediate student can be easily summarized here.

The classical accusative-infinitive construction for indirect statement gives way to a subordinate clause introduced by *quia/quod/quoniam* with the indicative or subjunctive mood, though the classical construction can still be found:

> Quem dicunt homines esse filium hominis?
> ("Who do people say the son of man is?")
>
> Scitote quia appropinquavit desolatio eius.
> ("Know that its desolation has grown near.")
>
> Scitote quoniam prope est regnum Dei.
> ("Know that the Kingdom of God is near.")

We see the beginning of compound progressive tenses in vulgate Latin, mostly in the imperfect tense:

> Et erat praedicans in synagogis Iudaeae.
> ("And he was preaching in the synagogues of Judea.")

. . . et ipse erat docens, et erant Pharisaei sedentes et legis doctores . . .
("... and he was teaching and the Pharisees and people educated in the Law were present . . .")

The infinitive is frequently used to show purpose after verbs implying motion, though the classical supine in *–um* and *ut/ne* plus the subjunctive have not completely vanished:

Tunc venit Iesus a Galilaeā in Iordanem ad Ioannem, ut baptizaretur ab eo.
("Then Jesus comes from Galilee to the Jordan to John to be baptized by him.")

Quid nobis et tibi, Iesu Nazarene? Venisti perdere nos?
("What business is there between you and us, Jesus of Nazareth? Have you come to destroy us?")

Words that are emphatic or indefinite in classical Latin become less so in vulgate Latin:

Colloquebantur ad invicem quidnam facerent Iesu.
("They were talking with one another about what [not 'what in the world'] they would do to Jesus.")

Et si domus in semetipsam dispertiatur, non poterit domus illa stare.
("And if a house is divided in itself [not 'in its very own self'], that house will not be able to stand.")

Multos enim sanavit, ita ut irruerent in eum, ut illum tangerent.
("For he cured so many that they rush to him in order to touch him.")

## *Notes about This Book*

The Vulgate texts in this book are in the public domain and are available at http://www.vatican.va/archive/bible/nova_vulgata/documents/nova-vulgata_novum-testamentum_lt.html.

The punctuation marks in the book are my own. I have tried to use conventions that suit modern tastes as much as possible. In particular, I've banished the semicolon, which was used extensively in earlier editions as a way of linking shorter sentences together. This not only made the narrative sometimes difficult to follow by creating long, periodic sentences, but it also created a false impression of the original. Koine Greek and vulgate Latin were as accessible to the average reader as a local newspaper would be to us. The Gospels in particular were born in oral traditions, where long sentences are practically nonexistent and sentences frequently begin with conjunctions.

The Synoptics insert the adverbial imperative "behold" (*ecce*) in the middle of a sentence to call attention to something surprising or worthy of close attention. It's difficult to know how to punctuate this, inasmuch as there's nothing like it in standard English. I've decided on a colon, following the Dumbarton Oaks Medieval Library edition of the Vulgate Bible. This preserves the slight interruption of thought that *ecce* implies. For example, *Tunc reliquit eum Diabolus, et ecce: angeli accesserunt et ministrabant ei,* "Then the Devil left him, and behold! Angels came and took care of him."

Long marks, and sometimes short marks, over vowels are used only to clarify the grammar of a word. For example:

The perfect *vēnit* is distinguished from the present *vĕnit.*

The adverb *hīc* is distinguished from the pronoun *hĭc.*

The ablative *hōc* is distinguished from the neuter accusative *hoc.*

The first declension ablative singular is always *-ā.*

The fourth declension genitive singular, and nominative and accusative plural, are *-ūs.*

I have capitalized the names of the Jewish sects of the period: *Pharisaei, Sadducaei, Herodiani.* I do not, however, capitalize any of the forms of the word for "scribes." Scribes, it seems to me, belonged to a profession rather than a party with an identifiable political or religious philosophy.

Religious terms are capitalized in accordance with the standard conventions: "Lord," "Holy Spirit," and "God," "Messiah," "Christ." I have not capitalized the expression "son of man," as it seems most likely to have meant merely a human being, and not a specific, named spiritual entity.

Similarly, I do not capitalize other uses of the word "son" in expressions such as "son of God." This is because it's difficult to know in each context what the figure in the story using the expression actually intends. The notion that someone could be a "son of God" was not uncommon at the time, and each instance of the expression need not imply a later theological meaning. I thought it best just to leave it indeterminate.

The running vocabulary lists facing the texts aren't comprehensive. (The glossary in the back of the book is.) They include only words that students are unlikely to have seen in first-year Latin. There is only one list per pericope and it includes the vocabulary from Mark and (when applicable) the other two Synoptic Gospels arranged alphabetically.

## *Suggestions for Using This Book*

I'd like to suggest a method of study to get the most out of your study time and to help develop your reading skills.

Preview the new vocabulary for a pericope before you start reading. This will build some momentum going into the text because so many of the words will not be new or will have obvious English derivatives.

Next, before you "translate" a single word in the section you're preparing, read through all the passages quickly, while you try as best you can to grasp the general sense. This is sometimes called "reading for comprehension." This is a technique, incidentally, that is regularly used by even the most advanced readers. After these initial steps—vocabulary preview and reading for comprehension—then it's time to get down to the nuts and bolts of the language. Again, don't read word for word, but read sentences. Pass your eyes over all the words in a sentence before you start looking things up. Try to get a feel for who's doing or saying what. Ask questions such as, "Where's the main verb?" "Where's the main clause?" "Are there subordinate clauses?" "Are there direct objects?" Once you're ready to start looking up words, look up only those that are completely unknown to you, not words that look familiar but you're not sure of. Once you've plugged in the unknown words, try to conjecture how the other words fit in. Constantly read through the entire sentence even as you're looking up vocabulary so that you'll know how this new bit of knowledge is fitting into the emerging syntax of the sentence. In other words, always keep your mind active. You'll make little progress in Latin if you use mere word substitution rather than deliberate translating.

Finally, when you're reading the parallel passages from the other Gospels, try as much as possible to read them at sight without referring to any supplemental aids. You'll find that much of it will be review, and you'll build up confidence that you can actually read Latin with comprehension on your own.

There is also a map provided on page 404 to help students visualize Jesus's travels.

# The Vulgate of Mark

# Chapter 1

The Gospel of Mark begins when Jesus is already a grown man, unlike the other two Synoptics. Jesus is baptized by John in the Jordan River, but his own ministry begins only after John is imprisoned by the authorities. He is driven out into the wilderness, where he is tested for forty days. Jesus returns and calls the first four of his followers. He immediately attracts attention among the local Jews in Galilee because of his cures, his exorcisms, and the unusual way he teaches in a synagogue. As the crowds of people seeking cures increase, Jesus finds it difficult to move around freely in public. At the end of the first chapter, he and his students leave his home district for the city of Capernaum on the shore of the Sea of Galilee.

# Mark 1:1–8

## *The First Days of Jesus's Ministry*

Mark's Gospel begins with the declaration by John the Baptist, a widely honored holy man at the time, that someone even greater than he is will arrive shortly. This was predicted in the Old Testament.

**1** Initium evangelii Iesu Christi filii Dei. **2** Sicut scriptum est in Isaiā prophetā, "Ecce: mitto angelum meum ante faciem tuam, qui praeparabit viam tuam.

### Matthew 3:1–11

**1** In diebus autem illis venit Ioannes Baptistā, praedicans in deserto Iudaeae **2** et dicens, "Paenitentiam agite. Appropinquavit enim regnum caelorum."

### Luke 3:3–16

**3** Et [Ioannes] venit in omnem regionem circa Iordanem, praedicans baptismum paenitentiae in remissionem peccatorum.

## Vocabulary

**ago, -ere, egi, actus,** to make; perform; do
**angelus, -i,** *m.,* messenger
**appropinquo (1)** + *dative,* to approach; arrive at
**baptismum, -i,** *n.,* baptism
**baptista, -ae,** *m.,* baptizer
**caelum, -i,** *n.,* sky; heaven
**Christus, -i,** *m.,* anointed one; Messiah
**desertum, -i,** *n.,* wilderness
**dies, -ei,** *m./f.,* day
**ecce,** behold
**evangelium, -ii,** *n.,* good news; good report
**facies, -ei,** *f.,* face; presence
**Iesus, -us** (*gen.* **-u,** *dat.* **-u,** *acc.* **-um,** *abl.* **-u**), *m.,* Jesus
**initium, -i,** *n.,* beginning
**Ioannes, -is,** *m.,* John
**Iordanes, -is,** *m.,* the Jordan River
**Isaias, -ae,** *m.,* Isaiah
**Iudaea, -ae,** *f.,* Judea
**mitto, -ere, misi, missus,** to send
**paenitentia, -ae,** *f.,* repentance
**peccatum, -i,** *n.,* sin; fault
**praedico (1),** to preach
**propheta, -ae,** *m.,* prophet
**regio, -ionis,** *f.,* area; region
**regnum, -i,** *n.,* kingdom
**remissio, -ionis,** *f.,* forgiveness; remission
**sicut,** thus; as
**via, -ae,** *f.,* way; road

## Historical and Grammatical Notes

### Mark 1:1–8

1. **Initium:** The opening of the Gospel isn't easy to follow. Mark begins with a fragmentary sentence, followed by a complicated Old Testament reference. It may be that the first verse was actually a subtitle for the manuscript (MS) that got worked into the text. Another possibility is that the Old Testament citation was inserted in between *Initium* and its verb *fuit* that comes two verses later. Leaving out the Old Testament text results in "The beginning of the good news about Jesus Christ, the Son of God, . . . was John the Baptist . . ." This not only makes the grammar easier to understand, but it's also consistent with events. John's voice in the wilderness predicts a great one who is to come shortly. This is the beginning of the good news about Jesus.

2. **Sicut scriptum est:** There are other reasons to suspect that the Old Testament citation is a later insertion. For one, this is the only time in Mark that a reference to the Old Testament is made by the narrator—by Mark, in this case. Everywhere else they are made by characters in the narrative. Secondly, it is the only citation from a *specific* book of the Old Testament. All the other references in Mark are more general. They refer simply to the Laws of Moses, for example, or to the prophet Isaiah personally and not to the book of Isaiah. Thirdly, the quotation does not come only from Isaiah. It actually combines two Old Testament references: *Ecce . . . tuam* is from Exodus 23:20 or Malachi 3:1; *vox . . . semitas eius* is from Isaiah 40:3.

# Mark 1:1–8 (cont.)

**3** Vox clamantis in deserto, 'Parate viam Domini. Rectas
facite semitas eius.' " **4** Fuit Ioannes Baptista in deserto,
praedicans baptismum paenitentiae in remissionem
peccatorum. **5** Et egrediebatur ad illum omnis Iudaeae
regio et Hierosolymitae universi, et baptizabantur ab
illo in Iordane flumine, confitentes peccata sua. **6** Et erat
Ioannes, vestitus pilis cameli et zonā pelliceā circa lumbos
eius, et locustas et mel silvestre edebat.

## Matthew 3:1–11 (cont.)

**3** Hĭc est enim qui dictus est per Isaiam prophetam, dicentem, "Vox
clamantis in deserto, 'Parate viam Domini. Rectas facite semitas
eius.' " **4** Ipse autem Ioannes habebat vestimentum de pilis cameli et
zonam pelliceam circa lumbos suos. Esca autem eius erat locustae et
mel silvestre. **5** Tunc exibat ad eum Hierosolyma et omnis Iudaea et
omnis regio circa Iordanem. **6** Et baptizabantur in Iordane flumine
ab eo, confitentes peccata sua.

## Luke 3:3–16 (cont.)

**4** Sicut scriptum est in libro sermonum Isaiae prophetae, "Vox
clamantis in deserto, 'Parate viam Domini. Rectas facite semitas
eius.' "

## Vocabulary

**baptizo (1),** to baptize
**camelus, -i,** *m.,* camel
**circa** + *accusative,* around; for
**clamo (1),** to cry out; shout
**confiteor, -fiteri, -fessus sum,** to confess; admit
**edo, -ere** *or* **esse, edi, essus,** to eat
**egredior, -i, -gressus sum,** to go out; depart
**esca, -ae,** *f.,* food
**exeo, -ire, -ii** *or* **-ivi, -itus,** to go out; leave
**flumen, -inis,** *n.,* river
**Hierosolyma, -ae,** *f.,* Jerusalem
**Hierosolymitas, -ae,** *m.,* resident of Jerusalem
**locusta, -ae,** *f.,* locust; grasshopper
**lumbus, -i,** *m.,* loin
**mel, mellis,** *n.,* honey
**pelliceus, -a, -um,** leather; made of animal skin
**pilus, -i,** *m.,* hair
**rectus, -a, -um,** straight
**semita, -ae,** *f.,* path
**sermo, -onis,** *m.,* talk; speech
**silvester, -tris, -tre,** of the woods; wild
**universus, -a, -um,** all; entire
**vestimentum, -i,** *n.,* clothing
**vestio, -ire, -ii** *or* **-ivi, -itus,** to dress
**vox, -cis,** *f.,* voice
**zona, -ae,** *f.,* belt

## Historical and Grammatical Notes

### Mark 1:1–8 (cont.)

5. **omnis Iudaeae regio et Hierosolymitae universi:** This indicates that John was respected by even the most devout Jews of the time. Judea and Jerusalem represent the heart of orthodox Judaism, unlike Jesus's homeland of Galilee, which had always been seen by devout Jews as somewhat out of the norm, overrun by foreigners and given to a relaxed observation of Mosaic law.

6. **Ioannes, vestitus pilis cameli . . .:** the traditional garb and behavior of a holy man. In this way, John is further identified with the prophet Elijah, whose return is a precondition for the final judgment (Mal 3:1 and 3:23–24).

### Matthew 3:1–11 (cont.)

3. **Vox clamantis in deserto:** Matthew improves on Mark's original by embedding the Old Testament prophecy as an object of the participle *dicentem* and by deleting the first half.

# Mark 1:1–8 (cont.)

**7** Et praedicabat, dicens, "Vĕnit fortior me post me cuius non sum dignus procumbens solvere corrigiam calceamentorum eius. **8** Ego baptizavi vos aquā. Ille vero baptizabit vos in Spiritu Sancto."

## Matthew 3:1–11 (cont.)

[*7–10 John denounces some Pharisees and Sadducees who had come to see him. He also proclaims that the end of time is near.*] **11** "Ego quidem vos baptizo in aquā in paenitentiam. Qui autem post me venturus est, fortior me est, cuius non sum dignus calceamenta portare. Ipse vos baptizabit in Spiritu Sancto et igni."

## Luke 3:3–16 (cont.)

[*5–14 John denounces the crowd for their hypocrisy and smugness. He answers questions about how one may be spared the coming wrath of God.*] **15** Existimante autem populo et cogitantibus omnibus in cordibus suis de Ioanne, ne forte ipse esset Christus, **16** respondit Ioannes, dicens omnibus, "Ego quidem aquā baptizo vos. Venit autem fortior me, cuius non sum dignus solvere corrigiam calceamentorum eius. Ipse vos baptizabit in Spiritu Sancto et igni . . ."

## Vocabulary

**aqua, -ae,** *f.,* water
**autem,** however, moreover
**calceamentum, -i,** *n.,* shoe
**cogito (1),** to think
**cor, cordis,** *n.,* heart
**corrigia, -ae,** *f.,* lace
**dignus, -a, -um,** + *genitive or ablative, or + infinitive,* worthy; worthy of; worthy to
**existimo (1),** to wonder
**forte,** by chance; perhaps
**fortis, -e,** strong; powerful
**procumbo, -cumbere, -cubui, -cubitus,** to lean down; fall forward
**quidem,** indeed; in fact
**solvo, -vere, -ui** *or* **-ii, -utus,** to set free; untie
**tunc,** then; thereupon
**vero,** truly; but

## Historical and Grammatical Notes

### Mark 1:1–8 (cont.)

7. **Vĕnit:** "there is coming." **fortior me:** *Me* is ablative of comparison: "stronger than I." John emphasizes his subordination to Jesus. There is evidence in all four Gospels that there was competition, and even conflict, between the followers of Jesus and the followers of John (Mark 2:18, for example, and Luke 3:15).

### Matthew 3:1–11 (cont.)

11. **Qui:** "he who will come after me." **venturus est:** = *veniet.* The paraphrastic future—the future active participle with a conjugated form of the verb *sum*—is used interchangeably with the simple future in vulgate Latin. **portare:** complementary infinitive after the adjective *dignus*: "worthy to carry." **igni:** The addition of fire to Mark's text can be taken as evidence that Mark was written before the destruction of the Temple in Jerusalem in 70 CE, whereas Matthew's and Luke's Gospels were written after. The sack of Jerusalem by the Romans culminated in the burning of the Temple, so the image of baptism by fire would have been a reminder to Christians that even the annihilation of the center of the Jewish world was part of God's plan.

### Luke 3:3–16 (cont.)

15. **Existimante . . . omnibus:** ablative absolute. **ne forte ipse esset Christus:** "whether he might not be the Christ."

# Mark 1:9–11

## *John Baptizes Jesus in the Jordan River*

After Jesus is baptized by John, an apparition and voice heard from the sky indicate his special nature.

**9** Et factum est in diebus illis, vēnit Iesus a Nazareth Galilaeae et baptizatus est in Iordane ab Ioanne. **10** Et statim ascendens de aquā vidit apertos caelos et Spiritum tamquam columbam descendentem in ipsum. **11** Et vox facta est de caelis, "Tu es filius meus dilectus. In te complacui."

### Matthew 3:13–17

**13** Tunc vĕnit Iesus a Galilaeā in Iordanem ad Ioannem, ut baptizaretur ab eo. **14** Ioannes autem prohibebat eum, dicens, "Ego a te debeo baptizari, et tu venis ad me?" **15** Respondens autem Iesus dixit ei, "Sine modo. Sic enim decet nos implere omnem iustitiam." Tunc dimittit eum. **16** Baptizatus autem Iesus confestim ascendit de aquā. Et ecce: aperti sunt ei caeli, et vidit Spiritum Dei descendentem sicut columbam et venientem super se. **17** Et ecce: vox de caelis, dicens, "Hĭc est filius meus dilectus, in quo mihi complacui."

### Luke 3:21–22

**21** Factum est autem, cum baptizaretur omnis populus, et, Iesu baptizato et orante, apertum est caelum. **22** Et descendit Spiritus Sanctus corporali specie sicut columba super ipsum. Et vox de caelo facta est, "Tu es filius meus dilectus. In te complacui mihi."

## Vocabulary

**aperio, -ire, -ui, -rtus,** to uncover
**ascendo, -ndere, -ndi, -nsus,** to rise
**columba, -ae,** *f.,* dove
**complaceo, -cere, -cui, -citus,** to be pleasing to
**confestim,** immediately
**decet, decuit,** *impers.,* it is fitting
**descendo, -ndere, -ndi, -nsus,** to descend
**dilectus, -a, -um,** beloved
**dimitto, -mittere, -misi, -missus,** to dismiss; forgive; divorce
**fio, fieri, factus est,** to happen
**Galilaea, -ae,** *f.,* Galilee
**impleo, -ere, -evi, -etus,** to fulfill
**iustitia, -ae,** *f.,* divine will; justice
**modo,** just now; recently
**Nazareth** *(indecl.),* Nazareth
**oro (1),** to pray
**sino, sinere, sivi, situs,** to allow, permit
**species, -ei,** *f.,* appearance
**statim,** immediately
**super** + *accusative or ablative,* upon; on; concerning
**tamquam,** as; like

## Historical and Grammatical Notes

### Mark 1:9–11

**9. factum est:** "it came about." This is a very common transitional introduction to a new pericope in Mark. It looks forward to the next event without necessarily attaching it chronologically to the previous one. Matthew tends to replace this expression with adverbs implying a more precise meaning, such as *tunc.*

**10. vidit:** The subject is John, since *ipsum* later in the sentence isn't reflexive. The participle *ascendens* is nominative because John would have been in the water with Jesus during the baptism: "John, coming out of the water, saw the sky open up and saw the Spirit, like a dove, coming down into [onto] to him."

**11. In te complacui:** "I have been pleased in [with] you." In classical Latin, this would have been *complacuisti mihi*: "you pleased me."

### Matthew 3:13–17

**13. a Galilaeā:** Why is Nazareth dropped from his Marcan source? A possible explanation is that according to Old Testament prophecy the Messiah was to come from Bethlehem (Mt 2:6). Matthew might have omitted Nazareth so as not to include details that would raise unnecessary questions. Luke will delete both Nazareth and Galilee, perhaps for the same reason.

**14. Ego a te debeo baptizari:** John asks a question that would have been obvious to Jesus's later followers, because baptism was preceded by a confession of sin.

### Luke 3:21–22

**21. Iesu . . . orante:** ablative absolute: "When Jesus had been baptized and was praying."

**22. corporali specie:** ablative of specification: "in bodily appearance." Luke makes it clear that this is no metaphor. This was a real, physical dove.

# Mark 1:12–13

## *The Temptation of Jesus in the Desert*

Jesus is driven out into the wilderness by a spirit immediately after his baptism, where he is subjected to forty days and nights of temptations and physical torment.

**12** Et statim Spiritus expellit eum in desertum.

### Matthew 4:1–11

**1** Tunc Iesus ductus est in desertum a Spiritu ut tentaretur a Diabolo.

### Luke 4:1–13

**1** Iesus autem plenus Spiritu Sancto regressus est ab Iordane et agebatur in Spiritu in deserto.

## Vocabulary

**Diabolus, -i,** *m.,* the Devil
**duco, ducere, duxi, ductus,** to lead; think; marry
**expello, -pellere, -puli, -pulsus,** to expel; throw out
**plenus, -a, -um** + *ablative or genitive,* filled by; full of
**regredior, -gredi, -gressus sum,** to withdraw from
**tento (1),** to tempt; taunt

## Historical and Grammatical Notes

### Mark 1:12–13

**12. Et statim:** The adverb *statim* nearly loses its basic meaning "immediately" in Mark and becomes merely a conventional way to begin a new pericope: "and thereupon" or "and next." Notice that both Matthew and Luke tend to replace it with the less abrupt conjunction *autem* or the adverb *tunc.* Some commentators, however, argue that this repeated use of *statim* in Mark builds up the sense of urgency and speed as the events leading to Jesus's death and resurrection unfold. **desertum:** "wilderness."

### Luke 4:1–13

**1. autem:** often best translated as "thereupon," or just "next." **ab Iordane:** Luke's chronology is tighter than Mark's or Matthew's. Jesus is driven out into the wilderness *immediately* after his baptism, not just some time after.

# Mark 1:12–13 (cont.)

**13** Et erat in deserto quadraginta diebus et tentabatur a Satanā. Eratque cum bestiis, et angeli ministrabant illi.

## Matthew 4:1–11 (cont.)

**2** Et cum ieiunasset quadraginta diebus et quadraginta noctibus, postea esuriit. [**3–*10*** *Matthew specifies how the Diabolos tempts Jesus.*] **11** Tunc reliquit eum Diabolus, et ecce: angeli accesserunt et ministrabant ei.

## Luke 4:1–13 (cont.)

**2** Diebus quadraginta et tentabatur a Diabolo. Et nihil manducavit in diebus illis, et, consummatis illis, esuriit. [**3–*12*** *Luke details the several temptations that Jesus resists.*] **13** Et consummatā omni tentatione, Diabolus recessit ab illo usque ad tempus.

## Vocabulary

**accedo, -cedere, -cessi, -cessus,** to draw near
**bestia, -ae,** *f.,* wild animal
**consummo, -ere, -psi, -ptus,** to use up; spend
**esurio, -ire, —, -tus,** to be hungry
**ieiuno (1),** to fast
**manduco (1),** to eat
**ministro (1)** + *dative,* to take care of; tend to
**quadraginta,** forty
**recedo, -cedere, -cessi, -cessum,** to withdraw
**relinquo, -liqui, -lectus,** to leave behind
**Satanas, -ae,** *m.,* Satan
**tentatio, -ionis,** *f.,* temptation
**usque,** from everywhere; up until

## Historical and Grammatical Notes

### Mark 1:12–13 (cont.)

13. **Satanā:** from the Hebrew *satan,* "adversary." The Greek *diabole* comes from the verb *diaballō,* "to accuse" or "to slander." This retains the sense that Satan is like a corrupt prosecutor, who tempts people to commit a crime and then arraigns them in court when they do. In this passage, the Diabolos tempts Jesus to sin (if that's possible), but this is an essential service to prove something about Jesus. The Holy Spirit, after all, drives Jesus out in the desert *in order* that he may be tempted by the Diabolos. In his other appearances in the Synoptic Gospels, however, Satan doesn't appear to be performing any useful purpose beyond tormenting people with illness and insanity, all small-scale troublemaking unworthy of the archenemy of God. **quadraginta diebus:** = *dies,* accusative of duration of time: "for forty days." Forty days is a traditional extent of time for Old Testament prophets to endure a test or challenge (Ex 24:18; Dt 9:18, 25;1 Kgs 19:8). **illi:** dative after *ministrabant*: "they took care of him."

### Matthew 4:1–11 (cont.)

2. **ieiunasset:** = *ieiunavisset.* The *–vi–* of the third principal part of first conjugation verbs is regularly dropped from some perfect tense forms in both classical and vulgate Latin. *Laudavissem,* for example, can be shortened to *laudassem; laudavisse* can be written as *laudasse.* This is called syncopation. So we can say that *ieiunasset* (< *ieiunavisset*) is a syncopated pluperfect subjunctive. This can occur in a small number of third conjugation verbs: *nosse* < *novisse; nosti* < *novisti.* Both Matthew and Luke emphasize that Jesus doesn't eat until after the forty days and nights have been completed. This may be to clarify, or add to, Mark's account, where Jesus is not specifically said to have fasted during his ordeal.

### Luke 4:1–13 (cont.)

13. **consummatā omni tentatione:** ablative absolute: "after each temptation had been played out."

# Mark 1:14–15

## *John Is Arrested and Jesus Begins His Ministry*

John is arrested and Jesus's ministry begins.

**14** Postquam autem traditus est Ioannes, vēnit Iesus
in Galilaeam, praedicans evangelium Dei **15** et dicens,
"Impletum est tempus, et appropinquavit regnum Dei.
Paenitemini et credite evangelio."

### Matthew 4:12–17

**12** Cum autem audisset quod Ioannes traditus esset, secessit in
Galilaeam. [***13–16*** *Jesus fulfills prophecies from Isaiah concerning
the Messiah by going into the towns of Zabulon and Naphthali.*] **17**
Exinde coepit Iesus praedicare et dicere, "Paenitentiam agite,
appropinquavit enim regnum caelorum."

## Vocabulary

**coepi, -isse, -tus,** to begin
**credo, -ere, -idi, -itus,** to believe; believe in
**exinde,** next; thereupon
**paeniteor, -eri,** to repent
**secedo, -cedere, -cessi, -cessus,** to go away
**trado, -dere, -didi, -ditus,** to hand over; betray

## Historical and Grammatical Notes

### Mark 1:14–15

**14. traditus est Ioannes:** The verb *trado* suggests that he was betrayed. We know why John was arrested but not how. This will be discussed at 6:14–29. **Paenitemini:** second person plural imperative, "Repent!" In classical Latin the verb is impersonal: *me paenitet*: "it causes me regret." **credite evangelio:** *Evangelio* is dative: "believe in the good news." Mark provides us a summary of Jesus's message: (1) *impletum est tempus,* (2) *appropinquavit regnum Dei,* and (3) people should repent and believe in the message.

### Matthew 4:12–17

**12. quod . . . esset:** Indirect statement in vulgate Latin is usually a subordinate clause introduced by the conjunctions *quod* or *quia* with the indicative or subjunctive mood, without any difference in meaning. The classical Latin formulation of the accusative/infinitive does appear in vulgate Latin, but it is somewhat rare.

# Mark 1:16–20

## *The Calling of Jesus's First Disciples*

Jesus calls the first four of his disciples while he is passing by the shore of the Sea of Galilee. They put down their fishing gear and follow him.

**16** Et praeteriens secus mare Galilaeae vidit Simonem et
Andream fratrem Simonis mittentes in mare. Erant enim
piscatores. **17** Et dixit eis Iesus, "Vĕnite post me, et faciam
vos fieri piscatores hominum." **18** Et protinus, relictis
retibus, secuti sunt eum.

## Matthew 4:18–22

**18** Ambulans autem iuxta mare Galilaeae, vidit duos fratres,
Simonem, qui vocatur Petrus, et Andream fratrem eius, mittentes
rete in mare. Erant enim piscatores. **19** Et ait illis, "Vĕnite post me, et
faciam vos piscatores hominum." **20** At illi continuo, relictis retibus,
secuti sunt eum.

## Luke 5:2–11

**2** Et vidit duas naves stantes secus stagnum. Piscatores autem
descenderant de illis et lavabant retia. **3** Ascendens autem in unam
navem, quae erat Simonis, rogavit eum a terrā reducere pusillum.
Et sedens docebat de naviculā turbas. **4** Ut cessavit autem loqui,
dixit ad Simonem, "Duc in altum et laxate retia vestra in capturam."
**5** Et respondens Simon dixit, "Praeceptor, per totam noctem
laborantes nihil cepimus. In verbo autem tuo laxabo retia." **6** Et
cum hoc fecissent, concluserunt piscium multitudinem copiosam.
Rumpebantur autem retia eorum. **7** Et annuerunt sociis qui erant in
aliā navi ut venirent et adiuvarent eos. Et venerunt et impleverunt
ambas naviculas, ita ut mergerentur. **8** Quod cum videret Simon
Petrus, procidit ad genua Iesu, dicens, "Exi a me, quia homo peccator
sum, Domine." **9** Stupor enim circumdederat eum et omnes qui cum
illo erant in capturā piscium, quos ceperant.

## Vocabulary

**adiuvo, -iuvare, -iuvi, -iutus,** to help
**alius, -a, -ud,** other
**altus, -a, -um,** high; deep
**ambo, -ae, -o,** both
**ambulo (1),** to walk
**Andreas, -ae,** *m.,* Andrew
**annuo, -nuere, -nui, -nutus,** to nod to; signal to
**captura, -ae,** *f.,* catch; take
**cesso (1),** to cease
**circumdo, -dăre, -dedi, -datus,** to envelop; surround
**concludo, -dere, -si, -sus,** to encompass; close up on
**continuo,** directly, immediately
**doceo, -ere, -ui, -tus,** to teach; preach
**frater, -tris,** *m.,* brother
**genu, -us,** *n.,* knee
**iuxta** + *accusative,* close to
**laboro (1),** to struggle
**lavo, -are, -avi, -atus** *or* **lotus,** to wash
**laxo (1),** to spread out
**loquor, loqui, locutus sum,** to speak
**mergo, -gere, -si, -sus,** to cause to sink
**peccator, -oris,** *m.,* a sinner
**piscator, -oris,** *m.,* fisherman
**piscis, -is,** *m.,* fish
**praeceptor, -oris,** *m.,* teacher
**praetereo, -ire, -ii** *or* **-ivi, -itus,** to pass by
**procido, -cidere, -cidi,** to fall before
**protinus,** straightaway
**pusillum,** a little
**quia,** because; since; that
**rete, -is,** *n.,* net
**rogo (1),** to ask
**rumpo, -ere, rupi, ruptus,** to burst
**secus** + *accusative,* along; nearby
**sequor, sequi, secutus sum,** to follow; come next
**Simon, -is,** *m.,* Simon
**socius, -i,** *m.,* friend
**stagnum, -i,** *n.,* lake
**sto, -are, steti, status,** to stand; stop
**stupor, -oris,** *m.,* astonishment

## Historical and Grammatical Notes

### Mark 1:16–20

**16. praeteriens:** Jesus is walking along the shore of the Sea of Galilee. Here the verb must mean "passing along." **mittentes:** "casting [nets]." Jesus calls two pairs of brothers as his first followers. They are (1) Simon, later given the name Peter, (2) his brother Andrew, and the two brothers (3) John and (4) Jacob, whom we call James by tradition. This James must not be confused with another James, a brother of Jesus, who appears later in Mark. (See the note at 6:3.)

**17. faciam . . . hominum:** "I'll make you fishermen of men."

### Luke 5:2–11

**3. reducere pusillum:** Jesus gets into Simon's boat and asks him to push it out from the shore. From there Jesus can address the people gathered to hear him.

**4. Ut:** With the indicative, *ut* means "when" or "as." **cessavit . . . loqui:** "stopped talking." **in capturam:** "for the catch."

**5. In verbo . . . tuo:** "at your word" or "on your authority."

**7. ut venirent et adiuvarent:** indirect command after *annuerunt.*

# Mark 1:16–20 (cont.)

**19** Et progressus pusillum vidit Iacobum Zebedaei et
Ioannem fratrem eius, et ipsos in navi componentes retia.
**20** Et statim vocavit illos, et, relicto patre suo Zebedaeo in
navi cum mercennariis, abierunt post eum.

## Matthew 4:18–22 (cont.)

**21** Et procedens inde vidit alios duos fratres, Iacobum Zebedaei et
Ioannem fratrem eius, in navi cum Zebedaeo patre eorum reficientes
retia sua. Et vocavit eos. **22** Illi autem statim, relictā navi et patre suo,
secuti sunt eum.

## Luke 5:2–11 (cont.)

**10** Similiter autem et Iacobum et Ioannem, filios Zebedaei, qui erant
socii Simonis. Et ait ad Simonem Iesus, "Noli timere. Ex hōc iam
homines eris capiens." **11** Et subductis ad terram navibus, relictis
omnibus, secuti sunt illum.

## Vocabulary

**abeo, -ire, -ii** *or* **-ivi, -itus,** to depart; leave
**ait, aiunt,** he says/they say
**compono, -ponere, -posui, -positus,** to collect together
**Iacobus, -i,** *m.,* Jacob = James
**inde,** thereupon
**mercennarius, -i,** *m.,* employee; hired man
**nolo, nolle, nolui,** not to want
**procedo, -cedere, -cessi, -cessus,** to go forth
**reficio, -ficere, -feci, -fectus,** to repair
**similiter,** in the same way; similarly
**subduco, -ducere, -duxi, -ductus,** to bring up; dock
**Zebedaeus, -i,** *m.,* Zebedee

## Historical and Grammatical Notes

### Mark 1:16–20 (cont.)

**19. Iacobum Zebedaei:** "James, the son of Zebedee."

**20. relicto patre suo Zebedaeo in navi cum mercennariis:** ablative absolute: "with his father Zebedee having been left in the boat with the workmen."

### Luke 5:2–11 (cont.)

**10. Noli timere:** *Noli* is the imperative of the verb *nolo* ("not to wish"), which is used to express a negative command: "Don't be afraid." **Ex hōc iam homines eris capiens:** *Homines* is the accusative object of the future periphrastic progressive *eris capiens*: "from now on, you will be catching men."

# Mark 1:21–22

## *Jesus Teaches in a Synagogue*

Jesus shocks a congregation in a synagogue in Capernaum by departing from the regular practice of simply commenting on scripture. He speaks in his own words as if they are on par with scripture.

**21** Et ingrediuntur Capharnaum. Et statim Sabbatis
ingressus synagogam docebat. **22** Et stupebant super
doctrinā eius. Erat enim docens eos quasi potestatem
habens et non sicut scribae.

# Vocabulary

**doctrina, -ae,** *f.,* teaching
**ingredior, ingredi, ingressus sum,** to enter into
**potestas, -tatis,** *f.,* power; authority
**quasi,** as if; like
**Sabbatum, -i,** *n.,* the Sabbath
**scriba, -ae,** *m.,* a scribe
**stupeo, -ere, -ui,** to be astonished

# Historical and Grammatical Notes

## Mark 1:21–22

**21. Sabbatis:** ablative of time when: "on the Sabbath." The singular and plural of the word for "Sabbath" don't differ at all in meaning. **docebat:** A regular practice in a synagogue was to read and expound upon a passage from Scripture.

**22. stupebant:** Jesus's reading of the text differed from the usual practice because, evidently, he was proclaiming his own thoughts as if they were on par with Scripture. We can well imagine the reaction of a congregation if, after his sermon, their pastor were to say, "That's what Scripture says. And I say . . ." **scribae:** The scribes were literate men who had studied Scripture and the laws derived from it. They were employed by different Jewish sects and by the Temple authorities as living reference libraries. They may be compared to modern-day lawyers in that they were versed in the texts of the laws, without necessarily being committed to one particular method of interpretation.

## Synoptic Parallels

There are no parallels to this event in Matthew and Luke. Jesus is going to visit another synagogue later in Mark and again will surprise the congregation because of the way he teaches. Matthew and Luke have parallels for this later event. Matthew and Luke may have omitted this particular episode here because they thought these two passages in Mark were describing the same thing.

# Mark 1:23–28

## *Jesus Frees a Man from a Demon in the Synagogue*

Jesus casts out a demon that recognizes he is a divine being and speaks to him. Jesus commands it to keep silent. The witnesses in the synagogue are astonished, and the news of Jesus's power spreads throughout Galilee.

**23** Et statim erat in synagogā eorum homo in spiritu
immundo, et exclamavit, **24** dicens, "Quid nobis et tibi,
Iesu Nazarene? Venisti perdere nos? Scio qui sis: Sanctus
Dei." **25** Et comminatus est ei Iesus, dicens, "Obmutesce
et exi de homine!" **26** Et discerpens eum spiritus
immundus et exclamans voce magnā exivit ab eo. **27** Et
mirati sunt omnes, ita ut conquirerent inter se, dicentes,
"Quidnam est hoc? Doctrina nova cum potestate? Et
spiritibus immundis imperat, et oboediunt ei?" **28** Et
processit rumor eius statim ubique in omnem regionem
Galilaeae.

## Luke 4:33–37

**33** Et in synagogā erat homo habens spiritum daemonii immundi. Et
exclamavit voce magnā, **34** "Sine! Quid nobis et tibi, Iesu Nazarene?
Venisti perdere nos? Scio te qui sis: Sanctus Dei." **35** Et increpavit
illi Iesus, dicens, "Obmutesce et exi ab illo!" Et cum proiecisset
illum daemonium in medium, exiit ab illo nihilque illum nocuit.
**36** Et factus est pavor in omnibus, et colloquebantur ad invicem,
dicentes, "Quod est hoc verbum, quia in potestate et virtute imperat
immundis spiritibus, et exeunt?" **37** Et divulgabatur fama de illo in
omnem locum regionis.

## Vocabulary

**ad invicem,** in turn; to one another
**colloquor, -qui, -cutus sum,** to converse
**comminor, -ari, -atus sum** + *dative,* to curse; threaten
**conquiro, -rere, -sivi** *or* **-sii, -situs,** to ask questions; wonder
**daemonium, -i,** *n.,* demon
**discerpo, -ere, -si, -tus,** to tear apart
**divulgo (1),** to spread
**immundus, -a, -um,** unclean
**impero (1)** + *dative,* to command
**increpo (1),** to scold; grumble at
**miror, -ari, -atus sum,** to be astonished
**Nazarenus, -a, -um,** of Nazareth
**noceo, -ere, -ui, -itum,** to harm
**obmutesco, -ere, -tui,** to become silent
**oboedio, -ire, -ivi, -itus** + *dative,* to be obedient to
**pavor, -oris,** *m.,* fear; dread
**perdo, -dere, -didi, -ditus,** to destroy
**proicio, -icere, -ieci, -iectus,** to cast out in front of
**quisnam, quidnam,** whoever, whatever
**rumor, -oris,** *m.,* reputation
**scio, -ire, -ii** *or* **-ivi, -itus,** to know
**ubique,** everywhere
**virtus, -tutis,** *f.,* power

## Historical and Grammatical Notes

### Mark 1:23–28

**24. Quid nobis et tibi:** "What do we have to do with each other?" Jewish traditions envisioned a lively world of spirit beings. Usually these beings stayed out of each other's affairs when visiting earth. It was natural that this unclean spirit would protest Jesus's interference, and that people who saw the exorcism would think that Jesus was from this spiritual world. **perdere:** In vulgate Latin infinitives are more often used to show purpose than the classical *ut/ne* + the subjunctive. **qui:** = *quis.* **sis:** subjunctive in indirect question.

**25. ei:** dative after *comminatus est.*

**26. voce magnā:** ablative of manner.

**27. ita ut:** = *ut.* **Quidnam:** Vulgate Latin uses emphatic or indefinite forms where no such significance is evident. *Quidnam,* "whatever," can be translated simply as "what." **spiritibus:** dative after imperative. **ei:** dative after *oboediunt.*

### Luke 4:33–37

**34. Sine:** "leave us alone."

**35. illi:** dative after *increpavit.* **in medium:** "into the middle [of the room]." **nihilque illum nocuit:** "and he did him no harm." In classical Latin, *nocuit* would be followed by the dative case.

**36. hoc verbum:** "this teaching." The people in the synagogue connect Jesus's power over demons to the nature of his teachings. **in potestate et virtute:** "with authority and power."

# Mark 1:29–34

## *Jesus Cures a Fever and Casts Demons Out of Others*

Jesus is taken to the home of Simon and Andrew. There he cures Simon's mother-in-law of a fever. Many more ill people are brought to him for cures and exorcisms. As before, the evil spirits know who Jesus is.

**29** Et protinus egredientes de synagogā venerunt in
domum Simonis et Andreae cum Iacobo et Ioanne. **30**
Socrus autem Simonis decumbebat febricitans. Et statim
dicunt ei de illā. **31** Et accedens elevavit eam apprehensā
manu, et dimisit eam febris. Et ministrabat eis. **32** Vespere
autem facto, cum occĭdisset sol, afferebant ad eum omnes
male habentes et daemonia habentes, **33** et erat omnis
civitas congregata ad ianuam. **34** Et curavit multos, qui
vexabantur variis languoribus, et daemonia multa eiecit et
non sinebat loqui daemoniā, quoniam sciebant eum.

## Matthew 8:14–16

**14** Et cum venisset Iesus in domum Petri, vidit socrum eius iacentem
et febricitantem. **15** Et tetigit manum eius, et dimisit eam febris.
Et surrexit et ministrabat ei. **16** Vespere autem facto, obtulerunt ei
multos daemonia habentes et eiciebat spiritūs verbo et omnes male
habentes curavit.

## Luke 4:38–41

**38** Surgens autem de synagogā introivit in domum Simonis. Socrus
autem Simonis tenebatur magnā febri. Et rogaverunt illum pro eā.
**39** Et stans super illam imperavit febri, et dimisit illam. Et continuo
surgens ministrabat illis. **40** Cum sol autem occĭdisset, omnes qui
habebant infirmos variis languoribus ducebant illos ad eum. At ille
singulis manūs imponens curabat eos. **41** Exibant autem daemonia
a multis, clamantia et dicentia, "Tu es filius Dei." Et increpans non
sinebat ea loqui, quia sciebant ipsum esse Christum.

## Vocabulary

**affero, -ferre, -tuli, -latus,** to bring to
**apprehendo, -dere, -di, -sus,** to take hold of
**congrego (1),** to gather; assemble together
**curo (1),** to heal
**decumbo, -cumbere, -cubui,** to recline; be bedridden
**eicio, -icere, -ieci, -iectus,** to throw out; expel
**elevo (1),** to lift up
**febricito (1),** to have a fever
**febris, -is,** *f.,* fever
**iaceo, -ere, -cui, -itum,** to be lying down
**ianua, -ae,** *f.,* door; gate
**impono, -ponere, -posui, -positus,** to place on
**infirmus, -a, -um,** weak; sick
**introeo, -ire, -ii** *or* **-ivi, -itus,** to enter
**languor, -is,** *m.,* disease; ailment
**male,** badly
**manus, -us,** *f.,* hand
**occĭdo, -cidere, -cĭdi, -cāsum,** to fall, sink
**singulis,** one at a time, individually
**socrus, -us,** *m./f.,* father- or mother-in-law
**sol, -is,** *m.,* sun
**surgo, -gere, -rexi, -rectus,** to get up; rise up
**tango, tangere, tetigi, tactus,** to touch
**teneo, -ere, -ui, -ntus,** to hold
**vesper, -eris** *or* **-eri,** *m.,* evening; evening star
**vexo (1),** to disturb; make ill; torment

## Historical and Grammatical Notes

### Mark 1:29–34

**32. male habentes:** "being ill."

**34. multos:** "he cured many who were sick with different illnesses." It's not clear in Mark whether Jesus cured them all or cured many of them. Compare this with Matthew and Luke, who insist that Jesus cured each and every one of the ill brought to him.

### Matthew 8:14–16

**14. Petri:** Simon has not yet been renamed "Peter" at this point in Matthew. That doesn't happen until much later in Matthew at 16:13–19. It could be that Matthew's audience was so familiar with the name Peter that they would not have realized that Simon and Peter were in fact the same person, so Matthew uses the name Peter to avoid any misunderstanding. Indeed, at 4:18, when Matthew first mentions Peter, he foreshadows the change of his name.

**16. omnes male habentes curavit:** "he cured *all* those being ill."

### Luke 4:38–41

**41. quia sciebant ipsum esse Christum:** They knew not just that Jesus was a spiritual being, but that he was the Messiah himself. This would mean also that they knew that the current order of things was coming to an end and that the Kingdom of God was nigh.

# Mark 1:35–39

## *Jesus Prays in Solitude*

Jesus goes off early in the morning to pray by himself. Simon and others go to look for him. When they find him, he tells them that it's time to move on to another district so that his ministry can continue there as well.

**35** Et diluculo valde mane surgens egressus est et abiit in
desertum locum ibique orabat. **36** Et persecutus est eum
Simon et qui cum illo erant. **37** Et cum invenissent eum,
dixerunt ei, "Omnes quaerunt te."

### Luke 4:42–44

**42** Factā autem die, egressus ibat in desertum locum, et turbae requirebant eum et venerunt usque ad ipsum et detinebant illum, ne discederet ab eis.

## Vocabulary

**detineo, -tinere, -tinui, -tentus,** to restrain; impede
**diluculum, -i,** *n.,* dawn
**discedo, -cedere, -cessi, -cessus,** to leave; get away
**ibique,** there; in that place
**invenio, -ire, -vēni, -ventus,** to find
**mane,** in the morning; at dawn
**persequor, -qui, -secutus sum,** to follow after; look for
**quaero, -rere, -sivi, -situs,** to look for; ask about
**requiro, -quirere, -quisivi** *or* **-quisii, -quisitus,** to look for; ask after
**valde,** really; very much

## Historical and Grammatical Notes

### Mark 1:35–39

**35. diluculo valde mane:** "early in the morning." Why does Jesus withdraw early in the morning to be alone and why does he want to move on to another place to continue his ministry? As we saw in 1:14–15, Jesus's ministry is not about curing the sick. It's about delivering the message that the time has been fulfilled, the Kingdom of God is approaching, and people should repent and believe in the Word. In Mark and Luke, Jesus says "I've come to preach." Yet his reputation as a miracle healer is what is bringing in the crowds. In Mark, we see Jesus become annoyed that his true message is not getting through. **orabat:** This is the first time we see Jesus praying, a detail that Luke curiously omits.

**36. qui cum illo erant:** "those who were with him [Simon]." This isn't the *turbae* we see in Luke. It's Jesus's followers, not the mob. This is made clear in verse 38, where Jesus says to them, "Let's go elsewhere." He takes them with him. In Luke, however, he tells the crowd that he has to go. The *turbae* might have gone with him, but Jesus doesn't invite them to. In fact, they had just tried to restrain him from leaving.

### Luke 4:42–44

**42. turbae:** This is the multitude, not the circle of Jesus's followers, as we have in Mark. Luke makes some significant changes. In Mark, Simon (Peter) has a privileged role in this scene and appears to be leading Jesus's closest followers, *qui cum illo erant.* In Luke, however, Simon plays no role whatsoever, and it's the crowd that catches up with Jesus. Jesus goes to pray in Mark, but Luke doesn't tell us why Jesus goes into the desert. The crowd in Mark merely asks a question. In Luke it seems to hinder him from going on further. Is there any significance to these changes? **ne discederet ab eis:** a negative jussive noun clause: "they kept him from getting away from them." The crowd wouldn't let him leave. Jesus has to explain why he needs to go, and it's not to cure other people. It's to spread the news about the Kingdom of God.

# Mark 1:35–39 (cont.)

**38** Et ait illis, "Eamus alibi in proximos vicos, ut et ibi praedicem. Ad hoc enim veni." **39** Et vēnit praedicans in synagogis eorum per omnem Galilaeam et daemonia eiciens.

## Luke 4:42–44 (cont.)

**43** Quibus ille ait, "Et aliis civitatibus oportet me evangelizare regnum Dei, quia ideo missus sum." **44** Et erat praedicans in synagogis Iudaeae.

## Vocabulary

**alibi,** elsewhere
**evangelizo (1),** to preach; spread the word about
**ideo,** on this account; therefore
**oportet, -uit,** to be necessary; appropriate
**proximus, -a, -um,** nearby
**vicus, -i,** *m.,* village

## Historical and Grammatical Notes

### Mark 1:35–39 (cont.)

**38. Eamus:** "Let's go." Jesus is including Simon and *qui cum illo erant.* Presumably the crowd has been left behind. **Ad hoc:** that is, "to preach." Jesus may be weary of performing miracle cures. His mission is to preach, not heal.

**39. et daemonia eiciens:** This is deleted in Luke, where Jesus is said to be preaching only. He may be throwing out demons, but why would Luke discard these words? Could it be that these three words were added to Mark after Luke received his copy of Mark's Gospel? That is, the version of Mark that Luke was working from isn't the same in all the details as the one we have. The end of sentences is a convenient place for later copyists to add material they may think is helping the original become clearer or more forceful. That's for the very simple reason that there is space there for a few extra words before the end of the line is reached. But if it's a correct interpretation of this section that Jesus wants to get away from healing and back to preaching, then despite this copyist's best intention, adding these words obscures, rather than amplifies, the sense of the original.

# Mark 1:40–45

## *Jesus Heals a Leper*

Jesus heals a leper. He orders him to go to a priest to offer the traditional thank offerings for the cure. Despite being told not to tell anyone what has happened, the healed man spreads the news about Jesus's amazing powers. Jesus finds it difficult to move around freely in public because of the size of the crowds that he is starting to attract.

**40** Et vĕnit ad eum leprosus, deprecans eum et genu
flectens et dicens ei, "Si vis, potes me mundare." **41** Et
misertus, extendens manum suam, tetigit eum, et ait illi,
"Volo. Mundare!" **42** Et statim discessit ab eo lepra, et
mundatus est.

## Matthew 8:1–4

**1** Cum autem descendisset de monte, secutae sunt eum turbae
multae. **2** Et ecce: leprosus veniens adorabat eum, dicens, "Domine,
si vis, potes me mundare." **3** Et, extendens manum, tetigit eum,
dicens, "Volo. Mundare!" Et confestim mundata est lepra eius.

## Luke 5:12–16

**12** Et factum est, cum esset in unā civitatum, et ecce: vir plenus
leprā. Et videns Iesum et procidens in faciem, rogavit eum, dicens,
"Domine, si vis, potes me mundare." **13** Et extendens manum tetigit
illum, dicens, "Volo. Mundare!" Et confestim lepra discessit ab illo.

## Vocabulary

**adoro (1),** to pray to; curse
**deprecor, -ari, -atus sum,** to beg
**extendo, -dere, -di, -tus** *or* **-sus,** to extend; reach out
**flecto, -ctere, -xi, -ctus,** to bend
**lepra, -ae,** *f.,* leprosy
**leprosus, -a, -um,** afflicted with leprosy; a leper
**misereor, -eri, -rtus sum** + *genitive,* to feel sorry for; take pity on
**mundo (1),** to heal; make whole
**possum, posse, potui,** to be able
**volo, velle, volui, voliturus,** to wish; want

## Historical and Grammatical Notes

### Mark 1:40–45

**41. misertus:** There is a manuscript dispute in the original Greek. A major variant reading says that Jesus was enraged, not moved to pity, by the man. **manum suam:** object of the participle *extendens,* which leaves *eum* as the object of *tetigit.* Touching a leper was an extraordinary act. **Mundare:** Despite its resemblance to a present infinitive, this is the second person passive imperative—"Be healed."

### Matthew 8:1–4

**1. de monte:** There is no account of how Jesus came to be on a mountain between this scene and what had come before, where Jesus had delivered his unusual sermon, speaking unlike the scribes. As we saw in Mark, this pericope isn't connected with its immediate context.

# Mark 1:40–45 (cont.)

**43** Et infremuit in eum statimque eiecit illum, **44** et dicit
ei, "Vide nemini quidquam dixeris. Sed vade. Ostende
te sacerdoti et offer pro emundatione tuā, quae praecepit
Moyses, in testimonium illis." **45** At ille egressus coepit
praedicare multum et diffamare sermonem, ita ut iam non
posset manifesto in civitatem introire, sed foris in desertis
locis erat. Et conveniebant ad eum undique.

## Matthew 8:1–4 (cont.)

**4** Et ait illi Iesus, "Vide nemini dixeris. Sed vade. Ostende te sacerdoti et offer munus, quod praecepit Moyses, in testimonium illis."

## Luke 5:12–16 (cont.)

**14** Et ipse praecepit illi, ut nemini diceret, sed, "Vade. Ostende te
sacerdoti et offer pro emundatione tuā, sicut praecepit Moyses,
in testimonium illis." **15** Perambulabat autem magis sermo de
illo, et conveniebant turbae multae, ut audirent et curarentur ab
infirmitatibus suis. **16** Ipse autem secedebat in desertis et orabat.

# Vocabulary

**convenio, -venire, -vēni, -ventus,** to fit
**diffamo (1),** to spread around
**emundatio, -ionis,** *f.*, healing; cure
**foris,** outside
**infremo, -ere, -ui,** to growl at; roar, rage
**magis,** more; even more; greater
**manifesto,** openly
**multum,** greatly; much
**munus, -eris,** *n.*, gift; offering
**ostendo, -dere, -ndi, -tus** *or* **-sus,** to show
**perambulo (1),** to spread out; get around
**praecipio, -cipere, -cepi, -ceptus** + *dative,* to instruct; order
**quisquam, quaequam, quicquam** *or* **quidquam,** anyone; anything
**sacerdos, -otis,** *m.*, priest
**undique,** from everywhere
**vado,** to go; walk

# Historical and Grammatical Notes

## Mark 1:40–45 (cont.)

**43. infremuit:** Here there is no doubt that Jesus is being stern, if not threatening, in Mark. A variant for this reading of Mark has *comminatus est ei*: "he threatened him." An angry, or at least frustrated, Jesus at this point is certainly dramatically understandable. He wants to preach the imminent arrival of the Kingdom of God, and yet again and again people seek him out only to heal their ailments.

**44. Vide nemini quidquam dixeris:** "See [to it that] to no one you say anything" = "see to it that you say nothing to anyone." **Ostende te:** To be admitted back into society, the leper had to present himself to the priest, who would verify that the disease was gone (Lv 14:1–32). Despite Jesus's orders, the man doesn't keep quiet about it. The result is that Jesus can no longer go out openly in public without attracting a mob.

**45. ita ut:** Mark is explicit that Jesus goes into the wilderness because the crowds have grown too large—to no effect, though, because they find him even there. Matthew doesn't mention the crowds at all, and Luke merely says that Jesus cured the people who'd come to him and then he withdrew.

## Luke 5:12–16 (cont.)

**15. Perambulabat:** The leper isn't faulted for having disobeyed Jesus. The word of what happened simply got around.

# Chapter 2

As Jesus's reputation and following grow, he is increasingly drawn into conflict with religious and political authorities. Even disciples of John the Baptist charge Jesus and his followers with being lax about observing basic religious practices. Jesus responds to these complaints with parables, thus opening a repeated theme in Mark's Gospel. Even his closest associates have difficulty understanding his true teachings and apprehending his identity.

# Mark 2:1–12

## *Jesus Heals a Paralytic*

Jesus is staying in a private home in Capernaum when a paralytic is brought to him. The size of the crowd in front of the house forces them to lower the man's stretcher into the house through a hole that they dig through the ceiling. Jesus shocks some scribes present at the scene not by curing the man, which he does, but by proclaiming that his sins have been forgiven. Only God, they insist, can forgive sin.

**1** Et iterum intravit Capharnaum post dies, et auditum
est quod in domo esset. **2** Et convenerunt multi, ita ut non
amplius caperentur neque ad ianuam. Et loquebatur eis
verbum. **3** Et veniunt ferentes ad eum paralyticum, qui a
quattuor portabatur. **4** Et cum non possent offerre eum illi
prae turbā, nudaverunt tectum ubi erat, et perfodientes
summittunt grabatum, in quo paralyticus iacebat. **5** Cum
vidisset autem Iesus fidem illorum, ait paralytico, "Fili,
dimittuntur peccata tua." **6** Erant autem illic quidam de
scribis sedentes et cogitantes in cordibus suis, **7** "Quid hĭc
sic loquitur? Blasphemat! Quis potest dimittere peccata
nisi solus Deus?"

### Matthew 9:1–8

**1** Et ascendens in naviculam transfretavit et vĕnit in civitatem suam.
**2** Et ecce: offerebant ei paralyticum iacentem in lecto. Et videns
Iesus fidem illorum dixit paralytico, "Confide, fili. Remittuntur
peccata tua." **3** Et ecce: quidam de scribis dixerunt intra se, "Hĭc
blasphemat."

### Luke 5:17–26

**17** Et factum est in unā dierum, et ipse erat docens, et erant
Pharisaei sedentes et legis doctores, qui venerant ex omni castello
Galilaeae et Iudaeae et Ierusalem. Et virtus Domini erat ei ad
sanandum. **18** Et ecce: viri portantes in lecto hominem, qui erat

paralyticus, et quaerebant eum inferre et ponere ante eum. **19** Et
non invenientes quā parte illum inferrent prae turbā, ascenderunt
supra tectum et per tegulas summiserunt illum cum lectulo in
medium ante Iesum. **20** Quorum fidem ut vidit, dixit, "Homo,
remittuntur tibi peccata tua." **21** Et coeperunt cogitare scribae et
Pharisaei, dicentes, "Quis est hĭc qui loquitur blasphemias? Quis
potest dimittere peccata nisi solus Deus?"

# Vocabulary

**amplius,** anymore; more; further
**blasphemo (1),** to blaspheme
**castellum, -i,** *n.,* fort; village
**confido, -dere, -sus sum** + *dative,* to have faith; trust in
**doctor, -oris,** *m.,* teacher
**fides, -ei,** *f.,* faith
**grabatum, -i,** *n.,* stretcher
**illic,** there; in that place
**intro (1),** to enter into
**lectulum, -i,** *n.,* bed; couch
**lectus, -i,** *m.,* couch
**paralyticus, -i,** *m.,* paralytic
**pars, partis,** *f.,* part; area
**perfodio, -odere, -odi, -ossus,** to dig through
**Pharisaeus, -i,** *m.,* a Pharisee
**quidam, quaedam, quod[d]am,** a certain; some
**remitto, -mittere, -misi, -missus,** to send back
**sano (1),** to heal
**sedeo, sedere, sedi, sessus,** to sit
**summitto, -mittere, -misi, -missus,** to send underneath; lower
**tectum, -i,** *n.,* dwelling; roof
**tegula, -ae,** *f.,* rafter
**transfreto (1),** to cross over

# Historical and Grammatical Notes

## Mark 2:1–12

**1. post dies:** "after a few days." **quod in domo esset:** indirect statement: "that he was at home." **domo:** Jesus's biological family has probably relocated to Capernaum, but this could mean that Jesus was at his familial home, the place where he personally was living, or the house of his host while he was visiting.

**2. neque ad ianuam:** "not even at the door." That is, there were so many people gathering that even the porch of the house was overcrowded.

**4. prae turbā:** "because of the crowd." **ubi erat:** "where Jesus was." **perfodientes:** Since the house was made of dried mud brick, the image of the men "digging through" to get in is very fitting.

**5. dimittuntur peccata tua:** This is the only cure effected by forgiving sin. The rest are worked through the casting out of demons or by some other means.

## Matthew 9:1–8

**2. ei:** dative after the compound verb *offerebant.*

# Mark 2:1–12 (cont.)

**8** Quo statim cognito Iesus spiritu suo quia sic cogitarent
intra se dicit illis, “Quid ista cogitatis in cordibus vestris? **9**
Quid est facilius: dicere paralytico, ‘Dimittuntur peccata
tua,’ an dicere, ‘Surge et tolle grabatum tuum et ambula’?
**10** Ut autem sciatis quia potestatem habet filius hominis
in terrā dimittendi peccata”—ait paralytico—**11** “Tibi
dico, surge! Tolle grabatum tuum et vade in domum
tuam.” **12** Et surrexit et protinus, sublato grabato, abiit
coram omnibus, ita ut admirarentur omnes et glorificarent
Deum, dicentes, “Numquam sic vidimus!”

## Matthew 9:1–8 (cont.)

**4** Et cum vidisset Iesus cogitationes eorum, dixit, “Ut quid
cogitatis mala in cordibus vestris? **5** Quid enim est facilius: dicere,
‘Dimittuntur peccata tua,’ aut dicere, ‘Surge et ambula?’ **6** Ut sciatis
autem quoniam filius hominis habet potestatem in terrā dimittendi
peccata”—tunc ait paralytico—”Surge! Tolle lectum tuum et
vade in domum tuam.” **7** Et surrexit et abiit in domum suam. **8**
Videntes autem turbae timuerunt et glorificaverunt Deum, qui dedit
potestatem talem hominibus.

## Luke 5:17–26 (cont.)

**22** Ut cognovit autem Iesus cogitationes eorum, respondens dixit ad
illos, “Quid cogitatis in cordibus vestris? **23** Quid est facilius: dicere,
‘Dimittuntur tibi peccata tua,’ an dicere, ‘Surge et ambula?’ **24** Ut
autem sciatis quia filius hominis potestatem habet in terrā dimittere
peccata”—ait paralytico—“Tibi dico, surge! Tolle lectulum tuum
et vade in domum tuam.” **25** Et confestim surgens coram illis tulit
in quo iacebat, et abiit in domum suam, magnificans Deum. **26** Et
stupor apprehendit omnes, et magnificabant Deum. Et repleti sunt
timore, dicentes, “Vidimus mirabilia hodie.”

## Vocabulary

**admiror -ari, -miratus sum,** to admire; be amazed
**cogitatio, -ionis,** *f.*, thought
**cognosco, -oscere, -ovi, -itus,** to come to know; recognize
**coram** + *ablative,* before; in front of
**facilis, -e,** easy
**magnifico (1),** to fuss over; make a big deal of
**mirabilis, -e,** wonderful; miraculous
**pono, ponere, posui, positus,** to put; place
**repleo, -ere, -evi, -etus,** to fill up
**talis, -e,** such; so great a(n)
**timeo, -ere, -ui,** to fear; be afraid
**tollo, tollere, sustuli, sublatus,** to lift up; destroy

## Historical and Grammatical Notes

### Mark 2:1–12 (cont.)

**8. Quo . . . intra se:** a very convoluted expression that may be clearer if reordered thus and with the elements of the ablative absolute underscored: *quo quia sic cogitarent spiritu suo intra se cognito, Iesus . . .* "Then with it [*quo*] being known [*cognito*] that they were thinking in this way in their minds among themselves, Jesus . . ." What makes this difficult is that the nominative *Iesus* is inserted into the middle of an ablative absolute construction: *Quo . . . cognito.* The clause *quia sic* is a complement to the pronoun *quo,* which serves to explain what is known. Note how Matthew and Luke rephrase and simplify this difficult expression. **Quid ista cogitatis:** *Ista* is neuter accusative plural and direct object of *cogitatis*: "Why are you thinking those things?"

**10. Ut:** This purpose clause is without an explicit main clause: "So you'll know . . ." **dimittendi:** gerund functioning as a complementary genitive of *potestatem*: "has the power of forgiving."

### Luke 5:17–26 (cont.)

**17. ei:** dative of possession: "there was to him the power" or "he had the power" of the Lord to heal.

**19. quā parte:** indirect question: "where they might bring him in before the crowd."

**20. Quorum . . . vidit:** = *Ut* (when) *vidit fidem eorum.*

**22. Quid cogitatis:** "What are you thinking in your hearts?"

**25. tulit in quo iacebat:** Supply *lectulum* after *tulit.*

# Mark 2:13–17

## *Levi (Matthew) Is Called; Publicans and Sinners*

Jesus calls the toll collector Levi. Jesus's easy association with the impure in Galilee causes the scribes of the Pharisees to object that he is not observing the traditional purity regulations expected of all good Jews.

**13** Et egressus est rursus ad mare, omnisque turba
veniebat ad eum, et docebat eos. **14** Et cum praeteriret,
vidit Levin Alphaei sedentem ad teloneum, et ait illi,
"Sequere me." Et surgens secutus est eum. **15** Et factum
est cum accumberet in domo illius et multi publicani et
peccatores simul discumbebant cum Iesu et discipulis
eius. Erant enim multi et sequebantur eum.

## Matthew 9:9–13

**9** Et cum transiret inde Iesus vidit hominem sedentem in teloneo,
Matthaeum nomine, et ait illi, "Sequere me." Et surgens, secutus
est eum. **10** Et factum est discumbente eo in domo, ecce: multi
publicani et peccatores venientes simul discumbebant cum Iesu et
discipulis eius.

## Luke 5:27–32

**27** Et post haec exiit et vidit publicanum, nomine Levi, sedentem ad
teloneum, et ait illi, "Sequere me." **28** Et relictis omnibus, surgens
secutus est eum. **29** Et fecit ei convivium magnum Levi in domo
suā. Et erat turba multa publicanorum et aliorum, qui cum illis erant
discumbentes.

# Vocabulary

**accumbo, -cumbere, -cubui, -cubitus,** to recline at the dinner table
**convivium, -i,** *n.,* party; feast
**discumbo, -cumbere, -cubui, -cubitum,** to recline at the dinner table
**publicanus, -i,** *m.,* tax collector; public contractor
**rursus,** again
**simul,** at the same time
**teloneum, -i,** *n.,* tollbooth; tax table

# Historical and Grammatical Notes

## Mark 2:13–17

**14. Levin:** accusative of "Levi." Matthew changes the name to "Matthew." Luke retains Mark's "Levi." Levi, the son of Alphaeus, is not otherwise known in the New Testament. The name doesn't appear in the list of the canonical Twelve at Mark 3:13–19. Is Levi just another name for Matthew, a son of Alphaeus? Or was there some ambiguity about who was being called in this pericope, an ambiguity that Matthew tried to correct by renaming Levi to Matthew?

**15. Et factum est cum:** "And then there came [a time] when . . ." **multi publicani et peccatores:** *Publicani,* essentially, were civil servants, as we might call them today, working for the Roman administration. Some of them would have been tax collectors, but there were many other duties that they may have performed. Levi was indeed a tax collector, or at least a tollbooth attendant where fees were collected, because he was found *ad teloneum.* The problem that the Pharisees and their scribes had was not that Jesus associated with these people, but that he was eating with them, and, presumably, eating at the house of a *publicanus.* Pharisaic law was nowhere more particular and detailed than in matters of ritual cleanliness and food. They strictly forbade eating with the unclean, defined generally as anyone who wasn't Jewish. Jesus doesn't challenge their laws or say that they should be repealed across the board. He says only that his special mission exempts him.

## Luke 5:27–32

**29. aliorum:** "foreigners." Thus Luke clarifies what the Pharisees mean. Jesus should not be eating with them not merely because of what they do, but because of who they are. It would have been difficult in a diverse region such as Galilee not to have contact, and even friendships, with Greeks, Romans, and many other people of foreign extraction.

# Mark 2:13–17 (cont.)

**16** Et scribae Pharisaeorum, videntes quia manducaret
cum peccatoribus et publicanis, dicebant discipulis eius,
"Quare cum publicanis et peccatoribus manducat?" **17**
Et Iesus hoc audito ait illis, "Non necesse habent sani
medicum, sed qui male habent. Non veni vocare iustos sed
peccatores."

## Matthew 9:9–13 (cont.)

**11** Et videntes Pharisaei dicebant discipulis eius, "Quare cum
publicanis et peccatoribus manducat magister vester?" **12** At ille
audiens ait, "Non est opus valentibus medico, sed male habentibus.
**13** Euntes autem discite quid est: 'Misericordiam volo et non
sacrificium.' Non enim veni vocare iustos sed peccatores."

## Luke 5:27–32 (cont.)

**30** Et murmurabant Pharisaei et scribae eorum adversus discipulos
eius, dicentes, "Quare cum publicanis et peccatoribus manducatis
et bibitis?" **31** Et respondens Iesus dixit ad illos, "Non egent qui sani
sunt medico, sed qui male habent. **32** Non veni vocare iustos sed
peccatores in paenitentiam."

## Vocabulary

**adversus** + *accusative,* to; against
**bibo, -ere, -ii,** to drink
**disco, discere, didici,** to learn
**egeo, -ere, -ui** + *ablative,* to need
**iustus, -a, -um,** righteous
**medicus, -i,** *m.,* doctor
**misericordia, -ae,** *f.,* pity; sympathy; mercy
**murmuro (1),** to whisper; murmur
**opus, -eris,** *n.,* + *dative,* work; task; duty; a need for
**quare,** for what/which reason; why

## Historical and Grammatical Notes

### Mark 2:13–17 (cont.)

17. **sani:** subject of *habent*: "it is not necessary [that] the healthy have a doctor." **vocare:** infinitive showing purpose.

### Matthew 9:9–13 (cont.)

12. **male habentibus:** "for those holding badly" = "for the sick."

13. **Euntes autem discite:** "Go and learn."

### Luke 5:27–32 (cont.)

31. **Non egent qui sani sunt medico:** "Those who are well don't need a doctor."

# Mark 2:18–20

## *Fasting and the Law*

Some followers of John, accompanied by the Pharisees, ask Jesus why his disciples don't observe the ritual fast days. Jesus replies with his first parable.

**18** Et erant discipuli Ioannis et Pharisaei ieiunantes. Et veniunt et dicunt illi, "Cur discipuli Ioannis et discipuli Pharisaeorum ieiunant, tui autem discipuli non ieiunant?"
**19** Et ait illis Iesus, "Numquid possunt convivae nuptiarum quamdiu sponsus cum illis est ieiunare? Quanto tempore habent secum sponsum non possunt
ieiunare. **20** Venient autem dies, cum auferetur ab eis sponsus, et tunc ieiunabunt in illā die."

### Matthew 9:14–15

**14** Tunc accedunt ad eum discipuli Ioannis, dicentes, "Quare nos et Pharisaei ieiunamus frequenter, discipuli autem tui non ieiunant?"
**15** Et ait illis Iesus, "Numquid possunt convivae nuptiarum lugere quamdiu cum illis est sponsus? Venient autem dies, cum auferetur ab eis sponsus, et tunc ieiunabunt."

### Luke 5:33–35

**33** At illi dixerunt ad eum, "Discipuli Ioannis ieiunant frequenter et obsecrationes faciunt, similiter et Pharisaeorum. Tui autem
edunt et bibunt." **34** Quibus Iesus ait, "Numquid potestis convivas
nuptiarum, dum cum illis est sponsus, facere ieiunare? **35** Venient
autem dies, et cum ablatus fuerit ab illis sponsus, tunc ieiunabunt in illis diebus."

## Vocabulary

**aufero, auferre, abstuli, ablatus,** to take away
**conviva, -ae,** *m.*, invited guest
**frequenter,** frequently; often
**lugeo, -gere, -xi, -ctus,** to lament
**numquid,** *interrogative to begin a question,* what
**nuptiae, -arum,** *f. pl.*, wedding festivities
**obsecratio, -ionis,** *f.*, supplication; prayer
**quamdiu,** how long; so long as
**sponsus, -i,** *m.*, groom

## Historical and Grammatical Notes

### Mark 2:18–20

**18. erant:** the vulgate compound imperfect: "the Pharisees and disciples of John were fasting." We have in this passage evidence that there were followers of John the Baptist who didn't accept Jesus as their leader, but continued to be loyal to John. At the beginning of Mark's Gospel, it appears that Jesus is but another follower of John, and that he struck out on his own when John was arrested by Herod Antipas, the local ruler in Judea. It's clear from this passage that some of John's original followers became followers of Jesus. There are some who remained loyal to John and thought that some of Jesus's teachings were at odds with John's.

**20. cum auferetur ab eis sponsus:** Jesus's answer must have been shocking. He is stating as clearly as he ever says anything in a parable that his presence alone is enough to suspend the practice of fasting. This is Jesus's first parable in Mark. The word "parable" is little more than a transliteration of a Greek word, and though in modern times it has come to mean something quite specific, it originally means any number of ways of illustrating a point. There's no one way to translate the word since it covers such a wide range of possibilities: metaphor, allegory, analogy, even riddle.

### Luke 5:33–35

**34. potestis:** "can you make [*facere*] the guests at a wedding party fast while the groom is with them?"

# Mark 2:21–22

## *Two Parables about the Old and the New*

Jesus uses two more parables to illustrate his understanding of the proper role of the Law: New wine is not put into an old wine skin and one does not patch an old garment with new cloth.

**21** "Nemo assumentum panni rudis assuit vestimento veteri, alioquin supplementum aufert aliquid ab eo, novum a veteri, et peior scissura fit.

### Matthew 9:16–17

**16** "Nemo autem immittit commissuram panni rudis in vestimentum vetus. Tollit enim supplementum eius a vestimento, et peior scissura fit.

### Luke 5:36–39

**36** Dicebat autem et similitudinem ad illos, "Nemo abscindit commissuram a vestimento novo et immittit in vestimentum vetus, alioquin et novum rumpet, et veteri non conveniet commissura a novo.

## Vocabulary

**alioquin,** otherwise
**assumentum, -i,** *n.,* swath
**assuo, -suere, -sui, -sutus,** to sew on
**commissura, -ae,** *f.,* seam; stitch
**immitto, -mittere, -misi, -missus,** to insert
**pannus, -i,** *m.,* piece of cloth
**peior, peius,** worse
**rudis, -e,** rough; raw
**scissura, -ae,** *f.,* rip; tear
**supplementum, -i,** *n.,* patch
**vetus, -eris,** old

## Historical and Grammatical Notes

### Mark 2:21–22

**21. novum a veteri:** "the new patch [takes something] from the old [garment]." That is, it tears the old garment because the new patch is likely to shrink as it ages, whereas the old garment has already shrunk to its final size. The general sense of these two very famous parables is clear enough: The old and the new don't mix. But what is Jesus saying is the old and what is he saying is the new? It's not easy to decide in this context. The Pharisees tried to interpret the old, Mosaic laws in light of new realities, in much the same way that the US Constitution is constantly being supplemented by the creation of new laws that try to apply to new conditions that the Constitution could never have envisioned. In this analogy, therefore, Jesus would appear to be attacking what the Pharisees do: making new laws to supplement the old laws. Further, the context is that Jesus has just violated a rule developed by the Pharisees, not one that was part of the Mosaic code. It makes perfect sense that Jesus would assail them for creating new laws and trying to fit them onto the old laws.

### Matthew 9:16–17

**16. supplementum:** *Supplementum* is the subject of *tollit*: "its patch pulls away from the garment."

# Mark 2:21–22 (cont.)

**22** Et nemo mittit vinum novellum in utres veteres,
alioquin dirumpet vinum utres. Et vinum perit et utres.
Sed vinum novum in utres novos."

## Matthew 9:16–17 (cont.)

**17** Neque mittunt vinum novum in utres veteres, alioquin rumpuntur utres, et vinum effunditur, et utres pereunt. Sed vinum novum in utres novos mittunt, et ambo conservantur."

## Luke 5:36–39 (cont.)

**37** Et nemo mittit vinum novum in utres veteres, alioquin rumpet
vinum novum utres et ipsum effundetur, et utres peribunt. **38** Sed
vinum novum in utres novos mittendum est. **39** Et nemo bibens
vetus vult novum. Dicit enim, 'Vetus melius est!' "

## Vocabulary

**abscindo, -scindere, -scidi, -scissus,** to cut away; cut out
**aliquis, aliquid,** someone; something
**dirumpo, -rumpere, -rupi, -ruptus,** to burst
**effundo, -fundere, -fudi, -fusus,** to pour out
**novellus, -a, -um,** new
**pereo, -ire, -ii** *or* **-ivi, -itus,** to be destroyed; perish
**similitudo, -inis,** *f.*, likeness; comparison; parable; riddle
**uter, utris,** *m.*, leather bag; skin for wine

## Historical and Grammatical Notes

### Mark 2:21–22 (cont.)

22. **vinum novellum:** Why would new wine ruin old wineskins? An apparent answer is that as it ferments, it gives off gas. The old skin would not be able to expand enough to keep from rupturing. So new wine should be put only into new, more flexible skins. So what are the analogs to the new wine and the old wineskins? In the context of this passage, the old wineskins would be Mosaic laws as recorded in the Torah, and the new wine is the Pharisaic laws. Luke, at least, seems to have understood it this way because of the sentence he adds at the end: "the old wine is better than the new wine." So where does that leave us? In these two parables, Jesus appears to be saying that the old, original Mosaic laws are superior to modern laws, and one damages Moses's original intent by trying to patch on new laws. Jesus and his followers therefore don't feel bound by the new laws of the Pharisees and others, but adhere to the more ancient Mosaic laws.

### Luke 5:36–39 (cont.)

36. **veteri:** dative after *conveniet*: "and the patch from the new garment will not fit the old garment."

# Mark 2:23–28

## *Working on the Sabbath*

Jesus's alleged indifference to the Law reaches a climax when he does not keep his followers from working on the Sabbath. Jesus counters that King David once ate the sacred bread from the Temple, which is a clear violation of sacred law.

**23** Et factum est, cum ipse Sabbatis ambularet per sata,
discipuli eius coeperunt praegredi vellentes spicas. **24**
Pharisaei autem dicebant ei, "Ecce: quid faciunt Sabbatis,
quod non licet?" **25** Et ait illis, "Numquam legistis quid
fecerit David, quando necessitatem habuit et esuriit ipse et
qui cum eo erant?

## Matthew 12:1–8

**1** In illo tempore abiit Iesus Sabbatis per sata. Discipuli autem eius
esurierunt et coeperunt vellere spicas et manducare. **2** Pharisaei
autem videntes dixerunt ei, "Ecce: discipuli tui faciunt quod non
licet facere Sabbato." **3** At ille dixit eis, "Non legistis quid fecerit
David, quando esuriit, et qui cum eo erant?

## Luke 6:1–5

**1** Factum est autem in Sabbato, cum transiret per sata, et vellebant
discipuli eius spicas et manducabant confricantes manibus. **2**
Quidam autem Pharisaeorum dixerunt, "Quid facitis, quod non licet
in Sabbatis?" **3** Et respondens Iesus ad eos dixit, "Nec hoc legistis
quod fecit David, cum esurisset ipse et qui cum eo erant?

## Vocabulary

**confrico (1),** to rub together
**lego, legere, legi, lectus,** to pick; read
**licet, licere, licuit** + *dative and infinitive,* it is permitted
**sata, -orum,** *n. pl.,* grain; crops
**spica, -ae,** *f.,* ear of grain
**vello, vellere, velli** *or* **vulsi** *or* **volsi, vulsus** *or* **volsus,** to pick

## Historical and Grammatical Notes

### Mark 2:23–28

23. **praegredi:** "began to get ahead of him." Matthew and Luke both omit this detail and say simply that his disciples picked the grain and removed the chaff.

24. **quid . . . licet:** "why [*quid*] do they do on the Sabbath what [it] is not permitted to do?"

25. **quid fecerit David:** perfect subjunctive in indirect question: "what David did." Again, we see Jesus replying to a question not by replying to it, but by asking another question that seems to change the subject. David didn't perform any work on the Sabbath, so referring to this passage doesn't justify Jesus's indifference to this particular restriction. Jesus's reply is much more radical. He is countering with a fundamental assault on what the Law really is. How do we know what the Law is when we see it broken even by the most revered figures? Further, Jesus appears to be implying a comparison between himself and David: "David broke the Law, didn't he? Why would you expect me to be bound by it?" **quando . . . erant:** "when he and those who were with him had need."

# Mark 2:23–28 (cont.)

**26** Quomodo introivit in domum Dei sub Abiathar
principe sacerdotum et panes propositionis manducavit,
quos non licet manducare nisi sacerdotibus, et dedit
etiam eis qui cum eo erant?" **27** Et dicebat eis, "Sabbatum
propter hominem factum est, et non homo propter
Sabbatum. **28** Itaque dominus est filius hominis etiam
Sabbati."

## Matthew 12:1–8 (cont.)

**4** Quomodo intravit in domum Dei et panes propositionis comedit,
quod non licebat ei edere neque his, qui cum eo erant, nisi solis
sacerdotibus? **5** Aut non legistis in Lege quia Sabbatis sacerdotes
in Templo Sabbatum violant et sine crimine sunt? **6** Dico autem
vobis quia Templo maior est hīc. **7** Si autem sciretis quid est,
'Misericordiam volo et non sacrificium,' numquam condemnassetis
innocentes. **8** Dominus est enim filius hominis Sabbati."

## Luke 6:1–5 (cont.)

**4** Quomodo intravit in domum Dei et panes propositionis sumpsit
et manducavit et dedit his qui cum ipso erant, quos non licet
manducare nisi tantum sacerdotibus?" **5** Et dicebat illis, "Dominus
est Sabbati filius hominis."

## Vocabulary

**comedo, -edere** *or* **-esse, -edi, -esus,** to eat
**crimen, -inis,** *n.,* crime
**etiam,** even still; be that as it may
**innocens, -ntis,** innocent
**Lex, Legis,** *f.,* the Laws; the Pentateuch
**maior, maius,** greater
**panis, -is,** *m.,* bread; loaf
**sumo, sumere, sumpsi, sumptus,** to take up
**quando,** when; *after* **ne,** ever; in any way
**tantum,** only

## Historical and Grammatical Notes

### Mark 2:23–28 (cont.)

**26. Abiathar principe:** Modern commentators are quick to note an error in Mark: The priest in the Old Testament reference (1 Sm 21) was Abimelek, not his son Abiathar. Further, Abimelek was not the high priest. Both Matthew and Luke correct this error by omitting any mention of the priest involved in the story. Whatever its cause or source—Jesus, Mark, or Peter (who tradition holds is Mark's source)—the fact that such an easily corrected mistake was retained in the manuscript tradition shows how determined the copyists were to preserve the precise reading of the original, even when that meant passing along imperfections and passages that were difficult to understand.

**28. filius hominis:** Jesus, and only Jesus, uses this expression about himself and it's impossible to know how his first followers would have understood it. Jesus could have meant anything from a human being to the figure seen in Daniel 7:13. It could very well be just a literal rendering into Greek, and then into Latin, of the Aramaic expression that means simply "a human being." The last interpretation makes perfect sense in this context, where Jesus is saying that the Sabbath is for human beings and not the other way around.

### Matthew 12:1–8 (cont.)

**5. sacerdotes . . . violant:** The priests are implicated presumably because they allowed David to take the bread.

**6. Templo:** ablative of comparison after *maior.* **hīc:** "here." It could refer to the place in the Temple where the display bread was set out. It could also refer to the place where Jesus has just shown mercy to his followers because of their hunger.

**7. Si autem sciretis quid est . . . innocentes:** "If you had known what this means—I want mercy, not sacrifice—you would never have condemned the innocent." *Condemnassetis* is a syncopated form of *condemnavissetis.*

# Chapter 3

Chapter 3 begins the development of another main idea in the Gospel, the demands of discipleship. As Jesus's reputation begins to grow outside of Galilee, he picks out twelve of his followers to help him spread his message. The logistics of managing large crowds begin to become an issue for Jesus and his followers. Many people are so anxious to see him that they come without any concern for how they will provide for themselves. Because he casts out demons, the Pharisees allege that Jesus's power comes from Satan. Jesus replies with another parable. Jesus turns away his family, who've come because they fear that he has gone mad. He says that his true family are those who are doing the will of God.

# Mark 3:1–7

## *Jesus Heals on the Sabbath*

The Pharisees and their scribes follow Jesus into another synagogue, where they tempt Jesus to perform a miraculous cure on the Sabbath. Jesus sees through their trap and challenges them with a question they refuse to answer. He performs the healing, which causes the Pharisees to begin colluding with the Herodians to destroy Jesus.

**1** Et introivit iterum in synagogam. Et erat ibi homo
habens manum aridam. **2** Et observabant eum, si Sabbatis
curaret illum, ut accusarent eum. **3** Et ait homini habenti
manum aridam, "Surge in medium." **4** Et dicit eis, "Licet
Sabbatis bene facere an male? Animam salvam facere an
perdere?" At illi tacebant.

### Matthew 12:9–14

**9** Et cum inde transisset, venit in synagogam eorum. **10** Et ecce:
homo manum habens aridam. Et interrogabant eum, dicentes,
"Licet Sabbatis curare?" ut accusarent eum. **11** Ipse autem dixit illis,
"Quis erit ex vobis homo, qui habeat ovem unam et, si ceciderit haec
Sabbatis in foveam, nonne tenebit et levabit eam? **12** Quanto igitur
melior est homo ove! Itaque licet Sabbatis bene facere."

### Luke 6:6–11

**6** Factum est autem in alio Sabbato, ut intraret in synagogam
et doceret. Et erat ibi homo, et manus eius dextra erat arida. **7**
Observabant autem illum scribae et Pharisaei, si Sabbato curaret, ut
invenirent accusare illum. **8** Ipse vero sciebat cogitationes eorum,
et ait homini qui habebat manum aridam, "Surge et sta in medium."
Et surgens stetit. **9** Ait autem ad illos Iesus, "Interrogo vos, si licet
Sabbato bene facere an male, animam salvam facere an perdere?"

## Vocabulary

**aridus, -a, -um,** dry; dried out
**cado, cadere, cecidi, casus,** to fall; fall on; attack
**dexter, -tra, -trum,** right; on the right
**fovea, -ae,** *f.*, ditch
**levo (1),** to lift up
**ovis, -is,** *f.*, sheep
**taceo, -ere, -ui, -itus,** to be silent

## Historical and Grammatical Notes

### Mark 3:1–7

**1. in synagogam:** We can see a crescendo effect of Jesus's violations of the Law. He had gone so far as to ignore the work restrictions of the Sabbath, but that occurred out in a field. The violation that begins chapter 3 is both on the Sabbath and in full view of the pious at a synagogue. This pericope would have been a fine conclusion to chapter 2, whose theme was Jesus's growing difficulties with the Law.

**2. Sabbatis:** ablative of time. **curaret:** subjunctive in indirect question.

**4. Licet Sabbatis bene facere an male:** The Pharisees can't answer these questions easily. Besides, they aren't there to defend themselves, but to find a reason to condemn Jesus. They're not interested in debating the Law with another wayward Jew, but in enforcing it.

### Matthew 12:9–14

**10. interrogabant:** This scene has all the appearances of being a trap set by the Pharisees. In none of the Synoptics does the ill man actually ask Jesus for a cure. He is simply presented to Jesus, and the Pharisees wait to see what he does.

**11. Ipse autem dixit illis:** As we've seen before, Matthew adds an explanatory verse to his source to clarify—we might say demystify—the original. But does it help? The man with the withered hand will not die if he is not treated immediately; presumably the lamb that has fallen into the ditch will. This is an evocative metaphor, but it is entirely irrelevant to the situation at hand. Jesus doesn't cure the man's withered hand to save his life. His purpose is to infuriate the Pharisees.

### Luke 6:6–11

**7. invenirent:** "find a way to accuse him."

# Mark 3:1–7 (cont.)

**5** Et circumspiciens eos cum irā, contristatus super caecitate cordis eorum, dicit homini, "Extende manum." Et extendit, et restituta est manus eius. **6** Et exeuntes Pharisaei statim cum Herodianis consilium faciebant adversus eum quomodo eum perderent. **7** Et Iesus cum discipulis suis secessit ad mare.

## Matthew 12:9–14 (cont.)

**13** Tunc ait homini, "Extende manum tuam." Et extendit, et restituta est sana sicut altera. **14** Exeuntes autem Pharisaei consilium faciebant adversus eum, quomodo eum perderent.

## Luke 6:6–11 (cont.)

**10** Et circumspectis omnibus illis, dixit illi, "Extende manum tuam." Et fecit. Et restituta est manus eius. **11** Ipsi autem repleti sunt insipientiā et colloquebantur ad invicem quidnam facerent Iesu.

## Vocabulary

**caecitas, -tatis,** *f.*, blindness
**circumspicio, -spicere, -spexi, -spectus,** to look around; examine
**contristatus, -a, -um,** sad
**Herodianus, -i,** *m.*, a Herodian
**insipientia, -ae,** *f.*, stupidity; ignorance
**restituo, -tuere, -tui, -tutus,** to restore; make whole

## Historical and Grammatical Notes

### Mark 3:1–7 (cont.)

**6. cum Herodianis:** The Herodians might have been upper-class Jews seeking power and prestige for themselves and their circle by associating with Herod Antipas, the local ruler. They might have been Hellenized Jews, who sincerely believed that assimilation into Greek and Roman culture represented a better future for the Jewish nation and were taking steps to bring their people into the wider world. Another possibility is that they were people who thought that accommodation with the Roman authorities was the best way to avoid the wrath of Rome, which had come down on the Jews frequently in the past few generations. Most likely, it was a combination of motives that mingled what they saw as a worthy cause with self-interest.

### Luke 6:6–11 (cont.)

**10. circumspectis:** ablative absolute: "when all of them around had been looked at." This is a very powerful touch. Jesus looked at each one of them individually.

**11. quidnam facerent:** This is an indirect question, probably representing an original deliberative question: "what they should do to Jesus."

# Mark 3:7–12

## *Jesus Silences Demons*

Jesus begins attracting throngs of people from outside of Galilee. He casts out many evil spirits, who as before know who he is.

**7** Et multa turba a Galilaeā secuta est et a Iudaeā **8** et ab
Hierosolymis et ab Idumaeā et qui trans Iordanem et
circa Tyrum et Sidonem—multitudo magna—audientes
quae faciebat, venerunt ad eum. **9** Et dixit discipulis
suis, ut navicula sibi praesto esset propter turbam, ne
comprimerent eum. **10** Multos enim sanavit, ita ut
irruerent in eum, ut illum tangerent, quotquot habebant
plagas. **11** Et spiritūs immundi, cum illum videbant,
procidebant ei et clamabant, dicentes, "Tu es filius Dei!"
**12** Et vehementer comminabatur eis, ne manifestarent
illum.

## Vocabulary

**comprimo, -primere, -pressi, -pressus,** to press up against
**irruo, -ere, -rui, -rutus,** to rush toward
**manifesto (1),** to make clear; reveal; expose
**plaga, -ae,** *f.,* wound; ailment
**praesto,** *indecl.,* available; at hand

## Historical and Grammatical Notes

### MARK 3:7–12

**8. multitudo magna:** Jesus's reputation is spreading through all the regions of Palestine, including Judea, the heart of orthodox Judaism.

**11. Tu es filius Dei:** Many figures in the Old Testament were called the "Son of God," mostly as a way of underscoring their political authority. In this passage, it should not be taken as indicating the second person of the Trinity, as that theological understanding took centuries to develop fully.

# Mark 3:13–19

## *The Twelve Apostles Are Appointed*

Jesus picks twelve of his many followers for a special role in his ministry.

**13** Et ascendit in montem et vocat ad se quos voluit ipse,
et venerunt ad eum. **14** Et fecit Duodecim, ut essent cum
illo, et ut mitteret eos praedicare, **15** habentes potestatem
eiciendi daemonia. **16** Et imposuit Simoni nomen
Petrum. **17** Et Iacobum Zebedaei et Ioannem fratrem
Iacobi, et imposuit eis nomina Boanerges, quod est "Filii
tonitrui." **18** Et Andream et Philippum et Bartholomaeum
et Matthaeum et Thomam et Iacobum Alphaei et
Thaddaeum et Simonem Chananaeum **19** et Iudam
Iscarioth, qui et tradidit illum.

## Matthew 10:1–4

**1** Et convocatis Duodecim discipulis suis, dedit illis potestatem
spirituum immundorum, ut eicerent eos et curarent omnem
languorem et omnem infirmitatem. **2** Duodecim autem apostolorum
nomina sunt haec: primus Simon, qui dicitur Petrus, et Andreas
frater eius, et Iacobus Zebedaei et Ioannes frater eius, **3** Philippus et
Bartholomaeus, Thomas et Matthaeus publicanus, Iacobus Alphaei
et Thaddaeus, **4** Simon Chananaeus et Iudas Iscariotes, qui et
tradidit eum.

## Luke 6:12–16

**12** Factum est autem in illis diebus, exiit in montem orare et erat
pernoctans in oratione Dei. **13** Et cum dies factus esset, vocavit
discipulos suos, et elegit duodecim ex ipsis, quos et apostolos
nominavit: **14** Simonem, quem et cognominavit Petrum, et
Andream fratrem eius et Iacobum et Ioannem et Philippum et
Bartholomaeum **15** et Matthaeum et Thomam et Iacobum Alphaei
et Simonem, qui vocatur Zelotes, **16** et Iudam Iacobi et Iudam
Iscarioth, qui fuit proditor.

## Vocabulary

**Boanerges,** *indecl.,* Sons of Thunder
**cognomino (1),** to give as a second name; give as a nickname
**eligo, -ligere, -legi, -lectus,** to pick out
**oratio, -ionis,** *f.,* prayer
**pernocto (1),** to spend the night
**proditor, -oris,** *m.,* traitor
**Zelotes, -ae,** *m.,* the eager one; zealous one

## Historical and Grammatical Notes

### Mark 3:13–19

**18. Matthaeum:** This is generally assumed to be Levi from Mark 2:14.

### Matthew 10:1–4

**1. curarent . . . infirmitatem:** In Mark, Jesus selects the Twelve for three purposes: (1) to be with him, presumably as assistants, (2) to preach, and (3) to have power over demons.

### Luke 6:12–16

**13. quos et apostolos nominavit:** "whom he also called 'Apostles.' " The word "apostle" means literally "one who is sent out." Mark doesn't use the word until the disciples have actually been sent out on a mission at 6:30.

**15. Zelotes:** Simon is given this nickname to underscore his enthusiasm for Jesus and his message, not to identify him with the group of revolutionaries known as the Zealots who were active in the final insurrection against Rome in 66–70 CE. Simon the Zealot is not heard of again in any of the Gospels.

# Mark 3:20–21

## *The Crowds Have Nothing to Eat; Jesus's People Think That He Is Mad*

The enormous size of the crowds that Jesus is attracting is again emphasized. They are following him without any regard for how they will provide for themselves. Seeing the crowds, Jesus's family thinks that he has gone mad and tries to restrain him.

**20** Et vĕnit ad domum. Et convĕnit iterum turba, ita
ut non possent neque panem manducare. **21** Et cum
audissent sui, exierunt tenere eum. Dicebant enim, "In
furorem versus est."

## Vocabulary

**contra,** to the other side
**digitus, -i,** *m.,* finger
**furor, -oris,** *m.,* madness; rage
**vel,** or; either; perhaps
**verto, -ere, -i, versus,** to turn to; go

## Historical and Grammatical Notes

### Mark 3:20–21

**20. ita ut:** result clause: "such [a size] that." **neque:** "they didn't even have bread to eat," let alone anything else.

**21. audissent:** What did they hear? Probably both that Jesus was back in Capernaum and that there were huge crowds following him. **sui:** It's tempting and probably accurate to translate *sui* as "his family," though strictly speaking it could mean just "his associates" or "friends." **tenere:** infinitive to show purpose: "They came out to get him."

# Mark 3:22–30

## *Some Scribes Claim That Jesus Must Be in League with Satan*

The scribes argue that Jesus must be casting out demons with Satan's permission. Jesus's reply is that it would make no sense for Satan to cast out his own underlings. Jesus illustrates his point with two parables.

**22** Et scribae, qui ab Hierosolymis descenderant,
dicebant, "Beelzebul habet," et "In principe daemonum
eicit daemonia." **23** Et convocatis eis, in parabolis dicebat
illis, "Quomodo potest Satanas Satanam eicere? **24** Et si
regnum in se dividatur, non potest stare regnum illud. **25**
Et si domus in semetipsam dispertiatur, non poterit domus
illa stare. **26** Et si Satanas consurrexit in semetipsum et
dispertitus est, non potest stare, sed finem habet.

### Matthew 12:24–32

**24** Pharisaei autem audientes dixerunt, "Hĭc non eicit daemones nisi
in Beelzebul, principe daemonum." **25** Sciens autem cogitationes
eorum dixit eis, "Omne regnum divisum contra se desolatur, et
omnis civitas vel domus divisa contra se non stabit. **26** Et si Satanas
Satanam eicit, adversus se divisus est. Quomodo ergo stabit regnum
eius? **27** Et si ego in Beelzebul eicio daemones, filii vestri in quo
eiciunt? Ideo ipsi iudices erunt vestri. **28** Si autem in Spiritu Dei ego
eicio daemones, igitur pervēnit in vos regnum Dei.

### Luke 11:15–22

**15** Quidam autem ex eis dixerunt, "In Beelzebul principe
daemoniorum eicit daemonia." **16** Et alii tentantes signum de
caelo quaerebant ab eo. **17** Ipse autem sciens cogitationes eorum
dixit eis, "Omne regnum in seipsum divisum desolatur, et domus
supra domum cadit. **18** Si autem et Satanas in seipsum divisus est,
quomodo stabit regnum ipsius? quia dicitis in Beelzebul eicere me

daemonia. **19** Si autem ego in Beelzebul eicio daemonia, filii vestri in quo eiciunt? Ideo ipsi iudices vestri erunt. **20** Porro si in digito Dei eicio daemonia, profecto pervēnit in vos regnum Dei.

## Vocabulary

**Beelzebul,** *indecl.,* Beelzebul; Satan
**consurgo, -gere, -rexi, -rectus,** to rise up against
**daemon, -is,** *m.,* demon
**desolo (1),** to abandon; desert
**digitum, -i,** *n.,* finger; *also* **digitus, -i,** *m.*
**dispertio, -ire, -ii** *or* **-ivi, -itus,** to apportion out; divide
**divido, -videre, -visi, -visus,** to divvy up
**iudex, -icis,** *m.,* judge
**porro,** at a distance; furthermore
**profecto,** certainly

## Historical and Grammatical Notes

### Mark 3:22–30

**22. scribae, qui ab Hierosolymis:** The fact that these scribes are from Jerusalem indicates that Jesus is being investigated by the highest religious authorities.

**23. in parabolis:** "in riddles."

### Matthew 12:24–32

**24. daemones nisi:** "this man does not cast out demons if not in the name of Beelzebul."

**27. in quo:** "in whose [name]." **Ideo ipsi iudices erunt vestri:** If the Pharisees are right that casting out demons is proof that one is in league with Satan, then what about the followers of the Pharisees? Don't they cast out demons? Wouldn't that mean that they too are in Satan's camp?

**28. pervēnit in vos regnum Dei:** "if I'm casting out demons, then the Kingdom of God has come for you." The Pharisees claim that they have the power to cast out demons, and now they accuse Jesus, an outsider, of having the same power. This would be a sure sign that God is about to end the current order of things, where only the Jewish authorities have powers from God.

### Luke 11:15–22

**16. Et alii tentantes signum de caelo quaerebant ab eo:** "And others, making a trial of him, were asking him for a sign from heaven." Presumably they would withdraw their charge if Jesus could get some sign from God that he is working his will.

**18. eicere me daemonia:** *me daemonia eicere* would be the more natural word order. The Latin follows exactly the word order in Greek, which is also somewhat unusual.

# Mark 3:22–30 (cont.)

**27** Nemo autem potest in domum fortis ingressus vasa
eius diripere, nisi prius fortem alliget. Et tunc domum
eius diripiet. **28** Amen dico vobis, omnia dimittentur
filiis hominum peccata et blasphemiae, quibus
blasphemaverint. **29** Qui autem blasphemaverit in
Spiritum Sanctum non habet remissionem in aeternum,
sed reus est aeterni delicti." **30** Quoniam dicebant,
"Spiritum immundum habet."

## Matthew 12:24–32 (cont.)

**29** Aut quomodo potest quisquam intrare in domum fortis et vasa
eius diripere, nisi prius alligaverit fortem? Et tunc domum illius
diripiet. **30** Qui non est mecum contra me est. Et qui non congregat
mecum spargit. **31** Ideo dico vobis, omne peccatum et blasphemia
remittetur hominibus, Spiritūs autem blasphemia non remittetur. **32**
Et quicumque dixerit verbum contra filium hominis, remittetur ei.
Qui autem dixerit contra Spiritum Sanctum, non remittetur ei neque
in hoc saeculo neque in futuro."

## Luke 11:15–22 (cont.)

**21** Cum fortis armatus custodit atrium suum, in pace sunt ea quae
possidet. **22** Si autem fortior illo superveniens vicerit eum, universa
arma eius auferet in quibus confidebat, et spolia eius distribuet."

## Vocabulary

**alligo (1),** to bind; tie up
**atrium, -i,** *n.,* central room
**custodio, -ire, -ii** *or* **-ivi, -itus,** to guard; watch over
**delictum, -i,** *n.,* crime
**diripio, -ripere, -ripui, -reptus,** to steal; rob
**distribuo, -uere, -ui, -utus,** to distribute
**possideo, -sidere, -sedi, -sessus,** to own
**prior, prius,** earlier
**proficio, -ficere, -feci, -fectum,** to work; succeed
**quicumque, quaecumque, quodcumque,** whosoever; whatsoever
**reus, -a, -um,** accused; guilty of
**saeculum, -i,** *n.,* generation; age; the people of an age
**spargo, -gere, -si, -sus,** to scatter
**spolia, -orum,** *n. pl.,* goods; spoils
**supervenio, -venire, -vēni, -ventus,** to fall upon; attack
**vasum, -i,** *n.,* vase
**vinco, vincere, vici, victus,** to overcome; vanquish

## Historical and Grammatical Notes

### Mark 3:22–30 (cont.)

28. **quibus:** literally, "the blasphemies with which they blaspheme." **blasphemaverint:** The future perfect is used as an indefinite in these legalist contexts: "whosoever has blasphemed."

29. **blasphemaverit:** "whosoever has blasphemed." The passage closes with one of the more challenging passages in the Gospels for the early Christians, for it says that not all sins can be forgiven. What is a blasphemy against the Holy Spirit? Mark gives us a hint of how he understands it at verse 30. Anyone who has seen Jesus's miracles and believes that he is an agent of evil is so blind as to be incorrigible.

### Matthew 12:24–32 (cont.)

30. **Qui non . . . spargit:** "He who is not with me is against me; he who does not gather with me, scatters." Indifference to Jesus's message is not an option. The time has come and everyone, willing or unwilling, will be swept up in the events that are at hand.

# Mark 3:31–35

## *Jesus's True Family*

Jesus's family wishes to speak to him, but he refuses to see them. Jesus says his real family are those who are doing God's will.

**31** Et vĕnit mater eius et fratres eius, et foris stantes
miserunt ad eum vocantes eum. **32** Et sedebat circa eum
turba, et dicunt ei, "Ecce: mater tua et fratres tui et sorores
tuae foris quaerunt te." **33** Et respondens eis ait, "Quae est
mater mea et fratres mei?" **34** Et circumspiciens eos qui in
circuitu eius sedebant, ait, "Ecce: mater mea et fratres mei.
**35** Qui enim fecerit voluntatem Dei, hĭc frater meus et
soror mea et mater est."

### Matthew 12:46–50

**46** Adhuc eo loquente ad turbas, ecce: mater et fratres eius stabant
foris quaerentes loqui ei. **47** Dixit autem ei quidam, "Ecce: mater
tua et fratres tui foris stant quaerentes loqui tecum." **48** At ille
respondens dicenti sibi ait, "Quae est mater mea, et qui sunt fratres
mei?" **49** Et extendens manum suam in discipulos suos dixit, "Ecce:
mater mea et fratres mei. **50** Quicumque enim fecerit voluntatem
Patris mei, qui in caelis est, ipse meus frater et soror et mater est."

### Luke 8:19–21

**19** Venerunt autem ad illum mater et fratres eius, et non poterant
adire ad eum prae turbā. **20** Et nuntiatum est illi, "Mater tua et
fratres tui stant foris volentes te videre." **21** Qui respondens dixit
ad eos, "Mater mea et fratres mei hi sunt qui verbum Dei audiunt et
faciunt."

## Vocabulary

**adhuc,** still
**circuitus, -us,** *m.*, circle
**voluntas, -tatis,** *f.*, will

## Historical and Grammatical Notes

### Mark 3:31–35

**31. mater eius et fratres eius:** Many try to argue that *fratres* (*adelphoi* in Greek) actually means "cousins," thus preserving Mary's perpetual virginity. Where, incidentally, is Joseph, Mary's husband? There's no biblical evidence for anything about him after the narratives of Jesus's birth and early years.

**35. fecerit:** perfect subjunctive as an indefinite: "whosoever has done the will of God." The use of the perfect subjunctive in proclamations like this give it a legal ring. Eventually some of Jesus's family will come around. His brother James will become the leader of the Jesus movement in Jerusalem.

### Matthew 12:46–50

**48. dicenti sibi:** Take *sibi* as the indirect object of the participle: "to the one talking to him."

### Luke 8:19–21

**19. non poterant adire:** Jesus's family came to hear him speak but couldn't because of the size of the crowd. This is how Luke understands the scene. They haven't come to him out of concern for his actions or to talk with him. They were simply looking for special seating.

**21. Qui respondens dixit ad eos:** *Qui* = *Is*. Luke simplifies this scene. In his version, Jesus doesn't address an inner circle or direct his reply to his disciples. He appears to address the entire crowd and calls all of them his new family.

# Chapter 4

Chapter 4 focuses on the nature and purpose of Jesus's parables. His first parable, the parable of the sower, accounts for why only a few people will take his words to heart. When they're away from the crowd, Jesus's disciples ask him why he teaches in parables. He explains that it is to hide his teaching from those he wishes not to save. He then explicates the meaning of the parable of the sower to them in private. This is followed by three other parables derived from agriculture to illustrate how the Kingdom of God will slowly grow and how the disciples will play a central role in spreading light in the world. The chapter ends with the only nature miracle in Mark, when Jesus commands a storm to recede.

# Mark 4:1–9

## *The Parable of the Sower*

Preaching before a large crowd, Jesus uses a parable of a sower to demonstrate why his words will take root in only a very few people who hear them.

**1** Et iterum coepit docere ad mare. Et congregatur ad
eum turba plurima, ita ut in navem ascendens sederet in
mari, et omnis turba circa mare super terram erant. **2** Et
docebat eos in parabolis multa, et dicebat illis in doctrinā
suā: **3** "Audite. Ecce: exiit seminans ad seminandum. **4**
Et factum est, dum seminat, aliud cecidit circa viam, et
venerunt volucres et comederunt illud. **5** Aliud cecidit
super petrosā, ubi non habebat terram multam, et statim
exortum est, quoniam non habebat altitudinem terrae.
**6** Et quando exortus est sol, exaestuavit, et eo quod non
haberet radicem, exaruit.

## Matthew 13:1–9

**1** In illo die exiens Iesus de domo sedebat secus mare. **2** Et congregatae
sunt ad eum turbae multae, ita ut in naviculam ascendens sederet, et
omnis turba stabat in litore. **3** Et locutus est eis multa in parabolis,
dicens, "Ecce: exiit qui seminat seminare. **4** Et dum seminat, quaedam
ceciderunt secus viam, et venerunt volucres et comederunt ea. **5** Alia
autem ceciderunt in petrosā, ubi non habebant terram multam. Et
continuo exorta sunt, quia non habebant altitudinem terrae. **6** Sole
autem orto, aestuaverunt, et quia non habebant radicem, aruerunt.

## Luke 8:4–8

**4** Cum autem turba plurima conveniret, et de singulis civitatibus
properarent ad eum, dixit per similitudinem: **5** "Exiit, qui seminat,
seminare semen suum. Et dum seminat ipse, aliud cecidit secus viam
et conculcatum est, et volucres caeli comederunt illud. **6** Et aliud
cecidit super petram et natum aruit, quia non habebat umorem.

## Vocabulary

**altitudo, -inis,** *f.*, height; depth
**conculco (1),** to walk on; trample
**exaestuo (1),** to grow hot; be scorched
**exaresco, -escere, -ui,** to dry up
**exorior, -iri, -tus sum,** to rise up
**litus, -oris,** *n.*, shore
**nascor, -i, natus sum,** to be born
**petra, -ae,** *f.*, rock
**petrosus, -a, -um,** rocky
**propero (1),** to rush; hurry
**radix, -cis,** *f.*, root
**semen, -inis,** n., seed
**semino (1),** to sow seeds
**umor, -oris,** m., moisture
**volucris, -is,** *f.*, bird

## Historical and Grammatical Notes

### Mark 4:1–9

**2. docebat eos . . . dicebat illis:** Jesus teaches the outsiders (*eos*) in parables, but he explains his meaning to his inner circle (*illis*).

**4. aliud:** "one [of them]." This begins a series of distributives with *aliud*: "one . . . another . . . another . . ." First a seed is eaten before it sprouts, next a seed sprouts upward too quickly and can't survive the heat, then a seed that sprouts and grows is crowded out by weeds and can't produce, and finally a seed on good soil and in a good location grows and produces abundantly.

**6. eo quod:** "because [of the fact] that."

### Matthew 13:1–9

**3. qui seminat:** "he who sows" = "a sower."

### Luke 8:4–8

**5. seminare:** infinitive showing purpose: "The sower went out to sow."

**6. natum [semen] aruit:** "when the seed sprouted it dried out." **quia non habebat umorem:** This seedling doesn't die because of lack of moisture per se. As any gardener knows, a seed that is planted on hard soil will sprout up quickly but will not be able to establish a healthy root system. When hot weather comes, the seedling dries out because it can't draw moisture out of the soil to sustain it.

# Mark 4:1–9 (cont.)

**7** Et aliud cecidit in spinas, et ascenderunt spinae
et suffocaverunt illud, et fructum non dedit. **8** Et
alia ciderunt in terram bonam et dabant fructum.
Ascendebant et crescebant et afferebant unum triginta
et unum sexaginta et unum centum." **9** Et dicebat, "Qui
habet aures audiendi audiat."

## Matthew 13:1–9 (cont.)

**7** Alia autem ceciderunt in spinas, et creverunt spinae et
suffocaverunt ea. **8** Alia vero ceciderunt in terram bonam et dabant
fructum, aliud centesimum, aliud sexagesimum, aliud tricesimum.
**9** Qui habet aures audiat."

## Luke 8:4–8 (cont.)

**7** Et aliud cecidit inter spinas, et simul exortae spinae suffocaverunt
illud. **8** Et aliud cecidit in terram bonam et ortum fecit fructum
centuplum." Haec dicens clamabat, "Qui habet aures audiendi audiat."

## Vocabulary

**auris, -is,** *m.*, ear
**centuplus, -a, -um,** a hundredfold
**cresco, crescere, crevi, cretus,** to grow; increase
**fructus, -us,** *m.*, fruit
**sexaginta,** sixty
**spina, -ae,** *f.*, thorn
**suffoco (1),** to choke out; suffocate

## Historical and Grammatical Notes

### Mark 4:1–9 (cont.)

**8. unum . . . centum: literally:** "a thirty and a sixty and a one hundred." Clearly, Jesus doesn't mean to be precise. This is just a poetic way of saying "abundantly."

**9. audiendi:** gerund in the genitive, but it's best translated as if it were dative "for hearing." This could mean that there are some who will never understand Jesus's meaning because they don't have "ears to hear."

### Matthew 13:1–9 (cont.)

**8. aliud . . . tricesimum:** "one hundred [times], another sixty [times], another thirty [times]."

### Luke 8:4–8 (cont.)

**8. ortum [semen] fecit:** "springing up, the [seed] makes . . ."

# Mark 4:10–12

## *The Purpose of Teaching in Parables*

In one of the most difficult passages to understand in the Gospels, Jesus tells his disciples that he cloaks his true meaning in parables to keep outsiders from understanding his words and converting.

**10** Et cum esset singularis, interrogaverunt eum, hi qui circa eum erant cum Duodecim, parabolas.

### Matthew 13:10–13

**10** Et accedentes discipuli dixerunt ei, "Quare in parabolis loquĕris eis?"

### Luke 8:9–10

**9** Interrogabant autem eum discipuli eius quae esset haec parabola.

## Vocabulary

**singularis, -e,** alone

## Historical and Grammatical Notes

### MARK 4:10–12

**10. singularis:** "by himself," or "without a crowd around him." **eum . . . parabolas:** double accusative after *interrogaverunt*: "they questioned him [about] the parables." It's clear by his answer that the question was not about the meaning of this particular parable, but about why he uses parables in general.

### MATTHEW 13:10–13

**10. Quare in parabolis loquĕris eis:** Matthew understands the original question in Mark as a general one: "Why do you speak to them in *parabolae*?" Luke, by contrast, thinks that the question was about the meaning of this particular *parabola*.

### LUKE 8:9–10

**9. esset:** the subjunctive in indirect question: "his disciples asked him what this parable was."

# Mark 4:10–12 (cont.)

**11** Et dicebat eis, "Vobis datum est mysterium regni Dei.
Illis autem qui foris sunt in parabolis omnia fiunt, **12** ut
videntes videant et non videant, et audientes audiant et
non intellegant, ne quando convertantur, et dimittatur
eis."

## Matthew 13:10–13 (cont.)

**11** Qui respondens ait illis, "Quia vobis datum est nosse mysteria
regni caelorum, illis autem non est datum. **12** Qui enim habet,
dabitur ei, et abundabit. Qui autem non habet, et quod habet
auferetur ab eo. **13** Ideo in parabolis loquor eis, quia videntes non
vident et audientes non audiunt neque intellegunt."

## Luke 8:9–10 (cont.)

**10** Quibus ipse dixit, "Vobis datum est nosse mysteria regni Dei,
ceteris autem in parabolis, ut videntes non videant et audientes non
intellegant."

## Vocabulary

**abundo (1),** to overflow; be abundant
**ceterus, -a, -um,** other
**converto, -tere, -ti, -sus,** to turn toward
**nosco, noscere, novi, notus,** to come to know; recognize

## Historical and Grammatical Notes

### Mark 4:10–12 (cont.)

**12. ne quando convertantur, et dimittatur eis:** "lest at any time they should be converted and their sins should be forgiven them" (King James Version). These very perplexing verses come directly from Isaiah 6:9–10. The meaning of his words is clear, but can Jesus really have said this? Jesus appears to be saying that his words have such power that anyone and everyone hearing them will be converted and forgiven. Teaching in parables therefore is a way of selecting only those whom he wants to convert. These select few will understand, but the rest will be confused. This is hard enough to accept theologically, but his explanation appears also to contradict the parable of the sower that he has just narrated to the crowd. There we understood Jesus to mean that the Word will flourish if it is sown in the right soil. Here, by contrast, the word has such power that it will flourish anywhere, but Jesus will sow it only in certain places. Needless to say, this passage figures prominently in Lutheranism and other forms of Protestantism, which argue that God has elected certain people for salvation and others for eternal damnation. Both Matthew and Luke delete Mark's final six words, perhaps because they found them troubling.

### Matthew 13:10–13 (cont.)

**11. Qui:** = *Is.* **nosse:** a syncopated form of *novisse*. Though the form is perfect, don't translate it as "to have known," but "to know." The perfect tense of ingressive verbs (those having the –sc– infix in the present system) is best translated into English as a present tense; the pluperfect as a perfect or preterit; the future perfect as a future.

**13. vident . . . audiunt . . . intellegunt:** Matthew changes the mood of his original material to change Mark's original purpose clauses to simple statements of fact. In Matthew, Jesus speaks to the outsiders not *so that* they won't understand but because they *don't* understand. Both Matthew and Luke delete the most troubling words from Mark and the original verses in Isaiah.

# Mark 4:13–20

## *The Parable of the Sower Explained*

Jesus returns to the parable of the sower and explains its hidden meaning to his followers. The seed is the message, and it will take root and flourish only in the rare places where conditions are right.

**13** Et ait illis, "Nescitis parabolam hanc? Et quomodo
omnes parabolas cognoscetis? **14** Qui seminat verbum
seminat. **15** Hi autem sunt qui circa viam ubi seminatur
verbum. Et cum audierint, confestim vĕnit Satanas
et aufert verbum quod seminatum est in eos. **16** Et hi
sunt qui super petrosā seminantur. Qui cum audierint
verbum, statim cum gaudio accipiunt illud, **17** et non
habent radicem in se, sed temporales sunt. Deinde ortā
tribulatione vel persecutione propter verbum, confestim
scandalizantur.

### Matthew 13:18–23

**18** "Vos ergo audite parabolam seminantis. **19** Omnis qui audit
verbum regni et non intellegit, vĕnit Malus et rapit quod seminatum
est in corde eius. Hĭc est qui secus viam seminatus est. **20** Qui autem
supra petrosā seminatus est, hĭc est qui verbum audit et continuo
cum gaudio accipit illud. **21** Non habet autem in se radicem, sed
est temporalis. Factā autem tribulatione vel persecutione propter
verbum, continuo scandalizatur.

### Luke 8:11–15

**11** "Est autem haec parabola. Semen est verbum Dei. **12** Qui autem
secus viam sunt qui audiunt. Deinde vĕnit Diabolus et tollit verbum
de corde eorum, ne credentes salvi fiant. **13** Qui autem supra petram,
qui cum audierint, cum gaudio suscipiunt verbum. Et hi radices non
habent, qui ad tempus credunt, et in tempore tentationis recedunt.

## Vocabulary

**accipio, -cipere, -cepi, -ceptus,** to get; acquire; take up
**nescio, -ire, -ii** *or* **-ivi, -itus,** not to know
**scandalizo (1),** to cause to stumble
**temporalis, -e,** temporary
**tribulatio, -ionis,** *f.,* tribulation

## Historical and Grammatical Notes

### Mark 4:13–20

**13. Nescitis:** This is a fair question because the parable of the sower isn't one of Jesus's more challenging ones.

**16. petrosā:** Supply *terrā*. **seminantur:** Jesus's explication is a little hard to follow because he uses the verb *semino* in different senses. In verses 14 and 15, it's the seed/Word that is being sown. In verse 16, the verb *seminantur* means not that the people are being sown like seeds, but that they are being sown *with* seed. It appears that Luke recognized this dual use of *semino*, a problem he avoided by not using the verb at all. Matthew does a lot of rephrasing as well.

**17. Deinde ortā tribulatione:** This sentence looks very much like a later addition to the original text of Mark. Jesus has just explained what happens to a seed that springs up too quickly. Since it doesn't have roots, the seedling lives only a short while. It's not that it's squeezed out by something external to it—it wouldn't survive under any conditions. Luke deletes the lines, possibly because he too thought that they didn't fit with the context.

### Matthew 13:18–23

**19. Omnis qui . . .:** The relative clause is grammatically detached from the main clause of the sentence, though the general meaning is clear. A seed that is picked up off the ground by the crow/devil is analogous to the Word that was received but not understood. It's not easy to translate the sentence smoothly: "When any one heareth the word of the kingdom and understandeth it not, then cometh the wicked one and catcheth away that which was sown in his heart" (King James Version).

### Luke 8:11–15

**12. ne credentes salvi fiant:** "so that they won't believe and be saved." Luke understands Mark differently from Matthew. Matthew thinks that Jesus meant to say that the seed/Word was stolen by the evil one *because* it was not understood. Luke says that Satan steals the seed/Word *so that* it won't be understood.

**13. tentationis:** Luke simplifies Mark by compressing the list of temptations and trials into this one word: "in a time of temptation they draw back."

# Mark 4:13–20 (cont.)

**18** Et alii sunt qui in spinis seminantur. Hi sunt qui verbum audierunt, **19** et aerumnae saeculi et deceptio divitiarum et circa reliqua concupiscentiae introeuntes suffocant verbum, et sine fructu efficitur. **20** Et hi sunt qui super terram bonam seminati sunt. Qui audiunt verbum et suscipiunt et fructificant unum triginta et unum sexaginta et unum centum."

## Matthew 13:18–23 (cont.)

**22** Qui autem est seminatus in spinis, hĭc est qui verbum audit, et sollicitudo saeculi et fallacia divitiarum suffocat verbum, et sine fructu efficitur. **23** Qui vero in terrā bonā seminatus est, hĭc est qui audit verbum et intellegit et fructum affert et facit aliud quidem centum, aliud autem sexaginta, porro aliud triginta."

## Luke 8:11–15 (cont.)

**14** Quod autem in spinis cecidit, hi sunt qui audierunt et a sollicitudinibus et divitiis et voluptatibus vitae euntes suffocantur et non referunt fructum. **15** Quod autem in bonam terram, hi sunt qui in corde bono et optimo audientes verbum retinent et fructum afferunt in patientiā."

# Vocabulary

**aerumna, -ae,** *f.*, hardship
**concupiscentia, -ae,** *f.*, lust
**divitiae, -arum,** *f. pl.*, wealth
**efficio, -ficere, -feci, -fectus,** to produce; end up; come about
**fallacia, -ae,** *f.*, deceit
**fructifico (1),** to produce fruit
**sollicitudo, -inis,** *f.*, care; anxiety

# Historical and Grammatical Notes

### Luke 8:11–15 (cont.)

**14. Quod:** Until now, the parts of the analogy had been introduced with *qui*: "those who . . ." It's clearly a continuation of the same idea, but now it seems that Luke returns to the idea of the seed/Word as that which is sown.

**15. in patientiā:** "in enduring." Though the Latin root verb *patior* could mean "to suffer" as in physical or emotional torment, the original Greek text (*en hupomonē*) means only "patience." This curious addition in Luke comes at the end of a sentence, where, as we've seen before at Mark 1:38, there may have been room for an extra word or two. This prepositional phrase may have been added by an earnest copyist who thought that he was helping Luke make his point.

# Mark 4:21–25

## *The Light and the Bushel*

In the first of a sequence of three parables, Jesus tells his followers that no one puts a candle under a basket, but rather it should be set out in the open so that its light can be seen.

**21** Et dicebat illis, "Numquid vĕnit lucerna ut sub modio
ponatur aut sub lecto? Nonne ut super candelabrum
ponatur? **22** Non enim est aliquid absconditum, nisi ut
manifestetur, nec factum est occultum, nisi ut in palam
veniat. **23** Si quis habet aures audiendi, audiat." **24** Et
dicebat illis, "Videte quid audiatis. In quā mensurā mensi
fueritis remetietur vobis et adicietur vobis. **25** Qui enim
habet dabitur illi. Et qui non habet etiam quod habet
auferetur ab illo."

### Matthew 5:14–16

**14** "Vos estis lux mundi. Non potest civitas abscondi supra montem
posita, **15** neque accendunt lucernam et ponunt eam sub modio,
sed super candelabrum, ut luceat omnibus qui in domo sunt. **16** Sic
luceat lux vestra coram hominibus, ut videant vestra bona opera et
glorificent Patrem vestrum, qui in caelis est."

### Luke 8:16–18

**16** "Nemo autem lucernam accendens opeirt eam vaso aut subtus
lectum ponit, sed supra candelabrum ponit, ut intrantes lumen
videant lumen. **17** Non enim est occultum, quod non manifestetur,
nec absconditum, quod non cognoscatur et in palam veniat. **18**
Videte ergo quomodo audiatis: qui enim habet, dabitur illi, et
quicumque non habet, etiam quod putat se habere auferetur ab illo."

# Vocabulary

**abscondo, -dere, -di** *or* **-didi, -ditus,** to hide; conceal
**accendo, -dere, -di, -sus,** to kindle; set on fire
**candelabrum, -i,** *n.,* lampstand
**luceo, -cere, -xi,** to shine
**lucerna, -ae,** *f.,* lamp
**lumen, -inis,** *n.,* light
**lux, lucis,** *m.,* light; dawn
**mensura, -ae,** *f.,* measure
**metior, -iri, mensus sum,** to measure out; reckon; judge
**modium, -ii,** *n.,* basket
**palam,** openly; **in palam,** in the open
**remetior, -iri, -mensus sum,** to measure out again

# Historical and Grammatical Notes

## Mark 4:21–25

**21. Nonne:** expects a positive answer: "It comes to be put on a candelabra, doesn't it?" What is the light? If we connect verse 22 to this sentence, it seems that the light is some truth that had been hidden but is now being revealed. This truth or light could be any number of things: Jesus's true nature, the truth about the Kingdom of God that has been growing secretly and steadily, the true meaning of the parables that only the disciples can understand . . .

**23. Si quis:** "if someone/anyone" (*si* [*ali*]*quis*). Jesus repeats this formula (omitted in both Matthew and Luke) that calls to mind the special understanding only the disciples have. It could be setting up the next two verses, which can be paraphrased as "You who have already been given the ability to understand will be given even more of the truth. The others who don't have this ability will sink even further into the darkness as time goes on." On the other hand, verses 24–25 may be continuing the metaphor implied in *sub modio* above. The image that emerges is one of a customer at a bazaar who has a bushel basket for his purchases. His *modium* will be filled up.

## Matthew 5:14–16

**14. Vos estis lux mundi:** There is no question how Matthew understands this parable. Jesus's followers will be the light of the world and they will be the "city on the hill."

**15. accendunt:** Who are the "they" of the verb? The residents of the city on the hill? Matthew omits *sub lecto*. It doesn't add much to the parable, and in fact detracts from it: "under a bushel" *and* "under a bed"?

## Luke 8:16–18

**18. Videte ergo quomodo audiatis:** "Therefore take heed what you hear." What is the significance of the change from Mark's *quid* to *quomodo*? **quod putat se habere auferetur ab illo:** "that which he thinks he has will be taken away from him." Luke's view of the have-nots is even bleaker than Mark's. In Luke, these people only *think* they have something. In Mark, they have very little, but at least they have something.

# Mark 4:26–29

## *The Kingdom of God Compared to an Ear of Grain*

The next parable shows how the Kingdom of God is able to grow even if no one detects it. Just as no one can see a seed sprouting and growing, so the Kingdom of God has been growing while no one knew what was happening.

**26** Et dicebat, "Sic est regnum Dei, quemadmodum
si homo iaciat sementem in terram, **27** et dormiat et
exsurgat nocte ac die, et semen germinet et increscat,
dum nescit ille. **28** Ultro terra fructificat primum herbam,
deinde spicam, deinde plenum frumentum in spicā. **29** Et
cum se produxerit fructus, statim mittit falcem, quoniam
adest messis."

## Vocabulary

**dormio, -ire, -ii** *or* **-ivi, -itus,** to sleep
**exsurgo, -gere, -rexi,** to rise up
**falx, falcis,** *f.,* sickle
**germino (1),** to bud; germinate
**incresco, -escere, -evi,** to increase; grow
**messis, -is,** *f.,* harvest
**quemadmodum,** just as; how
**semens, -ntis,** *f.,* the act of sowing; seeding
**ultro,** on its own; without being asked

## Historical and Grammatical Notes

### Mark 4:26–29

**29. se produxerit fructus:** Some important manuscripts delete *se,* resulting in "And when it produces fruits," taking *fructūs* to be accusative plural, direct object of *produxerit.* Others have *ex se*: "And when by itself it produces fruits." As it is, however, it can be translated "And when the fruit has produced itself," taking *fructus* as the nominative singular subject of *produxerit.*

# Mark 4:30–34

## *The Kingdom of God Compared to the Mustard Seed*

Jesus illustrates that not only is the Kingdom of God growing undetected, but it began from the smallest seed and will grow into the largest plant in the garden.

**30** Et dicebat, "Quomodo assimilabimus regnum Dei aut
in quā parabolā ponemus illud? **31** Sicut granum sinapis,
quod cum seminatum fuerit in terrā, minus est omnibus
seminibus quae sunt in terrā. **32** Et cum seminatum
fuerit, ascendit et fit maius omnibus holeribus et facit
ramos magnos, ita ut possint sub umbrā eius aves caeli
habitare." **33** Et talibus multis parabolis loquebatur eis
verbum, prout poterant audire. **34** Sine parabolā autem
non loquebatur eis. Seorsum autem discipulis suis
disserebat omnia.

## Matthew 13:31–32

**31** Aliam parabolam proposuit eis, dicens, "Simile est regnum
caelorum grano sinapis, quod accipiens homo seminavit in agro suo,
**32** quod minimum quidem est omnibus seminibus. Cum autem
creverit, maius est holeribus et fit arbor, ita ut volucres caeli veniant
et habitent in ramis eius."

## Luke 13:18–19

**18** Dicebat ergo, "Cui simile est regnum Dei, et cui simile existimabo
illud? **19** Simile est grano sinapis, quod acceptum homo misit in
hortum suum, et crevit et factum est in arborem, et volucres caeli
requieverunt in ramis eius."

## Vocabulary

**arbor, -oris,** *m./f.,* tree
**assimilo (1),** to compare to
**avis, -is,** *f.,* bird
**dissero, -ere, -ui, -tus,** to discuss
**granum, -i,** *n.,* grain
**holus, -eris,** *n.,* vegetable plant
**hortus, -i,** *m.,* garden
**minimus, -a, -um,** least; smallest
**prout,** insofar as
**ramus, -i,** *m.,* branch
**requiesco, -escere, -evi, -etus,** to rest
**seorsum,** apart; separately
**sinapis, -is,** *n.,* mustard plant
**umbra, -ae,** *f.,* shade

## Historical and Grammatical Notes

### Mark 4:30–34

**30. Quomodo assimilabimus regnum:** "How will we illustrate the kingdom?"

**31. omnibus seminibus:** ablative of comparison after *minus.*

**33. prout poterant audire:** "such as they were able to hear." This repeats the theme that only some would be able to understand Jesus's true meaning.

**34. Seorsum:** "privately."

### Matthew 13:31–32

**31. grano:** dative complement of *simile.*

**32. omnibus seminibus:** Supply *in.*

### Luke 13:18–19

**19. quod acceptum homo misit in hortum suum:** *Acceptum* agrees with *quod,* but that's hard to translate literally: "which, when obtained, the man sows in his garden." Try to break the sentence into two clauses: "which a man acquires and sows into his garden." **factum est:** "turns into."

# Mark 4:35–41

## *Jesus Quells a Storm*

Jesus and his disciples are crossing a body of water (likely the Sea of Galilee) at night when a storm suddenly comes up. Jesus orders the storm to abate. His disciples are alarmed that he should have such power.

**35** Et ait illis illā die, cum sero esset factum, "Transeamus
contra." **36** Et dimittentes turbam, assumunt eum, ut
erat, in navi. Et aliae naves erant cum illo. **37** Et exoritur
procella magna venti, et fluctūs se mittebant in navem,
ita ut iam impleretur navis. **38** Et erat ipse in puppi supra
cervical dormiens. Et excitant eum et dicunt ei, "Magister,
non ad te pertinet quia perimus?" **39** Et exsurgens
comminatus est vento et dixit mari, "Tace! Obmutesce!"
Et cessavit ventus, et facta est tranquillitas magna. **40** Et
ait illis, "Quid timidi estis? Necdum habetis fidem?" **41** Et
timuerunt magno timore et dicebant ad alterutrum, "Quis,
putas, est iste, quia et ventus et mare oboediunt ei?"

## Matthew 8:18–27

**18** Videns autem Iesus turbas multas circum se iussit ire trans
fretum. [**19–22** *A scribe comes to Jesus and says, "Teacher, I will follow
you wherever you go." Jesus replies cryptically, "Foxes have their dens,
and the birds of the sky have their nests, but the Son of Man has no place
to lay his head." One of his disciples says to Jesus, "Lord, let me go bury
my father first." Jesus replies, "Follow me and let the dead bury their
dead."*] **23** Et ascendente eo in naviculam, secuti sunt eum discipuli
eius. **24** Et ecce: motus magnus factus est in mari, ita ut navicula
operiretur fluctibus. Ipse vero dormiebat. **25** Et accesserunt et
suscitaverunt eum, dicentes, "Domine, salva nos! Perimus!" **26**
Et dicit eis, "Quid timidi estis, modicae fidei?" Tunc surgens
increpavit ventis et mari, et facta est tranquillitas magna. **27** Porro
homines mirati sunt, dicentes, "Qualis est hĭc, quia et venti et mare
oboediunt ei?"

## Luke 8:22–25

**22** Factum est autem in unā dierum, et ipse ascendit in navem et
discipuli eius, et ait ad illos, "Transfretemus trans stagnum." Et
ascenderunt. **23** Navigantibus autem illis, obdormivit. Et descendit
procella venti in stagnum, et complebantur et periclitabantur.
**24** Accedentes autem suscitaverunt eum, dicentes, "Praeceptor,
praeceptor, perimus!" At ille surgens increpavit ventum et
tempestatem aquae, et cessaverunt, et facta est tranquillitas. **25** Dixit
autem illis, "Ubi est fides vestra?" Qui timentes mirati sunt dicentes
ad invicem, "Quis, putas, hĭc est, quia et ventis imperat et aquae, et
oboediunt ei?"

## Vocabulary

**alteruter, alterutera, alteruterum,** one another
**assumo, -ere, -psi, -ptus,** to take up as a companion; take aside
**cervical, -is,** *n.,* pillow
**compleo, -ere, -evi, -etus,** to fill up
**excito (1),** to rouse; awaken
**fluctus, -us,** *m.,* flood; wave
**fretum, -i,** *n.,* strait; body of water
**iubeo, -bere, -ssi, -ssus,** to order
**necdum,** not yet
**obdormio, -ire, -ivi** *or* **-ii, -itus,** to fall asleep
**operio, -ire, -ui, -tus,** to cover over
**periclito (1),** to be in danger
**procella, -ae,** *f.,* storm
**puppis, -is,** *f.,* stern
**qualis, -e,** what sort; such a sort
**sero,** late at night
**ventus, -i,** *m.,* wind; a windstorm

## Historical and Grammatical Notes

### Mark 4:35–41

**36. ut erat:** "just as he was." **aliae naves:** The event was witnessed by others.

**37. fluctūs se mittebant:** literally: "threw themselves against [or upon] the boat."

**38. non ad te pertinet:** "it doesn't bother you," or "have you no concern."

**39. comminatus est vento . . .:** Jesus treats the storm and the sea in the same way he'd dealt with demons. *Vento* is dative after *comminatus est.*

**41. Quis, putas, est iste:** *Putas* is almost parenthetical: "Who is this man, do you suppose, that . . ."

### Matthew 8:18–27

**26. modicae fidei:** genitive of description: "[you] of little faith."

### Luke 8:22–25

**23. et complebantur et periclitabantur:** Supply *naves* as the subject.

**25. Qui:** = *Ei.*

# Chapter 5

This chapter has only two stories, and both are longer and more detailed than the short pericopes of the first four chapters. In the first of the two, Jesus leaves the traditional homeland of the Jewish people to cast out the collection of demons famously known as "Legion." In the second, Jesus returns to Galilee and performs two miracles, one of his own will and another because a woman touched his garment while he was passing through a crowd.

# Mark 5:1–20

## *The Gerasene Demoniac; a Herd of Swine Possessed*

Jesus crosses over the Sea of Galilee to an area known as Decapolis (Ten Cities), where he cures an exceptionally powerful possession. A man was the victim of thousands of different demons, a condition that gave him supernatural strength. Jesus casts them all out and allows them to take over a herd of pigs, which then rushes over a cliff to the sea below. Jesus instructs the cured man to proclaim the miracle, and not to keep it secret. The local people are disturbed and ask Jesus to leave their area.

**1** Et venerunt trans fretum maris in regionem
Gerasenorum. **2** Et exeunte eo de navi, statim occurrit
ei de monumentis homo in spiritu immundo, **3** qui
domicilium habebat in monumentis. Et neque catenis
iam quisquam eum poterat ligare, **4** quoniam saepe
compedibus et catenis vinctus dirupisset catenas et
compedes comminuisset, et nemo poterat eum domare.
**5** Et semper nocte ac die in monumentis et in montibus
erat clamans et concidens se lapidibus.

## Matthew 8:28–34

**28** Et cum venisset trans fretum in regionem Gadarenorum, occurrerunt ei duo habentes daemonia, de monumentis exeuntes, saevi nimis, ita ut nemo posset transire per viam illam.

## Luke 8:26–39

**26** Enavigaverunt autem ad regionem Gergesenorum, quae est
contra Galilaeam. **27** Et cum egressus esset ad terram, occurrit
illi vir quidam de civitate, qui habebat daemonia et iam tempore multo vestimento non induebatur neque in domo manebat sed in monumentis.

## Vocabulary

**catena, -ae,** *f.,* chain
**comminuo, -uere, -ui, -utus,** to weaken; make smaller; crumble to pieces
**compes, -edis,** *f.,* shackles
**concido, -dere, -di, -sus,** to cut up
**domicilium, -ii,** *n.,* home
**domo (1),** to subdue, tame
**induo, -uere, -ui, -utus,** to put on; clothe
**lapis, -idis,** *m.,* stone
**monumentum, -i,** *n.,* grave; tomb
**nimis,** excessively; very
**occurro, -currere, -curri** *or* **-cucurri, -cursum** + *dative,* to meet; encounter
**saevus, -a, -um,** savage; wild
**vincio, -cire, -xi, -ctus,** to bind

## Historical and Grammatical Notes

### Mark 5:1–20

**1. trans fretum maris:** i.e., across the Sea of Galilee. This takes Jesus out of Jewish lands and into territory that is mostly pagan.

**4. nemo poterat eum domare:** The possessed man could not be helped by the local people and their spiritual healers. Jesus demonstrates his power by exorcising the demons that the local pagan priests were unable to overcome.

### Matthew 8:28–34

**28. duo habentes:** Matthew's version has two men possessed by the demons, and there are other significant changes to Mark's original version, not the least of which is that the collection of demons is not named. These are simply two men who've been possessed by demons.

### Luke 8:26–39

**27. vir quidam de civitate:** Luke specifies that the man is from a city and thus presumably known to other people. That is, he wasn't someone without family and acquaintances. Consequently, Jesus's exorcism will not pass unnoticed.

# Mark 5:1–20 (cont.)

**6** Et videns Iesum a longe cucurrit et adoravit eum, **7** et
clamans voce magnā dicit, "Quid mihi et tibi, Iesu, fili Dei
Altissimi? Adiuro te per Deum ne me torqueas." **8** Dicebat
enim illi, "Exi, spiritus immunde, ab homine."

## Matthew 8:28–34 (cont.)

**29** Et ecce: clamaverunt, dicentes, "Quid nobis et tibi, fili Dei?
Venisti huc ante tempus torquere nos?"

## Luke 8:26–39 (cont.)

**28** Is ut vidit Iesum exclamans procidit ante illum et voce magnā
dixit, "Quid mihi et tibi est, Iesu, fili Dei Altissimi? Obsecro te ne
me torqueas." **29** Praecipiebat enim spiritui immundo ut exiret ab
homine. (Multis enim temporibus arripiebat illum, vinciebatur
catenis et compedibus custoditus. Et, ruptis vinculis, agebatur a
daemonio in desertā.)

## Vocabulary

**adiuro (1),** to swear to; swear by
**arripio, -ripere, -ripui, -reptus,** to lay hold of
**longe,** far from
**obsecro (1),** to implore; beg
**torqueo, -quere, -si, -tus,** to torture

## Historical and Grammatical Notes

### Mark 5:1–20 (cont.)

**6. Quid mihi et tibi:** As noted before at Mark 1:24 when we first saw this formulation, Jewish tradition held that the world was populated with supernatural beings who were able to recognize each other. For the most part, they stayed out of each other's way when they were visiting the earth. Hence the question from one supernatural being to another would be perfectly appropriate: "What's your business here?" **Dei Altissimi:** This isn't a Jewish formula for God; it's from pagan cults. It's understandable that the demons, who are inhabiting pagan lands, should address Jesus this way.

**7. ne me torqueas:** Demons need to reside in a body, and perhaps being expelled is a kind of suffering.

### Luke 8:26–39 (cont.)

**29. spiritui immundo:** dative after *praecipiebat.*

# Mark 5:1–20 (cont.)

**9** Et interrogabat eum, "Quod tibi nomen est?" Et
dicit ei, "Legio nomen mihi est, quia multi sumus." **10**
Et deprecabatur eum multum, ne se expelleret extra
regionem. **11** Erat autem ibi circa montem grex porcorum
magnus pascens. **12** Et deprecati sunt eum, dicentes,
"Mitte nos in porcos, ut in eos introeamus." **13** Et concessit
eis. Et exeuntes spiritūs immundi introierunt in porcos. Et
magno impetu grex ruit per praecipitium in mare, ad duo
milia, et suffocabantur in mari.

## Matthew 8:28–34 (cont.)

**30** Erat autem longe ab illis grex porcorum multorum pascens. **31**
Daemones autem rogabant eum, dicentes, "Si eicis nos, mitte nos
in gregem porcorum." **32** Et ait illis, "Ite." Et illi exeuntes abierunt
in porcos. Et ecce: impetu abiit totus grex per praeceps in mare, et
mortui sunt in aquis.

## Luke 8:26–39 (cont.)

**30** Interrogavit autem illum Iesus, dicens, "Quod tibi nomen est?"
At ille dixit, "Legio," quia intraverunt daemonia multa in eum. **31** Et
rogabant eum ne imperaret illis ut in abyssum irent. **32** Erat autem
ibi grex porcorum multorum pascentium in monte. Et rogaverunt
eum ut permitteret eis in illos ingredi. Et permisit illis. **33** Exierunt
ergo daemonia ab homine et intraverunt in porcos, et impetu abiit
grex per praeceps in stagnum et suffocatus est.

## Vocabulary

**concedo, -cedere, -cessi, -cessus** + *dative,* to allow; grant to
**extra** + *accusative,* besides; out of; not including
**grex, gregis,** *m.,* flock; herd
**impetus, -us,** *m.,* rush
**legio, -ionis,** *f.,* legion
**milia, -ium,** *n. pl.* + *genitive,* thousands
**pasco, pascere, pavi, pastus,** to feed; pasture; *in the passive voice,* to graze
**permitto, -mittere, -misi, -missus** + *dative,* to allow
**porcus, -i,** *m.,* pig

## Historical and Grammatical Notes

### Mark 5:1–20 (cont.)

9. **Legio:** A Roman legion was somewhere between three and six thousand men. Note the shifting number of the verbs. Legion *says* to Jesus, but later *they* beg Jesus.

13. **per praecipitium:** "headlong." **ad duo milia:** "approximately two thousand."

### Matthew 8:28–34 (cont.)

32. **Et illi exeuntes abierunt in porcos:** The demons aren't given permission by Jesus to take up residence in the herd of pigs; they simply go there on their own.

### Luke 8:26–39 (cont.)

31. **Et rogabant eum ne imperaret illis ut in abyssum irent:** Luke includes an explanation of why the demons asked to be allowed to take over the herd of pigs. Expelling evil spirits from a body is tantamount to destroying them. What the demons don't realize, however, is that they are so powerful that even a herd of two thousand pigs can't contain them. The pigs are instantly driven so insane that they rush off the cliff and into the water.

# Mark 5:1–20 (cont.)

**14** Qui autem pascebant eos fugerunt et nuntiaverunt in
civitatem et in agros. Et egressi sunt videre quid esset facti.
**15** Et veniunt ad Iesum, et vident illum qui a daemonio
vexabatur sedentem vestitum et sanae mentis, eum qui
Legionem habuerat, et timuerunt. **16** Et qui viderant
narraverunt illis qualiter factum esset ei qui daemonium
habuerat, et de porcis. **17** Et rogare eum coeperunt ut
discederet a finibus eorum. **18** Cumque ascenderet
navem qui daemonio vexatus fuerat deprecabatur eum ut
esset cum illo. **19** Et non admisit eum, sed ait illi, "Vade
in domum tuam ad tuos et annuntia illis quanta tibi
Dominus fecerit et misertus sit tui." **20** Et abiit et coepit
praedicare in Decapoli quanta sibi fecisset Iesus, et omnes
mirabantur.

## Matthew 8:28–34 (cont.)

**33** Pastores autem fugerunt et venientes in civitatem nuntiaverunt
omnia et de his qui daemonia habuerant. **34** Et ecce: tota civitas exiit
obviam Iesu, et, viso eo, rogabant ut transiret a finibus eorum.

## Luke 8:26–39 (cont.)

**34** Quod ut viderunt factum qui pascebant fugerunt et nuntiaverunt
in civitatem et in villas. **35** Exierunt autem videre quod factum
est, et venerunt ad Iesum et invenerunt hominem sedentem, a
quo daemonia exierant, vestitum ac sanā mente ad pedes Iesu, et
timuerunt. **36** Nuntiaverunt autem illis hi qui viderant quomodo
sanus factus esset qui a daemonio vexabatur. **37** Et rogaverunt illum
omnis multitudo regionis Gergesenorum ut discederet ab ipsis, quia
timore magno tenebantur. Ipse autem ascendens navem reversus
est. **38** Et rogabat illum vir a quo daemonia exierant ut cum eo esset.
Dimisit autem eum dicens: **39** "Redi domum tuam et narra quanta
tibi fecit Deus." Et abiit per universam civitatem praedicans quanta
illi fecisset Iesus.

## Vocabulary

**admitto, -mittere, -misi, -missus,** to allow; permit; let in
**annuntio (1),** to announce
**fines, -ium,** *f. pl.,* borders; land
**fugio, fugere, fugi, fugiturus,** to flee
**mens, mentis,** *f.,* mind
**morior, -i, mortuus sum,** to die
**obviam** + *dative,* up to
**pes, pedis,** *m.,* foot
**qualiter,** just as
**quantus, -a, -um,** how many; as many
**revertor, -verti, -versus sum,** to turn back; go away

## Historical and Grammatical Notes

### Mark 5:1–20 (cont.)

**14. quid esset facti:** *Facti* is genitive of the whole after the neuter pronoun *quid*: "what [of] deed there was." In Luke this changes to *quid factum est,* which is much better grammatically: "what had happened."

**15. sanae mentis:** genitive of description. **eum qui Legionem habuerat:** This clause seems superfluous, and many manuscripts omit it.

**17. ut discederet a finibus eorum:** The loss of so many pigs could not have been well received, no matter what the reason. It's also possible that the local pagans didn't want to have such a powerful representative of a god most of them didn't worship.

**19. non admisit eum:** Jesus has a more important assignment for him. He is to be a constant reminder to the pagans of the area of the power of God. **quanta:** accusative object of *fecerit.* Mark mixes two constructions: "how many things the Lord did for you and [that] he took pity on you."

# Mark 5:21–43

## *A Woman Touches Jesus's Garment and Is Healed; The Healing of the Daughter of Jairus*

Returning to Galilee, Jesus is again faced with a crowd seeking cures and miracles. Among them is the leader of a local congregation, Jairus, who begs him to come heal his daughter. A woman afflicted with an ailment touches Jesus's shirt as he passes by and she is healed. At Jairus's house, Jesus is told that the girl has died, but Jesus cures her.

**21** Et cum transcendisset Iesus in navi rursus trans fretum,
convēnit turba multa ad illum, et erat circa mare. **22** Et
vĕnit quidam de archisynagogis, nomine Iairus. Et videns
eum procidit ad pedes eius, **23** et deprecatur eum multum,
dicens, "Filiola mea in extremis est. Veni. Impone manūs
super eam, ut salva sit et vivat." **24** Et abiit cum illo. Et
sequebatur eum turba multa et comprimebant illum.

### Matthew 9:18–26

**18** Haec illo loquente ad eos, ecce: princeps unus accessit et adorabat
eum, dicens, "Filia mea modo defuncta est. Sed veni. Impone
manum tuam super eam et vivet." **19** Et surgens Iesus sequebatur
eum et discipuli eius.

### Luke 8:40–56

**40** Cum autem rediret Iesus, excepit illum turba. Erant enim omnes
exspectantes eum. **41** Et ecce: vĕnit vir, cui nomen Iairus, et ipse
princeps synagogae erat, et cecidit ad pedes Iesu rogans eum ut
intraret in domum eius, **42** quia filia unica erat illi fere annorum
duodecim, et haec moriebatur. Et dum iret, a turbis comprimebatur.

## Vocabulary

**archisynagogus, -i,** *m.,* a leader of a synagogue
**defungor, -i, -functus sum,** to be deceased; pass away; have done with
**exspecto (1),** to wait for
**fere,** almost; nearly
**filiola, -ae,** *f.,* little daughter
**princeps, -cipis,** *m.,* leader
**unicus, -a, -um,** sole; only
**vivo, vivere, vixi, victus,** to live

## Historical and Grammatical Notes

### Mark 5:21–43

**21. trans fretum:** Jesus passes back to the other side of the Sea of Galilee.

**22. quidam de archisynagogis:** This person is identified as *princeps unus* in Matthew and *princeps synagogae* in Luke. We can be certain at least that he was a local Jewish leader. That he should beg Jesus for a cure shows both his desperation and the widening acceptance of the reality of Jesus's powers. **nomine:** "Jairus by name." The fact that Mark mentions his name might mean that he was known to Mark's audience.

**23. Filiola:** "daughter" or "little daughter." Vulgate Latin often adds suffixes to stems without altering the base meaning. **in extremis:** "gravely ill." She isn't dead in Matthew's account, though she's very close to it.

### Matthew 9:18–26

**18. Filia mea modo defuncta est:** "my daughter just died." There's no question in Matthew that Jesus brings back someone from the dead in this episode.

# Mark 5:21–43 (cont.)

**25** Et mulier, quae erat in profluvio sanguinis annis duodecim, **26** et fuerat multa perpessa a compluribus medicis et erogaverat omnia sua, nec quidquam profecerat, sed magis deterius habebat, **27** cum audisset de Iesu, vēnit in turbā retro et tetigit vestimentum eius. **28** Dicebat enim, "Si vel vestimenta eius tetigero, salva ero." **29** Et confestim siccatus est fons sanguinis eius, et sensit corpore quod sanata esset a plaga.

## Matthew 9:18–26 (cont.)

**20** Et ecce: mulier, quae sanguinis fluxum patiebatur duodecim annis, accessit retro et tetigit fimbriam vestimenti eius. **21** Dicebat enim intra se, "Si tetigero tantum vestimentum eius, salva ero."

## Luke 8:40–56 (cont.)

**43** Et mulier quaedam erat in fluxu sanguinis ab annis duodecim, quae in medicos erogaverat omnem substantiam suam nec ab ullo potuit curari, **44** accessit retro et tetigit fimbriam vestimenti eius, et confestim stetit fluxus sanguinis eius.

## Vocabulary

**complures, -a,** very many
**erogo (1),** to spend
**fimbria, -ae,** *f.,* border; tassel; edge
**fluxus, -us,** *m.,* flow
**fons, -ntis,** *m.,* source; origin
**mulier, -is,** *f.,* woman; wife
**patior, -i, passus sum,** to suffer; endure
**perpetior, -peti, -pessus sum,** to endure
**profluvium, -ii,** *n.,* flow
**retro,** behind
**sanguis, -inis,** *m.,* blood
**sentio, -tire, -si, -sus,** to feel; perceive
**sicco (1),** to dry out
**ullus, -a, -um,** any; anyone, anything

## Historical and Grammatical Notes

### Mark 5:21–43 (cont.)

**25–27. Et . . . eius:** This is an unusually lengthy sentence for Mark. The main clause comes only after a string of subordinate clauses: "And a woman—who . . . when she heard about Jesus came from behind in the crowd and touched his clothing."

**25. mulier:** Later Christian tradition calls this anonymous woman Veronica.

**26. magis deterius:** Translate *magis* as "rather": "but rather she was worse."

**28. tetigero:** future perfect indicative in the protasis of a future more vivid condition.

**29. corpore:** = *in corpore suo.*

### Matthew 9:18–26 (cont.)

**20. fimbriam vestimenti eius:** She didn't get a good hold of Jesus's clothing as she did in Mark, but just barely touched the fringes. That's all it takes to effect the cure.

### Luke 8:40–56 (cont.)

**43. nec ab ullo potuit curari:** Tradition has it that Luke was a physician by trade. Perhaps this is why he excised Mark's additional comment that the woman actually got worse under the care of her doctors.

# Mark 5:21–43 (cont.)

**30** Et statim Iesus cognoscens in semetipso virtutem quae
exierat de eo conversus ad turbam aiebat, "Quis tetigit
vestimenta mea?" **31** Et dicebant ei discipuli sui, "Vides
turbam comprimentem te, et dicis, 'Quis me tetigit?' " **32**
Et circumspiciebat videre eam quae hoc fecerat. **33** Mulier
autem timens et tremens, sciens quod factum esset in se,
vēnit et procidit ante eum et dixit ei omnem veritatem. **34**
Ille autem dixit ei, "Filia, fides tua te salvam fecit. Vade in
pace et esto sana a plagā tuā."

## Matthew 9:18–26 (cont.)

**22** At Iesus conversus et videns eam dixit, "Confide, filia. Fides tua te
salvam fecit." Et salva facta est mulier ex illā horā.

## Luke 8:40–56 (cont.)

**45** Et ait Iesus, "Quis est qui me tetigit?" Negantibus autem
omnibus, dixit Petrus, "Praeceptor, turbae te comprimunt et
affligunt." **46** At dixit Iesus, "Tetigit me aliquis. Nam et ego novi
virtutem de me exisse." **47** Videns autem mulier quia non latuit,
tremens vĕnit et procidit ante eum et ob quam causam tetigerit eum
indicavit coram omni populo et quemadmodum confestim sanata
sit. **48** At ipse dixit illi, "Filia, fides tua te salvam fecit. Vade in pace."

## Vocabulary

**affligo, -gere, -xi, -ctus,** to brush up against
**causa, -ae,** *f.,* legal case; crime
**indico (1),** to explain
**lateo, -ere, -ui,** to be concealed; hidden
**nego (1),** to deny
**ob** + *accusative,* on account of
**tremo, -ere, -ui,** to tremble

## Historical and Grammatical Notes

### Mark 5:21–43 (cont.)

**30. in semetipso:** "within himself." This is an intensive form of the third person reflexive pronoun ( *se* + *met* + *ipso*). **virtutem:** Both Matthew and Luke omit this. In Mark it does appear that Jesus senses a lessening of his power as some is drained off to heal the woman of her ailment. This notion that Jesus can be temporarily weakened is wholly inconsistent with the emerging understanding that Jesus's powers are unbounded and equal to that of God's.

**31. Vides turbam . . .:** This almost seems an impertinent, sarcastic question.

**33. sciens quod factum esset in se:** "knowing what had happened to her."

**34. fides tua:** Her belief is that Jesus's power radiates from him and can be accessed even without his willing it. This is what distinguishes her from the many other people who were touching him without being healed.

### Matthew 9:18–26 (cont.)

**22. At Iesus conversus:** Matthew's reworking of Mark goes beyond merely compressing out needless information. Major elements in Mark's version are that Jesus felt power flowing out of him, that his disciples asked him an ironic question, and that the woman was afraid that Jesus would be angry with her. All of this is absent in Matthew. There must be a purpose for such a drastic revision. Matthew seems to want to emphasize the role of faith in both these stories.

### Luke 8:40–56 (cont.)

**45. comprimunt et affligunt:** Peter is assigned this comment in Luke, and the sassy follow-up question that was in Mark is deleted.

**47. coram omni populo:** The miracle and conversation has many witnesses.

# Mark 5:21–43 (cont.)

**35** Adhuc eo loquente, veniunt ab archisynagogo,
dicentes, "Filia tua mortua est. Quid ultra vexas
magistrum?" **36** Iesus autem, verbo quod dicebatur audito,
ait archisynagogo, "Noli timere. Tantummodo crede!"
**37** Et non admisit quemquam sequi se nisi Petrum et
Iacobum et Ioannem fratrem Iacobi. **38** Et veniunt ad
domum archisynagogi. Et videt tumultum et flentes et
eiulantes multum, **39** et ingressus ait eis, "Quid turbamini
et ploratis? Puella non est mortua, sed dormit." **40** Et
irridebant eum. Ipse vero, eiectis omnibus, assumit patrem
puellae et matrem et qui secum erant, et ingreditur ubi
erat puella. **41** Et tenens manum puellae ait illi, "Talitha
qum," quod est interpretatum,"Puella, tibi dico, surge!"
**42** Et confestim surrexit puella et ambulabat. Erat enim
annorum duodecim. Et obstupuerunt continuo stupore
magno. **43** Et praecepit illis vehementer ut nemo id sciret,
et dixit dari illi manducare.

## Matthew 9:18–26 (cont.)

**23** Et cum venisset Iesus in domum principis et vidisset tibicines et
turbam tumultuantem, **24** dicebat, "Recedite. Non est enim mortua
puella, sed dormit." Et deridebant eum. **25** At cum eiecta esset turba,
intravit et tenuit manum eius, et surrexit puella. **26** Et exiit fama
haec in universam terram illam.

## Luke 8:40–56 (cont.)

**49** Adhuc illo loquente, vĕnit quidam e domo principis synagogae,
dicens, "Mortua est filia tua. Noli amplius vexare magistrum." **50**
Iesus autem, audito hoc verbo, respondit ei, "Noli timere. Crede
tantum, et salva erit." **51** Et cum venisset domum, non permisit
intrare secum quemquam nisi Petrum et Ioannem et Iacobum et
patrem puellae et matrem. **52** Flebant autem omnes et plangebant

illam. At ille dixit, "Nolite flere. Non est enim mortua, sed dormit."
**53** Et deridebant eum scientes quia mortua esset. **54** Ipse autem
tenens manum eius clamavit, dicens, "Puella, surge!" **55** Et reversus
est spiritus eius, et surrexit continuo. Et iussit illi dari manducare. **56**
Et stupuerunt parentes eius, quibus praecepit ne alicui dicerent quod
factum erat.

## Vocabulary

**derideo, -dere, -si, -sus,** to laugh at
**eiulo (1),** to wail
**fleo, -ere, -evi, -etus,** to cry
**hora, -ae,** *f.*, time; hour
**interpretatus, -a, -um,** translated
**irrideo, -dere, -si, -sus,** to laugh at
**pastor, -oris,** *m.*, shepherd
**plango, -gere, -xi, -ctus,** to wail
**ploro (1),** to cry
**tantummodo,** just; only
**tibicen, -inis,** *m.*, flute player
**tumultuor, -ari, -atus sum,** to make a disturbance
**tumultus, -us,** *m.*, uproar
**turbo (1),** to stir up; disturb
**ultra,** any longer, anymore

## Historical and Grammatical Notes

### Mark 5:21–43 (cont.)

**35. veniunt ab archisynagogo:** "come from the leader of the synagogue." As the *archisynagogus* is with Jesus, this has to mean that some of his friends, or his people, come to tell him that his daughter has died.

**36. Noli timere:** negative imperative: "Don't be afraid."

**37. nisi Petrum et Iacobum et Ioannem:** the first time they are singled out among the Twelve. Matthew and Luke omit this, perhaps to avoid stoking conflict among later Christians as to whether there was a hierarchy of disciples.

**41. Talitha qum:** Remarkably, both Matthew and Luke omit what is arguably a direct citation of Jesus's actual words in his native Aramaic.

**42. Erat enim annorum duodecim:** Why is this bit of information included? It almost appears to be an afterthought in Mark, whereas Luke weaves it more naturally into the narrative. Matthew deletes it. It may tie this cure with the healing of the bleeding woman. The girl is on the verge of the beginning of her menstrual cycles, and the woman has an irregularity with the same.

**43. praecepit illis vehementer:** because this is no typical cure. He actually brings someone back from dead, even though he tries to conceal what happened by saying that she was only asleep. She was dead, and everyone knew it. **manducare:** Eating shows that she is not a phantom. She's fully back among the living.

### Matthew 9:18–26 (cont.)

**23. tibicines et turbam:** The mourners have already arrived.

# Chapter 6

Mark returns to the subject of discipleship and its perils in chapter 6. Jesus himself finds that his hometown and even his own family reject him. He sends out his disciples on their missions and predicts that they too will come upon people who are hostile to them. At verse 14 the narrative leaves Jesus for the first and only time in Mark. It moves to the court of Herod Antipas where John the Baptist meets his fate. The scene then shifts back to Jesus. The apostles have returned, and Jesus miraculously feeds a crowd of five thousand. Finally, Jesus walks across the water to catch up with his disciples, who had departed in a boat from the shore. They are astonished by Jesus's powers, showing once again that they fail to apprehend his true nature.

# Mark 6:1–6

## *Jesus Has No Respect in His Hometown*

Jesus returns to his hometown, which only Luke names as Nazareth. Some who hear him speak in a synagogue are amazed by his wisdom and powers. His family and others are "scandalized." The local people challenge him to perform miracles as he has in other places, but because of their disbelief he can bring about only a few ordinary cures.

**1** Et egressus est inde et vĕnit in patriam suam, et
sequuntur illum discipuli sui. **2** Et facto Sabbato, coepit
in synagogā docere. Et multi audientes admirabantur,
dicentes, "Unde huic haec, et quae est sapientia quae data
est illi, et virtutes tales quae per manūs eius efficiuntur? **3**
Nonne iste est faber, filius Mariae et frater Iacobi et Iosetis
et Iudae et Simonis? Et nonne sorores eius hīc nobiscum
sunt?" Et scandalizabantur in illo.

### Matthew 13:54–58

**54** Et veniens in patriam suam, docebat eos in synagogā eorum,
ita ut mirarentur et dicerent, "Unde huic sapientia haec et virtutes?
**55** Nonne hĭc est fabri filius? Nonne mater eius dicitur Maria, et
fratres eius Iacobus et Ioseph et Simon et Iudas? **56** Et sorores eius
nonne omnes apud nos sunt? Unde ergo huic omnia ista?" **57** Et
scandalizabantur in eo.

### Luke 4:16–24

**16** Et vēnit Nazareth, ubi erat nutritus, et intravit secundum
consuetudinem suam die Sabbati in synagogam et surrexit legere.
[**17–22** *Jesus reads and comments on a passage from Isaiah. Everyone
is astonished by his words and asks . . .*] "Nonne hĭc filius est Ioseph?"
**23** Et ait illis, "Utique dicetis mihi hanc similitudinem, 'Medice,
cura teipsum. Quanta audivimus facta in Capharnaum, fac et hīc in
patriā tuā.' "

## Vocabulary

**consuetudo, -inis,** *f.,* habit; custom
**faber, fabri,** *m.,* craftsman
**nutrio, -ire, -ii** *or* **-ivi, -itus,** to raise; bring up
**sapientia, -ae,** *f.,* wisdom
**secundum** + *accusative,* according to; along
**utique,** most assuredly

## Historical and Grammatical Notes

### Mark 6:1–6

1. **inde et vĕnit in patriam suam:** Jesus leaves the city of Capernaum, which is on the north shore of the Sea of Galilee and goes south and west. **in patriam suam:** generally understood to mean Nazareth, not just the region where he was raised. Luke makes sure there is no doubt by replacing this expression with *Nazareth.*

2. **Unde huic haec . . .:** As we've seen before, Mark often writes very difficult sentences. Add *veniunt* after the first *haec*: "From where do these things come to him, and what is this wisdom that is given to him and [from where] do such powers [come to him] that are accomplished through his hands?" As is his standard practice, Matthew considerably simplifies this sentence in his reworking. Luke deletes it altogether.

3. **Nonne:** "Is this not . . ."? **filius Mariae:** It is remarkable that he is called the son of Mary and not of Joseph, his father. This may indicate a suspicion among the local people that Jesus was her illegitimate son. **et frater Iacobi . . .:** Defenders of the notion that Mary was forever a virgin argue that *frater* should be taken to mean "cousin."

### Matthew 13:54–58

54. **Et veniens . . .:** Matthew's extensive reworking of Mark shows his typical approach. He greatly simplifies complex expression in the narrative, while treating Jesus's actual words conservatively. **nutritus est:** "where he was raised," not necessarily where he was born.

55. **Nonne hĭc est fabri filius:** Jesus is not a *faber* as in Mark; in Matthew he is only *filius fabri.* (Again, why isn't Joseph mentioned by name?) This slight change—from *faber* to *filius fabri*—may reflect a cultural disdain for manual laborers. Jesus isn't himself a lowly workman; he was merely the son of a lowly workman.

### Luke 4:16–24

23. **Utique dicetis:** Jesus is anticipating their request for a miracle of some sort to verify what they've heard he's been doing elsewhere.

# Mark 6:1–6 (cont.)

**4** Et dicebat eis Iesus, "Non est propheta sine honore nisi in patriā suā et in cognatione suā et in domo suā." **5** Et non poterat ibi virtutem ullam facere, nisi paucos infirmos impositis manibus curavit. **6** Et mirabatur propter incredulitatem eorum. Et circumibat castella, in circuitu docens.

## Matthew 13:54–58 (cont.)

Iesus autem dixit eis, "Non est propheta sine honore nisi in patriā et in domo suā." **58** Et non fecit ibi virtutes multas propter incredulitatem illorum.

## Luke 4:16–24 (cont.)

**24** Ait autem, "Amen dico vobis, 'Nemo propheta acceptus est in patriā suā.' "

## Vocabulary

**cognatio, -ionis,** *m.,* family; relations

**incredulitas, -tatis,** *f.,* disbelief

## Historical and Grammatical Notes

### Mark 6:1–6 (cont.)

4. **Non est propheta:** "There is no prophet without honor except . . ." That is, a prophet has honor everywhere but at his own home. **et in cognatione suā:** "and among his family."

5. **Et non poterat:** Jesus could not perform any significant miracles in his hometown, aside from healing a few ill people. Even then he had to work hard at it. He couldn't heal them at a distance with the power of his word only. He had to put his hands on them directly. We're not told explicitly why his powers were reduced. We're given a hint, however, at a possibility. The disbelief of the local people held Jesus back. Clearly this is an unacceptable possibility for the early followers of Jesus. As Jesus's status rose, it was unthinkable that his power could in any way be limited or thwarted. Matthew simply says that Jesus did not perform any *potestates* because of their disbelief, probably as a way of punishing them. Luke recasts the scene completely. In Luke, Jesus appears to be responding to a request for miraculous signs of his power. This would be understandable enough. A local boy returns home and claims to have supernatural powers. "Let him prove it," the people may say. "Do here what we've heard you've done elsewhere."

### Matthew 13:54–58 (cont.)

58. **Et non fecit ibi virtutes:** Jesus would have been able to work miracles had he wanted to, not, as in Mark, because he couldn't. As Jesus's supernatural status grew in the earliest church, any evidence that his powers could be checked or limited in any way became problematic.

# Mark 6:7–13

## *Jesus Gives Instructions to the Twelve and Sends Them Out*

Jesus summons the Twelve, whom he'd already selected from his larger entourage at 3:13–19, and sends them out. They are to travel in extreme poverty, taking with them only a walking stick, sandals, and one tunic. They are forbidden to carry food or even to bring a pouch to hold a coin if one is given to them. They should stay only where they and their message are welcomed.

**7** Et convocat Duodecim et coepit eos mittere binos et
dabat illis potestatem in spiritūs immundos. **8** Et praecepit
eis, ne quid tollerent in viā nisi virgam tantum, non
panem, non peram neque in zonā aes, **9** sed ut calcearentur
sandaliis et ne induerentur duabus tunicis.

### Matthew 10:5–15

**5** Hos Duodecim misit Iesus praecipiens eis et dicens, "In viam
gentium ne abieritis, et in civitates Samaritanorum ne intraveritis. **6**
Sed potius ite ad oves quae perierunt domūs Israel. **7** Euntes autem
praedicate dicentes, 'Appropinquavit regnum caelorum.' **8** Infirmos
curate, mortuos suscitate, leprosos mundate, daemones eicite. Gratis
accepistis, gratis date. **9** Nolite possidere aurum neque argentum
neque pecuniam in zonis vestris, **10** non peram in viā neque duas
tunicas neque calceamenta neque virgam. Dignus enim est operarius
cibo suo.

### Luke 9:1–6

**1** Convocatis autem Duodecim, dedit illis virtutem et potestatem
super omnia daemonia, et ut languores curarent, **2** et misit illos
praedicare regnum Dei et sanare infirmos. **3** Et ait ad illos, "Nihil
tuleritis in viā neque virgam neque peram neque panem neque
pecuniam, neque duas tunicas habeatis.

## Vocabulary

**argentum, -i,** *n.,* silver
**aurum, -i,** *n.,* gold
**bini, -ae, -a,** two by two; in pairs
**calceo (1),** to put on shoes; wear shoes
**cibum, -i,** *n.,* food
**gentes, -ium,** *m. pl.,* the nations; Gentiles; non-Jews
**gratis,** freely
**operarius, -ii,** *m.,* laborer
**pecunia, -ae,** *f.,* money
**pera, -ae,** *f.,* pouch; bag
**potius,** rather
**sandalium, -ii,** *n.,* sandals
**tunica, -ae,** *f.,* tunic; shirt
**virga, -ae,** *f.,* walking stick

## Historical and Grammatical Notes

### Mark 6:7–13

**7. eos mittere binos:** Only Mark says that Jesus sent them out in pairs.

**8. ne quid:** = *ne aliquid,* a negated indirect command: "that they not take anything." **nisi virgam tantum:** "except for a walking stick only." **neque in zonā aes:** "and not even a penny in their belt."

**9. duabus tunicis:** The Twelve are sent off in extreme poverty and are to endure all manner of physical hardship. This includes subjecting themselves to cold, without the benefit of wearing more than one layer of clothing.

### Matthew 10:5–15

**5. Hos:** Matthew blends this story in with the time Jesus first picked out the Twelve from his entourage. This occurred just after Jesus had been tempted by Satan in the wilderness at the very beginning of his ministry.

**5–6. In viam gentium ne abieritis . . . ad oves quae perierunt domūs Israel:** How does this square with the notion that Jesus's message and offer of salvation is for the whole world? One possible answer is that Jesus meant this to be a temporary measure. The message is first for the Jews.

**8. mortuos suscitate:** There are no recorded instances of the Apostles bringing the dead back to life in the Gospels. Only Jesus has this ability and he uses it rarely. This passage in Matthew, moreover, is the only suggestion in the Gospels that they had this power. Acts, however, contains two such occasions: 9:36–42, when Peter brings Tabitha back to life, and 20:9–12, when Paul resurrects Eutychus.

**10. Dignus enim est operarius cibo suo:** "the workman earns his bread." Jesus sends out the Apostles in the most extreme poverty. In Matthew and Luke they are not even allowed shoes! They are to earn their keep wherever they go.

### Luke 9:1–6

**3. Nihil tuleritis:** The perfect subjunctive is frequently used in vulgate Latin for negative commands, whereas classical Latin would use the imperative of the verb *nolo.* Here classical Latin might have written *nolite nihil ferre.*

# Mark 6:7–13 (cont.)

**10** Et dicebat eis, “Quocumque introieritis in domum,
illic manete, donec exeatis inde. **11** Et quicumque locus
non receperit vos nec audierint vos, exeuntes inde excutite
pulverem de pedibus vestris in testimonium illis.” **12** Et
exeuntes praedicaverunt, ut paenitentiam agerent. **13**
Et daemonia multa eiciebant et ungebant oleo multos
aegrotos et sanabant.

## Matthew 10:5–15 (cont.)

**11** In quamcumque civitatem aut castellum intraveritis, interrogate
quis in eā dignus sit, et ibi manete donec exeatis. **12** Intrantes autem
in domum, salutate eam. **13** Et si quidem fuerit domus digna, veniat
pax vestra super eam. Si autem non fuerit digna, pax vestra ad
vos revertatur. **14** Et quicumque non receperit vos neque audierit
sermones vestros, exeuntes foras de domo vel de civitate illā, excutite
pulverem de pedibus vestris. **15** Amen dico vobis, tolerabilius
erit terrae Sodomorum et Gomorraeorum in die iudicii quam illi
civitati.”

## Luke 9:1–6 (cont.)

**4** Et in quamcumque domum intraveritis, ibi manete et inde exite. **5**
Et quicumque non receperint vos, exeuntes de civitate illā pulverem
pedum vestrorum excutite in testimonium supra illos.” **6** Egressi
autem circumibant per castella evangelizantes et curantes ubique.

## Vocabulary

**aegrotus, -a, -um,** sick
**donec,** while; until
**excutio, -cutere, -cussi, -cussus,** to shake off
**foras,** outside
**iudicium, -ii,** *n.,* judgment
**oleum, -i,** *n.,* oil
**pax, pacis,** *f.,* peace
**pulvis, -eris,** *m.,* dust
**quocumque,** to wheresoever
**saluto (1),** to greet; bless
**tolerabilis, -e,** tolerable
**ungo, -ere, unxi, unctus,** to put oil on; oil

## Historical and Grammatical Notes

### Mark 6:7–13 (cont.)

**10. illic manete, donec exeatis inde:** This can't mean "stay there until you leave," which would be fatuous advice indeed. Try "stay there [in that person's house] until you leave [the area]."

**11. Et quicumque locus non receperit vos nec audierint vos:** another fractured sentence: "and whatever place does not welcome you and [wherever] they don't listen to you." The connection with the main clause of the sentence is loose. It may be taken as a protasis of a conditional sentence: "if a place doesn't welcome you and if they don't listen to you."

### Matthew 10:5–15 (cont.)

**11. interrogate quis in eā dignus sit, et ibi manete donec exeatis:** They should ask who in the city is worthy and they should stay with him until they leave.

**12. salutate eam:** The Apostles have a quasi-magical power granted to them. Blessing a house confers something special and lasting, even if the people inside don't truly deserve it. This is why Jesus instructs them to revoke their blessing if the people living there don't turn out to be worthy of it.

**15. terrae:** locative case: "in the land."

# Mark 6:14–29

## *What Herod and Others Think Jesus Is; The Imprisonment and Execution of John the Baptist*

Herod Antipas, the ruler over Galilee, is beginning to hear rumors about Jesus. Some even think that Jesus is John the Baptist returned from the dead. Herod had been tricked into executing John earlier by his wife, Herodias. At a banquet, Herodias's daughter had danced so well for the guests that Herod promised her anything she desired as a reward. Herodias told her to ask for the head of John the Baptist on a plate.

**14** Et audivit Herodes rex. Manifestum enim factum est
nomen eius. Et dicebant, "Ioannes Baptista resurrexit a
mortuis, et propterea inoperantur virtutes in illo." **15** Alii
autem dicebant, "Elias est." Alii vero dicebant, "Propheta
est, quasi unus ex prophetis." **16** Quo audito, Herodes
aiebat, "Quem ego decollavi, Ioannem, hĭc resurrexit!"

### Matthew 14:1–12

**1** In illo tempore audivit Herodes tetrarcha famam Iesu, **2** et ait
pueris suis, "Hĭc est Ioannes Baptista. Ipse surrexit a mortuis, et ideo
virtutes operantur in eo."

### Luke 9:7–9

**7** Audivit autem Herodes tetrarcha omnia, quae fiebant, et
haesitabat, eo quod diceretur a quibusdam, "Ioannes surrexit a
mortuis." **8** A quibusdam vero, "Elias apparuit." Ab aliis autem,
"Propheta unus de antiquis surrexit." **9** Et ait Herodes, "Ioannem ego
decollavi. Quis autem est iste, de quo audio ego talia?" Et quaerebat
videre eum.

# Vocabulary

**appareo, -ere, -ui, -itum,** to appear
**decollo (1),** to decapitate
**haesito (1),** to hesitate; doubt
**Herodes, -is,** *m.,* Herod
**inopero (1),** to work; to perform
**propterea,** for that reason
**tetrarcha, -ae,** *m.,* tetrarch

# Historical and Grammatical Notes

## Mark 6:14–29

**14. Herodes rex:** Matthew and Luke give Herod the lesser title of *tetrarcha* (literally, "ruler of a fourth part"). After the death of Herod the Great in 4 BCE, the unified kingdom was split up, and the area of Galilee was given to this Herod, who often bears the epithet Antipas to distinguish him from his father and from one of his brothers, who was also named Herod. Since he was ruler over Galilee, it's natural that he should have gotten wind of Jesus's activities in his district. This pericope, however, is only loosely connected with the immediate context and could have been inserted nearly anywhere in the chronology of the early days of Jesus's ministry. It has the classical folktale motif of the hasty promise, and it breaks Mark's singular focus on Jesus. Indeed, it is the only scene in Mark when Jesus isn't "on stage."

**16. hĭc resurrexit:** Did Herod Antipas really believe that John had come back to life? He does in Mark, and Matthew follows Mark. In Luke, however, Herod dismisses these rumors.

## Matthew 14:1–12

**1. Iesu:** genitive.

## Luke 9:7–9

**7. haesitabat:** In Luke, Herod doesn't believe that John has come back from the dead, but he is concerned, as a leader should be, that some of his subjects do. Luke's Herod is both more sensible and more ruthless. He is solely responsible for John's execution. There's no talk of how Herod found himself trapped by a rash promise and a vengeful wife. It's somewhat curious, though, that Luke deletes this part of the story. Luke, we should remember, has more of an interest in John than either Mark or Matthew. His is the only Gospel that talks about John's own miraculous birth. This omission of Herod's promise, along with the unusual nature of this episode in Mark, may indicate that it was inserted into Mark at a later date, after Luke had obtained his copy of Mark and after he had written his own Gospel.

**9. iste:** Jesus. Herod's reaction to the rumors is practical and direct: "John? I gave the orders to execute him myself! Who's this new person I'm hearing all these things about?"

# Mark 6:14–29 (cont.)

**17** Ipse enim Herodes misit ac tenuit Ioannem et vinxit
eum in carcere propter Herodiadem, uxorem Philippi
fratris sui, quia duxerat eam. **18** Dicebat enim Ioannes
Herodi, "Non licet tibi habere uxorem fratris tui." **19**
Herodias autem insidiabatur illi et volebat occīdere eum
nec poterat.

## Matthew 14:1–12 (cont.)

**3** Herodes enim tenuit Ioannem et alligavit eum et posuit in carcere
propter Herodiadem uxorem, Philippi fratris sui. **4** Dicebat enim
illi Ioannes, "Non licet tibi habere eam." **5** Et volens illum occīdere,
timuit populum, quia sicut prophetam eum habebant.

# Vocabulary

**carcer, -eris,** *m.,* prison
**Herodias, -adis,** *f.,* Herodias
**insidio (1)** + *dative,* to plot against
**occīdo, -cīdere, -cīdi, -cīsus,** to kill
**uxor, -oris,** *f.,* wife

# Historical and Grammatical Notes

## Mark 6:14–29 (cont.)

**17. propter Herodiadem:** According to the story, Herod Antipas had seduced the wife of his brother, Philip. She divorced Philip and then married Herod. Herodias was also the daughter of another of Herod's brothers, which means she was Herod's niece as well as his new wife. John spoke out against the marriage—we're not told on what basis—and was imprisoned. This story shows that John was more than a mere prophet preaching the impending arrival of the Kingdom of God. He was involved with the court politics of the day to such an extent that the ruler took notice of his comments and had to act against them if they in any way threatened the legitimacy of his power. Ruling over Jewish subjects required at least the fiction of observing Jewish religious practices. **duxerat eam:** "had married her."

**18. Non licet:** Mark doesn't tell us why the marriage was illegitimate. The violation might be that Philip was still alive. If he were dead, then Herod would have been expected to marry his widow if he was not already married.

**19. Herodias:** Herod's wife is the engine behind this plot. Does this protect Herod, or does it make him seem weak and an even worse leader than if he had been personally responsible for John's execution?

## Matthew 14:1–12 (cont.)

**5. Et volens illum occīdere:** Matthew seems to be trying to diminish Herodias's role in the plot, but as a result his narrative is problematic. At first Herod himself wants to kill John, but he refrains from so doing out of fear of what the people think of him. Then Salome makes the request, forewarned by her mother that . . . what? . . . that Herod would make her his thoughtless promise? Then, Herod is sad that he's been trapped into giving the order because of the promise. In Matthew, Herod wants to execute John and then he *doesn't* want to execute John.

# Mark 6:14–29 (cont.)

**20** Herodes enim metuebat Ioannem, sciens eum virum
iustum et sanctum, et custodiebat eum, et, audito eo,
multum haesitabat et libenter eum audiebat. **21** Et cum dies
opportunus accidisset, quo Herodes natali suo cenam fecit
principibus suis et tribunis et primis Galilaeae, **22** cumque
introisset filia ipsius Herodiadis et saltasset, placuit Herodi
simulque recumbentibus. Rex ait puellae, "Pete a me, quod
vis, et dabo tibi." **23** Et iuravit illi multum, "Quidquid
petieris a me, dabo tibi, usque ad dimidium regni mei." **24**
Quae cum exisset, dixit matri suae, "Quid petam?" At illa
dixit, "Caput Ioannis Baptistae." **25** Cumque introisset
statim cum festinatione ad regem, petivit, dicens, "Volo
ut protinus des mihi in disco caput Ioannis Baptistae."
**26** Et contristatus rex propter iusiurandum et propter
recumbentes noluit eam decipere. **27** Et statim misso
spiculatore rex praecepit afferri caput eius. Et abiens
decollavit eum in carcere, **28** et attulit caput eius in disco,
et dedit illud puellae, et puella dedit illud matri suae. **29**
Quo audito, discipuli eius venerunt et tulerunt corpus eius
et posuerunt illud in monumento.

## Matthew 14:1–12 (cont.)

**6** Die autem natalis Herodis saltavit filia Herodiadis in medio
et placuit Herodi, **7** unde cum iuramento pollicitus est ei dare
quodcumque postulasset. **8** At illa, praemonita a matre suā,
"Da mihi," inquit, "hīc in disco caput Ioannis Baptistae." **9** Et
contristatus rex propter iuramentum et eos qui pariter recumbebant
iussit dari, **10** misitque et decollavit Ioannem in carcere. **11** Et
allatum est caput eius in disco et datum est puellae, et tulit matri
suae. **12** Et accedentes discipuli eius tulerunt corpus et sepelierunt
illud et venientes nuntiaverunt Iesu.

# Vocabulary

**accido, -cidere, -cidi,** to happen
**caput, -itis,** *n.,* head
**cena, -ae,** *f.,* meal
**contristo (1),** to make sad
**decipio, -cipere, -cepi, -ceptus,** to mislead; deceive
**discus, -i,** *m.,* plate
**festinatio, -ionis,** *f.,* haste
**inquit, inquunt,** he/she/it says; they say
**iuramentum, -i,** *n.,* oath
**iuro (1),** to swear an oath
**iusiurandum, iurisiurandi,** *n.,* oath
**libenter,** freely; with pleasure
**metuo, -uere, -ui, -utus,** to fear; respect
**natalis, -e,** birth; birthday
**opportunus, -a, -um,** suitable
**pariter,** equally; alongside
**polliceor, -eri, -itus sum,** to promise
**postulo (1),** to ask for
**praemoneo, -ere, -ui, -itus,** to forewarn
**salto (1),** to dance
**sepelio, sepelire, sepelii, sepultus,** to bury; give the funeral rites
**spiculator, -oris,** *m.,* scout; spy
**tribunus, -i,** *m.,* tribune; politician

# Historical and Grammatical Notes

## Mark 6:14–29 (cont.)

**20. multum haesitabat:** "he had lots of doubts." Probably Herod listened to John on more issues than just his marriage to Herodias. He's a rather sympathetic figure in Mark, even if he's a weak ruler and dominated by his wife.

**22. saltasset:** *saltavisset.*

**22. Rex ait puellae:** Later sources give her the name Salome.

**23. iuravit illi multum:** Herod makes the same offer twice in Mark. This could be the result of two different sources from which Mark built his version. Another possibility is that Mark accurately repeated his one source, where Herod in fact insisted that she accept his offer. This would be understandable under the circumstances, where presumably there was a great deal of wine flowing.

**24. Quae cum exisset:** Herodias would not have been invited into the hall with the guests. Salome left the hall and spoke with her mother, then returned with her (i.e., her mother's) wish.

**25. Volo ut protinus:** Surely Herod was expecting a much less gruesome request. This narrative seems to be a reworking of the folktale motif of the hasty promise. It's difficult to believe that a ruler would decapitate a man he thought to be just merely because of a drunken offer he made to a child. Luke, it seems, thought that there was no historical basis for it and deleted it all.

## Matthew 14:1–12 (cont.)

**9. iussit dari:** "he ordered that it be granted."

**10. misit:** "he gave the order."

**12. Iesu:** Here it's dative.

# Mark 6:30–44

## *The Apostles Report to Jesus; The Feeding of the Five Thousand*

The Twelve return and report to Jesus what they have done. A large crowd has followed them back, and Jesus instructs the Twelve to go with him to a secluded area where they can rest and have something to eat. The crowd follows. Jesus compares them to a herd of wandering sheep. Jesus miraculously provides fish and bread for them all.

**30** Et convenientes apostoli ad Iesum renuntiaverunt illi
omnia quae egerant et docuerant. **31** Et ait illis, "Venite
vos ipsi seorsum in desertum locum et requiescite
pusillum." Erant enim qui veniebant et redibant multi, et
nec manducandi spatium habebant. **32** Et abierunt in navi
in desertum locum seorsum. **33** Et viderunt eos abeuntes
et cognoverunt multi. Et pedestre de omnibus civitatibus
concurrerunt illuc et praevenerunt eos. **34** Et exiens vidit
multam turbam et misertus est super eos, quia erant sicut
oves non habentes pastorem, et coepit docere illos multa.

## Matthew 14:13–21

**13** Quod cum audisset Iesus, secessit inde in naviculā in locum
desertum seorsum. Et cum audissent, turbae secutae sunt eum
pedestres de civitatibus. **14** Et exiens vidit turbam multam et
misertus est eorum et curavit languidos eorum.

## Luke 9:10–17

**10** Et reversi apostoli narraverunt illi quaecumque fecerunt.
Et assumptis illis, secessit seorsum ad civitatem quae vocatur
Bethsaida. **11** Quod cum cognovissent turbae, secutae sunt illum.
Et excepit illos et loquebatur illis de regno Dei et eos qui curā
indigebant sanabat.

## Vocabulary

**indigeo, -ere, -ui** + *ablative,* to be in need of
**languidus, -a, -um,** sick
**pedester, -tris, -tre,** on foot
**praevenio, -venire, -vēni, -ventus,** to come before; anticipate
**spatium, -ii,** *n.,* space; time

## Historical and Grammatical Notes

### Mark 6:30–44

**30. apostoli:** This is the first and only time Mark refers to the Twelve as Apostles. It fits the context nicely because they had been "sent out" for a specific purpose and have now returned. **illi:** dative.

**31. Erant enim qui veniebant et redibant multi:** "For many were those who were coming and going." The Apostles needed rest because they had been coping with a large, disorganized crowd of people. This verse also sets up Jesus's likening the crowd to a flock of sheep without a shepherd.

**32. in navi:** The Twelve took a small boat down the shore to a private spot, but the crowd recognized who they were and arrived at the place before they disembarked.

**34. Et exiens:** Jesus apparently went with the Twelve on the boat because he is with them when the crowd arrives, even though at verse 31 he told the Apostles to go off by themselves.

### Matthew 14:13–21

**14. curavit languidos eorum:** "cured their ailments." Mark says that Jesus taught them many things, presumably cloaked in parables.

### Luke 9:10–17

**11. et loquebatur illis de regno Dei et eos qui curā indigebant sanabat:** Jesus preaches *and* heals their ailments in Luke. This seemingly unimportant detail presents an interesting question. Did Luke get the idea that Jesus preached from Mark and the idea that he healed from Matthew? That is, did Luke write his Gospel using both Mark and Matthew as his sources? The consensus is that he did not have Matthew's Gospel, but small details like this have to be accounted for somehow.

# Mark 6:30–44 (cont.)

**35** Et cum iam hora multa facta esset, accesserunt discipuli eius, dicentes, "Desertus est locus hĭc, et hora iam est multa. **36** Dimitte illos, ut euntes in villas et vicos in circuitu emant sibi quod manducent." **37** Respondens autem ait illis, "Date illis vos manducare." Et dicunt ei, "Euntes emamus denariis ducentis panes et dabimus eis manducare?" **38** Et dicit eis, "Quot panes habetis? Ite. Videte." Et cum cognovissent, dicunt, "Quinque et duos pisces."

## Matthew 14:13–21 (cont.)

**15** Vespere autem facto, accesserunt ad eum discipuli, dicentes, "Desertus est locus, et hora iam praeteriit. Dimitte turbas, ut euntes in castella emant sibi escas." **16** Iesus autem dixit eis, "Non habent necesse ire. Date illis vos manducare." **17** Illi autem dicunt ei, "Non habemus hīc nisi quinque panes et duos pisces." **18** Qui ait, "Afferte illos mihi huc."

## Luke 9:10–17 (cont.)

**12** Dies autem coeperat declinare, et accedentes Duodecim dixerunt illi, "Dimitte turbam, ut euntes in castella villasque quae circa sunt divertant et inveniant escas, quia hīc in loco deserto sumus." **13** Ait autem ad illos, "Vos date illis manducare." At illi dixerunt, "Non sunt nobis plus quam quinque panes et duo pisces, nisi forte nos eamus et emamus in omnem hanc turbam escas."

## Vocabulary

**declino (1),** to fall; go down
**denarius, -ii,** *m.,* coin
**emo, emere, emi, emptus,** to buy

## Historical and Grammatical Notes

### Mark 6:30–44 (cont.)

**35. iam hora multa facta esset:** "the hour was late." Both Matthew and Luke rephrase this somewhat unusual expression: *hora iam praeteriit* (Matthew) and *Dies . . . coeperat declinare* (Luke).

**36. Dimitte . . .:** This is a remarkable scene. The Twelve give Jesus an order—"Send them away." Jesus counters with *Date illis vos manducare. Feed them yourselves.* The Apostles then ask a flippant question. **Euntes emamus denariis ducentis panes et dabimus eis manducare?:** "We should go out and buy bread for twenty denarii and give it to them to eat?" Twenty *denarii* isn't meant to be a fixed amount. It was proverbial to denote a vast sum. The disciples are asking, "And where are we going to come up with the twenty *denarii* it will take to feed them?" Let's not forget that the Twelve have just returned from a mission on which they were to take no money or accept any. Are we witnessing some conflict between Jesus and his disciples? a growing irritation with his expectations?

**38. Ite. Videte:** "Come. Watch this."

# Mark 6:30–44 (cont.)

**39** Et praecepit illis, ut accumbere facerent omnes
secundum contubernia super viride fenum. **40** Et
discubuerunt secundum areas per centenos et per
quinquagenos. **41** Et acceptis quinque panibus et duobus
piscibus, intuens in caelum benedixit et fregit panes et
dabat discipulis suis, ut ponerent ante eos, et duos pisces
divisit omnibus.

## Matthew 14:13–21 (cont.)

**19** Et cum iussisset turbas discumbere supra fenum, acceptis quinque panibus et duobus piscibus, aspiciens in caelum benedixit et fregit et dedit discipulis panes, discipuli autem turbis.

## Luke 9:10–17 (cont.)

**14** Erant enim fere viri quinque milia. Ait autem ad discipulos suos,
"Facite illos discumbere per convivia ad quinquagenos." **15** Et ita
fecerunt et discumbere fecerunt omnes. **16** Acceptis autem quinque
panibus et duobus piscibus, respexit in caelum et benedixit illis et
fregit et dabat discipulis suis, ut ponerent ante turbam.

## Vocabulary

**area, -ae,** *f.*, ground
**benedico, -cere, -xi, -ctus,** to bless
**contubernium, -ii,** *n.*, dwelling place
**fenum, -i,** *n.*, hay
**frango, frangere, fregi, fractus,** to break
**intueor, -eri, -itus sum,** to look carefully upon
**viridis, -e,** green

## Historical and Grammatical Notes

### Mark 6:30–44 (cont.)

**39. secundum contubernia:** "by tent company." It makes sense that such a large crowd would be divided up into smaller groups to facilitate the distribution of food. The people are milling about—coming and going, as Mark said above—like a leaderless flock of sheep, so simply setting out the bread and fish would have been impractical and would surely have led to turmoil. Probably what Jesus ordered his disciples to do was to set up a certain number of feeding stations (*secundum contubernia*) and assign everyone in the crowd to one of them.

**40. per centenos et per quinquagenos:** There is no agreement on the significance of these very precise numbers, which Matthew and Luke both omit. The undeniable effect of such exactness, though, at least reinforces the sense that this is an eyewitness account.

# Mark 6:30–44 (cont.)

**42** Et manducaverunt omnes et saturati sunt. **43** Et
sustulerunt fragmenta duodecim cophinos plenos, et de
piscibus. **44** Et erant, qui manducaverunt panes, quinque
milia virorum.

## Matthew 14:13–21 (cont.)

**20** Et manducaverunt omnes et saturati sunt. Et tulerunt reliquias
fragmentorum duodecim cophinos plenos. **21** Manducantium autem
fuit numerus fere quinque milia virorum, exceptis mulieribus et
parvulis.

## Luke 9:10–17 (cont.)

**17** Et manducaverunt et saturati sunt omnes. Et sublatum est quod
superfuit illis fragmentorum cophini duodecim.

## Vocabulary

**cophinus, -i,** *m.,* basket
**parvulus, -i,** *m.,* child
**reliquiae, -arum,** *f. pl.,* leavings
**saturo (1),** to fill up; satisfy
**supersum, -esse, -fui,** to be left over

## Historical and Grammatical Notes

### Mark 6:30–44 (cont.)

**43. sustulerunt fragmenta duodecim cophinos plenos:** "they took up twelve baskets full for crumbs." The implication of the number twelve is that the twelve disciples, each with one basket, cleaned up the area. A *cophinus* was not a standard unit of measure, so it's not possible to estimate how much they swept up. We do get a feel, at the very least, for how large this miracle was. Twelve baskets of crumbs, even if they were small baskets, is a lot and could only have been produced by a very large banquet. What's of more interest, however, is why the disciples swept up after the meal. There would have been no pressing need to gather up fragments of fish bone and skin and crumbs from the bread. It all could have been left on the ground. There must have been a reason that this is emphasized in Mark. Perhaps the loaves and fish had been endowed with some divine presence that couldn't be left out in the open for animals or other people to consume. Matthew and Luke both retain this odd detail contrary to their usual habit of cutting Mark's narrative down. They must have thought that it was essential as well.

### Matthew 14:13–21 (cont.)

**20. tulerunt . . . plenos:** "they took away the leavings of the fragments, twelve full baskets."

**21. Manducantium:** genitive plural of the present active participle, best taken here as a substantive: "the number of those eating." **exceptis mulieribus et parvulis:** "not counting the women and children." This doesn't mean the women and children didn't eat. It probably means that five thousand men were given bread and fish, which they then took back to any women and children in their care. Still, it's an interesting clarification of what Mark appears to mean by *quinque milia <u>virorum</u>*.

# Mark 6:45–52

## *Jesus Walks on Water*

Jesus dismisses the crowd and sends his disciples up the coast to Bethsaida. Looking down from where he has gone to pray, Jesus sees that their boat is in trouble out on the water because of a sudden storm. Jesus walks out over the water to save them. His disciples are shocked and still cannot understand who Jesus is.

**45** Et statim coegit discipulos suos ascendere navem,
ut praecederent trans fretum ad Bethsaidam, dum ipse
dimitteret populum. **46** Et cum dimisisset eos, abiit in
montem orare.

## Matthew 14:22–34

**22** Et statim iussit discipulos ascendere in naviculam et praecedere
eum trans fretum, donec dimitteret turbas. **23** Et dimissis turbis,
ascendit in montem solus orare. Vespere autem facto, solus erat ibi.

## Vocabulary

**coago, -agere, -egi, -actus,** to force; order

## Historical and Grammatical Notes

### Mark 6:45–52

**45. coegit:** The verb suggests some urgency. **praecederent:** Bethsaida is only a few miles up the coast from where the last miracle occurred, and there is a small hill in between. Jesus was probably intending to walk to Bethsaida and catch up with them there. **trans fretum:** "across the river [Jordan]." Bethsaida isn't "across the sea." It is on the other side of the Jordan River from Capernaum and from the field where the miracle occurred.

### Luke

At this point we have the beginning of what's called Luke's Great Omission. Luke leaves out everything from here until Mark 8:27. One explanation for this silence is that he was working from a copy of Mark that didn't include this section. Scholars speak of an Ur-Mark, which means an early version of Mark, to which more material was added at different times and at different places until finally we have the Mark that comes down to us. It's possible, if an Ur-Mark existed, that Matthew and Luke had different versions of Mark. This would explain why Matthew includes parallels to Mark 6:45–8:27 and Luke does not. Luke may have deliberately left this material out for his own reasons, or it might be that his copy of Mark was damaged, missing a few pages, or different from the one Matthew used for his source. But this is all very contentious, and theoretically there may have been many Ur-Marks. Whatever we make of the theory of Ur-Marks, Luke's Great Omission is one of the great mysteries in the Synoptic Problem.

# Mark 6:45–52 (cont.)

**47** Et cum sero factum esset, erat navis in medio mari,
et ipse solus in terrā, **48** et videns eos laborantes in
remigando. Erat enim ventus contrarius eis, circa
quartam vigiliam noctis vĕnit ad eos ambulans super
mare et volebat praeterire eos. **49** At illi, ut viderunt
eum ambulantem super mare, putaverunt phantasma
esse et exclamaverunt, **50** omnes enim eum viderunt et
conturbati sunt. Statim autem locutus est cum eis et dicit
illis, "Confidite. Ego sum. Nolite timere!"

## Matthew 14:22–34 (cont.)

**24** Navicula autem iam multis stadiis a terrā distabat fluctibus
iactata. Erat enim contrarius ventus. **25** Quartā autem vigiliā noctis
vēnit ad eos ambulans supra mare. **26** Discipuli autem, videntes eum
supra mare ambulantem, turbati sunt, dicentes, "Phantasma est." Et
prae timore clamaverunt. **27** Statimque Iesus locutus est eis, dicens,
"Habete fiduciam. Ego sum. Nolite timere!"

## Vocabulary

**contrarius, -a, -um,** contrary; opposing
**disto, -stare, -steti, -status,** to be away from
**iacto (1),** to buffet; shake; brandish
**phantasma, -atis,** *n.,* ghost
**remigo (1),** to row
**stadium, -ii,** *n.,* a stade (a distance of about two hundred yards)
**vigilia, -ae,** *f.,* watch

## Historical and Grammatical Notes

### Mark 6:45–52 (cont.)

**48. laborantes in remigando:** They are rowing against the wind, which is pushing them back to where they set out. **circa quartam vigiliam noctis:** sometime between 3 and 6 a.m. **praeterire eos:** Jesus wants to go (*praeter*) beyond them, but what does that mean? If the boat is being pushed by the wind, Jesus is going to have to angle his approach to cut it off. Going "beyond" it and waiting for it to be blown toward him would be a sensible way of catching up with it.

**49. phantasma:** This is a Greek neuter in the accusative singular. Here it's the accusative subject of the infinitive in indirect statement.

### Matthew 14:22–34 (cont.)

**24. multis stadiis a terrā:** It may be that even in Matthew's day there were some who figured that Jesus was actually on the shore and that the disciples made a mistake about what they saw. To make sure that this objection was answered, Matthew tells us that the boat was several hundred yards away from the coast. There is no way they could have seen anyone walking on the shore, particularly in the dark of night. This creates another difficulty, however. Given their destination, which is on the same side of the sea, there would have been no reason for them to have gone so far off from the shore.

# Mark 6:45–52 (cont.)

**51** Et ascendit ad illos in navem, et cessavit ventus. Et
valde nimis intra se stupebant, **52** non enim intellexerant
de panibus, sed erat cor illorum obcaecatum.

## Matthew 14:22–34 (cont.)

[**28–31** *For a while, Peter walks on the water too, but he loses faith and begins to sink. He is saved by Jesus and the two of them walk to the boat over the waves.*] **32** Et cum ascendissent in naviculam, cessavit
ventus. **33** Qui autem in naviculā erant, adoraverunt eum, dicentes,
"Vere filius Dei es!" **34** Et cum transfretassent, venerunt in terram
Gennesaret.

## Vocabulary

**obcaecatus, -a, -um,** blinded

## Historical and Grammatical Notes

### Mark 6:45–52 (cont.)

**51. Et ascendit ad illos in navem:** The somewhat clumsy Latin accurately translates the equally clumsy Greek ("he embarked near them into the boat").

**52. sed erat cor illorum obcaecatum:** After having seen Jesus feed the multitude the day before, the disciples should not have been at a loss at further evidence of Jesus's power.

### Matthew 14:22–34 (cont.)

**28–31.** Where did Matthew get the report that Peter also walked on the water? It's not in Mark, and, if it had happened, that's very surprising. Peter is traditionally believed to be Mark's source. Surely if he had also walked on the water, Peter would have included the fact in his telling of the event, and Mark would have passed it along.

**33. Vere filius Dei es:** It would be hard to imagine how Matthew's conclusion of this pericope could be any different than Mark. In Mark, the disciples are completely in the dark about Jesus's true nature after these two miracles. In Matthew they see clearly who he is. Matthew's consistent desire to protect and elevate the twelve disciples in light of their growing stature in the early church is on vivid display in this passage.

**34. Gennesaret:** The winds push the boat back even beyond where it had set out from.

# Mark 6:53–56

## *Jesus Heals the Sick in Gennesaret*

Jesus and his disciples land at Gennesaret, a town on the shore of the Sea of Galilee. The local people recognize who he is and bring as many as they can for healing. He allows many people to touch him and be healed.

**53** Et cum transfretassent in terram, pervenerunt
Gennesaret et applicuerunt. **54** Cumque egressi essent
de navi, continuo cognoverunt eum, **55** et percurrentes
universam regionem illam coeperunt in grabatis eos qui se
male habebant circumferre, ubi audiebant eum esse. **56** Et
quocumque introibat in vicos aut in civitates vel in villas,
in plateis ponebant infirmos. Et deprecabantur eum, ut vel
fimbriam vestimenti eius tangerent. Et quotquot tangebant
eum salvi fiebant.

### Matthew 14:34–36

**34** Et cum transfretassent, venerunt in terram Gennesaret. **35**
Et cum cognovissent eum viri loci illius, miserunt in universam
regionem illam et obtulerunt ei omnes male habentes, **36** et rogabant
eum, ut vel fimbriam vestimenti eius tangerent. Et quicumque
tetigerunt salvi facti sunt.

## Vocabulary

**applico (1),** to steer toward; put in at

**percurro, percurrere, percurri** *or* **percucurri, percursus,** to run through

**platea, -ae,** *f.,* broad street; major road

**quotquot,** as many as

## Historical and Grammatical Notes

### Mark 6:53–56

**53. Et cum transfretassent . . . applicuerunt:** Though the general sense is clear, the grammar of this verse is far from straightforward. First they land, then they go to Gennesaret (which is not directly on the coast), and then they dock their boat (where, back on the coast?). Matthew's revision clears away these problems.

**54. egressi essent . . . cognoverunt:** We have a change of subject from the subordinate to the main clause: "When they [the disciples] got off the boat, they [the local people] immediately recognized him [Jesus]." Note how Matthew avoids this ambiguity in his version.

**55. coeperunt . . . circumferre:** *coeperunt circumferre eos qui se male habebant in grabatis.* **ubi:** "wherever." Wherever the word got out that Jesus was nearby, the people gathered up their ill friends and family and brought them to him.

**56. vel:** "if only," just as it was used in 5:28, when a cure was effected merely by touching the edge of his garment. The word may have spread that the woman who touched his clothing was healed.

### Matthew 14:34–36

**35. miserunt:** "they sent word."

**36. rogabant eum:** Matthew's *rogabant* seems much less pleading than Mark's verb *deprecabantur.* We've seen before in Mark that Jesus isn't entirely happy with his popular role as a miracle healer. Perhaps the verb Mark uses shows us that the people had to do more than just ask for cures. They had to beg for them. Even then, Jesus doesn't make any effort to heal them. He just walks through the crowds and people touch *him.*

# Chapter 7

Chapter 7 continues to develop the charge that Jesus and his followers are outside of the Jewish mainstream because they don't observe the Law. First there is the question of washing before eating. Jesus replies with a radical critique of the source of these purity laws and by charging the Pharisees with manufacturing new laws out of the old to suit their own purposes. His example is how Jews can avoid the commandment to honor one's parents by simply declaring their wealth as a gift to the Temple. Outside of the traditional Jewish lands, he transgresses the barrier between Jew and non-Jew by healing the daughter of a Syrophoenician woman. The chapter ends with a healing, omitted by Matthew and Luke, that Jesus appears to have some difficulty performing.

# Mark 7:1–23

## *Question about Ritual Washing*

Some Pharisees complain that Jesus's followers eat with ritually unclean hands and don't respect the traditions of their elders. Jesus counters that they have created their self-serving collection of laws that don't interpret, but vitiate, Mosaic Law. If they understood the intent of the Law correctly, they would see that physical impurity is nothing compared to spiritual impurity.

**1** Et conveniunt ad eum Pharisaei et quidam de scribis
venientes ab Hierosolymis. **2** Et cum vidissent quosdam
ex discipulis eius communibus manibus, id est non lotis,
manducare panes. **3** Pharisaei enim et omnes Iudaei, nisi
pugillo lavent manūs, non manducant, tenentes traditionem
seniorum, **4** et a foro nisi baptizentur, non comedunt, et alia
multa sunt, quae acceperunt servanda: baptismata calicum
et urceorum et aeramentorum et lectorum. **5** Et interrogant
eum Pharisaei et scribae, "Quare discipuli tui non ambulant
iuxta traditionem seniorum, sed communibus manibus
manducant panem?" **6** At ille dixit eis, "Bene prophetavit
Isaias de vobis hypocritis, sicut scriptum est, 'Populus hĭc
labiis me honorat, cor autem eorum longe est a me. **7** In
vanum autem me colunt docentes doctrinas praecepta
hominum.' **8** Relinquentes mandatum Dei tenetis
traditionem hominum."

### Matthew 15:1–20

**1** Tunc accedunt ad Iesum ab Hierosolymis Pharisaei et scribae,
dicentes, **2** "Quare discipuli tui transgrediuntur traditionem
seniorum? Non enim lavant manūs suas, cum panem manducant."

## Vocabulary

**aeramentum, -i,** *n.*, bronze vessel
**baptisma, -atis,** *n.*, washing
**calix, -icis,** m., cup
**colo, colere, colui, cultus,** to worship; tend; devote oneself to
**communis, -e,** common; unwashed
**honoro (1),** to honor
**hypocrita, -ae,** *m.*, hypocrite; dissembler
**labia, -ae,** *f.*, lip
**mandatum, -i,** *n.*, command
**praeceptum, -i,** *n.*, commandment; order; precept; teaching
**pugillo,** carefully
**seniores, -ium,** *m. pl.*, elders
**urceus, -i,** *m.*, pitcher

## Historical and Grammatical Notes

### Mark 7:1–23

**1. ab Hierosolymis:** They are from the capital city and may be a part of an official inquiry from the highest authorities.

**3–4. Pharisaei . . . lectorum:** These verses are almost certainly an explanatory comment for non-Jews written on the margins of a manuscript and then inserted into the text at some point in the history of its transmission. Cutting them out results in a smooth sentence starting in verse 2: "when they saw some of his disciples eat bread with common, that is unclean, hands, the Pharisees and scribes asked him . . ."

**4. a foro nisi baptizentur, non comedunt:** "[coming] from the marketplace, they don't eat unless they wash." It's likely in a crowded market that a Jew would come into physical contact with non-Jews, who were considered ritually unclean by strict Jewish practice. **quae acceperunt servanda:** "which they received as things to be preserved."

**7. docentes doctrinas praecepta hominum:** "teaching the *praecepta* of men as *doctrinas*." Jesus is making a distinction between divine doctrine and the human interpretation of divine law. The Pharisees insisted that, though infallible, the Mosaic laws needed to be interpreted to make them applicable to current realities. They further claimed that these interpretations had equal status as the original Mosaic laws. Jesus is thus directly attacking the Pharisees and their religious philosophy.

# Mark 7:1–23 (cont.)

**9** Et dicebat illis, "Bene irritum facitis praeceptum
Dei, ut traditionem vestram servetis. **10** Moyses enim
dixit, 'Honora patrem tuum et matrem tuam,' et, 'Qui
maledixerit patri aut matri, morte moriatur.' **11** Vos autem
dicitis, 'Si dixerit homo patri aut matri, "Corban," quod
est "donum," quodcumque ex me tibi profuerit,' **12** ultra
non permittitis ei facere quidquam patri aut matri, **13**
rescindentes verbum Dei per traditionem vestram, quam
tradidistis. Et similia huiusmodi multa facitis."

## Matthew 15:1–20 (cont.)

**3** Ipse autem respondens ait illis, "Quare et vos transgredimini
mandatum Dei propter traditionem vestram? **4** Nam Deus dixit,
'Honora patrem tuum et matrem,' et 'Qui maledixerit patri vel
matri, morte moriatur.' **5** Vos autem dicitis, 'Quicumque dixerit
patri vel matri, "Munus est quodcumque ex me profuerit," **6** non
honorificabit patrem suum.' Et irritum fecistis verbum Dei propter
traditionem vestram. **7** Hypocritae! Bene prophetavit de vobis
Isaias dicens: **8** 'Populus hĭc labiis me honorat, cor autem eorum
longe est a me. **9** Sine causā autem colunt me docentes doctrinas
mandata hominum.' "

## Vocabulary

**huiusmodi,** of this kind
**irritus, -a, -um,** invalid; useless
**maledico, -dicere, -dixi, -dictus** + *dative,* to curse
**mors, mortis,** *f.,* death
**prosum, prodesse, profui,** to be helpful to; be useful to
**rescindo, -scindere, -scidi, -scissus,** to rescind; repeal

## Historical and Grammatical Notes

### Mark 7:1–23 (cont.)

**9. Bene:** Take this as ironic: "you've done a good job making the commandment of God null and void!" Jesus doesn't stop with the accusation that the Pharisees create new laws and suppose that they are equivalent to Mosaic law. He continues with an even more serious charge: They find ways to cancel out the Law altogether. Jesus accuses the Pharisees of not even doing what they claim to be doing, which is to try to extend the application of the Law to new situations. They are willingly and knowingly voiding Mosaic law. The legal declaration of *corban* is an example.

**10. maledixerit:** perfect subjunctive in a legal formulation is common: "who(soever) has cursed." **morte moriatur:** literally, "let him die by death."

**11. "Corban," quod est "donum," quodcumque ex me tibi profuerit:** *Quodcumque ex me tibi profuerit* is a noun clause acting as the subject of an implied verb *est*: "whatsoever from me would be useful to you [is] 'corban,' which means 'gift.' " Anything declared a "corban" in this way was forever the possession of God. This, in practice, is a sly way children could exempt themselves from helping their parents and from having to obey the central Mosaic imperative to honor one's father and mother.

**12. ultra non permittitis:** "from then on you don't allow him." The perversion of the Mosaic commandment is complete. Not only is the child exempted from honoring his father and mother, he's not even allowed to do so after the declaration of "corban."

**13. huiusmodi:** complementary genitive after *similia*: "many things of this sort."

### Matthew 15:1–20 (cont.)

**5. Munus:** "an offering" to the Temple.

**9. Sine causā:** "Without justification." Jesus mocks the formal, legalistic diction of the Pharisees. This could be translated "They have no case."

# Mark 7:1–23 (cont.)

**14** Et advocatā iterum turbā, dicebat illis, "Audite me, omnes, et intellegite. **15** Nihil est extra hominem introiens in eum quod possit eum coinquinare. Sed quae de homine procedunt, illa sunt quae coinquinant hominem!" [**16** Si quis habet aures audiendi audiat.] **17** Et cum introisset in domum a turbā, interrogabant eum discipuli eius parabolam. **18** Et ait illis, "Sic et vos imprudentes estis? Non intellegitis quia omne extrinsecus introiens in hominem non potest eum coinquinare, **19** quia non introit in cor eius sed in ventrem et in secessum exit, purgans omnes escas?"

## Matthew 15:1–20 (cont.)

**10** Et convocatā ad se turbā, dixit eis, "Audite et intellegite. **11** Non quod intrat in os coinquinat hominem, sed quod procedit ex ore, hoc coinquinat hominem!" [***12–14*** *Jesus doesn't care whether the Pharisees are scandalized by his attack. He says they are no better than the blind leading the blind.*] **15** Respondens autem Petrus dixit ei, "Edissere nobis parabolam istam." **16** At ille dixit, "Adhuc et vos sine intellectu estis? **17** Non intellegitis quia omne quod in os intrat in ventrem vadit et in secessum emittitur?

## Vocabulary

**advoco (1),** to summon
**coinquino (1),** to defile
**edissero, -ere, -ui, -tus,** to explain
**extrinsecus,** from the outside
**imprudens, -ntis,** foolish
**os, oris,** *n.,* mouth; speech
**secessus, -us,** *m.,* departure
**venter, -tris,** *m.,* stomach

## Historical and Grammatical Notes

### Mark 7:1–23 (cont.)

**15. Nihil est:** "there is nothing." **quod possit:** subjunctive in a relative clause of characteristic. **Sed quae . . . illa:** The relative clause is appositional to the demonstrative: "but that which . . . those are things that . . ."

**16. Si quis:** This verse almost certainly was not in Mark's original. It adds nothing to the narrative and is not attested in some of the major manuscripts.

**17. a turbā:** "away from the crowd." **eum . . . parabolam:** a double accusative after *interrogabant*: "asked him about the parable." It's easy to see in this verse why "parable" is not always a good translation of *parabola*. "Metaphor," "saying," "analogy," "example," or even "riddle" might all be better ways of expressing the sense intended here.

**19. purgans:** What does this participle agree with? Grammatically, it would have to go with *omne,* but that's a problem. In this passage, Jesus is objecting to the Pharisees' fussy regulations about washing. He's saying that food, which is something that comes from the outside, can't pollute a man. The *omne,* therefore, is the food. But if *purgans* agrees with *omne* above, we have the food purging itself, rather than being purged. It's the body via the alimentary canal that purges food. The participial phrase floats at the end of the sentence, almost like an absolute clause. This is another example of Mark's relaxed conversational style that Matthew and Luke tighten up in their reworkings.

### Matthew 15:1–20 (cont.)

**11. Non quod intrat in os coinquinat hominem:** "It is not that which goes into the mouth that defiles a man."

**15. Edissere:** infinitive as imperative: "[Would you care] to explain?"

# Mark 7:1–23 (cont.)

**20** Dicebat autem, "Quod de homine exit, illud coinquinat hominem. **21** Ab intus enim de corde hominum cogitationes malae procedunt—fornicationes, furta, homicidia, **22** adulteria, avaritiae, nequitiae, dolus, impudicitia, oculus malus, blasphemia, superbia, stultitia— **23** omnia haec mala ab intus procedunt et coinquinant hominem."

## Matthew 15:1–20 (cont.)

**18** Quae autem procedunt de ore de corde exeunt, et ea coinquinant hominem. **19** De corde enim exeunt cogitationes malae, homicidia, adulteria, fornicationes, furta, falsa testimonia, blasphemiae. **20** Haec sunt quae coinquinant hominem. Non lotis autem manibus manducare non coinquinat hominem."

## Vocabulary

**adulterium, -ii,** *n.*, adultery
**avaritia, -ae,** *f.*, greed
**dolus, -i,** *m.*, deceit; trick
**furtum, -i,** *n.*, theft
**homicidium, -ii,** *n.*, homicide; murder
**impudicitia, -ae,** *f.*, shamelessness
**nequitia, -ae,** *f.*, evildoing
**oculus, -i,** *m.*, eye
**superbia, -ae,** *f.*, pride

## Historical and Grammatical Notes

### Mark 7:1–23 (cont.)

**20. Quod de homine exit, illud coinquinat hominem:** "what comes from [one man] is what corrupts [another man] if it is something that comes from the heart of a man." Jesus's parable focuses on the Pharisaic idea that certain foods and even the bodies of Gentiles are a physical source of spiritual contamination. Jesus's reply is that you can't become polluted by touching a Gentile or by eating the wrong foods. The kind of pollution that matters is spiritual in nature.

**21–22. fornicationes . . . stultitia:** Are these a list of *cogitationes malae*? That is, is Jesus saying something like this: "for it's from the heart that evil thoughts come forth, evil thoughts such as *fornicationes, furta, homicidia* . . ."? Or is he saying something like this: "for it's from the inside, from the heart, that evil thoughts come forth, and *fornicationes, furta, homicidia* . . ."? What did Matthew think?

### Matthew 15:1–20 (cont.)

**19. cogitationes malae:** Should *malae* be followed by a comma or by a colon? If we use a comma, we're supposing that Jesus sees a distinction between evil thoughts and what follows. This is a defensible position because the six vices that follow are actions and not just thoughts. Using a colon, however, means that Jesus is saying that the six are a type of thought. That's also possible because you can't commit any of these evil actions without thinking about it first.

**20. manducare:** gerund, subject of *coinquinat*: "eating with uncleaned hands does not defile a man."

# Mark 7:24–30

## *Jesus Heals the Daughter of a Gentile*

Jesus travels well outside of Galilee and Jewish lands. The people there have heard of him, and he can't hide from his reputation. At first Jesus rebuffs a woman (named "Justa" in later traditions) with surprising cruelty, but he relents when she pleases him with her ready wit and humility. Jesus heals the woman's daughter with his word and sends her away.

**24** Inde autem surgens abiit in fines Tyri et Sidonis. Et
ingressus domum neminem voluit scire et non potuit
latere. **25** Sed statim ut audivit de eo mulier, cuius habebat
filia spiritum immundum, veniens procidit ad pedes eius.
**26** Erat autem mulier Graeca, Syrophoenissa genere. Et
rogabat eum ut daemonium eiceret de filiā eius.

### Matthew 15:21–28

**21** Et egressus inde Iesus, secessit in partes Tyri et Sidonis. **22** Et
ecce: mulier Chananaea a finibus illis egressa clamavit, dicens,
"Miserere mei, Domine, fili David! filia mea male a daemonio
vexatur." **23** Qui non respondit ei verbum. Et accedentes discipuli
eius rogabant eum, dicentes, "Dimitte eam, quia clamat post nos."

# Historical and Grammatical Notes

## Mark 7:24–30

**24. Inde:** There is no explanation provided as to why Jesus would have made this journey forty miles away from Galilee and traditional Jewish lands. **domum:** He didn't necessarily stay with Gentiles. There surely would have been Jews living in this region.

**25. statim ut audivit de eo mulier:** "right when a woman heard about him . . . she . . ."

**26. Syrophoenissa genere:** *Genere* is an ablative of specification: "a Syrophoenician by race." Syria and Phoenicia were organized into one administrative district by the Romans, hence the compound adjective is appropriate.

## Matthew 15:21–28

**22. Chananaea:** "a Canaanite woman." This adjective is even more contemptuous than Mark's *Syrophoenissa*. **fili David:** It's somewhat surprising that a non-Jew would address Jesus with the very Jewish expression "Son of David."

**23. Qui:** = *is*. **non respondit:** This could imply contempt, or it could reflect Jesus's wish not to be identified. His disciples seem to confirm the latter interpretation. They ask Jesus to send her away because she is making such a fuss over them (*quia clamat post nos*) that others will come running to see what all the commotion is about.

# Mark 7:24–30 (cont.)

**27** Et dicebat illi, "Sine prius saturari filios. Non est enim
bonum sumere panem filiorum et mittere catellis." **28** At
illa respondit et dicit ei, "Domine, etiam catelli sub mensā
comedunt de micis puerorum." **29** Et ait illi, "Propter hunc
sermonem, vade. Exiit daemonium de filiā tuā." **30** Et cum
abisset domum suam, invēnit puellam iacentem supra
lectum et daemonium exisse.

## Matthew 15:21–28 (cont.)

**24** Ipse autem respondens ait, "Non sum missus nisi ad oves quae
perierunt domūs Israel." **25** At illa venit et adoravit eum, dicens,
"Domine, adiuva me!" **26** Qui respondens ait, "Non est bonum
sumere panem filiorum et mittere catellis." **27** At illa dixit, "Etiam,
Domine, nam et catelli edunt de micis quae cadunt de mensā
dominorum suorum." **28** Tunc respondens Iesus ait illi, "O mulier,
magna est fides tua! Fiat tibi sicut vis." Et sanata est filia illius ex
illā horā.

## Vocabulary

**catellus, -i,** *m.*, puppy

**mica, -ae,** *f.*, crumb

## Historical and Grammatical Notes

### Mark 7:24–30 (cont.)

**27. Sine:** imperative of *sino*: "Allow [it]." **prius:** Jesus's first mission is to the Jews. **catellis:** Jews used this pejorative term to refer to Gentiles.

**29. Exiit daemonium de filiā:** the only example in Mark of an exorcism/cure performed at a distance. All the others require Jesus's near presence and are accompanied by an explicit act or direct command.

**30. invēnit puellam iacentem supra lectum et daemonium exisse:** a zeugma, where one word is followed by two or more different grammatical constructions. Some examples in English would be "I like candy and to go to the zoo"; "I ate my breakfast with great pleasure, a spoon, and my friends." In Latin and Greek poetry a zeugma can be used for specific, intentional effects, but it's rare in prose. In this case, the verb *invēnit* is followed both by an accusative object and by an indirect statement: "she found her daughter lying on a couch and [found] that the demon had left."

### Matthew 15:21–28 (cont.)

**28. magna est fides tua:** Matthew makes a significant change. In Mark, Jesus grants the woman's request because of her *sermo*. In Matthew, her *fides* is key. This might reflect the fact that, by the time of Matthew, the possibility of salvation had indisputably been extended to Gentiles.

# Mark 7:31–37

## *Jesus Heals a Deaf and Blind Man*

Only Mark reports this cure. In this healing, Jesus appears to act more like a traditional medicine man by looking up to heaven, groaning, touching the patient, and even spitting to bring about the cure.

**31** Et iterum exiens de finibus Tyri vēnit per Sidonem
ad mare Galilaeae inter medios fines Decapoleos. **32** Et
adducunt ei surdum et mutum et deprecantur eum, ut
imponat illi manum. **33** Et apprehendens eum de turbā
seorsum misit digitos suos in auriculas eius et exspuens
tetigit linguam eius, **34** et suspiciens in caelum ingemuit
et ait illi, "Effetha," quod est, "Adaperire." **35** Et statim
apertae sunt aures eius, et solutum est vinculum linguae
eius, et loquebatur recte. **36** Et praecepit illis ne cui
dicerent. Quanto autem eis praecipiebat, tanto magis plus
praedicabant. **37** Et eo amplius admirabantur, dicentes,
"Bene omnia fecit, et surdos facit audire et mutos loqui!"

## Vocabulary

**adaperio, -ire, -ui, -tus,** to open; reveal
**auricula, -ae,** *f.*, ear
**exspuo, -uere, -ui, -utus,** to spit
**ingemo, -ere, -ui,** to groan
**lingua, -ae,** *f.*, tongue
**mutus, -a, -um,** mute; dumb
**recte,** correctly; properly
**surdus, -a, -um,** deaf

## Historical and Grammatical Notes

### Mark 7:31–37

**33. exspuens:** This probably means that he spat on the man's tongue. The only other time Jesus spits during a cure is at Mark 8:23, an episode that, like this one, Matthew and Luke also delete.

**36. Quanto . . . praedicabant:** "by how much he instructed them [not to spread the word], by that much they spread the word more."

**37. eo amplius:** "all the more."

# Chapter 8

Chapter 8 appears to fall into two most unrelated sections with no thematic unity linking them together. Verses 1–26 contain a collection of events that don't move the story line forward or add new experiences to what is already known to Jesus and his followers. Luke omits them all. Jesus again feeds a large crowd, confronts the Pharisees, chastises his followers for their forgetfulness, and heals a blind man. After verse 27, however, the story of Jesus progresses. Peter alone among the disciples recognizes that Jesus is not just another prophet but the Messiah. Following up on that revelation, Jesus makes the first predictions of his fate: how he is going to be killed by the authorities and is going to rise from the dead three days later. Peter is harshly rebuked by Jesus when he prays that it won't happen. Jesus then reminds them of the cost of discipleship. If they give up all the attachments they have to the world and even to themselves, he says, they will be glorified in the Kingdom of God, which will arrive before this generation has passed.

# Mark 8:1–10

## *Feeding of the Four Thousand*

Jesus again feeds a large crowd that has followed him into a remote area. The differences from the feeding of the five thousand from 6:31–44 are so slight that it could very well be just a another account of the same event.

**1** In illis diebus iterum cum turba multa esset nec haberent
quod manducarent, convocatis discipulis, ait illis, **2**
"Misereor super turbam, quia iam triduo sustinent me
nec habent quod manducent. **3** Et si dimisero eos ieiunos
in domum suam, deficient in viā. Et quidam ex eis de
longe venerunt." **4** Et responderunt ei discipuli sui, "Unde
istos poterit quis hīc saturare panibus in solitudine?" **5**
Et interrogabat eos, "Quot panes habetis?" Qui dixerunt,
"Septem." **6** Et praecipit turbae discumbere supra terram.
Et accipiens septem panes, gratias agens fregit et dabat
discipulis suis, ut apponerent. Et apposuerunt turbae. **7**
Et habebant pisciculos paucos. Et benedicens eos iussit
hos quoque apponi. **8** Et manducaverunt et saturati sunt.
Et sustulerunt quod superaverat de fragmentis, septem
sportas. **9** Erant autem quasi quattuor milia. Et dimisit eos.
**10** Et statim ascendens navem cum discipulis suis vēnit in
partes Dalmanutha.

## Matthew 15:32–39

**32** Iesus autem convocatis discipulis suis dixit, "Misereor turbae,
quia triduo iam perseverant mecum et non habent quod manducent.
Et dimittere eos ieiunos nolo, ne forte deficiant in viā." **33** Et dicunt
ei discipuli, "Unde nobis in deserto panes tantos, ut saturemus
turbam tantam?" **34** Et ait illis Iesus, "Quot panes habetis?" At illi
dixerunt, "Septem et paucos pisciculos." **35** Et praecepit turbae, ut
discumberet super terram. **36** Et accipiens septem panes et pisces et
gratias agens fregit et dedit discipulis, discipuli autem turbis. **37** Et
comederunt omnes et saturati sunt. Et quod superfuit de fragmentis

tulerunt septem sportas plenas. **38** Erant autem qui manducaverant quattuor milia hominum extra mulieres et parvulos. **39** Et dimissis turbis, ascendit in naviculam et vēnit in fines Magadan.

## Vocabulary

**appono, -ponere, -posui, -positus** + *dative,* to set before; serve
**deficio, -ficere, -feci, -fectus,** to fail; fall down; run out; collapse
**ieiunus, -a, -um,** fasting; hungry
**pisciculus, -i,** *m.,* little fish
**solitudo, -inis,** *f.,* solitude; wilderness
**sporta, -ae,** *f.,* basket
**sustineo, -tinere, -tinui,** to hold up; stop; support; endure
**triduum, -i,** *n.,* a three-day period; three days

## Historical and Grammatical Notes

### Mark 8:1–10

**1. In illis diebus iterum:** This miracle is only loosely tied in with the context by this vague expression. It may have happened somewhere near Dalmanutha, but unfortunately Dalmanutha is wholly unknown. Some manuscripts offer Mageda or Magada in its place, but their whereabouts are also unknown. This sentence is unpolished: "In those days again when there was a large crowd and they didn't have anything to eat, the disciples being summoned, he said to them."

**3. dimisero:** future perfect in the protasis of a future more vivid condition.

**4. Unde . . . quis:** "So who will be able . . . or from where will anyone . . ." taking *unde* as the interrogative, and *quis* as *aliquis*. Either way, the question seems impertinent and odd. Didn't the disciples see Jesus feed an even larger crowd before?

**6. turbae:** dative after *praecipit*: "he gave an order to the crowd to . . ." **apposuerunt turbae:** *Turbae* is dative: "they set it out for the crowd."

**8. septem sportas:** appositional to *quod*: "they took away what was left from the crumbs, seven baskets (full)."

### Matthew 15:32–39

**33. Unde nobis:** The question is certainly less sarcastic here.

**36. discipuli autem turbis:** Supply *dederunt.*

# Mark 8:11–13

## *Some Pharisees Request a Miracle*

Some Pharisees engage Jesus in a discussion, finally asking him for a miracle to prove his status. He refuses.

**11** Et exierunt Pharisaei et coeperunt conquirere cum eo,
quaerentes ab illo signum de caelo, tentantes eum. **12** Et
ingemiscens spiritu suo ait, "Quid generatio ista quaerit
signum? Amen dico vobis, non dabitur generationi isti
signum." **13** Et dimittens eos, iterum ascendens abiit
trans fretum.

### Matthew 16:1–4

**1** Et accesserunt ad eum Pharisaei et Sadducaei tentantes
et rogaverunt eum, ut signum de caelo ostenderet eis. **2** At
ille respondens ait eis, "Facto vespere dicitis, 'Serenum erit,
rubicundum est enim caelum.' **3** Et mane, 'Hodie tempestas,
rutilat enim triste caelum.' Faciem quidem caeli diiudicare nostis,
signa autem temporum non potestis? **4** Generatio mala et adultera
signum quaerit et signum non dabitur ei, nisi signum Ionae." Et,
relictis illis, abiit.

## Vocabulary

**adulterus, -a, -um,** debauched; adulterous
**diiudico (1),** to judge
**generatio, -ionis,** *f.,* generation; nation
**ingemisco, -ere, -ui,** to sigh; groan
**Ionas, -ae,** *m.,* Jonah
**rubicundus, -a, -um,** red
**rutilo (1),** to grow red
**serenus, -a, -um,** calm
**tristis, -e,** sad; gloomy

## Historical and Grammatical Notes

### Mark 8:11–13

**11. signum:** The Pharisees are not unaware of Jesus's powers. Mark says that they witnessed several miracles with their own eyes. What more evidence do they need, particularly after this impressive miracle of feeding such a large crowd? But the question may be different from what it appears. This is the first time the word *signum* has been used in Mark, so it may be that the Pharisees aren't interested merely in another demonstration of his powers. They may be requesting proof—a sign—that he is truly a prophet sent by God with the proper authority that prophets are traditionally granted. It's one thing to acknowledge his special powers; it's entirely another to elevate him to the level of an Isaiah or Elijah. We can only guess just what such a *signum* would be.

**12. Quid:** "Why?"

### Matthew 16:1–4

**1. Sadducaei:** Though the Pharisees and the Sadducees differ on important doctrine, they would both agree that a true and fully authorized prophet in their midst would have to be taken seriously. It's not surprising to see them on the same side on this question. Does Jesus have any evidence that he is more than just a magician?

**2. Serenum erit:** Think of the adage in English: "Red sky at night, sailor's delight. / Red sky at morning, sailor's warning." Jesus counters that they can see the signs of the weather, but can't they recognize the *signa temporum*? This is something they should be skilled in.

**4. nisi signum Ionae:** There won't be any sign given this generation, "except for the sign of Jonah." Matthew appears to have had two sources for this pericope. He has a version that came before at 12:38–41 and this one at 16:1–4. Both of Matthew's versions have tie-ins with the "sign of Jonah." The first one explains the connection explicitly as presaging the resurrection: "For just as Jonah was three days and three nights in the belly of the great fish, so will the son of man be three days and three nights in the heart of the earth" (12:40).

# Mark 8:14–21

## *The Disciples Have No Bread*

The disciples realize that they forgot to bring food, but they should know that Jesus will provide for them. Embedded in this rather straightforward narrative, is a reference to "yeast of the Pharisees and of Herod." Its significance is not elucidated in the context in which it appears.

**14** Et obliti sunt sumere panes, et nisi unum panem non
habebant secum in navi. **15** Et praecipiebat eis, dicens,
"Videte! Cavete a fermento Pharisaeorum et fermento
Herodis!" **16** Et disputabant ad invicem, quia panes non
haberent. **17** Quo cognito, ait illis, "Quid disputatis, quia
panes non habetis? Nondum cognoscitis nec intellegitis?
Caecatum habetis cor vestrum? **18** Oculos habentes non
videtis? Et aures habentes non auditis?

## Matthew 16:5–12

**5** Et cum venissent discipuli trans fretum, obliti sunt panes
accipere. **6** Iesus autem dixit illis, "Intuemini et cavete a fermento
Pharisaeorum et Sadducaeorum." **7** At illi cogitabant inter se,
dicentes, "Panes non accepimus." **8** Sciens autem Iesus dixit, "Quid
cogitatis inter vos, modicae fidei, quia panes non habetis?

## Vocabulary

**caveo, cavere, cavi, cautus,** to beware of
**fermentum, -i,** *n.,* yeast
**nondum,** not yet
**obliviscor, -i, oblitus sum** + *infinitive or genitive,* to forget

## Historical and Grammatical Notes

### Mark 8:14–21

**14. nisi unum panem:** They "did not have but one loaf."

**15. Videte! Cavete:** The disciples don't reply to Jesus's enigmatic remark. This suggests that we have two different sayings that are spliced together into one scene. **a fermento:** Jesus could be referring generally to the plot that the Pharisees and Herod are devising against Jesus, but it's an odd way to put it. Perhaps Jesus is using "yeast" as a general metaphor. The passage focuses on the blindness of his disciples. Jesus may be saying that they've become distracted or blinded by the complex teachings of the Pharisees and the temptations of accommodation with the Roman authorities, as is represented by Herod. This is why they fail to understand the meaning of the miracles he has been performing in plain sight.

### Matthew 16:5–12

**7. cogitabant:** Changing Mark's *disputabant* improves the image of the disciples. They aren't quarreling with one another but calmly considering what they should do.

# Mark 8:14–21 (cont.)

Nec recordamini, **19** quando quinque panes fregi in
quinque milia, quot cophinos fragmentorum plenos
sustulistis?" Dicunt ei, "Duodecim." **20** "Quando
illos septem in quattuor milia, quot sportas plenas
fragmentorum tulistis?" Et dicunt ei, "Septem." **21** Et
dicebat eis, "Nondum intellegitis?"

## Matthew 16:5–12 (cont.)

**9** Nondum intellegitis neque recordamini quinque panum quinque
milium hominum, et quot cophinos sumpsistis? **10** Neque septem
panum quattuor milium hominum, et quot sportas sumpsistis? **11**
Quomodo non intellegitis quia non de panibus dixi vobis? Sed cavete
a fermento Pharisaeorum et Sadducaeorum." **12** Tunc intellexerunt
quia non dixerit cavendum a fermento panum sed a doctrinā
Pharisaeorum et Sadducaeorum.

## Vocabulary

**recordor, -ari, -atus sum,** to remember

## Historical and Grammatical Notes

### Mark 8:14–21 (cont.)

**19. quinque panes:** Jesus reminds them not just of the events but of the specific details to bring home the fact that they really happened. Once Jesus fed five thousand with five loaves of bread, and there were twelves baskets full of crumbs left over. Another time he fed four thousand with seven loaves, and there were seven baskets left over. It may be, as well, that there is some additional numerological significance to these numbers and combinations. What that might be is pure speculation.

### Matthew 16:5–12 (cont.)

**11. Quomodo . . . dixi vobis?:** Matthew protects the disciples against the ignorance they're charged with in Mark. There they failed to see that Jesus would and could provide them something as simple as bread. Jesus even grilled them on the details of the miraculous feedings in a way that borders on insult. Matthew, however, relocates the expression about the "yeast" of Jesus's opponents in a place that makes it appear more organically related to the context. He also has Jesus say that these miracles weren't about bread at all, but about teachings of the Pharisees and the Sadducees, a rather subtle point that they can be forgiven for having missed.

**12. cavendum a fermento panum:** Supply *esse* to complete the indirect statement: "caution should be taken about the yeast of bread."

# Mark 8:22–26

## *Jesus Heals a Blind Man in Bethsaida*

Only Mark has this pericope. Jesus spits on the blind man and even appears to have some difficulty effecting the cure. He has to take it in steps.

**22** Et veniunt Bethsaida. Et adducunt ei caecum et rogant
eum ut illum tangat. **23** Et apprehendens manum caeci
eduxit eum extra vicum. Et exspuens in oculos eius,
impositis manibus ei, interrogabat eum, "Vides aliquid?"
**24** Et aspiciens dicebat, "Video homines, quia velut
arbores video ambulantes." **25** Deinde iterum imposuit
manūs super oculos eius, et coepit videre et restitutus est,
et videbat clare omnia. **26** Et misit illum in domum suam,
dicens, "Nec in vicum introieris."

## Vocabulary

**clare,** clearly
**educo, -ducere, -duxi, -ductus,** to draw out
**velut,** like

## Historical and Grammatical Notes

### Mark 8:22–26

**22. Bethsaida:** accusative case. Motion toward a named city does not require the preposition *ad*.

**23. extra vicum:** This cure is unique for several reasons, one of which is that Jesus moves his patient elsewhere before he works his miracle. We can only speculate as to why. Perhaps Gentiles were more numerous in Bethsaida. If so, Jesus may not have wanted to show non-Jews the extent of his powers. **Vides aliquid?:** Jesus has to check the progress of the cure to verify that he's on the right track. Why? Was it in some way difficult to perform? A reason Matthew deleted this pericope might have been that it implied that Jesus struggles with this cure.

**24. velut arbores:** The man wasn't blind from birth. He had a memory of what men and trees looked like.

**26. in vicum:** This could be merely a variation of the "don't tell anyone" motif we've seen so often. It may be, however, that this pericope preserves the notion that Jesus's cures and message were meant for Jews first, not for Gentiles. **introieris:** As in classical Latin, the perfect subjunctive can be used for a negative imperative: "See to it that you don't go into the village."

# Mark 8:27–30

## *The Faith of Peter*

While traveling well outside of Jewish lands, Jesus asks his disciples what people are saying about him. They answer that most everyone thinks he's one of the prophets come back to life. Then he asks what *they* think he is. Peter says he is the Messiah. Jesus neither affirms nor denies it.

**27** Et egressus est Iesus et discipuli eius in castella
Caesareae Philippi. Et in viā interrogabat discipulos
suos, dicens eis, "Quem me dicunt esse homines?" **28**
Qui responderunt illi, dicentes, "Ioannem Baptistam,
alii Eliam, alii vero unum de prophetis." **29** Et ipse
interrogabat eos, "Vos vero quem me dicitis esse?"
Respondens Petrus ait ei, "Tu es Christus." **30** Et
comminatus est eis ne cui dicerent de illo.

## Matthew 16:13–20

**13** Venit autem Iesus in partes Caesareae Philippi et interrogabat
discipulos suos, dicens, "Quem dicunt homines esse filium
hominis?" **14** At illi dixerunt, "Alii Ioannem Baptistam, alii autem
Eliam, alii vero Ieremiam, aut unum ex prophetis." **15** Dicit illis, "Vos
autem quem me esse dicitis?" **16** Respondens Simon Petrus dixit,
"Tu es Christus, filius Dei vivi." **17** Respondens autem Iesus dixit
ei, "Beatus es, Simon Bariona, quia caro et sanguis non revelavit tibi
sed Pater meus, qui in caelis est. **18** Et ego dico tibi, tu es Petrus, et
super hanc petram aedificabo ecclesiam meam, et portae inferi non
praevalebunt adversum eam. **19** Tibi dabo claves regni caelorum.
Et quodcumque ligaveris super terram, erit ligatum in caelis, et
quodcumque solveris super terram, erit solutum in caelis." **20** Tunc
praecepit discipulis ut nemini dicerent quia ipse esset Christus.

## Luke 9:18–21

**18** Et factum est, cum solus esset orans, erant cum illo discipuli, et
interrogavit illos, dicens, "Quem me dicunt esse turbae?" **19** At illi
responderunt et dixerunt, "Ioannem Baptistam, alii autem Eliam, alii

vero, 'Propheta unus de prioribus surrexit.' " **20** Dixit autem illis, "Vos autem quem me esse dicitis?" Respondens Petrus dixit, "Christum Dei." **21** At ille increpans illos praecepit ne cui dicerent hoc . . .

## Vocabulary

**aedifico (1),** to build
**beatus, -a, -um,** blessed; happy
**caro, carnis,** *f.,* flesh
**clavis, -is,** *f.,* key
**ecclesia, -ae,** *f.,* church
**inferum, -i,** *n.,* the lower place; the underworld
**praevaleo, -ere, -ui,** to prevail; succeed; be victorious
**revelo (1),** to reveal

## Historical and Grammatical Notes

### Mark 8:27–30

**27. in castella:** This is probably just a way of saying "into the outskirts" or "into the region" of Caesarea Philippi, i.e., Jesus didn't go into the city itself, but he was making stops in the district.

**28. Ioannem Baptistam . . .:** Everyone recognizes that Jesus is more than a medicine man and miracle worker, but only Peter knows the truth.

**29. Christus:** This is Greek for the Hebrew *Messiah,* "the one anointed."

### Matthew 16:13–20

**14. Ieremiam:** It makes sense that Jeremiah would be added to the list of possibilities. He was an early example of a "suffering servant," who was maltreated by those whom he tried to help.

**17. Beatus es:** Matthew adds much to Mark's original. Until now, only other spiritual beings recognized Jesus for who is. Now one of the disciples has progressed in his understanding of the unfolding events so that he has attained a supernatural view of reality.

**18–19. Tu es Petrus . . .:** Jesus renames Simon to Peter, a play on words with the Greek *petra.* There are perhaps no more hotly contested verses in Matthew's Gospel. They are the foundation of the Roman Catholic church, which tradition holds was founded by the Apostle Peter during his mission to Rome. Since then, all Popes claim to be occupying the seat of Peter with all the authority granted to him by Jesus. This notion is known as the "Petrine Theory of Papal Succession." The objection to this reading is that there is nothing like these verses in Mark or Luke. If Peter himself is the primary source for Mark's gospel, it's hard to understand why this would not have been in Mark. Matthew's source for Jesus's comment is unknowable.

### Luke 9:18–21

The Great Omission of Luke ends with this pericope.

# Mark 8:31–33

## *The First Prediction of the Suffering and Resurrection of Jesus*

Following directly upon Peter's confession, Jesus explains to his disciples that he will have to suffer at the hands of his enemies and then be resurrected after three days. Peter objects and is rebuked by Jesus.

**31** Et coepit docere illos, "Oportet filium hominis multa
pati et reprobari a senioribus et a summis sacerdotibus et
scribis et occīdi et post tres dies resurgere." **32** Et palam
verbum loquebatur.

### Matthew 16:21–23

**21** Exinde coepit Iesus ostendere discipulis suis quia oporteret eum ire Hierosolymam et multa pati a senioribus et principibus sacerdotum et scribis et occīdi et tertiā die resurgere.

### Luke 9:21–22

[**21** At ille increpans illos praecepit ne cui dicerent hoc,] **22** dicens,
"Oportet filium hominis multa pati et reprobari a senioribus et principibus sacerdotum et scribis et occīdi et tertiā die resurgere."

## Vocabulary

**reprobo (1),** to disapprove of; condemn; reject
**tertius, -a, -um,** third

## Historical and Grammatical Notes

### Mark 8:31–33

**31. coepit docere illos:** Who are the *illos*? If it's only the disciples, we have another example of Jesus's secret teachings meant for his inner circle. **pati:** This sentence isn't easy to disentangle. With *reprobari* it seems that a list of things Jesus will endure is starting. *Et a summis sacerdotibus et scribis* seems to be appositional to *senioribus*. Finally *occīdi* ends the bad things that will happen to Jesus, because what comes next is a triumph: *resurgere*. An idiomatic translation is hard to come by without considerably rewriting the original: "The son of man is to suffer many things. He will be rejected and put to death by the leaders—all the way from the high priests down to the lowly scribes. And then he is to rise again after three days."

**32. palam:** "plainly" or "openly" in the presence of outsiders.

### Matthew 16:21–23

**21. discipulis:** Matthew's understanding of Mark's *illos* is pretty obvious. He told only his disciples what lay before him as the *Christus*.

### Luke 9:21–22

Luke greatly simplifies the scene and preserves only what is essential: Peter recognized that Jesus was the Messiah and the Messiah must suffer and be resurrected.

# Mark 8:31–33 (cont.)

Et apprehendens eum Petrus coepit increpare eum. **33** Qui
conversus et videns discipulos suos comminatus est Petro
et dicit, "Vade retro me, Satana, quoniam non sapis quae
Dei sunt, sed quae sunt hominum."

## Matthew 16:21–23 (cont.)

**22** Et assumens eum Petrus coepit increpare illum, dicens, "Absit a
te, Domine! Non erit tibi hoc." **23** Qui conversus dixit Petro, "Vade
post me, Satana! Scandalum es mihi, quia non sapis ea quae Dei sunt,
sed ea quae hominum!"

## Vocabulary

**sapio, -ere, -ivi** *or* **-ii,** to know; be wise about

**scandalum, -i,** *n.,* impediment; stumbling block

## Historical and Grammatical Notes

### Mark 8:31–33 (cont.)

**33. videns discipulos suos:** Jesus rebukes Peter while looking at his disciples. This has more power than if he'd glowered at Peter alone. Jesus is publicly humiliating Peter in front of the others. **Satana:** Jesus knows that he must suffer real torment, and finding an excuse to avoid his fate would be very tempting, even for Jesus. This is why he calls Peter *Satan,* the one who tempts. It's not because Peter is speaking plain evil, but because he is tempting Jesus to think that he needn't suffer. **non sapis quae Dei sunt, sed quae sunt hominum:** "you don't understand the things that are of God but the things that are of men." Jesus effectively undoes the compliment he paid Peter in the previous pericope. Trying to persuade Jesus that he doesn't have to suffer death at the hands of his enemies is of course a very natural and humane thing to do. But to know that it has to be this way is to know the will of God. Peter also exhibits a flawed understanding of the Messiah. The Messiah will not be a conquering, heroic, military leader. The events inaugurated by his appearance will be subtle and difficult to understand.

### Matthew 16:21–23 (cont.)

**22. Absit a te:** Matthew reports Peter's words: "May this be far from you" or "May this not be yours."

**23. Scandalum es mihi:** i.e., "You are a stumbling block." This isn't because what Peter is saying is not effective in creating doubts in Jesus; it's because it is. Critics of the Theory of Petrine Succession, incidentally, are quick to point out that directly after Jesus gives him the keys to heaven and hell in Matthew, Peter proves himself to be unworthy and even worse than the other disciples.

# Mark 8:34–9:1

## *How to Follow Jesus*

Jesus tells his disciples and others that they will have to give up all they have to follow him. In exchange, they will have a special place in the Kingdom of God, which is coming soon.

**34** Et convocatā turbā cum discipulis suis, dixit eis, "Si quis vult post me sequi, deneget semetipsum et tollat crucem suam et sequatur me. **35** Qui enim voluerit animam suam salvam facere perdet eam. Qui autem perdiderit animam suam propter me et evangelium salvam eam faciet. **36** Quid enim prodest homini, si lucretur mundum totum et detrimentum faciat animae suae? **37** Quid enim dabit homo commutationem pro animā suā?

### Matthew 16:24–28

**24** Tunc Iesus dixit discipulis suis, "Si quis vult post me venire, abneget semetipsum et tollat crucem suam et sequatur me. **25** Qui enim voluerit animam suam salvam facere, perdet eam. Qui autem perdiderit animam suam propter me, inveniet eam. **26** Quid enim prodest homini, si mundum universum lucretur, animae vero suae detrimentum patiatur? Aut quam dabit homo commutationem pro animā suā?

### Luke 9:23–27

**23** Dicebat autem ad omnes, "Si quis vult post me venire, abneget semetipsum et tollat crucem suam cotidie et sequatur me. **24** Qui enim voluerit animam suam salvam facere, perdet illam. Qui autem perdiderit animam suam propter me, hĭc salvam faciet illam. **25** Quid enim proficit homo, si lucretur universum mundum, se autem ipsum perdat vel detrimentum sui faciat?

## Vocabulary

**commutatio, -ionis,** *f.*, exchange
**cotidie,** daily
**crux, crucis,** *f.*, cross
**denego (1),** to deny
**lucro (1),** to gain

## Historical and Grammatical Notes

### Mark 8:34–9:1

35. **Qui enim voluerit:** The perfect subjunctive is used in legalistic formulae like this: "whosoever wished" = "he who wishes." Evidence of the total commitment and self-denial needed to follow Jesus is a complete rejection of all personal gain. But Jesus goes further. Even wanting to save your soul is a sign that you're not truly following Jesus. Is this degree of self-denial possible? It seems difficult to believe that a true follower of Jesus would be completely indifferent to the salvation of his eternal soul. Matthew alters a single word in Mark's formulation and makes it less striking.

36. **Quid enim prodest homini:** "What gain is it for a man." We can understand the requirement to cast off worldly ambitions and concerns. One could argue, however, that rejecting worldly concerns in fact reveals a concern for the soul, and in the previous verse Jesus has explicitly said that wishing to save one's soul is incompatible with true discipleship.

### Matthew 16:24–28

25. **inveniet eam:** "Will find it" makes the conflict in Mark less striking. Mark first says that the wish for salvation proves an unworthiness to follow Jesus, but then he says that following Jesus is the way to personal salvation. The tension between these two propositions is obvious. Is it possible for anyone in this world to follow Jesus without an interest in the eternal reward it promises? And yet such an interest is an insuperable barrier to true discipleship. Changing Mark's *salvam eam faciet* to *inveniet eam* deflects the problem somewhat, while not completely resolving it. It's still a paradox at the heart of the Christian life.

26. **vero:** "but."

### Luke 9:23–27

25. **Quid enim proficit homo:** "what has a man earned." Mark's original is an economic metaphor. *Proficit* is another way of saying the same thing. Luke drops the verse "what payment will he offer in exchange for his soul" perhaps because he thought that the economic metaphor had already been established.

# Mark 8:34–9:1 (cont.)

**38** Qui enim me confusus fuerit et mea verba in generatione istā adulterā et peccatrice, et filius hominis confundetur eum, cum venerit in gloriā Patris sui cum angelis sanctis."

## Matthew 16:24–28 (cont.)

**27** Filius enim hominis venturus est in gloriā Patris sui cum angelis suis, et tunc reddet unicuique secundum opus eius.

## Luke 9:23–27 (cont.)

**26** Nam qui me erubuerit et meos sermones, hunc filius hominis erubescet, cum venerit in gloriā suā et Patris et sanctorum angelorum.

## Vocabulary

**confundo, -fundere, -fudi, -fusus,** to blend together; bewilder

**erubesco, -escere, -ui,** to blush; be ashamed of

**peccatrix, -cis,** sinful

## Historical and Grammatical Notes

### Mark 8:34–9:1 (cont.)

**38. confusus fuerit:** perfect subjunctive: "whosoever has been ashamed of me and my words." The verb *confundo* is being used as if it were deponent, hence the accusative objects *me* and *mea verba.* This is still an odd way of putting it. Jesus is saying that someone who denies or is not proud of Jesus and his message will be treated likewise when the Kingdom of God arrives. Matthew recasts the phrase to make it clearer, but Luke retains Mark's idea that it's not so much evildoing that will cost a person at the end of time as it is hesitation or shame about Jesus.

### Matthew 16:24–28 (cont.)

**27. reddet unicuique secundum opus eius:** "he will pay back to each person according to his work." This completely eliminates the puzzling way Mark expresses it. We're not talking about shame or some other emotional response to Jesus and his message, but what a follower does about it. This is action, which is a much more measurable, tangible proof of an inward disposition.

# Mark 8:34–9:1 (cont.)

**9:1** Et dicebat illis, "Amen dico vobis, sunt quidam de hīc stantibus qui non gustabunt mortem, donec videant regnum Dei venisse in virtute."

## Matthew 16:24–28 (cont.)

**28** Amen dico vobis, sunt quidam de hīc stantibus qui non gustabunt mortem, donec videant filium hominis venientem in regno suo."

## Luke 9:23–27 (cont.)

**27** Dico autem vobis vere, sunt aliqui hīc stantes qui non gustabunt mortem, donec videant regnum Dei."

## Vocabulary

**gusto (1),** to taste

## Historical and Grammatical Notes

### Mark 8:34–9:1 (cont.)

**9:1. qui . . . in virtute:** The prediction of an imminent end of time becomes increasingly problematic for the Jesus movement as the decades roll on after Jesus's death. If Mark was assembled in 70 CE, one could still make the case that Jesus's statement could be borne out, as it was possible for a young man in the crowd still to be alive forty years later. But with Matthew and Luke (written somewhere around 90–110), clearly something had to be explained. Matthew makes subtle changes to Mark to soften the paradox, but Luke retains the original nearly word for word. One proposed solution is that the Kingdom of God, which is what they're to see, is not the end of time that everyone was expecting after all. Instead it is a process, one that begins with the resurrection and the arrival of the Holy Spirit among Jesus's discouraged followers, as recorded in the opening verses of Acts.

### Matthew 16:24–28 (cont.)

**28. filium hominis venientem:** The son of man has already been identified as Jesus. The Kingdom of God is to bring an end of the current order. That hadn't happened by the time Jesus appears to have said it would, and early followers of Jesus had to be aware that they'd misunderstood something. Matthew makes this subtle adjustment by not referring explicitly to the Kingdom of God, but more equivocally to the "kingdom of the son of man." What that means is another question.

# Chapter 9

In chapter 9 Jesus's nature is more explicitly revealed than before. Three of his disciples see him transformed into his true nature, and he is seen talking with Elijah and Moses. The chapter also explores what the disciples can expect when Jesus is no longer with them. They fail to cast out a demon on their own, they quarrel over which of them is the most important, they are chastised for having stopped another miracle worker from curing others, and they are reminded of the supreme importance of avoiding sin at any cost.

# Mark 9:2–10

## *The Transfiguration of Jesus*

Jesus is transformed into a resplendent being before the eyes of Peter, James, and John. They see him talking with Elijah and Moses, and a voice from a cloud proclaims him to be its beloved son. Jesus tells them not to reveal what they have seen until after he has risen from the dead.

**2** Et post dies sex assumit Iesus Petrum et Iacobum et
Ioannem, et ducit illos in montem excelsum seorsum
solos. Et transfiguratus est coram ipsis. **3** Et vestimenta
eius facta sunt splendentia, candida nimis, qualia fullo
super terram non potest tam candida facere. **4** Et apparuit
illis Elias cum Moyse, et erant loquentes cum Iesu.

### Matthew 17:1–9

**1** Et post dies sex assumit Iesus Petrum et Iacobum et Ioannem
fratrem eius et ducit illos in montem excelsum seorsum. **2** Et
transfiguratus est ante eos. Et resplenduit facies eius sicut sol.
Vestimenta autem eius facta sunt alba sicut lux. **3** Et ecce: apparuit
illis Moyses et Elias cum eo loquentes.

### Luke 9:28–36

**28** Factum est autem post haec verba fere dies octo, et assumpsit
Petrum et Ioannem et Iacobum et ascendit in montem ut oraret. **29**
Et facta est, dum oraret, species vultūs eius altera, et vestitus eius
albus, refulgens. **30** Et ecce: duo viri loquebantur cum illo—et erant
Moyses et Elias— **31** qui visi in gloriā dicebant exodum eius quam
completurus erat in Ierusalem. **32** Petrus vero et qui cum illo gravati
erant somno. Et evigilantes viderunt gloriam eius et duos viros qui
stabant cum illo.

## Vocabulary

**candidus, -a, -um,** bright
**evigilo (1),** to wake up
**excelsus, -a, -um,** high
**exodus, -i,** *f.,* way out; death
**fullo, -onis,** *m.,* fuller
**gravo (1),** to burden; weigh down
**refulgeo, -gere, -si,** to shine back
**resplendeo, -ere,** to shine
**sex,** six
**splendentius, -a, -um,** radiant
**vultus, -us,** *m.,* face

## Historical and Grammatical Notes

### Mark 9:2–10

**2. post dies sex:** This is the only pericope introduced with such a precise chronology. Others begin with something vaguer, such as *statim, in illis diebus,* or just the conjunction *et.* Matthew follows Mark. Luke is also precise, though he changes the number of days to eight. Why such precision? It may be that the event was so exceptional that even its exact position in the chronology of events was preserved in the oral tradition. **in montem excelsum:** Mt. Tabor, about eleven miles to the southeast of the Sea of Galilee, is the traditional location. **transfiguratus est:** We can only guess in what way Jesus was transfigured. Mark mentions simply that his clothing shone with a brilliance never seen on earth. Matthew and Luke both add that Jesus's face shone, too.

**3. qualia fullo super terram non potest tam candida facere:** literally, "such as a fuller on the earth is not able to make so white." A fuller cleans and thickens cotton or wool. In one of the steps of the process, the cloth was immersed in tubs of urine, which acted as a whitener. Matthew and Luke both omit Mark's homely image of the fuller, perhaps because they thought it unnecessary or unseemly.

**4. Elias cum Moyse:** Jesus was destined to perfect or supersede the Law, embodied in the person of Moses, and to fulfill the prophecies about the Messiah, which Elijah represents. Moses and Elijah were to return to earth before the Messiah's arrival.

### Luke 9:28–36

**31. dicebant exodum eius:** "were discussing his death." Only Luke claims to know what the three were talking about.

# Mark 9:2–10 (cont.)

**5** Et respondens Petrus ait Iesu, "Rabbi, bonum est
nos hīc esse. Et faciamus tria tabernacula: tibi unum et
Moysi unum et Eliae unum." **6** Non enim sciebat quid
responderet, erant enim exterriti. **7** Et facta est nubes
obumbrans eos, et vēnit vox de nube, "Hĭc est filius meus
dilectus. Audite illum." **8** Et statim circumspicientes
neminem amplius viderunt nisi Iesum tantum secum.
**9** Et descendentibus illis de monte, praecepit illis ne
cui quae vidissent narrarent, nisi cum filius hominis a
mortuis resurrexerit. **10** Et verbum continuerunt apud se,
conquirentes quid esset illud, "A mortuis resurgere."

## Matthew 17:1–9 (cont.)

**4** Respondens autem Petrus dixit ad Iesum, "Domine, bonum est
nos hīc esse. Si vis, faciam hīc tria tabernacula, tibi unum et Moysi
unum et Eliae unum." **5** Adhuc eo loquente, ecce: nubes lucida
obumbravit eos. Et ecce: vox de nube, dicens, "Hĭc est filius meus
dilectus, in quo mihi bene complacui. Ipsum audite." **6** Et audientes
discipuli ceciderunt in faciem suam et timuerunt valde. **7** Et accessit
Iesus et tetigit eos dixitque eis, "Surgite et nolite timere." **8** Levantes
autem oculos suos, neminem viderunt nisi solum Iesum. **9** Et
descendentibus illis de monte, praecepit eis Iesus, dicens, "Nemini
dixeritis visionem, donec filius hominis a mortuis resurgat."

## Luke 9:28–36 (cont.)

**33** Et factum est, cum discederent ab illo, ait Petrus ad Iesum,
"Praeceptor, bonum est nos hīc esse. Et faciamus tria tabernacula,
unum tibi et unum Moysi et unum Eliae," nesciens quid diceret.
**34** Haec autem illo loquente, facta est nubes et obumbravit eos. Et
timuerunt, intrantibus illis in nubem. **35** Et vox facta est de nube,
dicens, "Hĭc est filius meus electus. Ipsum audite." **36** Et dum fieret
vox, inventus est Iesus solus. Et ipsi tacuerunt et nemini dixerunt in
illis diebus quidquam ex his quae viderant.

# Vocabulary

**lucidus, -a, -um,** full of light
**obumbro (1),** to cast a shadow on
**tabernaculum, -i,** *n.,* tent

# Historical and Grammatical Notes

## MARK 9:2–10 (CONT.)

**5. Iesu:** dative. **tabernacula:** "tents."

**6. Non enim sciebat quid responderet, erant enim exterriti:** "for he didn't know what to say because they were terrified." Mark's editorial comment implies that he couldn't make sense out of why Peter offered to set up tents. Shock, disbelief, and disorientation are certainly natural enough responses to what they had seen.

**7. Hĭc est filius meus dilectus. Audite illum:** There are obvious parallels to Jesus's baptism, where the voice from heaven says (1:11) *Tu es filius meus dilectus. In te complacui.*

**9. ne cui:** *ne alicui.* **nisi cum:** "except when." Clearly this means "until after," but it's an odd way to put it. Matthew and Luke apparently thought so, too. Watch how they recast Mark's expression.

**10. conquirentes quid esset illud:** When Jesus first mentioned his resurrection from the dead at 8:31, the disciples didn't have any questions. It does seem strange that they should wonder what it means now. Matthew and Luke drop the line.

## MATTHEW 17:1–9 (CONT.)

**6. ceciderunt in faciem suam:** Matthew dramatizes what Mark meant by *territi sunt.*

## LUKE 9:28–36 (CONT.)

**33. cum discederent:** when Moses and Elijah were leaving, and Jesus was by himself.

**34. Et timuerunt, intrantibus illis in nubem:** "and they were afraid [because] they entered into the cloud." What is the setting here? A heavy cloud comes and shades the disciples, and then Moses, Elijah, and Jesus enter the cloud and that terrifies the disciples? Is the cloud up in the sky or should we envision it as on the ground?

# Mark 9:11–13

## *Jesus Answers a Question about Elijah*

According to Old Testament prophecy, Elijah must come before the Messiah to set everything right, so why, the disciples ask, should the Messiah suffer and die? Jesus explains to the disciples that Elijah had in fact returned in the person of John the Baptist.

**11** Et interrogabant eum, dicentes, "Quid ergo dicunt scribae quia Eliam oporteat venire primum?" **12** Qui ait illis, "Elias veniens primo restituit omnia. Et quomodo scriptum est super filio hominis, ut multa patiatur et contemnatur? **13** Sed dico vobis, et Elias vēnit et fecerunt illi quaecumque volebant, sicut scriptum est de eo."

### Matthew 17:10–13

**10** Et interrogaverunt eum discipuli, dicentes, "Quid ergo scribae dicunt quod Eliam oporteat primum venire?" **11** At ille respondens ait, "Elias quidem venturus est et restituet omnia. **12** Dico autem vobis quia Elias iam venit, et non cognoverunt eum. Sed fecerunt in eo quaecumque voluerunt. Sic et filius hominis passurus est ab eis." **13** Tunc intellexerunt discipuli quia de Ioanne Baptistā dixisset eis.

# Historical and Grammatical Notes

## Mark 9:11–13

**11. interrogabant:** We don't know the subject of the verb. It's either his disciples or the crowd. **scribae:** It's altogether fitting that the scribes would have this question. Being masters of the texts, they would know that Elijah must return *primum*. We can well imagine how this question came up. If the followers of Jesus were claiming, as they probably were, that Jesus was the Messiah, the scribes would have countered by saying, "Impossible. Elijah has to come back first, as we know from Malachi [3:22]." The scribes would also have been well prepared for claims like this. Jesus was not the first or the only one of the period to declare that he was king of the Jews.

**12. Elias veniens primo restituit omnia:** The question is not whether, but why, Elijah has to come first. **ut multa patiatur et contemnatur:** a somewhat rare use of *ut* to introduce indirect statement: "that he is to suffer and be condemned?" Curiously, there is no specific Old Testament text behind Jesus's claim.

**13. illi:** dative; the antecedent is Elijah: "they did to him whatever they wanted." There is no indication in Malachi that Elijah was to suffer on his return.

## Matthew 17:10–13

**10. discipuli:** Matthew removes the ambiguity of the subject of *interrogabant* in Mark.

**11. venturus est:** Jesus answers in the voice of the scribes as if the return of Elijah has yet to happen: "When he comes he will . . ." Then Jesus returns to his own voice: "But Elijah *has* come."

**13. quia de Ioanne Baptistā dixisset eis:** "that he was talking to them about John the Baptist." Matthew's editorial comment would be useful for an audience unfamiliar with past events in Israel.

# Mark 9:14–29

## *The Disciples Cannot Heal a Boy*

The disciples try and fail to heal a boy. Jesus casts out the demon and then comforts them by explaining that this was an extreme case.

**14** Et venientes ad discipulos viderunt turbam magnam
circa eos et scribas conquirentes cum illis. **15** Et
confestim omnis populus videns eum stupefactus est,
et accurrentes salutabant eum. **16** Et interrogavit eos,
"Quid inter vos conquiritis?" **17** Et respondit ei unus
de turbā, "Magister, attuli filium meum ad te habentem
spiritum mutum. **18** Et ubicumque eum apprehenderit,
allidit eum, et spumat et stridet dentibus et arescit. Et
dixi discipulis tuis ut eicerent illum, et non potuerunt."
**19** Qui respondens eis dicit, "O generatio incredula,
quamdiu apud vos ero? Quamdiu vos patiar? Afferte
illum ad me."

### Matthew 17:14–20

**14** Et cum venissent ad turbam, accessit ad eum homo genibus
provolutus ante eum **15** et, dicens, "Domine, miserere filii mei, quia
lunaticus est et male patitur, nam saepe cadit in ignem et crebro in
aquam. **16** Et obtuli eum discipulis tuis, et non potuerunt curare
eum." **17** Respondens autem Iesus ait, "O generatio incredula et
perversa, quousque ero vobiscum? Usquequo patiar vos? Afferte huc
illum ad me."

### Luke 9:37–42

**37** Factum est autem in sequenti die, descendentibus illis de monte,
occurrit illi turba multa. **38** Et ecce: vir de turbā exclamavit, dicens,
"Magister, obsecro te, respice in filium meum, quia unicus est mihi.
**39** Et ecce: spiritus apprehendit illum, et subito clamat, et dissipat
eum cum spumā et vix discedit ab eo dilanians eum. **40** Et rogavi

discipulos tuos ut eicerent illum, et non potuerunt." **41** Respondens autem Iesus dixit, "O generatio infidelis et perversa, usquequo ero apud vos et patiar vos? Adduc huc filium tuum."

## Vocabulary

**allido, -dere, -si, -sus,** to strike
**aresco, -escere, -ui,** to become dry
**dilanio (1),** to tear to pieces
**dissipo (1),** to disperse; scatter
**quousque,** until when
**respicio, -spicere, -spexi, -spectus,** to have thought for; consider
**spumo (1),** to foam; froth
**strideo, -ere, -i** *or* **strido, -ere, -i,** to hiss; shriek
**ubicumque,** wherever; whenever
**usquequo,** until what point?

## Historical and Grammatical Notes

### Mark 9:14–29

**14. scribas conquirentes cum illis:** The disciples failed to effect a cure, and the scribes would undoubtedly be asking for an explanation.

### Matthew 17:14–20

**15. miserere:** second person singular imperative < *misereor* + objective genitive. **nam saepe cadit in ignem et crebro in aquam:** "for he often falls into the fire and frequently into the water." This is all that Matthew preserves from the horrific description of the possession in Mark. **crebro:** an adverb < *creber*: "frequently."

### Luke 9:37–42

**39. apprehendit illum:** Matthew avoided the switching back and forth of subjects in his rewrite of Mark, but we see traces of it in Luke: "[the spirit] takes him, and [the boy] cries out, and [the spirit] tears at him with foam [ = makes him foam at the mouth] and with difficulty it leaves him as it tears him to pieces."

# Mark 9:14–29 (cont.)

**20** Et attulerunt illum ad eum. Et cum vidisset illum,
spiritus statim conturbavit eum. Et corruens in terram
volutabatur spumans. **21** Et interrogavit patrem eius,
"Quantum temporis est ex quo hoc ei accidit?" At ille ait,
"Ab infantiā, **22** et frequenter eum etiam in ignem et in
aquas misit ut eum perderet. Sed si quid potes, adiuva nos,
misertus nostri." **23** Iesus autem ait illi, "Si potes! Omnia
possibilia credenti." **24** Et continuo exclamans pater pueri
aiebat, "Credo. Adiuva incredulitatem meam." **25** Et cum
videret Iesus concurrentem turbam, comminatus est
spiritui immundo, dicens illi, "Mute et surde spiritus, ego
tibi praecipio, exi ab eo et amplius ne introeas in eum."
**26** Et clamans et multum discerpens eum exiit. Et factus
est sicut mortuus, ita ut multi dicerent, "Mortuus est!" **27**
Iesus autem tenens manum eius elevavit illum, et surrexit.

## Matthew 17:14–20 (cont.)

**18** Et increpavit eum Iesus, et exiit ab eo daemonium, et curatus est puer ex illā horā.

## Luke 9:37–42 (cont.)

**42** Et cum accederet, elisit illum daemonium et dissipavit. Et increpavit Iesus spiritum immundum et sanavit puerum et reddidit illum patri eius.

## Vocabulary

**corruo, -ere, -i,** to fall; collapse
**elido, -dere, -si, -sus,** to break to pieces
**possibilis, -e,** doable; possible
**volutor, -ari, volutus sum,** to roll about

## Historical and Grammatical Notes

### Mark 9:14–29 (cont.)

**18. spumat:** change of subject to the boy.

**20. illum:** The antecedents for the pronoun *illum* will be switching back and forth between the boy, the spirit, the boy's father, and Jesus. Here it refers to the spirit.

**21. Quantum temporis est ex quo hoc ei accidit:** "How long has it been since this has been happening to him."

**22. perderet:** It has to mean "to kill" in this context and not "to perish": "often it even throws him into fire and into water to kill him." **si quid potes:** "if you are in any way able."

**23. Si potes!:** Jesus throws the request back to the man: "If *you* are able." There is no question that Jesus is still annoyed at being pestered again for another cure. First his disciples fail to bring about the cure, and now the son's father doesn't realize that he could cure his son himself if he just believed. **credenti:** dative complement after *possibilia*: "possible for one who believes."

**25. amplius ne introeas in eum:** "and no longer go into him."

**26. discerpens eum:** "shaking him to pieces."

### Matthew 17:14–20 (cont.)

**18. exiit ab eo daemonium:** "and the demon left him." This is hardly the way the demon departed in Mark.

### Luke 9:37–42 (cont.)

**42. illum:** "the boy." "As Jesus was approaching, the demon threw the boy down and tore at him." **reddidit illum patri eius:** Luke deletes Jesus's final words to the disciples. It might be that Luke understood them to be sarcastic in Mark and didn't want the disciples to be the object of his abuse. One widely noticed trend in the way Matthew and Luke edit the material they received from Mark is that they both try to make the disciples look better in the eyes of the early Christians. This may be another example of that effort.

# Mark 9:14–29 (cont.)

**28** Et cum introisset in domum, discipuli eius secreto interrogabant eum, "Quare nos non potuimus eicere eum?" **29** Et dixit illis, "Hoc genus in nullo potest exire nisi in oratione."

## Matthew 17:14–20 (cont.)

**19** Tunc accesserunt discipuli ad Iesum secreto et dixerunt, "Quare nos non potuimus eicere illum?" **20** Ille autem dicit illis, "Propter modicam fidem vestram. Amen quippe dico vobis, si habueritis fidem sicut granum sinapis, dicetis monti huic, 'Transi hinc illuc,' et transibit. Et nihil impossibile erit vobis."

## Historical and Grammatical Notes

### Mark 9:14–29 (cont.)

**29. in nullo:** Add *modo*: "in no way." **nisi in oratione:** It's not easy to understand what Jesus means by this. It appears that he is saying that the disciples have just encountered a demon they weren't trained to deal with. It takes prayer as an additional measure to cast this sort out. If this is the case, the disciples can't be faulted in any way. It was beyond their training. But this explanation would not account for Jesus's outburst at verse 19, where it's clear he thinks that they should have been able to deal with the spirit effectively. To account for that, verse 29 can be read as a sarcastic way of saying: "You forgot to pray, and that's something you should surely know by now!"

### Matthew 17:14–20 (cont.)

**20. Transi hinc illuc:** "Move from here to over there." An old joke shows how difficult it is to have this degree of faith. A man who's just read this passage decides he wants to move a huge boulder that's in the middle of his field. One night, he believes with all his strength that the boulder would be gone in the morning. The next day he's sees that it's still there, and he says to himself, "Ah . . . I knew it wouldn't work!"

# Mark 9:30–32

## *Jesus Predicts His Betrayal, Suffering, and Resurrection*

Jesus's prediction of his death and resurrection this time adds the detail that he is going to be betrayed.

**30** Et inde profecti peragrabant Galilaeam, nec volebat quemquam scire. **31** Docebat enim discipulos suos et dicebat illis, "Filius hominis traditur in manūs hominum, et occīdent eum, et occisus post tres dies resurget." **32** At illi ignorabant verbum et timebant eum interrogare.

### Matthew 17:22–23

**22** Conversantibus autem eis in Galilaeā, dixit illis Iesus, "Filius hominis tradendus est in manūs hominum, **23** et occīdent eum, et tertio die resurget." Et contristati sunt vehementer.

### Luke 9:43–45

**43** Stupebant autem omnes in magnitudine Dei, omnibusque mirantibus in omnibus, quae faciebat, dixit ad discipulos suos, **44** "Ponite vos in auribus vestris sermones istos, filius enim hominis futurum est ut tradatur in manūs hominum." **45** At illi ignorabant verbum istud, et erat velatum ante eos, ut non sentirent illud, et timebant interrogare eum de hoc verbo.

## Vocabulary

**conversor, -ari, -atus sum,** to abide in; stay in
**peragro (1),** to walk through; traverse
**proficiscor, -i, -fectus sum,** to set out
**velo (1),** to cover up; veil

## Historical and Grammatical Notes

### Mark 9:30–32

**30. nec volebat quemquam scire:** This isn't the first time that Jesus wants to be away from the crowds. He's a reclusive figure in Mark in comparison to the other two Synoptics. They strip out any mention that Jesus wants solitude in their rewrites.

**32. timebant eum interrogare:** After the rough treatment Peter got earlier, this is understandable in part. But the darkening of the reputation of the disciples continues. They don't understand Jesus, and they haven't the courage to ask. The distance between them and Jesus is widening.

### Matthew 17:22–23

**23. Et contristati sunt vehementer:** They understood Jesus's words, and their reaction is sorrow.

### Luke 9:43–45

**44. filius enim hominis futurum est ut tradatur:** *Filius* is the subject of *tradatur*: "It will come about that the son of man will be betrayed."

**45. erat velatum:** It wasn't the disciples' fault that they didn't understand. The truth was actively being kept from them. **ut non sentirent:** either a purpose or result clause. Either way, the practical significance is the same. There was a veil pulled over their eyes and they didn't understand.

# Mark 9:33–37

## *The Disciples Quarrel over Which of Them Is More Important*

Some of the disciples have been arguing over which of them is more important than the others and ask Jesus to settle the debate. Jesus tells them that they all must be humble.

**33** Et venerunt Capharnaum. Qui cum domi esset,
interrogabat eos, "Quid in viā tractabatis?" **34** At illi
tacebant, siquidem inter se in viā disputaverant quis esset
maior. **35** Et residens vocavit Duodecim et ait illis, "Si
quis vult primus esse, erit omnium novissimus et omnium
minister."

### Matthew 18:1–5

**1** In illā horā accesserunt discipuli ad Iesum, dicentes, "Quis putas maior est in regno caelorum?"

### Luke 9:46–48

**46** Intravit autem cogitatio in eos, quis eorum maior esset.

## Vocabulary

**novissimus, -a, -um,** newest; the very last
**resideo, -sidere, -sedi,** to sit down
**siquidem,** since indeed
**tracto (1),** to treat; consider

## Historical and Grammatical Notes

### Mark 9:33–37

**34. siquidem:** They have reason to keep quiet, given what they were arguing about. This is an untimely disagreement. They'd just failed to perform a simple cure and failed to understand Jesus's clear words about his death and resurrection. Instead of feeling elevated by their association with Jesus, they should be ashamed of themselves at about this point. It only goes to underscore just how out of touch they've become with Jesus and his mission. **quis esset maior:** subjunctive in indirect question. John, Peter, and James have been singled out before for special duties and privileges, so it makes sense that they are involved in this dispute.

**35. erit:** This verb is often translated as if it were a subjunctive: "If anyone wants to be first, he must/should be the last minister of all." But the verb is a future indicative (so also is the Greek: *estai*). It could be that the line really means that the desire to be first will be answered with the punishment of being placed last and being made to serve everyone else. This is somewhat different from the way the sentence is generally understood and translated. Matthew appears to have recognized the difficulty, and he reworks Mark's original. **novissimus:** "the last."

### Matthew 18:1–5

**1. in regno caelorum:** Matthew completely redoes this scene. In Mark, the disciples were quarrelling over who was the most important, and their concern was not explicitly about the future. To give them some cover, Matthew changes this to a question about the Kingdom of God and drops any reference to the idea that the disciples were having a spat about their role in it.

# Mark 9:33–37 (cont.)

**36** Et accipiens puerum, statuit eum in medio eorum, quem ut complexus esset, ait illis, **37** "Quisquis unum ex huiusmodi pueris receperit in nomine meo, me recipit, et, quicumque me susceperit, non me suscipit, sed eum qui me misit."

## Matthew 18:1–5 (cont.)

**2** Et advocans parvulum, statuit eum in medio eorum **3** et dixit, "Amen dico vobis: Nisi conversi fueritis et efficiamini sicut parvuli, non intrabitis in regnum caelorum. **4** Quicumque ergo humiliaverit se sicut parvulus iste, hĭc est maior in regno caelorum. **5** Et, qui susceperit unum parvulum talem in nomine meo, me suscipit."

## Luke 9:46–48 (cont.)

**47** At Iesus sciens cogitationem cordis illorum, apprehendens puerum statuit eum secus se **48** et ait illis, "Quicumque susceperit puerum istum in nomine meo, me recipit, et, quicumque me receperit, recipit eum qui me misit. Nam qui minor est inter omnes vos, hĭc maior est."

# Historical and Grammatical Notes

## Mark 9:33–37 (cont.)

**36. accipiens puerum:** The message of the child is that of self-effacement. At this time, only women would be expected to take care of children, a chore that would be beneath the dignity of a man.

**37. in nomine meo:** To be with Jesus, one has to abase himself to the level of a nonperson. Thus the added phrase may mean no more than "for my sake" or "with me in mind."

## Matthew 18:1–5 (cont.)

**3. Nisi conversi fueritis et efficiamini:** "Unless you will have changed your ways and made yourselves." **sicut parvuli:** Our modern, more romantic ideas of childhood make this easy to misunderstand. A child in Jesus's age was a nonperson, a virtual nothing. His message to the disciples is not that they need to be innocent and full of wonder. It's that the disciples need to have no expectation that they are deserving of anything, let alone a privileged place in heaven.

**4. in regno caelorum:** Matthew reiterates that the argument was about their place in the coming age, not in the present.

## Luke 9:46–48 (cont.)

**48. hĭc maior est:** Is this kind of pure abasement humanly possible, particularly if there's an expectation that it will be rewarded with glory? Jesus is not talking about a mere outward appearance of deference and humility. He's talking about a complete remaking of the human *psyche*.

# Mark 9:38–41

## *Someone Else Is Casting Out Demons in Jesus's Name*

John tells Jesus that they stopped someone from casting out demons because he wasn't one of the disciples. Jesus says that they should let him continue. If he's not against them, he says, he's with them.

**38** Dixit illi Ioannes, "Magister, vidimus quendam in
nomine tuo eicientem daemonia, et prohibebamus eum,
quia non sequebatur nos." **39** Iesus autem ait, "Nolite
prohibere eum. Nemo est enim, qui faciat virtutem in
nomine meo et possit cito male loqui de me. **40** Qui enim
non est adversum nos, pro nobis est. **41** Quisquis enim
potum dederit vobis calicem aquae in nomine, quia Christi
estis, amen dico vobis, non perdet mercedem suam."

## Luke 9:49–50

**49** Respondens autem Ioannes dixit, "Praeceptor, vidimus quendam
in nomine tuo eicientem daemonia et prohibuimus eum, quia non
sequitur nobiscum." **50** Et ait ad illum Iesus, "Nolite prohibere, qui
enim non est adversus vos, pro vobis est."

## Vocabulary

**merces, -cedis,** *f.*, reward; payment

**potus, -us,** *m.*, a drink

## Historical and Grammatical Notes

### MARK 9:38–41

39. **Nolite prohibere eum:** "Don't stop him." The disciples failed to execute a simple exorcism, misunderstood Jesus, and quarreled about which of them was the top disciple. Now John tells Jesus that they've stopped someone from casting out demons in Jesus's name because he wasn't one of their circle. Their response is motivated by jealousy and not by any concern for the person who was possessed. Jesus's reply probably wasn't what they wanted to hear. They had taken themselves to be Jesus's exclusive representatives and followers. Now they learn that there's nothing so special about them after all. Others can work miracles in Jesus's name as well. **faciat:** relative clause of characteristic. **possit cito male loqui de me:** "can't turn around and speak ill of me." This implies at least two things. One is that it does Jesus no harm to have his name invoked while good is being done. Another is that it underscores the point Jesus has been making: Healing the sick is not his mission. It's to call people to repent and to be ready for the Kingdom of God. This would account for his apparent indifference to this unnamed exorcist.

40. **Qui enim non est adversum nos, pro nobis est:** We can well imagine how this and the following verse would have caused some consternation among the first Christians. It clearly says that one needn't be a follower of Jesus to receive the rewards that a Christian merits. All a non-Christian need do is not oppose the church. On top of this, a non-Christian who aids a Christian receives a reward. Luke, writing during the first years of the Christian church, truncates this pericope to avoid most of these issues. This may also explain why Matthew deletes the entire scene.

41. **potum dederit vobis calicem aquae:** Take *calicem* as appositive to *potum*: "whosoever should give you a drink, a cup of water." **in nomine, quia Christi estis:** Some manuscripts insert *meo* after *nomine,* but this doesn't help explain *quia Christi estis*. Extended senses of the word *nomen* are "excuse," "sake," or "account," and they are well attested in classical Latin. *Quia Christi estis* would then be complementary to *nomine*: "whosoever shall give you a drink, a cup of water, *on account of the fact that* you are Christians . . ."

# Mark 9:42–48

## *Sayings on Scandal*

Jesus underlines the seriousness of the time with the most gruesome parables in the Synoptics. It would be better for someone caught causing a follower of Jesus to lose faith to be drowned than suffer the real punishment. It would be better for someone to mutilate himself to avoid temptation than to sin and be cast into hell.

**42** "Et quisquis scandalizaverit unum ex his pusillis credentibus in me, bonum est ei magis ut circumdetur mola asinaria collo eius et in mare mittatur.

### Matthew 18:6–9

**6** "Qui autem scandalizaverit unum de pusillis istis, qui in me credunt, expedit ei, ut suspendatur mola asinaria in collo eius et demergatur in profundum maris. **7** Vae mundo ab scandalis! Necesse est enim ut veniant scandala. Verum tamen vae homini per quem scandalum vĕnit!

### Luke 17:1–2

**1** Et ad discipulos suos ait, "Impossibile est ut non veniant scandala. Vae autem illi, per quem veniunt! **2** Utilius est illi, si lapis molaris imponatur circa collum eius et proiciatur in mare, quam ut scandalizet unum de pusillis istis."

## Vocabulary

**asinarius, -a, -um,** of a mule
**collum, -i,** *n.,* neck
**demergo, -gere, -si, -sus,** to sink; submerge
**expedio, -ire, -ii** *or* **-ivi, -tus,** to be ready; be at hand
**mola, -ae,** *f.,* millstone
**molaris, -is,** belonging to a millstone
**pusillus, -a, -um,** small; insignificant
**suspendo, -dere, -di, -sus,** to hang on; fix on
**utilis, -e,** useful
**vae,** woe

## Historical and Grammatical Notes

### Mark 9:42–48

**42. scandalizaverit:** The key to this passage is the meaning of the verb *scandalizo.* Unfortunately, its meaning is slippery. Its basic sense is "to cause to stumble" by putting a *scandalum* (a "trap" or "hindrance") in one's way. From there all manner of extended senses are possible, related to the idea of keeping someone back from his destination: "to distract and cause someone to forget his goal," "to cause such a stir that someone is distracted," or even "to throw something in someone's view that is so tempting that he forgets his goal." There is a lingering sense of all this in our modern usage of the word. Someone who is scandalized by something isn't just annoyed or offended. His life has been disrupted and put on hold. It's important to remember, however, that Jesus's teachings scandalized the scribes earlier. Surely this isn't to be taken to mean that he caused them to sin. He disrupted their normal expectations, and that caused them great offense. There's no easy way to translate this constellation of ideas simply into English. "To tempt to sin" may be the best compromise when it's thoroughly and clearly negative; "to shock" or "to stun" may be the best when it's less so. **ex his pusillis credentibus in me:** "from these insignificant ones who believe in me." Jesus is referring to the disciples. The child in the previous passages wasn't one of his believers, and children were used only to illustrate the degree of humility required of the disciples.

### Matthew 18:6–9

**7. ab scandalis:** "because of the stumbling blocks" = "reasons not to believe." **Verum tamen:** "But truly."

### Luke 17:1–2

**1. ad discipulos:** Luke normally follows Mark more closely than Matthew does, but in this case he thoroughly redoes Mark's material.

# Mark 9:42–48 (cont.)

**43** Et si scandalizaverit te manus tua, abscide illam.
Bonum est tibi debilem introire in vitam, quam
duas manūs habentem ire in gehennam, in ignem
inexstinguibilem. (**44**) **45** Et si pes tuus te scandalizat,
amputa illum. Bonum est tibi claudum introire in vitam,
quam duos pedes habentem mitti in gehennam. (**46**)
**47** Et si oculus tuus scandalizat te, eice eum. Bonum est
tibi luscum introire in regnum Dei, quam duos oculos
habentem mitti in gehennam, **48** ubi vermis eorum non
moritur, et ignis non exstinguitur."

## Matthew 18:6–9 (cont.)

**8** Si autem manus tua vel pes tuus scandalizat te, abscide eum et
proice abs te. Bonum tibi est ad vitam ingredi debilem vel claudum,
quam duas manūs vel duos pedes habentem mitti in ignem
aeternum. **9** Et si oculus tuus scandalizat te, erue eum et proice abs
te. Bonum tibi est unoculum in vitam intrare, quam duos oculos
habentem mitti in gehennam ignis."

# Vocabulary

**amputo (1),** to cut off
**claudus, -a, -um,** limping
**debilis, -e,** crippled; lame
**eruo, -ere, -i, -tus,** to dig out; tear out
**gehenna, -ae,** *f.*, hell; a dump heap
**luscus, -a, -um,** with one eye closed
**vermis, -is,** *m.*, worm

# Historical and Grammatical Notes

## Mark 9:42–48 (cont.)

**43. Et si scandalizaverit:** In verse 42, Jesus was talking about the disciples. Now he addresses them in the second person. **in vitam:** presumably a life in the Kingdom of God, i.e., eternal life. Most commentators insist that Jesus is being metaphorical, and not literally suggesting that Christians mutilate themselves for the sake of eternal life. But why couldn't Jesus have meant exactly what he said? The stakes are heaven or hell, an eternity of life in the presence of God or an eternity of punishment. What earthly convenience, even sight, would be preferable? Luke, at least, thought that he might have meant this literally, and for that reason he deletes the verses about self-mutilation. **in gehennam, in ignem inexstinguibilem:** *Gehenna,* usually translated as "hell," was the city dump outside the walls of Jerusalem, an all-encompassing image of rot and filth. Worms and fire were literally true in *gehenna*.

**(44) 45:** The text of Mark used for this book omits verse 44, which reads *ubi vermis eorum non moritur et ignis non extinguitur,* "where their worm does not die and the flame is not extinguished." Instead of renumbering the subsequent verses when a verse is deleted, the custom is to retain their original numbering. The omission of verse 44 can be justified in part by the repetition of the idea that the fire never goes out, an image already established in the previous verse. The image of the worm, however, may have been deemed excessively lurid and deleted purely for aesthetic reasons.

**(46) 47:** Verse 46 was merely a reiteration of 44, *ubi vermis eorum non moritur et ignis non extinguitur.* Deleting one or the other is easy to justify. Deleting both is more of a judgment call.

# Mark 9:49–50

## *Parable of Salt*

The meaning of the parable of salt is so obscure that there can be little doubt of its authenticity. If the Synoptics hadn't been thoroughly convinced that Jesus had said it, at least one of them would have been tempted to leave it out. Matthew and Luke make editorial changes to the original to try to unlock its significance.

> **49** Omnis enim igne salietur. **50** Bonum est sal. Quod si
> sal insulsum fuerit, in quo illud condietis? Habete in vobis
> sal et pacem habete inter vos."

### Matthew 5:13

> **13** Vos estis sal terrae. Quod si sal evanuerit in quo salietur? Ad nihilum valet ultra, nisi ut mittatur foras et conculcetur ab hominibus.

### Luke 14:34–35

> **34** "Bonum est sal. Si autem sal quoque evanuerit, in quo condietur?
> **35** Neque in terram neque in sterquilinium utile est, sed foras
> proiciunt illud. Qui habet aures audiendi audiat."

## Vocabulary

**condio, -ire, -ii** *or* **-ivi, -itus,** to season; spice
**evanesco, -escere, -ui,** to disappear
**sal, -is,** *n.,* salt
**salio, -ire, -ivi, -itus,** to salt
**sterquilinium, -ii,** *n.,* dung pit

## Historical and Grammatical Notes

### Mark 9:49–50

**49. Omnis enim igne salietur:** "For everyone is salted ( = seasoned) with fire." This verse could be the final line of the previous pericope, where fire was mentioned. It's an odd connection, however, because there was the fire of the city dump, which was thoroughly destructive. It could be another reference to the baptism by fire that distinguished Jesus from John the Baptist.

**50. Bonum est sal . . .:** "Salt is a good thing. But if the salt should be tasteless, in what will you flavor it." If for some reason the salt has gone flat, there's no other spice you can use to make it flavorful again. Salt flavors everything, but there's nothing to flavor salt. **Habete in vobis sal et pacem habete inter vos:** Having salt in oneself in Greek can mean to have a ready mind and sharp wit. Perhaps this is all this means: Be as shrewd as snakes and as innocent as doves. Above all, don't turn on one another.

### Matthew 5:13

**13. Vos estis sal terrae:** "You are the salt of the world." Matthew has moved this parable next to the one where Jesus calls his disciples "the light of the world." This definitely helps him to understand its meaning. Just as Jesus's disciples bring light into the world, so they bring salt. We can add that not only does salt add flavor, but before refrigeration, it was also critically important for preserving food. **in quo salietur:** "what can be used to preserve salt?" **Ad nihilum valet ultra, nisi ut mittatur foras:** "It's useful for nothing beyond being thrown out of doors." **et conculcetur ab hominibus:** Salt that's no longer fresh enough to use for food can be used to treat soil so that nothing would grow in it, and that would be a good thing for a dirt road or pathway.

### Luke 14:34–35

**35. neque in sterquilinium utile est:** "it is not useful even for a dung heap." Salt is useful in dung heaps to control infestations of insects and fungus. But, as Luke says, if the salt has lost its properties, it wouldn't be good even for that.

# Chapter 10

Chapter 10 focuses on the central question of Jesus's crucifixion: "How could the Messiah have endured such an inglorious death?" The answer is that the power of God is expressed in the world through powerlessness. Chapter 10's stories about children, the vanity of worldly riches, and the virtues of humility prepare the way for what is going to happen in Jerusalem.

# Mark 10:1–12

## *Departure for Jerusalem; Question about Divorce*

Jesus is now in Judea, the heart of the Jewish nation. Some Pharisees make a trial of him by asking a question about divorce. Jesus answers that even though Moses permitted divorce, he did so only because of the perversity of the human heart. In reality, divorce was not a part of God's original plan. When they're alone with him, his disciples ask him to explain his answer more fully. Jesus tells them that because divorce is never recognized in the eyes of God, all divorcees who remarry commit adultery.

**1** Et inde exsurgens vĕnit in fines Iudaeae ultra Iordanem,
et conveniunt iterum turbae ad eum, et, sicut consueverat,
iterum docebat illos. **2** Et accedentes Pharisaei
interrogabant eum, si licet viro uxorem dimittere,
tentantes eum. **3** At ille respondens dixit eis, "Quid vobis
praecepit Moyses?" **4** Qui dixerunt, "Moyses permisit
libellum repudii scribere et dimittere."

### Matthew 19:1–9

**1** Et factum est, cum consummasset Iesus sermones istos, migravit
a Galilaeā et vēnit in fines Iudaeae trans Iordanem. **2** Et secutae
sunt eum turbae multae, et curavit eos ibi. **3** Et accesserunt ad eum
Pharisaei, tentantes eum et dicentes, "Licet homini dimittere uxorem
suam quācumque ex causā?"

## Vocabulary

**consuesco, -escere, -evi, -etus,** to become accustomed
**libellus, -i,** *m.,* little book; writ
**migro (1),** to depart
**repudium, -ii,** *n.,* repudiation; divorce
**ultra** + *accusative,* beyond

## Historical and Grammatical Notes

### Mark 10:1–12

1. **in fines Iudaeae:** Like any other good Jew of the time, Jesus travels to Jerusalem to celebrate the Passover. This starts the sequence of final events that lead to his crucifixion. **iterum:** There's no mention of a previous journey to Judea in Mark. It probably just means that as usual, Jesus attracts a crowd. **sicut consueverat:** Don't translate as a pluperfect, even though that is the form. Verbs with the ingressive –sc– infix in the present system are phased out of the normal temporal order: A perfect is translated as a present, a pluperfect as a perfect, and a future perfect as a future. **si licet viro:** "whether it is permitted for a husband." **tentantes eum:** Why would this particular question be a way of making a trial of Jesus? It could be that Jewish divorce laws were so complicated that only experts, such as the scribes or Pharisees, could possibly hope to understand them. The Pharisees might merely be asking Jesus, a layman, a particularly involved question, hoping to catch him in some misunderstanding of a particular clause. If this is true, they could have asked about any difficult point of Jewish law. On the other hand, perhaps the Pharisees are trying to get Jesus into trouble with the authorities over some high-profile divorce going on in Jerusalem at the time. John the Baptist was arrested, after all, and finally executed because of his opinion about Herod Antipas's marriage.

4. **Moyses permisit libellum repudii scribere:** The Pharisees' answer is strictly legalistic. They don't address any potential religious or moral issue in divorce. They describe only the process.

### Matthew 19:1–9

2. **et curavit eos ibi:** Note the difference with Mark: *iterum docebat illos.*

3. **quācumque ex causā:** "for any reason whatsoever?" Perhaps Matthew didn't see the point of the Pharisees' question in Mark. It was probably well known that the Law permitted divorce in cases of infidelity (Dt 24:1). How could that be controversial? Matthew changes the question to not whether divorce is permissible, but whether there are any limitations on when a divorce is allowed. That would require a detailed knowledge of the Old Testament text that most Jews of the time couldn't be expected to have.

# Mark 10:1–12 (cont.)

**5** Iesus autem ait eis, "Ad duritiam cordis vestri scripsit
vobis praeceptum istud. **6** Ab initio autem creaturae
masculum et feminam fecit eos. **7** Propter hoc relinquet
homo patrem suum et matrem et adhaerebit ad uxorem
suam, **8** et erunt duo in carne unā. Itaque iam non sunt
duo sed una caro. **9** Quod ergo Deus coniunxit, homo non
separet." **10** Et domo iterum discipuli de hoc interrogabant
eum. **11** Et dicit illis, "Quicumque dimiserit uxorem suam
et aliam duxerit, adulterium committit in eam, **12** et si ipsa
dimiserit virum suum et alii nupserit, moechatur."

## Matthew 19:1–9 (cont.)

**4** Qui respondens ait, "Non legistis quia, qui creavit ab initio
masculum et feminam fecit eos, **5** et dixit, 'Propter hoc dimittet
homo patrem et matrem et adhaerebit uxori suae, et erunt duo in
carne unā?' **6** Itaque iam non sunt duo sed una caro. Quod ergo
Deus coniunxit, homo non separet." **7** Dicunt illi, "Quid ergo
Moyses mandavit dari libellum repudii et dimittere?" **8** Ait illis,
"Moyses ad duritiam cordis vestri permisit vobis dimittere uxores
vestras. Ab initio autem non sic fuit. **9** Dico autem vobis quia
quicumque dimiserit uxorem suam, nisi ob fornicationem, et aliam
duxerit, moechatur."

## Luke 16:18

**18** Omnis, qui dimittit uxorem suam et ducit alteram, moechatur, et
qui dimissam a viro ducit, moechatur.

# Vocabulary

**adhaereo, -haerere, -haesi, -haesus,** to adhere to; cling to
**coniungo, -gere, -xi, -ctus,** to join together
**creatura, -ae,** *f.*, creation
**duritia, -ae,** *f.*, hardness; stubbornness
**mando (1),** to entrust; commit; order
**moechor, -ari, moechatus sum,** to commit adultery
**nubo, nubere, nupsi, nuptum** + *dative,* to wed
**separo (1),** to separate

# Historical and Grammatical Notes

### Mark 10:1–12 (cont.)

**5. Ad duritiam:** "Because of the hardness." There's no evidence in the Old Testament text (Dt 24:1) that Moses allowed divorce only because of the perversity of his people. Though the Pharisees' reaction isn't recorded, Jesus's contention that he knows the real meaning of the text that the Pharisees don't get couldn't have gone over well.

**6. Ab initio . . . fecit eos:** Take *creaturae* as a complementary genitive after *initio*: "From the beginning of the creature [man], he made them male and female."

**10. Et domo iterum:** that is, back to where they are staying outside of Jerusalem.

### Matthew 19:1–9 (cont.)

**6. Quod ergo Deus coniunxit:** Matthew returns to his Mark source and Jesus's reference to the Genesis text, but in Matthew's new context, it is hard to follow. In Mark, the texts were used to show that divorce is never permissible because God joined the two together as one being. Matthew continues to acknowledge that divorce is permissible by the Law, though grudgingly because of man's perversity and weakness, and only in cases of infidelity. The Genesis texts, therefore, which were so powerful in Mark to establish the point that divorce is never in accord with God's ways, have become less meaningful in Matthew because of how he reworks the original question.

# Mark 10:13–16

## *Jesus Allows Children to Come to Him*

Jesus chastises the disciples for driving away people who were bringing children to him. This scene is as much another rebuke of the disciples as it is a restatement of what is required to enter the Kingdom of God: complete and abject humility.

**13** Et offerebant illi parvulos, ut tangeret illos. Discipuli
autem comminabantur eis. **14** At videns Iesus, indigne
tulit et ait illis, "Sinite parvulos venire ad me. Ne
prohibueritis eos. Talium est enim regnum Dei. **15** Amen
dico vobis, quisquis non receperit regnum Dei velut
parvulus, non intrabit in illud." **16** Et complexans eos
benedicebat imponens manūs super illos.

### Matthew 19:13–15

**13** Tunc oblati sunt ei parvuli, ut manūs eis imponeret et oraret.
Discipuli autem increpabant eis. **14** Iesus vero ait, "Sinite parvulos
et nolite eos prohibere ad me venire. Talium est enim regnum
caelorum." **15** Et cum imposuisset eis manūs, abiit inde.

### Luke 18:15–17

**15** Afferebant autem ad illum et infantes, ut eos tangeret. Quod cum
viderent, discipuli increpabant illos. **16** Iesus autem convocans illos
dixit, "Sinite pueros venire ad me et nolite eos vetare. Talium est
enim regnum Dei. **17** Amen dico vobis, quicumque non acceperit
regnum Dei sicut puer, non intrabit in illud."

## Vocabulary

**complexo (1),** to embrace
**indigne,** indignantly; with great displeasure
**infans, -ntis,** *m.,* child; infant
**veto (1),** to prevent; deny

## Historical and Grammatical Notes

### Mark 10:13–16

**13. comminabantur:** The disciples' reaction is nearly violent. We can imagine them shoving the children back and threatening the people with blows.

**14. indigne tulit:** "he took it indignantly," or "he was very upset." **Sinite parvulos venire ad me:** These lines and what follows might have been delivered in a tone of strongest rebuke to the disciples. If the lead-in adverb *indigne* isn't enough to indicate Jesus's fury, the words he uses insult the disciples and their pretention. **Talium est enim regnum Dei:** *Talium* is genitive plural—"of such people is the Kingdom of God."

**16. benedicebat imponens:** These actions emphasize Jesus's criticism of the disciples' behavior toward the crowd and the children. Jesus has never blessed and put his hands on the disciples.

### Matthew 19:13–15

**13. manūs eis imponeret et oraret:** This is a much more stately gesture than Mark's simple *tangeret.* **increpabant:** Matthew tones down the disciples' reaction: "shouted at them" instead of "threatened them."

**14. Iesus vero ait:** Any notion that Jesus was angry with the disciples is absent in Matthew. This changes the tone of the entire passage.

**15. imposuisset eis manūs:** It's interesting that Matthew doesn't follow Mark, who says that Jesus embraced the children and blessed them. In Matthew, Jesus merely puts his hands on them. It may be that the verb *benedico* was gaining a specialized sense after Mark. Matthew used the verb only six times and only in contexts of miracles or high religious importance, never to bless a person, let alone a child.

### Luke 18:15–17

**16. convocans:** This is a much calmer exchange with the disciples, more on the lines of friendly concern and teaching than the anger in Mark.

# Mark 10:17–31

## *What Following Jesus Requires*

Jesus places a nearly impossible requirement on a rich man as a condition for eternal life: He must give up his wealth to follow him. Seeing the rich man leave in disappointment, the disciples ask Jesus whether what they have done is enough be saved. Jesus doesn't answer the question directly, but he assures them that anyone who has given up everything will have eternal life.

**17** Et cum egrederetur in viam, accurrens quidam et, genu
flexo ante eum, rogabat eum, "Magister bone, quid faciam
ut vitam aeternam percipiam?" **18** Iesus autem dixit ei,
"Quid me dicis bonum? Nemo bonus, nisi unus Deus. **19**
Praecepta nosti: ne occīdas, ne adulteres, ne fureris, ne
falsum testimonium dixeris, ne fraudem feceris, honora
patrem tuum et matrem?" **20** Ille autem dixit ei, "Magister,
haec omnia conservavi a iuventute meā."

## Matthew 19:16–30

**16** Et ecce: unus accedens ait illi, "Magister, quid boni faciam, ut
habeam vitam aeternam?" Qui dixit ei, **17** "Quid me interrogas
de bono? Unus est bonus. Si autem vis ad vitam ingredi, serva
mandata."**18** Dicit illi, "Quae?" Iesus autem dixit, "Non homicidium
facies, non adulterabis, non facies furtum, non falsum testimonium
dices, **19** honora patrem et matrem et diliges proximum tuum sicut
teipsum." **20** Dicit illi adulescens, "Omnia haec custodivi. Quid
adhuc mihi deest?"

## Luke 18:18–30

**18** Et interrogavit eum quidam princeps, dicens, "Magister bone,
quid faciens vitam aeternam possidebo?" **19** Dixit autem ei Iesus,
"Quid me dicis bonum? Nemo bonus nisi solus Deus. **20** Mandata
nosti: non moechaberis, non occīdes, non furtum facies, non falsum
testimonium dices, honora patrem tuum et matrem." **21** Qui ait,
"Haec omnia custodivi a iuventute."

## Vocabulary

**adulescens, -entis,** *m.*, a young man
**adultero (1),** to commit adultery
**desum, -esse, -fui, -futurus** + *dative,* to be lacking (to)
**diligo, -ligere, -lexi, -lectus,** to esteem highly; love
**furor, -ari, -atus sum,** to steal
**iuventus, -tutis,** *f.*, youth
**proximus, -i,** *m.*, a neighbor

## Historical and Grammatical Notes

### Mark 10:17–31

**17. vitam aeternam:** This passage contains the only two references to eternal life as a reward for following Jesus in all of Mark. The rarity of the subject seems puzzling to modern readers, as the promise of life everlasting has become such an important part of the Christian religious life.

**18. Nemo bonus, nisi unus Deus:** "No one is good but God alone." This brief exchange has caused great problems for the church, as the earliest Christology identified Jesus as a perfect being in a special relationship with God himself. Moreover, this comment almost seems superfluous in the context. The point is not to initiate a discussion about God, Jesus, and his perfection, but to emphasize the nearly impossible degree of commitment needed to follow Jesus and to win eternal life. Matthew alters the question that the young man asked to avoid the problem, as we'll see, but Luke faithfully reproduces his Mark source.

**19. nosti:** = a syncopated form of *novisti.* **ne occīdas . . .:** There is only one command that actually requires action in this list. The rest are things someone shouldn't do.

### Matthew 19:16–30

**16. quid boni faciam:** "what good deed should I do?" Moving the adjective avoids the theological problem that's in Mark.

**17. Quid me interrogas de bono:** Matthew did preserve parts of Jesus's reply from Mark. But without the original question, it's a very odd exchange: "What good deed should I do?" "Why do you ask me about good? Only one is good."

**19. et diliges proximum tuum sicut teipsum:** This is Matthew's unique, though famous, addition to the list in Mark.

### Luke 18:18–30

**18. princeps:** not in a political sense. He is just a leading citizen.

# Mark 10:17–31 (cont.)

**21** Iesus autem intuitus eum dilexit eum et dixit illi, "Unum tibi deest. Vade! Quaecumque habes vende, et da pauperibus et habebis thesaurum in caelo. Et veni! Sequere me!" **22** Qui contristatus in hoc verbo, abiit maerens. Erat enim habens possessiones multas. **23** Et circumspiciens Iesus ait discipulis suis, "Quam difficile, qui pecunias habent, in regnum Dei introibunt."

## Matthew 19:16–30 (cont.)

**21** Ait illi Iesus, "Si vis perfectus esse, vade, vende, quae habes, et da pauperibus, et habebis thesaurum in caelo. Et veni! Sequere me." **22** Cum audisset autem adulescens verbum, abiit tristis, erat enim habens multas possessiones. **23** Iesus autem dixit discipulis suis, "Amen dico vobis, dives difficile intrabit in regnum caelorum.

## Luke 18:18–30 (cont.)

**22** Quo audito, Iesus ait ei, "Adhuc unum tibi deest. Omnia, quaecumque habes, vende et da pauperibus, et habebis thesaurum in caelo. Et veni! Sequere me!" **23** His ille auditis, contristatus est, quia dives erat valde. **24** Videns autem illum Iesus tristem factum dixit, "Quam difficile, qui pecunias habent, in regnum Dei intrant.

## Vocabulary

**dives, divitis,** rich
**maereo, -ere,** to be sad
**perficio, -ficere, -feci, -fectus,** to make perfect
**possessio, -ionis,** *f.*, possession
**thesaurus, -i,** *m.*, treasure
**vendo, -ere, -idi, -itus,** to sell

## Historical and Grammatical Notes

### Mark 10:17–31 (cont.)

**21. dilexit eum:** The other two Synoptics omit the fact that Jesus loved this young man. Why? We're in a string of events in Mark that diminish the stature of the disciples. This one is no exception. In Mark, it appears that Jesus could be looking for another disciple out of his irritation with the canonical Twelve. Matthew and Luke, whose tendency is to soften any criticism of the disciples, might have thought that the reaction reported in Mark went too far. **vende:** The young man may have been good in the conventional sense in that he honored his parents and refrained from evildoing, but all this is private virtue. Jesus lays on him a command that not only is active—"Give your possessions away"—but also involves the one thing that would have been difficult for the young man. Jesus knew what the one attachment the young man had to the world was. The pericope isn't about wealth per se; it's about what it takes to follow Jesus, and that may be different for each person.

### Matthew 19:16–30 (cont.)

**23. difficile:** Take this as an adverb: "with difficulty will a rich man enter the kingdom of the heavens."

### Luke 18:18–30 (cont.)

**23. His ille auditis:** = *His auditis, ille . . .*

**24. tristem factum:** Supply *esse*: "saw that he had become sad."

# Mark 10:17–31 (cont.)

**24** Discipuli autem obstupescebant in verbis eius. At Iesus
rursus respondens ait illis, "Filii, quam difficile est in
regnum Dei introire! **25** Facilius est camelum per foramen
acūs transire, quam divitem intrare in regnum Dei." **26**
Qui magis admirabantur, dicentes ad semetipsos, "Et
quis potest salvus fieri?" **27** Intuens illos Iesus ait, "Apud
homines impossibile est sed non apud Deum. Omnia enim
possibilia sunt apud Deum." **28** Coepit Petrus ei dicere,
"Ecce: nos dimisimus omnia et secuti sumus te."

## Matthew 19:16–30 (cont.)

**24** Et iterum dico vobis, facilius est camelum per foramen acūs
transire, quam divitem intrare in regnum Dei." **25** Auditis autem his,
discipuli mirabantur valde, dicentes, "Quis ergo poterit salvus esse?"
**26** Aspiciens autem Iesus dixit illis, "Apud homines hoc impossibile
est, apud Deum autem omnia possibilia sunt." **27** Tunc respondens
Petrus dixit ei, "Ecce: nos reliquimus omnia et secuti sumus te. Quid
ergo erit nobis?"

## Luke 18:18–30 (cont.)

**25** Facilius est enim camelum per foramen acūs transire, quam
divitem intrare in regnum Dei." **26** Et dixerunt, qui audiebant, "Et
quis potest salvus fieri?" **27** Ait autem illis, "Quae impossibilia sunt
apud homines, possibilia sunt apud Deum." **28** Ait autem Petrus,
"Ecce: nos dimisimus nostra et secuti sumus te."

## Vocabulary

**acus, -us,** *f.*, needle

**foramen, -inis,** *n.*, small opening; eye

## Historical and Grammatical Notes

### Mark 10:17–31 (cont.)

**25. camelum per foramen acūs:** This rather odd metaphor may be the result of a typographical error originating in the Greek. The Greek words for *camel* and *rope* differ by only one letter: *kamelos* ("camel") and *kamilos* ("rope"). The Aramaic original therefore could have been "It's more difficult for a rope to pass through the eye of a needle." This is a compelling correction, but the point of the imagery is the same whichever word is preserved: Only God could make it happen.

**28. nos dimisimus omnia:** "*we* have given up [our] things." The disciples are understandably worried about their own status. They've made the necessary sacrifices. Are they in the same position as the young man who can't demonstrate the final measure of conviction?

# Mark 10:17–31 (cont.)

**29** Ait Iesus, "Amen dico vobis, nemo est qui reliquerit
domum aut fratres aut sorores aut matrem aut patrem
aut filios aut agros propter me et propter evangelium, **30**
qui non accipiat centies tantum nunc in tempore hōc,
domos et fratres et sorores et matres et filios et agros cum
persecutionibus et in saeculo futuro vitam aeternam. **31**
Multi autem erunt primi novissimi, et novissimi primi."

## Matthew 19:16–30 (cont.)

**28** Iesus autem dixit illis, "Amen dico vobis quod vos, qui secuti estis
me, in regeneratione, cum sederit filius hominis in throno gloriae
suae, sedebitis et vos super thronos duodecim, iudicantes duodecim
tribus Israel. **29** Et omnis, qui reliquit domos vel fratres aut sorores
aut patrem aut matrem aut filios aut agros propter nomen meum,
centuplum accipiet et vitam aeternam possidebit. **30** Multi autem
erunt primi novissimi, et novissimi primi."

## Luke 18:18–30 (cont.)

**29** Qui dixit eis, "Amen dico vobis, nemo est qui reliquit domum aut
uxorem aut fratres aut parentes aut filios propter regnum Dei, **30** et
non recipiat multo plura in hoc tempore et in saeculo venturo vitam
aeternam."

## Vocabulary

**centies,** a hundredfold
**iudico (1),** to judge
**regeneratio, -ionis,** *f.*, rebirth
**tribus, -us,** *m.*, tribe

## Historical and Grammatical Notes

### MARK 10:17–31 (CONT.)

**30. qui non accipiat centies tantum nunc in tempore hōc:** "who would get one hundred times such as [he has] now in the present time." How are we to understand what these rewards are? The literal meaning of the words is that the faithful man will get even more of what he gave up: houses, brothers, sisters, mother, father, sons, and fields. Either we have a very materialistic understanding of the afterlife, or Jesus's words have to be taken metaphorically to mean fulfillment and redemption of that which was lost. **cum persecutionibus:** This parenthetical remark is sorely out of place in this position. Jesus is listing the goods that will accrue to anyone who makes the necessary sacrifices, and it's hard to understand why these goods will be granted in the future life *cum persecutionibus.* If there are trials to be endured for the faith, it would be more understandable for them to occur during the time of privation and sacrifice, not during the time of rewards and eternal life. It has all the appearance of being a note written in the margin of a manuscript by a later copyist or commentator, which was later incorporated into the text. Neither Matthew nor Luke has it in their text. Either they rejected it or their versions of Mark didn't have it.

### MATTHEW 19:16–30 (CONT.)

**28. Iesus autem dixit illis:** This verse has no precedent in Mark; Luke has nothing like it in his rewrite. There's no Old Testament source that predicts such an arrangement at the final judgment. It is consistent, however, with the exaltation of the disciples that's typical of Matthew. They're promised more than just eternal life in the Kingdom of Heaven. Jesus tells them that they are to occupy powerful positions and pass judgment on the tribes of Israel personally.

**29. centuplum accipiet:** Matthew eliminates the potential materialistic view of the afterlife in Mark by deleting *tantum nunc in tempore hōc.*

# Mark 10:32–34

## *Third Prediction of Jesus's Suffering*

Now that Jesus and his disciples are on the road to Jerusalem, the time frame becomes compressed and the events are described with greater precision. Even Jesus's prediction in the pericope is much more detailed, as it gets down the specifics of the abuse that he will endure.

**32** Erant autem in viā ascendentes in Hierosolymam, et praecedebat illos Iesus, et stupebant. Illi autem sequentes timebant. Et assumens iterum Duodecim coepit illis dicere quae essent ei eventura. **33** "Ecce: ascendimus in Hierosolymam. Et filius hominis tradetur principibus sacerdotum et scribis, et damnabunt eum morte et tradent eum gentibus **34** et illudent ei et conspuent eum et flagellabunt eum et interficient eum, et post tres dies resurget."

## Matthew 20:17–19

**17** Et ascendens Iesus Hierosolymam assumpsit Duodecim discipulos secreto et ait illis in viā, **18** "Ecce: ascendimus Hierosolymam, et filius hominis tradetur principibus sacerdotum et scribis, et condemnabunt eum morte **19** et tradent eum gentibus ad illudendum et flagellandum et crucifigendum, et tertiā die resurget."

## Luke 18:31–33

**31** Assumpsit autem Duodecim et ait illis, "Ecce: ascendimus Ierusalem, et consummabuntur omnia, quae scripta sunt per Prophetas de filio hominis: **32** tradetur enim gentibus et illudetur et contumeliis afficietur et conspuetur. **33** Et, postquam flagellaverint, occīdent eum, et die tertiā resurget."

## Vocabulary

**afficio, -ficere, -feci, -fectus,** to inflict upon; treat
**conspuo, -ui, -utus,** to spit on
**contumelia, -ae,** *f.*, insult; abuse
**crucifigo, -figere, -fixi, -fixus,** to crucify
**evenio, -venire, -vēni, -ventus,** to occur; happen to
**flagello (1),** to whip; scourge
**illudo, -dere, -si, -sus,** to laugh at; mock
**interficio, -ficere, -feci, -fectus,** to kill

## Historical and Grammatical Notes

### Mark 10:32–34

32. **stupebant:** The crowds were amazed, probably for the same reasons that they had been before: Jesus spoke not as a scribe would, but as one with authority equal to that of the sacred texts. **Illi autem sequentes timebant:** This group of people is probably the Twelve and a larger circle of regular followers. Their reaction, however, is new and quite understandable. It was one thing for Jesus to be preaching about the Kingdom of God out in the remote, semi-Jewish areas around Galilee. It was another thing entirely to bring his controversial ideas right into the very capital of the Jewish nation. His followers could have rightly predicted a firm response from Jewish authorities there, even without Jesus's prophetic statements.

33. **gentibus:** This would mean the Roman authorities. Roman rule was liberal as to the operation of local customs, but capital punishment had to be authorized and carried out by the orders of the Roman governor.

### Matthew 20:17–19

19. **crucifigendum:** "for crucifixion." Only Matthew specifies the method of the execution in this summary. The Romans used it almost exclusively for sedition.

### Luke 18:31–33

31. **omnia, quae scripta sunt per Prophetas de filio hominis:** Thus Luke creates the expectation that the events to come will fulfill a number of Old Testament prophecies about the son of man. Matthew's and Luke's accounts of the passion and resurrection are replete with allusions to Old Testament prophecies.

32. **tradetur enim gentibus:** Luke has a very notable omission in the sequence of events. In both Mark and Matthew, Jesus is handed over first to the chief priests and the scribes, and they are the ones who condemn Jesus to death. Then they—the chief priests and the scribes—hand Jesus over to the Romans (*gentibus*) for punishment and execution.

# Mark 10:35–45

## *James and John's Request*

The brothers James and John ask Jesus to grant them a special role at his side in the Kingdom of God. Jesus tells the brothers that he can't fulfill their request because the arrangements of the kingdom have already been made. The other disciples are angered by what the two have asked, but Jesus tells them that the rule of the kingdom will not be like what they see in the world of men.

**35** Et accedunt ad eum Iacobus et Ioannes filii Zebedaei
dicentes ei, "Magister, volumus ut, quodcumque
petierimus a te, facias nobis." **36** At ille dixit eis, "Quid
vultis ut faciam vobis?" **37** Illi autem dixerunt ei, "Da nobis
ut unus ad dexteram tuam et alius ad sinistram sedeamus
in gloriā tuā." **38** Iesus autem ait eis, "Nescitis quid petatis.
Potestis bibere calicem, quem ego bibo, aut baptismum,
quo ego baptizor, baptizari?"

### Matthew 20:20–28

**20** Tunc accessit ad eum mater filiorum Zebedaei cum filiis suis,
adorans et petens aliquid ab eo. **21** Qui dixit ei, "Quid vis?" Ait illi,
"Dic ut sedeant hi duo filii mei unus ad dexteram tuam et unus ad
sinistram in regno tuo." **22** Respondens autem Iesus dixit, "Nescitis
quid petatis. Potestis bibere calicem, quem ego bibiturus sum?"

### Luke 22:24–27

**24** Facta est autem et contentio inter eos, quis eorum videretur esse
maior.

## Vocabulary

**contentio, -ionis,** *f.*, conflict; argument

**sinister, -tra, -trum,** left; on the left

## Historical and Grammatical Notes

### Mark 10:35–45

**35. volumus . . . facias nobis:** literally, "we want that you do for us what we are asking from you."

**36. Quid vultis ut faciam vobis:** The tone of this pericope is unusually chatty. This could have been simplified to just "James and John came to Jesus and asked: Let us sit at your right and left hand in your glory." Watch how Matthew and Luke reduce the introduction.

**37. in gloriā tuā:** James and John may have been thinking of the rule on earth, as envisioned in Daniel 2:44.

**38. calicem . . . baptismum:** At the time of Mark, the cup and baptism had no specific metaphorical significance, though Jesus's meaning is clear. Jesus's cup is his destiny and baptism means being overwhelmed with emotions. Jesus surely is referring to his impending torture, crucifixion, and resurrection.

### Matthew 20:20–28

**20. mater filiorum Zebedaei:** To provide cover for James and John, Matthew has their mother ask Jesus the question. The two aren't even referred to by name. Christian tradition identifies her as Salome, one of the women in Jesus's entourage.

**22. Nescitis quid petatis:** Jesus's reply is not to Salome, but to James and John. Matthew may merely be returning to his source in Mark, despite the change he's made to the introduction. Another possibility is that Jesus suspected that Salome was merely relaying to Jesus a question that her sons had expressed to her first. Instead of answering Salome, therefore, he speaks to James and John directly.

### Luke 22:24–27

**24. contentio:** Luke completely hides what James and John were seeking for themselves and makes no mention of the fact that their request angered the other disciples. All these changes protect the reputation of the disciples in general and of James and John in particular, who were to become leaders of the Christian church.

# Mark 10:35–45 (cont.)

**39** At illi dixerunt ei, "Possumus." Iesus autem ait eis,
"Calicem quidem, quem ego bibo, bibetis et baptismum,
quo ego baptizor, baptizabimini. **40** Sedere autem ad
dexteram meam vel ad sinistram non est meum dare, sed
quibus paratum est." **41** Et audientes decem coeperunt
indignari de Iacobo et Ioanne.

## Matthew 20:20–28 (cont.)

Dicunt ei, "Possumus." **23** Ait illis, "Calicem quidem meum bibetis,
sedere autem ad dexteram meam et sinistram non est meum dare
illud, sed quibus paratum est a Patre meo." **24** Et audientes decem
indignati sunt de duobus fratribus.

## Historical and Grammatical Notes

### Mark 10:35–45 (cont.)

39. **Possumus:** James was the first disciple to be martyred (Acts 12:1) in 44 CE. Christian tradition, however, holds that John was the only disciple not to be martyred.

40. **quibus paratum est:** "those for whom it has been arranged." The seating arrangements have already been made and even Jesus can't change them. There is no Old Testament source for this.

41. **coeperunt indignari de Iacobo et Ioanne:** Their irritation is understandable. Jesus has already addressed the issue of hierarchy among the disciples. For them to bring it up yet again could be annoying, particularly when Jesus is aware that his painful death is drawing near. These words also give us a glimpse of some tension among them. It would be surprising if there had never been any conflicts among the disciples under the circumstances.

### Matthew 20:20–28 (cont.)

23. **sedere:** gerund, subject of *est*: "sitting at the right or left hand—it is not mine to give that."

24. **indignati sunt de duobus fratribus:** Why would the disciples be angry with the two if it was their mother who made the request? Again, either Matthew is mingling his new introduction with his original material in Mark, or he is suggesting that the other disciples also knew that the request had to have originated with James and John.

# Mark 10:35–45 (cont.)

**42** Et vocans eos Iesus ait illis, "Scitis quia hi, qui videntur
principari gentibus, dominantur eis, et principes eorum
potestatem habent ipsorum? **43** Non ita est autem in vobis,
sed quicumque voluerit fieri maior inter vos, erit vester
minister. **44** Et, quicumque voluerit in vobis primus esse,
erit omnium servus. **45** Nam et filius hominis non vēnit, ut
ministraretur ei, sed ut ministraret et daret animam suam
redemptionem pro multis."

## Matthew 20:20–28 (cont.)

**25** Iesus autem vocavit eos ad se et ait, "Scitis quia principes gentium
dominantur eorum et, qui magni sunt, potestatem exercent in eos?
**26** Non ita erit inter vos, sed quicumque voluerit inter vos magnus
fieri, erit vester minister, **27** et, quicumque voluerit inter vos primus
esse, erit vester servus. **28** Sicut filius hominis non vēnit ministrari
sed ministrare et dare animam suam redemptionem pro multis."

## Luke 22:24–27 (cont.)

**25** Dixit autem eis, "Reges gentium dominantur eorum, et, qui
potestatem habent super eos, benefici vocantur. **26** Vos autem non
sic, sed qui maior est in vobis, fiat sicut iunior, et, qui praecessor
est, sicut ministrator. **27** Nam quis maior est, qui recumbit, an qui
ministrat? Nonne qui recumbit? Ego autem in medio vestrum sum,
sicut qui ministrat."

# Vocabulary

**dominor, -ari, -atus sum** + *ablative or genitive,* to rule over

**exerceo, -ere, -ui, -itus,** to exercise; wield; employ

**iunior, -ius,** younger

**praecessor, -oris,** *m.,* superior; *literally,* one who walks in front

**principor, -ari,** to rule

# Historical and Grammatical Notes

## Mark 10:35–45 (cont.)

**42. principes eorum potestatem habent ipsorum:** "and that their leaders have power over them."

**43. voluerit:** We've seen the perfect subjunctive used before in statements that are meant to resemble a legal statute.

**45. ministraretur:** impersonal: "it be ministered to him," or more idiomatically in English: "that he be ministered to." **redemptionem pro multis:** There is no other instance of this precise formulation in the rest of the New Testament, and to many commentators it appears to be an insertion into the text from a later time. The idea that a sacrifice could act as a sacrificial ransom for the sins of others, however, was common enough in Jesus's day that this wouldn't have been unintelligible to his disciples. But Jesus had never referred to his death and resurrection as a redemptive act before.

## Matthew 20:20–28 (cont.)

**28. ministrari:** infinitive of purpose: "to be served."

## Luke 22:24–27 (cont.)

**26. ministrator:** It's important to avoid the modern connotations of "minister" or "administrator" in the Latin word. In modern usage, a minister or administrator is in charge of something and appoints tasks for subordinates. The Latin word means something closer to "servant" or even "waiter," as is clear in the next analogy Jesus uses to illustrate his point.

**27. Nam quis maior est . . . qui recumbit?:** "For who is more important? the guest at meal, or the waiter? Isn't it the guest at the meal"? **in medio vestrum:** *Vestrum* is genitive plural: "in the middle of you" or "in your midst." **sicut qui ministrat:** "just like a servant [or waiter]."

# Mark 10:46–52

## *A Blind Man Healed Near Jericho*

As he is leaving Jericho, Jesus restores a blind man's vision. This is the final cure recorded in Mark.

**46** Et veniunt Ierichum. Et proficiscente eo de Iericho
et discipulis eius et plurimā multitudine, filius Timaei
Bartimaeus caecus sedebat iuxta viam mendicans. **47**
Qui cum audisset quia Iesus Nazarenus est, coepit
clamare et dicere, "Fili David Iesu, miserere mei!" **48** Et
comminabantur ei multi ut taceret. At ille multo magis
clamabat, "Fili David, miserere mei!"

## Matthew 20:29–34

**29** Et egredientibus illis ab Iericho, secuta est eum turba multa. **30**
Et ecce: duo caeci sedentes secus viam audierunt quia Iesus transiret
et clamaverunt, dicentes, "Domine, miserere nostri, fili David!" **31**
Turba autem increpabat eos ut tacerent. At illi magis clamabant,
dicentes, "Domine, miserere nostri, fili David!"

## Luke 18:35–43

**35** Factum est autem, cum appropinquaret Iericho, caecus
quidam sedebat secus viam mendicans. **36** Et cum audiret turbam
praetereuntem, interrogabat quid hoc esset. **37** Dixerunt autem ei,
"Iesus Nazarenus transit." **38** Et clamavit, dicens, "Iesu, fili David,
miserere mei!" **39** Et qui praeibant increpabant eum ut taceret. Ipse
vero multo magis clamabat, "Fili David, miserere mei!"

## Vocabulary

**praeeo, -ire, -ii** *or* **-ivi, -itus,** to go before; go in front of

## Historical and Grammatical Notes

### Mark 10:46–52

**46. Ierichum:** Jericho is on the road from Galilee to Jerusalem. **proficiscente:** This is a participle in a rambling ablative absolute, which includes *discipulis* and *multitudine*. Grammatically it should be *proficiscentibus*. **Timaei Bartimaeus:** Nothing else is known about Bartimaeus or his father Timaeus. They may have been well-known figures in the area at the time, or were to become active in the early church. Otherwise, why would they be named?

**47. Iesus Nazarenus:** Readers of Mark didn't need to be reminded that Jesus is from Nazareth. Mark might be representing what Bartimaeus heard. He didn't hear that someone named Jesus was nearby. Jesus was a rather common name. He heard that Jesus of Nazareth was nearby. Another possibility is that Bartimaeus is revealing that he knows Jesus's secret. It was predicted that the Messiah would come from Nazareth. Whereas others might have just heard the name of the village in the adjective *Nazarenus*, Bartimaeus made the connection between it and the Messiah, hence his invocation when he addresses Jesus in the next verse. **Fili David Iesu:** Since the Messiah was to be a descendant of David, this is equivalent to calling Jesus the Messiah. Thus Bartimaeus exhibits his extraordinary faith, which will be rewarded later in the story.

**48. comminabantur ei multi:** Why? Because he was just another noisy beggar, or because he exclaimed the secret of Jesus's true identity out loud?

### Matthew 20:29–34

**30. duo caeci:** This is not the first time we've seen Matthew double the number of the afflicted (cf. the pericope of the Gerasene demoniac at Mt 8:28–34).

### Luke 18:35–43

**35. appropinquaret Iericho:** Unlike Mark and Matthew, the event occurs as the crowd is approaching Jericho.

**36. turbam praetereuntem:** "the passing crowd."

**39. qui praeibant:** This could mean either the ones who were the leaders of the crowd or just the ones who were in the front. **Ipse vero multo magis clamabat:** *Multo* is the ablative of degree of difference: "but he cried out much more" or "all the more."

# Mark 10:46–52 (cont.)

**49** Et stans Iesus dixit, "Vocate illum." Et vocant caecum dicentes ei, "Animaequior esto. Surge. Vocat te." **50** Qui, proiecto vestimento suo, exsiliens vēnit ad Iesum. **51** Et respondens ei Iesus dixit, "Quid vis tibi faciam?" Caecus autem dixit ei, "Rabboni, ut videam." **52** Et Iesus ait illi, "Vade! Fides tua te salvum fecit." Et confestim vidit et sequebatur eum in viā.

## Matthew 20:29–34 (cont.)

**32** Et stetit Iesus et vocavit eos et ait, "Quid vultis ut faciam vobis?" **33** Dicunt illi, "Domine, ut aperiantur oculi nostri." **34** Misertus autem Iesus tetigit oculos eorum, et confestim viderunt et secuti sunt eum.

## Luke 18:35–43 (cont.)

**40** Stans autem Iesus iussit illum adduci ad se. Et cum appropinquasset, interrogavit illum, **41**"Quid tibi vis faciam?" At ille dixit, "Domine, ut videam." **42** Et Iesus dixit illi, "Respice! Fides tua te salvum fecit." **43** Et confestim vidit et sequebatur illum magnificans Deum. Et omnis plebs, ut vidit, dedit laudem Deo.

## Vocabulary

**animaequus, -a, -um,** of good courage; of calm mind
**exsilio, -ire, -ui,** to spring forth; spring up
**laus, laudis,** *f.,* praise
**plebs, -is,** *f.,* the people; crowd
**respicio, -spicere, -spexi, -spectus,** to look around; look back

## Historical and Grammatical Notes

### Mark 10:46–52 (cont.)

**50. proiecto vestimento suo:** Bartimaeus is standing naked before Jesus, a detail that both Matthew and Luke delete.

**51. Quid vis tibi faciam:** Supply *ut* before *tibi.* **Rabboni:** Bartimaeus addresses Jesus with the formal Aramaic version of the title Rabbi. It shows that Bartimaeus was an unusually educated beggar, one who knew his Old Testament scriptures well enough to know that Jesus was the Messiah, and who could speak in formal Aramaic. Matthew and Luke change this to *Kyrie,* translated into Latin as *Domine,* since, presumably, their audience would not have known the meaning of the Aramaic.

### Matthew 20:29–34 (cont.)

**34. tetigit oculos eorum:** Remarkably, Matthew reports a different method of the cure. In Mark, the blind man was healed by his faith, but in Matthew Jesus touches the two blind men.

### Luke 18:35–43 (cont.)

**40. appropinquasset:** syncopated form of *appropinquavisset.*

**43. Deo:** an interesting comment. The common people praised God, and not Jesus, for the cure they'd witnessed.

# Chapter 11

Jesus and his followers arrive in Jerusalem for the Passover celebrations, but their presence is anything but peaceful. He first rides into the city in a miniature triumphal parade that seems to mock the splendor of the city. On his way into the city, he curses a fig tree, and he is quickly drawn into conflict with the authorities of the city. He chases off money changers and other merchants from the Temple compound and is challenged to explain by what authority he dares take such actions.

# Mark 11:1–11

## *The Triumphal Entry of Jesus into Jerusalem*

The way Jesus enters the city fulfills various Old Testament prophecies. He sends his followers inside to secure a young male colt, which he will ride into Jerusalem in a mock triumphal parade. His procession happens late in the evening, so shortly after he arrives inside the city, he withdraws again and spends the night on the nearby hill of Bethany with his disciples.

**1** Et cum appropinquarent Hierosolymae, Bethphage et
Bethaniae, ad montem Olivarum, mittit duos ex discipulis
suis **2** et ait illis, "Ite in castellum, quod est contra vos,
et statim introeuntes illud invenietis pullum ligatum,
super quem nemo adhuc hominum sedit. Solvite illum
et adducite. **3** Et si quis vobis dixerit, 'Quid facitis hoc?'
dicite, 'Domino necessarius est, et continuo illum remittit
iterum huc.' "

## Matthew 21:1–11

**1** Et cum appropinquassent Hierosolymis et venissent Bethfage
ad montem Oliveti, tunc Iesus misit duos discipulos, **2** dicens eis,
"Ite in castellum, quod contra vos est, et statim invenietis asinam
alligatam et pullum cum eā. Solvite et adducite mihi. **3** Et si quis
vobis aliquid dixerit, dicite, 'Dominus eos necessarios habet,' et
confestim dimittet eos."

## Luke 19:28–38

**28** Et his dictis, praecedebat, ascendens Hierosolymam. **29** Et
factum est, cum appropinquasset ad Bethfage et Bethaniam, ad
montem qui vocatur Oliveti, misit duos discipulos, **30** dicens, "Ite in
castellum, quod contra est. In quod introeuntes, invenietis pullum
asinae alligatum, cui nemo umquam hominum sedit. Solvite illum et
adducite. **31** Et si quis vos interrogaverit, 'Quare solvitis?' sic dicetis,
'Dominus eum necessarium habet.' "

## Vocabulary

**asina, -ae,** *f.,* female donkey

**pullus, -i,** *m.,* young animal; colt

## Historical and Grammatical Notes

### Mark 11:1–11

1. **Bethphage et Bethaniae, ad montem Olivarum:** These three sites are to the east of the city walls of Jerusalem.
2. **Ite in castellum:** not into Jerusalem, which could hardly be called a mere fort, but into the nearby village where they were staying. Lodgings in Jerusalem itself would have been hard to come by during the Passover. **quod est contra vos:** "which is in front of you." **pullum:** This could mean a young horse, donkey, or mule. Mark isn't interested in what animal Jesus rides into the city. The importance is that it isn't a magnificent steed.
3. **continuo illum remittit iterum huc:** "he brings it back immediately here again." *Remittet* would obviously make more sense here, and some Greek and Latin manuscripts do have the future.

### Matthew 21:1–11

2. **asinam alligatam et pullum:** Matthew again doubles Mark's number, this time for an identifiable purpose. His rewrite is designed to confirm the Old Testament prophecy (Zec 9:9) that the king will come on an ass *and* on the offspring of an ass.

### Luke 19:28–38

31. **habet:** "thinks."

# Mark 11:1–11 (cont.)

**4** Et abeuntes invenerunt pullum ligatum ante ianuam
foris in bivio et solvunt eum. **5** Et quidam de illic stantibus
dicebant illis, "Quid facitis solventes pullum?" **6** Qui
dixerunt eis, sicut dixerat Iesus. Et dimiserunt eis. **7** Et
ducunt pullum ad Iesum et imponunt illi vestimenta sua,
et sedit super eum.

## Matthew 21:1–11 (cont.)

**4** Hoc autem factum est, ut impleretur quod dictum est per
prophetam, dicentem, **5** "Dicite filiae Sion, 'Ecce: rex tuus venit
tibi, mansuetus et sedens super asinam et super pullum, filium
subiugalis.' " **6** Euntes autem discipuli fecerunt sicut praecepit illis
Iesus, **7** et adduxerunt asinam et pullum, et imposuerunt super eis
vestimenta sua, et sedit super ea.

## Luke 19:28–38 (cont.)

**32** Abierunt autem, qui missi erant, et invenerunt sicut dixit illis.
**33** Solventibus autem illis pullum, dixerunt domini eius ad
illos, "Quid solvitis pullum?" **34** At illi dixerunt, "Dominus eum
necessarium habet." **35** Et duxerunt illum ad Iesum. Et iactantes
vestimenta sua supra pullum, imposuerunt Iesum.

## Vocabulary

**bivium, -i,** *n.*, crossroads; intersection
**mansuesco, -escere, -evi, -etus,** to tame
**subiugalis, -e,** used to the yoke; broken

## Historical and Grammatical Notes

### Mark 11:1–11 (cont.)

**4. ante ianuam foris:** "the outside gate."

**6. dimiserunt eis:** "they let them [take the *pullus*]."

**7. vestimenta sua:** "their coats." Jesus's entry has all the appearances of a Roman triumphal procession in miniature. Jesus is a triumphant emperor, but in a wholly unexpected way. He will emerge victorious through his defeat.

### Matthew 21:1–11 (cont.)

**5. mansuetus:** refers to *rex*. The king is broken and tame. He is not a warrior as might be expected given the pageantry of the procession.

**7. imposuerunt . . . et sedit super ea:** The disciples put blankets on the animals and Jesus sits on the blankets. This is difficult to envision, but somehow Jesus is sitting on both animals. There is reason to believe that Zechariah's text really means one animal, but clearly Matthew saw it differently.

### Luke 19:28–38 (cont.)

**33. domini:** "owners."

# Mark 11:1–11 (cont.)

**8** Et multi vestimenta sua straverunt in viā, alii autem frondes, quas exciderant in agris. **9** Et qui praeibant et qui sequebantur clamabant, "Hosanna! Benedictus, qui venit in nomine Domini! **10** Benedictum, quod venit regnum patris nostri David! Hosanna in excelsis!" **11** Et introivit Hierosolymam in Templum. Et circumspectis omnibus, cum iam vespera esset hora, exivit in Bethaniam cum Duodecim.

## Matthew 21:1–11 (cont.)

**8** Plurima autem turba straverunt vestimenta sua in viā. Alii autem caedebant ramos de arboribus et sternebant in viā. **9** Turbae autem, quae praecedebant eum et quae sequebantur, clamabant, dicentes, "Hosanna filio David! Benedictus, qui venit in nomine Domini! Hosanna in altissimis!" **10** Et cum intrasset Hierosolymam, commota est universa civitas, dicens, "Quis est hic?" **11** Turbae autem dicebant, "Hĭc est Iesus, propheta a Nazareth Galilaeae."

## Luke 19:28–38 (cont.)

**36** Eunte autem illo, substernebant vestimenta sua in viā. **37** Et cum appropinquaret iam ad descensum montis Oliveti, coeperunt omnis multitudo discipulorum gaudentes laudare Deum voce magnā super omnibus, quas viderant, virtutibus, **38** dicentes, "Benedictus, qui venit rex in nomine Domini! Pax in caelo, et gloria in excelsis!"

## Vocabulary

**caedo, caedere, cecidi, caesus,** to beat; come down on
**commoveo, -movere, -movi, -motus,** to be in motion; aroused; stirred up
**descensus, -us,** *m.,* descent
**excido, -dere, -di, -sus,** to cut out
**frons, frondis,** *f.,* a leafy branch
**gaudeo, gaudere, gavisus sum,** to rejoice; be pleased
**sterno, sternere, stravi, stratus,** to spread; cover

## Historical and Grammatical Notes

### Mark 11:1–11 (cont.)

**8. frondes:** "branches with leaves." Though this is celebrated as Palm Sunday, none of the Synoptics specifically refer to palms.

**9. Hosanna:** This is Hebrew, meaning "save now," used in the Old Testament when people were begging a king for help or protection (2 Sm 14:4; 2 Kgs 6:26).

### Matthew 21:1–11 (cont.)

**8. straverunt:** The subject is the *turba,* taken as a singular collective, hence the plural verb.

### Luke 19:28–38 (cont.)

**37. omnis multitudo discipulorum:** Luke seems to be using the word *discipuli* loosely in the passage and not specifically the inner core of the Twelve. **super omnibus, quas viderant, virtutibus:** They praised God "for all the miracles [*virtutibus*] they had seen." We can see the beginning of the chain of reminiscences that eventually would become the Gospels.

# Mark 11:12–14

## *Jesus Curses a Fig Tree*

In the only example of a destructive miracle in the New Testament, Jesus curses a fig tree for not having produced fruit for him.

**12** Et altera die, cum exirent a Bethaniā, esuriit. **13**
Cumque vidisset a longe ficum habentem folia, vēnit si quid forte inveniret in eā. Et cum venisset ad eam, nihil invēnit praeter folia, non enim erat tempus ficorum. **14**
Et respondens dixit ei, "Iam non amplius in aeternum quisquam fructum ex te manducet." Et audiebant discipuli eius.

### Matthew 21:18–19

**18** Mane autem revertens in civitatem, esuriit. **19** Et videns fici
arborem unam secus viam, venit ad eam. Et nihil invēnit in eā nisi folia tantum, et ait illi, "Numquam ex te fructus nascatur in sempiternum." Et arefacta est continuo ficulnea.

## Vocabulary

**arefacio, -facere, -feci, -factus,** to make dry
**ficulnea, -ae,** *f.,* a fig tree
**ficus, -i,** *f.,* fig tree; a fig
**folium, -ii,** *n.,* a leaf
**praeter** + *accusative,* besides; except for

## Historical and Grammatical Notes

### Mark 11:12–14

**13. si quid forte . . .:** "if by chance he might find something on it." **tempus ficorum:** Take *ficorum* as "figs" this time, not as "fig trees" as before.

**14. in aeternum:** "forever." **audiebant discipuli:** Mark emphasizes the fact that there were witnesses to attest to what happened.

### Matthew 21:18–19

**19. in sempiternum:** This is a little more emphatic than Mark's *in aeternum*: "forever and ever."

# Mark 11:15–19

## *Jesus Chases Merchants from the Temple*

Jesus runs off merchants and money changers, who are conducting business within the Temple compound. The Temple authorities plot against Jesus but dare not take action against him openly because of his popularity with the crowds of pilgrims. Jesus leaves the city at the end of the day.

**15** Et veniunt Hierosolymam. Et cum introisset in
Templum, coepit eicere vendentes et ementes in Templo,
et mensas nummulariorum et cathedras vendentium
columbas evertit. **16** Et non sinebat ut quisquam vas
transferret per Templum.

### Matthew 21:12–13

**12** Et intravit Iesus in Templum et eiciebat omnes vendentes et ementes in Templo, et mensas nummulariorum evertit et cathedras vendentium columbas.

### Luke 19:45–48

**45** Et ingressus in Templum, coepit eicere vendentes,

## Vocabulary

**cathedra, -ae,** *f.*, chair; cushioned seat
**mensa, -ae,** *f.*, table
**nummularius, -i,** *m.*, a money changer
**vas, vasis,** *n.*, vessel; dish; utensil

## Historical and Grammatical Notes

### Mark 11:15–19

15. **in Templum:** The Temple was a vast complex with courtyards and stoas, some of which were specifically designated for buying and selling. Jesus runs off people who are conducting themselves according to standard practice of the time and are even serving the religious operation of the Temple. Some of the vendors are selling the doves that were the traditional offering the poor could afford. Worshippers wanting to make a financial offering had to exchange their ordinary imperial money for a ceremonial coin. **coepit eicere vendentes et ementes in Templo:** Jesus must have had a sizable following if he did anything more than overturn a few tables. The vendors and their customers would have had no reason to obey Jesus and cease their activities if he weren't backed up by others.

16. **ut quisquam vas transferret per Templum:** Mark alone says this, and we can only speculate about why Jesus imposes this prohibition. It may be that he is trying to impede the conduct of business by denying them their vases. Another possibility may be that the vases are themselves ritually unclean for some reason. It's possible, though unlikely, that the vases had images of the gods on them, making them offensive to the Jews in the Temple. Ordinary, utilitarian pottery wasn't usually painted.

### Matthew 21:12–13

Matthew seems not have had much interest in this event; he compresses Mark's account into two sentences.

### Luke 19:45–48

45. **vendentes:** Interestingly, Luke omits what was being bought and sold. Mark mentions items for sale that were specifically associated with the Temple rituals, but by deleting this and making Jesus's objections more general and vague, Luke may be protecting somewhat the priests of the Temple, who sanctioned this activity.

# Mark 11:15–19 (cont.)

**17** Et docebat, dicens eis, “Non scriptum est, ‘Domus mea domus orationis vocabitur omnibus gentibus’? Vos autem fecistis eam speluncam latronum.” **18** Quo audito, principes sacerdotum et scribae quaerebant quomodo eum perderent. Timebant enim eum, quoniam universa turba admirabatur super doctrinā eius. **19** Et cum vespera facta esset, egrediebantur de civitate.

## Matthew 21:12–13 (cont.)

**13** Et dicit eis, “Scriptum est, ‘Domus mea domus orationis vocabitur.’ Vos autem facitis eam speluncam latronum.”

## Luke 19:45–48 (cont.)

**46** dicens illis, “Scriptum est, ‘Et erit domus mea domus orationis.’ Vos autem fecistis illam speluncam latronum.” **47** Et erat docens cotidie in Templo. Principes autem sacerdotum et scribae et principes plebis quaerebant illum perdere, **48** et non inveniebant quid facerent. Omnis enim populus suspensus erat audiens illum.

## Vocabulary

**latro, -onis,** *m.*, outlaw; rebel

**spelunca, -ae,** *f.*, cave

## Historical and Grammatical Notes

### Mark 11:15–19 (cont.)

17. **Non scriptum est:** Isaiah 56:7. **speluncam latronum:** Jesus doesn't accuse the vendors of dishonesty per se, but a market such as this would inevitably bring with it haggling and deal making. Jesus objects to the presence of any kind of business in the Temple area, which makes them de facto pirates or brigands.

### Luke 19:45–48 (cont.)

47. **Et erat docens cotidie in Templo:** Only Luke includes this comment, which gives the priests sufficient motive to plot against Jesus. Again, the problem with the exchange of goods in the Temple area is deemphasized in Luke. The real objection in Luke is that Jesus is preaching. **principes plebis:** This is a new source of opposition to Jesus in the Gospels. Who are the elders of the common people, and why do they suddenly appear here? One area of the Temple was the meeting hall of the Sanhedrin, the supreme council, which was made up of representatives of three classes: the high priests, the scribes, and the leaders or elders of the people. It makes perfect sense, therefore, that this final group should be entering the picture now. They probably didn't have the operational capacity to send out investigators to report on Jesus when he was preaching in the north, as the Pharisees and the Sadducees did. This could explain why Jesus had had no interaction with the *principes plebis* until he arrived at Jerusalem.
48. **Omnis enim populus suspensus erat audiens illum:** "For the people all hung upon him, listening."

# Mark 11:20–26

## *The Power of Faith*

Jesus and the disciples come back to Jerusalem on the next day. Peter is amazed to see that the fig tree that had offended Jesus two days before is now parched and dead. Jesus tells the disciples that they would be able to have this kind of power, too, if they truly believed.

**20** Et cum mane transirent, viderunt ficum aridam factam
a radicibus. **21** Et recordatus Petrus dicit ei, "Rabbi, ecce:
ficus, cui maledixisti, aruit." **22** Et respondens Iesus ait
illis, "Habete fidem Dei! **23** Amen dico vobis, quicumque
dixerit huic monti, 'Tollere et mittere in mare,' et non
haesitaverit in corde suo, sed crediderit quia, quod dixerit,
fiat, fiet ei. **24** Propterea dico vobis, omnia, quaecumque
orantes petitis, credite quia iam accepistis, et erunt vobis.
**25** Et cum statis in oratione, dimittite, si quid habetis
adversus aliquem, ut et Pater vester, qui in caelis est,
dimittat vobis peccata vestra. **(26)**"

## Matthew 21:20–22

**20** Et videntes discipuli mirati sunt, dicentes, "Quomodo continuo
aruit ficulnea?" **21** Respondens autem Iesus ait eis, "Amen dico
vobis, si habueritis fidem et non haesitaveritis, non solum de
ficulneā facietis, sed et si monti huic dixeritis, 'Tolle et iacta te
in mare,' fiet. **22** Et omnia, quaecumque petieritis in oratione
credentes, accipietis."

## Vocabulary

**areo, -ere, arui,** to be dry

## Historical and Grammatical Notes

### Mark 11:20–26

**23. huic monti:** Possibly Jesus means Mt. Olive. **Tollere et mittere in mare:** second person singular imperative passives: "Raise yourself up and send yourself to the sea," or "Get up and go to the sea." **crediderit quia, quod dixerit, fiat, fiet ei:** "[whosoever] believes that what he says will happen will happen, it will happen for him." This is a little clumsy, to be sure, and there's no way to bring this over into smooth English without paraphrasing: "whosoever believes that what he says is going to happen, it will be granted him."

**25. dimittite, si quid habetis adversus aliquem:** No one should use the power of belief to make a curse come true: "forgive if you have something against someone."

### Matthew 21:20–22

**20. videntes discipuli mirati sunt, dicentes:** In Matthew, this event follows directly after Jesus has cursed the fig tree. **Quomodo continuo aruit ficulnea:** "How is it that the fig tree immediately became dry?"

**21. si monti huic dixeritis:** In Matthew the connection between the fig tree and the power of prayer is made much clearer than it was in Mark.

# Mark 11:27–33

## *Jesus Fends Off a Challenge from the Temple Authorities*

The various authorities and leaders in the city ask Jesus on what authority he has tried to expel the merchants and their customers from the Temple grounds. Jesus promises to answer if they will answer his question first: "Where did John the Baptist get *his* authority, from heaven or from other men?" They reply that they don't know. Jesus therefore refuses to answer their question.

**27** Et veniunt rursus Hierosolymam. Et cum ambularet
in Templo, accedunt ad eum summi sacerdotes et scribae
et seniores, **28** et dicebant illi, "In quā potestate haec
facis? vel quis tibi dedit hanc potestatem, ut ista facias?"
**29** Iesus autem ait illis,"Interrogabo vos unum verbum,
et respondete mihi, et dicam vobis, in quā potestate
haec faciam. **30** Baptismum Ioannis, de caelo erat an ex
hominibus? Respondete mihi."

## Matthew 21:23–27

**23** Et cum venisset in Templum, accesserunt ad eum docentem
principes sacerdotum et seniores populi, dicentes, "In quā potestate
haec facis?" et "Quis tibi dedit hanc potestatem?" **24** Respondens
autem Iesus dixit illis, "Interrogabo vos et ego unum sermonem,
quem si dixeritis mihi, et ego vobis dicam, in quā potestate haec
facio. **25** Baptismum Ioannis, unde erat, a caelo an ex hominibus?"

## Luke 20:1–8

**1** Et factum est in unā dierum, docente illo populum in Templo
et evangelizante, supervenerunt principes sacerdotum et scribae
cum senioribus, **2** et aiunt, dicentes ad illum, "Dic nobis: In quā
potestate haec facis? aut quis est qui dedit tibi hanc potestatem?" **3**
Respondens autem dixit ad illos, "Interrogabo vos et ego verbum, et
dicite mihi: **4** Baptismum Ioannis, de caelo erat an ex hominibus?"

# Historical and Grammatical Notes

### Mark 11:27–33

27. **summi sacerdotes et scribae et seniores:** the three groups that made up the Sanhedrin, which is the supreme council of the Jews. It's to be expected after yesterday's events that they would confront Jesus. His action against the merchants and their customers in the Temple ultimately is an attack on the Temple leaders, who authorize their activities.

28. **quis tibi dedit hanc potestatem:** These are two different questions. The first asks, in essence, whether Jesus claims to get his authority directly from God, which would mean that he claims to be a prophet, or whether is he operating under the orders of, or in the name of, someone else. The chief concern of the Temple authorities isn't theological per se at this point; it's one of authority. Jesus just caused an uproar in the Temple and they want to know where he gets the idea that he can tell them how to manage this sacred area.

30. **Baptismum Ioannis . . .:** "The baptism of John, was it from heaven or from men?" The question of where John got his authority to baptize gets right to the heart of the issue. John didn't have any status in the religious organization of his day, and yet he performed baptisms.

### Matthew 21:23–27

23. **docentem:** This is added by Matthew and Luke. In Mark, Jesus was only walking about in the Temple. This gives a different focus to the question he's asked. He's being asked not about his effort to cleanse the Temple the day before, but about the way he preaches.

24. **quem si dixeritis mihi:** Take *quem* as *et eam*: "and if you tell it to me" or literally, "which if you say to me."

# Mark 11:27–33 (cont.)

**31** At illi cogitabant secum, dicentes, "Si dixerimus, 'De caelo,' dicet, 'Quare ergo non credidistis ei?' **32** Si autem dixerimus, 'Ex hominibus . . .' " Timebant populum. Omnes enim habebant Ioannem quia vere propheta esset. **33** Et respondentes dicunt Iesu, "Nescimus." Et Iesus ait illis, "Neque ego dico vobis, in quā potestate haec faciam."

## Matthew 21:23–27 (cont.)

At illi cogitabant inter se, dicentes, "Si dixerimus, 'E caelo,' dicet nobis, 'Quare ergo non credidistis illi?' **26** Si autem dixerimus, 'Ex hominibus' . . . timemus turbam. Omnes enim habent Ioannem sicut prophetam." **27** Et respondentes Iesu dixerunt, "Nescimus."Ait illis et ipse, "Nec ego dico vobis in quā potestate haec facio."

## Luke 20:1–8 (cont.)

**5** At illi cogitabant inter se, dicentes, "Si dixerimus, 'De caelo,' dicet, 'Quare non credidistis illi?' **6** Si autem dixerimus, 'Ex hominibus,' plebs universa lapidabit nos. Certi sunt enim Ioannem prophetam esse." **7** Et responderunt se nescire unde esset. **8** Et Iesus ait illis, "Neque ego dico vobis in quā potestate haec facio."

## Vocabulary

**lapido (1),** to stone

## Historical and Grammatical Notes

### Mark 11:27–33 (cont.)

**32. Ex hominibus . . .:** They trail off and don't say what will happen if they choose the second possibility. It's an ellipsis, as if they needn't express openly what they all must realize. If they say that it comes from men, they'll have a riot on their hands.

**33. Nescimus:** This is the only way they could have answered, given their situation.

### Luke 20:1–8 (cont.)

**6. plebs universa lapidabit nos:** "the entire mob will stone us." Evidently Luke didn't like the ellipsis of his Mark source. They articulate their fear. **Certi sunt enim:** "For they are sure that . . ."

# Chapter 12

The setting of chapter 12 is in the Temple compound, where Jesus preaches and answers a series of questions about various matters. The people and authorities of Jerusalem might have known about Jesus only as a backwoods preacher who'd managed to attract a small but enthusiastic following in the hills of Galilee. This is an opportunity for them to put him to the test. After a parable of the tenant farmers and their absentee landlord, which is a thinly veiled attack on the religious establishment, Jesus is grilled on doctrinal and social questions: Should taxes be paid to Caesar? How can there be an afterlife? Can the body of Laws be simplified to one overriding commandment? Does the Messiah have to be a descendant of David? During these interrogations, Jesus warns people about the evil of the scribes and praises the gift of a few pennies from a poor window.

# Mark 12:1–12

## *The Parable of the Grape Grower*

The meaning of the parable of the grape grower is unusually transparent given how difficult to understand Jesus's parables can often be. God (the owner of the land) has set up his vineyard (Israel) and entrusted it to the care of tenants (priests and other officials of the Temple). They routinely ignore and abuse the owner's representatives (prophets), until finally the owner sends his own son (Jesus), whom they kill. The owner will respond by killing the tenants and giving the vineyard to the care of others (the followers of Jesus? the Gentiles? the Romans?). Jesus concludes the parable by quoting Psalm 118:22: God built the Temple starting with a discarded block. In the same way, another discarded block (Jesus himself) will be the foundation of the true Temple.

**1** Et coepit illis in parabolis loqui, "Vineam pastinavit
homo et circumdedit saepem et fodit lacum et aedificavit
turrim et locavit eam agricolis et peregre profectus est. **2**
Et misit ad agricolas in tempore servum, ut ab agricolis
acciperet de fructu vineae. **3** Qui apprehensum eum
caeciderunt et dimiserunt vacuum.

### Matthew 21:33–46

**33** "Aliam parabolam audite. Homo erat paterfamilias, qui plantavit
vineam et saepem circumdedit ei et fodit in eā torcular et aedificavit
turrim et locavit eam agricolis et peregre profectus est. **34** Cum autem
tempus fructuum appropinquasset, misit servos suos ad agricolas, ut
acciperent fructūs eius. **35** Et agricolae, apprehensis servis eius, alium
ceciderunt, alium occīderunt, alium vero lapidaverunt.

### Luke 20:9–19

**9** Coepit autem dicere ad plebem parabolam hanc, "Homo plantavit
vineam et locavit eam colonis et ipse peregre fuit multis temporibus.
**10** Et in tempore misit ad cultores servum, ut de fructu vineae darent
illi. Cultores autem caesum dimiserunt eum inanem.

# Vocabulary

**fodio, fodere, fodi, fossus,** to dig
**lacus, -us,** *m.,* pond
**loco (1),** to place; contract out to someone
**pastino (1),** to till and make furrows in the ground; prepare the land
**paterfamilias, patrisfamiliae,** *m.,* head of the household
**peregre,** abroad; away from home
**saepes, -is,** *f.,* fence; hedge
**torcular, -is,** *n.,* wine cellar
**turris, -is,** *f.,* tower
**vacuus, -a, -um,** empty; empty-handed
**vinea, -ae,** *f.,* vineyard

# Historical and Grammatical Notes

## Mark 12:1–12

**1. locavit eam agricolis:** Since it takes three years before his vines would produce any grapes, the landowner would need someone to cultivate and watch over them for that time.

**2. in tempore:** "when the harvest is due." **de fructu vineae:** "to get his take of the harvest."

**3. caeciderunt:** The verb can mean "to kill," but the context makes it clear that they only gave him a thrashing.

## Luke 20:9–19

**9. multis temporibus:** "for a long time."

**10. caesum:** "roughed up," not "killed."

# Mark 12:1–12 (cont.)

**4** Et iterum misit ad illos alium servum. Et illum in
capite vulneraverunt et contumeliis affecerunt. **5** Et
alium misit, et illum occīderunt, et plures alios, quosdam
caedentes, alios vero occīdentes. **6** Adhuc unum habebat,
filium dilectum. Misit illum ad eos novissimum, dicens,
'Reverebuntur filium meum.' **7** Coloni autem illi dixerunt
ad invicem, 'Hĭc est heres. Venite! Occīdamus eum, et
nostra erit hereditas.' **8** Et apprehendentes eum occīderunt
et eiecerunt extra vineam.

## Matthew 21:33–46 (cont.)

**36** Iterum misit alios servos plures prioribus, et fecerunt illis
similiter. **37** Novissime autem misit ad eos filium suum, dicens,
'Verebuntur filium meum.' **38** Agricolae autem videntes filium
dixerunt intra se, 'Hĭc est heres. Venite! Occīdamus eum et
habebimus hereditatem eius.' **39** Et apprehensum eum eiecerunt
extra vineam et occīderunt.

## Luke 20:9–19 (cont.)

**11** Et addidit alterum servum mittere. Illi autem hunc quoque
caedentes et afficientes contumelia dimiserunt inanem. **12** Et
addidit tertium mittere. Qui et illum vulnerantes eiecerunt. **13**
Dixit autem dominus vineae, 'Quid faciam? Mittam filium meum
dilectum. Forsitan hunc verebuntur.' **14** Quem cum vidissent coloni,
cogitaverunt inter se, dicentes, 'Hĭc est heres. Occīdamus illum, ut
nostra fiat hereditas.' **15** Et eiectum illum extra vineam occīderunt.

## Vocabulary

**forsitan,** perhaps
**hereditas, -tatis,** *f.*, inheritance
**heres, heredis,** *m./f.*, heir
**novissime,** at last; finally
**revereor, -eri, -itus sum,** to respect; revere
**vulnero (1),** to wound

## Historical and Grammatical Notes

### Mark 12:1–12 (cont.)

5. **et plures . . . occīdentes:** This is some very rough Latin, but the sense is clear. The landlord sent other representatives. The tenant farmers thrashed some and killed others. To disentangle the original, begin by taking the participles *caedentes* and *occīdentes* as nominatives agreeing with an implied *agricolae*. Then you'll see that *quosdam* and *alios* are their objects: "And again he sent another; and him they killed, and many others; beating some, and killing some."

6. **novissimum:** "as the very last one."

7. **nostra erit hereditas:** It may seem surprising that the farmers thought killing the rightful heir would result in their getting the land. It's possible they thought that the landlord had died, which would explain why the heir and not the landlord himself came to check up on them. If they killed the heir, so they thought, the land might pass to them on the grounds that it no longer had a legal owner.

### Matthew 21:33–46 (cont.)

36. **plures prioribus:** "more than before." In Matthew, the landlord sent out one set of three servants. The farmers beat up one, killed another, and stoned another (presumably to death). Now he sends out even more.

37. **Novissime:** "Finally."

39. **Et apprehensum . . . occīderunt:** In Mark, they first kill the landlord's son and then throw his dead body out of the vineyard. Matthew's reversal of the verbs *eiecerunt* and *occīderunt* makes the scene less savage.

### Luke 20:9–19 (cont.)

11. **addidit:** There is no easy way to translate this while remaining close to the Latin. One way is to capture the sense of repetition in *addidit* in an adverb and to translate the infinitive *mittere* as a finite verb: "again he sent a second servant" or just "he added to that a second servant."

12. **Qui et illum vulnerantes eiecerunt:** In Luke, the field hands kill only the landlord's son. They don't kill any of the other servants, though they give them a sound beating.

# Mark 12:1–12 (cont.)

**9** Quid ergo faciet dominus vineae? Veniet et perdet
colonos et dabit vineam aliis. **10** Nec Scripturam hanc
legistis, 'Lapidem quem reprobaverunt aedificantes, hĭc
factus est in caput anguli. **11** A Domino factum est istud
et est mirabile in oculis nostris'?" **12** Et quaerebant eum
tenere et timuerunt turbam. Cognoverunt enim quoniam
ad eos parabolam hanc dixerit. Et relicto eo abierunt.

## Matthew 21:33–46 (cont.)

**40** Cum ergo venerit dominus vineae, quid faciet agricolis illis?" **41**
Aiunt illi, "Malos male perdet et vineam locabit aliis agricolis, qui
reddant ei fructum temporibus suis." **42** Dicit illis Iesus, "Numquam
legistis in Scripturis, 'Lapidem quem reprobaverunt aedificantes,
hĭc factus est in caput anguli'? 'A Domino factum est istud et est
mirabile in oculis nostris.' **43** Ideo dico vobis quia auferetur a vobis
regnum Dei et dabitur genti facienti fructūs eius. **44** Et qui ceciderit
super lapidem istum confringetur. Super quem vero ceciderit,
conteret eum." **45** Et cum audissent principes sacerdotum et
Pharisaei parabolas eius, cognoverunt quod de ipsis diceret. **46** Et
quaerentes eum tenere, timuerunt turbas, quoniam sicut prophetam
eum habebant.

## Luke 20:9–19 (cont.)

Quid ergo faciet illis dominus vineae? **16** Veniet et perdet colonos
istos et dabit vineam aliis." Quo audito, dixerunt, "Absit!" **17**
Ille autem aspiciens eos ait, "Quid est ergo hoc, quod scriptum
est, 'Lapidem quem reprobaverunt aedificantes, hĭc factus est
in caput anguli?' **18** Omnis, qui ceciderit supra illum lapidem,
conquassabitur. Supra quem autem ceciderit, comminuet illum."
**19** Et quaerebant scribae et principes sacerdotum mittere in illum
manūs in illā horā et timuerunt populum. Cognoverunt enim quod
ad ipsos dixerit similitudinem istam.

## Vocabulary

**angulus, -i,** *m.*, angle; corner
**confringo, -fringere, -fregi, -fractus,** to break into pieces; shatter
**conquasso (1),** to shake apart; break to pieces
**contero, -terere, -trivi, -tritus,** to grind down

## Historical and Grammatical Notes

### Mark 12:1–12 (cont.)

**10. Nec Scripturam hanc legistis:** Jesus means Psalm 118:22–23: "The stone that the builders rejected has become the chief cornerstone. This is the Lord's doing. It is marvelous in our eyes." The scribes and other officials would have known this passage. Jesus is the rejected son of the landlord in the previous parable. In this parable, he is the rejected stone that the Lord will use to build his kingdom.

### Matthew 21:33–46 (cont.)

**40. venerit:** This is future perfect for an action before the future *faciet.*

**41. Aiunt illi:** Jesus lets the people respond to the question. This reduces Jesus's role in the implied threat against the Temple authorities. He doesn't say that the Lord will kill them; the people are led to that conclusion. **Malos male perdet:** "He will destroy those bad men badly." This has almost a childlike feel to it, capturing how the common people might have expressed it. **locabit aliis agricolis:** "he will lease it out to other farmers." **reddant:** subjunctive in a relative clause of characteristic, perhaps also implying purpose: "who would give him his produce at harvesttime."

**43. quia auferetur . . . fructūs eius:** Matthew makes the implied threat explicit. The notion that God had transferred the agreement he had with Israel to the first Christians had been growing in the decades after Jesus's death.

**45. quod de ipsis diceret:** indirect statement introduced by *quod*: "that he was talking about them."

### Luke 20:9–19 (cont.)

**16. Absit!:** "May it not happen!" It appears that the common people are siding with the rebellious tenants! That would be a natural enough inclination because absentee landlords are never popular figures. But Jesus nudges them to a correct understanding of this parable with the next parable. As the tenants rejected the landlord's son, so the builders rejected the stone that God will use as his cornerstone. We're not told whether this helped the people understand, but the Temple officials understood Jesus's meaning clearly.

**18. ceciderit, comminuet:** The subject of both verbs is an implied *lapis.*

**19. mittere in illum manūs:** "to get their hands on him."

# Mark 12:13–17

## *Render unto Caesar*

The cross-examination of Jesus in the Temple continues with the most dangerous question Jesus has been asked so far: Should taxes be paid to Rome? If he answers no, he would have been thought a political subversive and subject to punishment by the Roman authorities. If he answers yes, he would have been branded as just another accommodationist by the people. Jesus deftly disentangles himself from the trap they've set for him and leaves them speechless.

**13** Et mittunt ad eum quosdam ex Pharisaeis et Herodianis, ut eum caperent in verbo. **14** Qui venientes dicunt ei, "Magister, scimus quia verax es et non curas quemquam. Nec enim vides in faciem hominum, sed in veritate viam Dei doces. Licet dare tributum Caesari an non? Dabimus an non dabimus?"

### Matthew 22:15–22

**15** Tunc abeuntes Pharisaei consilium inierunt, ut caperent eum in sermone. **16** Et mittunt ei discipulos suos cum Herodianis, dicentes, "Magister, scimus quia verax es et viam Dei in veritate doces, et non est tibi cura de aliquo, non enim respicis personam hominum. **17** Dic ergo nobis quid tibi videatur: Licet censum dare Caesari an non?"

### Luke 20:20–26

**20** Et observantes miserunt insidiatores, qui se iustos simularent, ut caperent eum in sermone, et sic traderent illum principatui et potestati praesidis. **21** Et interrogaverunt illum, dicentes, "Magister, scimus quia recte dicis et doces et non accipis personam, sed in veritate viam Dei doces. **22** Licet nobis dare tributum Caesari an non?"

# Vocabulary

**census, -us,** *m.,* census
**ineo, -ire, -ii** *or* **-ivi, -itum,** to enter into; collude in
**insidiator, -oris,** *m.,* conspirator; someone who sets an ambush; spy
**praeses, -idis,** *m.,* governor; ruler of a district
**principatus, -us,** *m.,* imperial authority
**simulo (1),** to imitate; make a pretense of
**tributum, -i,** *n.,* tax
**verax, -acis,** truthful

# Historical and Grammatical Notes

## Mark 12:13–17

**13. mittunt ad eum:** The subject is probably the Temple officials—the priests, scribes, and elders. They send the Pharisees and the Herodians as spies to trick Jesus into making some remark that they can use to indict him before the Romans.

**14. non curas quemquam:** The sense is "you don't worry about what anyone thinks." **Nec enim vides in faciem hominum:** "you don't look into the face of people." They're saying that Jesus doesn't tailor his teachings to what the people want to hear. Another way to phrase this would be "You don't play up to the crowd." **Licet:** "Is it permitted," not "Is it necessary." This issue clearly is going to be complicated. There would be no clear statement either way in Mosaic Law. How could the Torah have drafted a provision for the Roman Empire? So this is a matter for laws derived from Mosaic Law. If it's prohibited, it would have to be on the basis of what could be interpreted from the Law—the prohibition against having other gods, for example. As this is their area of expertise, the Pharisees are again inviting Jesus to compete with them on their playing field. **tributum:** The Greek word in Mark is *kēnsos,* which is transliterated as *census* in Latin. It was Roman practice to collect a poll tax when people reported for the census, so the two—tax and census—are closely tied together. That's why it's not surprising to see Mark call it *tributum* and to see Matthew call it *census.*

## Matthew 22:15–22

**17. quid tibi videatur:** "what seems right to you" or "what you think."

## Luke 20:20–26

**20. qui se iustos simularent:** Thus Luke accounts for their flattery. **sic traderent illum principatui et potestati praesidis:** They were probably hoping that they could arrest him right on the spot if he'd answered that the tax needn't be paid.

**21. non accipis personam:** "you don't take account of anyone."

# Mark 12:13–17 (cont.)

**15** Qui sciens versutiam eorum ait illis, "Quid me tentatis? Afferte mihi denarium, ut videam." **16** At illi attulerunt. Et ait illis, "Cuius est imago haec et inscriptio?" Illi autem dixerunt ei, "Caesaris." **17** Iesus autem dixit illis, "Quae sunt Caesaris, reddite Caesari, et quae sunt Dei, Deo." Et mirabantur super eo.

## Matthew 22:15–22 (cont.)

**18** Cognitā autem Iesus nequitiā eorum, ait, "Quid me tentatis, hypocritae? **19** Ostendite mihi nomisma censūs." At illi obtulerunt ei denarium. **20** Et ait illis, "Cuius est imago haec et suprascriptio?" **21** Dicunt ei, "Caesaris." Tunc ait illis, "Reddite ergo, quae sunt Caesaris, Caesari, et quae sunt Dei, Deo." **22** Et audientes mirati sunt et, relicto eo, abierunt.

## Luke 20:20–26 (cont.)

**23** Considerans autem dolum illorum dixit ad eos, **24** "Ostendite mihi denarium. Cuius habet imaginem et inscriptionem?" **25** At illi dixerunt, "Caesaris." Et ait illis, "Reddite ergo, quae Caesaris sunt, Caesari, et quae Dei sunt, Deo." **26** Et non potuerunt verbum eius reprehendere coram plebe et mirati in responso eius tacuerunt.

## Vocabulary

**imago, -inis,** *f.*, image
**inscriptio, -ionis,** *f.*, inscription; title
**nomisma, -atis,** *n.*, coin
**versutia, -ae,** *f.*, craftiness; slyness

## Historical and Grammatical Notes

### Mark 12:13–17 (cont.)

15. **denarium:** A *denarius* is a day's wages for an unskilled laborer—not a great amount but more than insignificant. Besides, the value of the coin doesn't matter here. **Cuius est imago haec et inscriptio:** The coin would have had the image of Tiberius, the emperor after Augustus, and an inscription running around the edge: *Ti[berivs] Caesar Divi Avg[vsti] F[ilivs] Avgvstvs* "Caesar Augustus Tiberius, son of the Divine Augustus."

17. **Quae sunt Caesaris, reddite Caesari, et quae sunt Dei, Deo:** This is one of the most often quoted sayings of Jesus, and, not surprisingly, it has been variously interpreted. There are at least three broad possibilities: (1) Jesus is making a distinction between church and state, saying that each has its exclusive and legitimate spheres. (2) Jesus is evading the question and attacking the Pharisees who so quickly produced a Roman coin. He's saying to them that they have made their choice which side they're on and they should pay Caesar his taxes. Of course, they don't understand his intent. That's why they are stunned by the answer. (3) Jesus is making a distinction between the kingdoms of this world and God's kingdom: Give Caesar your worldly obedience, but your life belongs to God.

### Matthew 22:15–22 (cont.)

19. **nomisma censūs:** "the census coin." As noted above, registering for a census and paying a poll tax were nearly the same thing for a subject of the Roman Empire at this time.

### Luke 20:20–26 (cont.)

26. **reprehendere:** In this context, the sense of *reprehendere* is "to refute." **coram plebe:** Does this mean that they refrained from engaging him on this point further because they feared the crowd's reaction or because the noise and commotion of the crowd didn't give them a chance to reply? The latter seems the stronger choice. It's hard to believe that the crowd, who probably despised Rome and its taxes, would have been thrilled by Jesus's answer. Jesus answered that everyone should pay their taxes, both the tax they owe to Rome and the tax they owe to the Temple. That's hardly an invitation to revolt.

# Mark 12:18–27

## *The Sadducees' Question about the Afterlife*

The Sadducees didn't believe in an afterlife because it couldn't be found in the Laws. They confront Jesus with a legalist question, perhaps one of their standard "talking points," as an objection to a notion of the afterlife: "If a woman is married several times in her lifetime, whom will she be married to in the afterlife?" Jesus replies by charging the Sadducees with a primitive understanding of spiritual matters because Heaven will be unlike anything on this earth. In a close reading of a passage from Scripture, he then proves that there is in fact a reference in the Torah to everlasting life.

**18** Et veniunt ad eum Sadducaei, qui dicunt
resurrectionem non esse, et interrogabant eum, dicentes,
**19** "Magister, Moyses nobis scripsit, ut si cuius frater
mortuus fuerit et reliquerit uxorem et filium non reliquerit,
accipiat frater eius uxorem et resuscitet semen fratri suo.

## Matthew 22:23–33

**23** In illo die accesserunt ad eum Sadducaei, qui dicunt non esse
resurrectionem, et interrogaverunt eum, **24** dicentes, "Magister,
Moyses dixit, si quis mortuus fuerit non habens filios, ut ducat frater
eius uxorem illius et suscitet semen fratri suo.

## Luke 20:27–39

**27** Accesserunt autem quidam Sadducaeorum, qui negant esse
resurrectionem, et interrogaverunt eum, **28** dicentes, "Magister,
Moyses scripsit nobis, si frater alicuius mortuus fuerit habens
uxorem et hic sine filiis fuerit, ut accipiat eam frater eius uxorem et
suscitet semen fratri suo.

## Vocabulary

**resuscito (1),** to revive; renew

## Historical and Grammatical Notes

### MARK 12:18–27

**18. Sadducaei:** Jesus is confronted directly by the Sadducees for the first and only time in the Synoptics, and it's on an issue that they would have been instantly identified with. Because it was not explicitly stated in the Law, the Sadducees did not believe in a resurrection or an afterlife. It's true that the book of Daniel speaks repeatedly and explicitly about an afterlife, but the Sadducees focused their attention on the Pentateuch as the most authoritative foundation of the Jewish religion.

**19. Moyses nobis scripsit:** The Old Testament passage is Deuteronomy 25:2. **si cuius:** = *si alicuius*. **uxorem:** Supply *eam*: "take her as a wife." **fratri suo:** dative: "he should revive the seed for his brother."

### MATTHEW 22:23–33

**24. ut ducat frater eius uxorem illius:** The location of the *ut*, so far from the *dixit*, may make it hard to see that this is an indirect command: "Moses said . . . that his brother should marry his brother's wife."

### LUKE 20:27–39

**27. quidam:** nominative plural, not singular.

# Mark 12:18–27 (cont.)

**20** Septem fratres erant. Et primus accepit uxorem, et moriens non reliquit semen. **21** Et secundus accepit eam et mortuus est, non relicto semine. Et tertius similiter. **22** Et septem non reliquerunt semen. Novissima omnium defuncta est et mulier. **23** In resurrectione, cum resurrexerint, cuius de his erit uxor? Septem enim habuerunt eam uxorem."

## Matthew 22:23–33 (cont.)

**25** Erant autem apud nos septem fratres. Et primus, uxore ductā, defunctus est et non habens semen reliquit uxorem suam fratri suo. **26** Similiter secundus et tertius usque ad septimum. **27** Novissime autem omnium mulier defuncta est. **28** In resurrectione ergo, cuius erit de septem uxor? Omnes enim habuerunt eam?"

## Luke 20:27–39 (cont.)

**29** Septem ergo fratres erant. Et primus accepit uxorem et mortuus est sine filiis. **30** Et sequens **31** et tertius accepit illam. Similiter autem et septem non reliquerunt filios et mortui sunt. **32** Novissima mortua est et mulier. **33** Mulier ergo in resurrectione, cuius eorum erit uxor, si quidem septem habuerunt eam uxorem?"

## Historical and Grammatical Notes

### Mark 12:18–27 (cont.)

**20. Septem fratres erant:** The Sadducees ask a far-fetched question so as to cast scorn on the Pharisaic belief in an afterlife. It may be that this is one of many counterarguments that the Sadducees had ready at hand when they debated the Pharisees.

**22. Novissima:** best taken adverbially. **et mulier:** Take *et* as "as well": "the woman dies as well."

**23. cuius de his erit uxor:** "she will be the wife of which from these."

### Matthew 22:23–33 (cont.)

**25. apud nos:** Matthew seems to think that the Sadducees are talking about something that indeed happened: "There was among us a woman," not "Suppose that a woman . . ."

**28. cuius:** This is the interrogative pronoun: "whose of the seven will she be the wife?" or "of which of the seven . . ."

### Luke 20:27–39 (cont.)

**31. et tertius . . . mortui sunt:** The roughness of this sentence is not at all what we've grown accustomed to in Luke. There may be a manuscript problem because after *sequens* some major witnesses read *accepit illam et ipse mortuus est sine filio*: "married her and he died without a son." The next sentence would follow naturally: "And similarly seven didn't leave behind sons and died."

**33. si quidem septem habuerunt eam uxorem:** *Uxorem* could be appositional: "if indeed the seven had her as a wife." It could also be that *eam* is being used as a demonstrative adjective: "if indeed the seven had this wife."

# Mark 12:18–27 (cont.)

**24** Ait illis Iesus, "Non ideo erratis, quia non scitis
Scripturas neque virtutem Dei? **25** Cum enim a mortuis
resurrexerint, neque nubent neque nubentur, sed sunt
sicut angeli in caelis. **26** De mortuis autem quod resurgant,
non legistis in libro Moysis super rubum, quomodo dixerit
illi Deus, inquiens, 'Ego sum Deus Abraham et Deus Isaac
et Deus Iacob?' **27** Non est Deus mortuorum sed vivorum!
Multum erratis."

## Matthew 22:23–33 (cont.)

**29** Respondens autem Iesus ait illis, "Erratis nescientes Scripturas
neque virtutem Dei. **30** In resurrectione enim neque nubent neque
nubentur, sed sunt sicut angeli in caelo. **31** De resurrectione autem
mortuorum non legistis, quod dictum est vobis a Deo dicente, **32**
'Ego sum Deus Abraham et Deus Isaac et Deus Iacob?' Non est Deus
mortuorum sed viventium." **33** Et audientes turbae mirabantur in
doctrinā eius.

## Luke 20:27–39 (cont.)

**34** Et ait illis Iesus, "Filii saeculi huius nubunt et traduntur
ad nuptias. **35** Illi autem, qui digni habentur saeculo illo et
resurrectione ex mortuis neque nubunt neque ducunt uxores,
**36** neque enim ultra mori possunt, aequales enim angelis sunt et
filii sunt Dei, cum sint filii resurrectionis. **37** Quia vero resurgant
mortui, et Moyses ostendit secus rubum, sicut dicit Dominum Deum
Abraham et Deum Isaac et Deum Iacob. **38** Deus autem non est
mortuorum sed vivorum, omnes enim vivunt ei." **39** Respondentes
autem quidam scribarum dixerunt, "Magister, bene dixisti."

## Vocabulary

**aequalis, -e** + *dative,* equal

**rubus, -i,** *m.,* bush

## Historical and Grammatical Notes

### Mark 12:18–27 (cont.)

**25. neque nubent neque nubentur:** "they will neither marry nor be married." It seems that the Latin translation is trying to preserve the feel of the Greek, where the verb "to marry" is used in the active (*gamousin*) and then in the passive voice (*gamizontai*). But in so doing it uses the very unusual passive voice of the normally intransitive Latin verb *nubo*.

**26. inquiens:** a rare present participle from the verb *inquit*: "saying." **Abraham . . . Isaac . . . Iacob:** They are all genitives from indeclinable proper nouns.

**27. est Deus mortuorum:** This is an extremely close reading of the original text (Ex 3:6). Jesus's argument is that since God used the present tense—"I *am* the God . . ."—this must mean that he was and still is the God of the patriarchs. And that can be the case only if Abraham, Isaac, and Jacob are still alive. Presumably if they were dead, God would have said, "I *was* the God of Abraham, Isaac, and Jacob." It's particularly important that Jesus cite evidence from one of the first five books of the Old Testament, which the Sadducees held as especially authoritative. As we'll see at the beginning of the next pericope, a scribe in the audience was delighted by Jesus's refutation of the Sadducees, possibly because of the lawyerly precision of Jesus's reading.

### Luke 20:27–39 (cont.)

**35. habentur:** "are deemed." **resurrectione:** ablative of time: "at (the time of) the resurrection."

**37. sicut dicit . . .:** Supply *esse* to complete the indirect statement: *"Dominum [esse] Deum Abraham et [esse] Deum Isaac et Deum Iacob."*

# Mark 12:28–34

## *The Most Important Commandment*

Delighted by seeing him contradict the Sadducees on the key issue of the afterlife, a scribe asks Jesus a question about the Law: "What is the first commandment of all?" The exchange is cordial, and Jesus pays the scribe a rare compliment.

**28** Et accessit unus de scribis, qui audierat illos conquirentes, videns quoniam bene illis responderit, interrogavit eum, "Quod est primum omnium mandatum?"

### Matthew 22:34–40

**34** Pharisaei autem audientes quod silentium imposuisset Sadducaeis, convenerunt in unum. **35** Et interrogavit unus ex eis legis doctor, tentans eum, **36** "Magister, quod est mandatum magnum in Lege?"

### Luke 10:25–28

**25** Et ecce: quidam legis peritus surrexit tentans illum, dicens, "Magister, quid faciendo vitam aeternam possidebo?"

## Vocabulary

**peritus, -a, -um,** experienced; skilled    **silentium, -ii,** *n.,* silence

## Historical and Grammatical Notes

### Mark 12:28–34

**28. unus de scribis:** It makes perfect sense that an expert of the Law, which is what the scribes were, would ask this question. **quoniam bene illis responderit:** Mark makes it clear that the scribe was impressed with the way Jesus argued the point of the afterlife and recognizes that he has an unusually authoritative understanding of the texts. The question he asks is a sincere request for help with an issue he and the other experts were probably dealing with. Is the mass of laws reducible to a basic commandment from which the others are derived? It's important to note what the scribe is not asking. He is not asking whether one commandment is so archetypical that the others need not be observed.

### Matthew 22:34–40

**34. Pharisaei:** The Pharisees would have been delighted to see the Sadducees silenced on such an essential doctrine, particularly because Jesus appealed to a text that the Sadducees must admit is authoritative. **convenerunt in unum:** "they convened." This suggests some kind of a plot.

**35. unus ex eis legis doctor:** literally, "one from those of the law learned" = "one of those educated in the Law." **tentans:** This is an entirely different tone from Mark's original. There the scribe seemed impressed by Jesus and asks a sincere question. Matthew, by contrast, has a hard time saying anything favorable about the Pharisees or scribes, even when it's in his Mark source.

### Luke 10:25–28

**25. quid faciendo vitam aeternam possidebo:** Luke thoroughly reworks Mark's material. The interlocutor doesn't ask a legalistic question but one that bears on him personally: He wants eternal life. Jesus doesn't quote the Old Testament sources, but the man who asked the question does. It's only implied that these two commandments are the most important, and Jesus's reply could be read as a radical critique of the Law. If the man does just these two things, he will have eternal life. Aside from the Old Testament references, there isn't much left of Mark in Luke's version.

# Mark 12:28–34 (cont.)

**29** Iesus respondit, "Primum est, 'Audi, Israel. Dominus
Deus noster Dominus unus est, **30** et diliges Dominum
Deum tuum ex toto corde tuo et ex totā animā tuā et ex
totā mente tuā et ex totā virtute tuā.' **31** Secundum est
illud, 'Diliges proximum tuum tamquam teipsum.' Maius
horum aliud mandatum non est." **32** Et ait illi scriba,
"Bene, Magister, in veritate dixisti, unus est, et non est
alius praeter eum. **33** Et diligere eum ex toto corde et ex
toto intellectu et ex totā fortitudine et diligere proximum
tamquam seipsum maius est omnibus holocaustomatibus
et sacrificiis."

## Matthew 22:34–40 (cont.)

**37** Ait autem illi, "Diliges Dominum Deum tuum in toto corde tuo
et in totā animā tuā et in totā mente tuā. **38** Hoc est magnum et
primum mandatum. **39** Secundum autem simile est huic, 'Diliges
proximum tuum sicut teipsum.' **40** In his duobus mandatis universa
Lex pendet et Prophetae."

## Luke 10:25–28 (cont.)

**26** At ille dixit ad eum, "In Lege quid scriptum est? Quomodo legis?"
**27** Ille autem respondens dixit, "Diliges Dominum Deum tuum ex
toto corde tuo et ex totā animā tuā et ex omnibus viribus tuis et ex
omni mente tuā et proximum tuum sicut teipsum."

# Vocabulary

**holocaustoma, -atis,** *n.,* burnt offering

**pendeo, pendere, pependi,** to depend

# Historical and Grammatical Notes

## Mark 12:28–34 (cont.)

**29–30. Audi, Israel . . . ex totā virtute tuā:** Deuteronomy 6:4–5: *Audi, Israel! Dominus Deus noster Dominus unus est. Diliges Dominum Deum tuum ex toto corde tuo et ex totā animā tuā et ex totā fortitudine tuā*: "Listen, Israel. The Lord our God is one. Cherish the God your Lord with your whole heart and with all your mind and with all your strength."

**31. Secundum est illud:** excerpted from Leviticus 19:18. **Maius horum:** "Greater than these." The Greek genitive of comparison is retained in the Latin translation. Latin would use the ablative of comparison. Some manuscripts have *his* instead of the more difficult *horum*.

**32. Et ait illi scriba:** Only Mark reports the scribe's explication of Jesus's answer. He repeats verbatim what Jesus just told him and then adds something of his own.

**33. diligere . . . diligere:** Both gerunds are subjects of *est*: "to love him . . . and to love your neighbor . . . [are] greater." **omnibus holocautomatibus et sacrificiis:** a return to the ablative of comparison. The scribe doesn't necessarily mean that burnt offerings as sacrifices needn't be made. He might mean only that though they aren't specifically required, burnt offerings and sacrifices are still necessary expressions of the two basic commandments. The rest of the laws provide guidance as to how to implement what that means. All the scribe is objecting to here is that offering sacrifices in itself means nothing. It can't be a pro forma ritual. **holocaustomatibus:** *Holo* comes from the Greek word that means "whole" or "entire," and the *caust* stem means "burned." The Greek term *holocaust* describes the Jewish practice of burning the entire animal in a sacrifice instead of burning only the inedible parts, which was the usual Greek practice.

## Matthew 22:34–40 (cont.)

**40. pendet et Prophetae:** Jesus's summary is conservative. There's no hint that Jesus is saying that the other laws are optional. Matthew's interpretation is that all the other laws, and even the sayings of the prophets, are living statutes contained within these two basic precepts. They have authority, even if it's a derived authority.

# Mark 12:28–34 (cont.)

**34** Et Iesus videns quod sapienter respondisset, dixit illi, "Non es longe a regno Dei." Et nemo iam audebat eum interrogare.

## Luke 10:25–28 (cont.)

**28** Dixitque illi, "Recte respondisti. Hoc fac et vives."

## Vocabulary

**sapienter,** wisely

## Historical and Grammatical Notes

### Mark 12:28–34 (cont.)

**34. Non es longe a regno Dei:** Jesus is not in the habit of complimenting people in Mark, and certainly not someone allied with his adversaries. Why does he make an exception in this case? The scribe approvingly repeats Jesus's words, which isn't enough to win Jesus's praise. But the scribe continues with a correct inference about the Law: Mere obedience without inward conviction is meaningless. This might not be something that the scribe just now learned from Jesus. It may be something that the scribe, and perhaps other scribes, had already concluded from their own study. In any case, this exchange shows that far from being a monolithic body of like-minded thinkers, the scribes could have held diverse opinions about basic doctrine and about Jesus.

# Mark 12:35–37

## *Will the Messiah Be of the House of David?*

Now that Jesus has silenced the Sadducees and has answered a question to the scribe's satisfaction, Jesus begins teaching on his own and asking the crowd his own questions. It's difficult to understand, or perhaps to accept, what Jesus intends to teach with this first lesson, but it appears that he shows that the Messiah will *not* be from the house of David. He may be only inviting deeper inquiry by asking a provocative question, as good teachers often do.

**35** Et respondens Iesus dicebat docens in Templo,
"Quomodo dicunt scribae Christum filium esse David? **36**
Ipse David dixit in Spiritu Sancto, 'Dixit Dominus domino
meo, "Sede a dextris meis, donec ponam inimicos tuos sub
pedibus tuis." ' **37** Ipse David dicit eum dominum et unde
est filius eius?" Et multa turba eum libenter audiebat.

## Matthew 22:41–45

**41** Congregatis autem Pharisaeis, interrogavit eos Iesus, **42** dicens,
"Quid vobis videtur de Christo? Cuius filius est?" Dicunt ei, "David."
**43** Ait illis, "Quomodo ergo David in Spiritu vocat eum dominum,
dicens, **44** 'Dixit Dominus domino meo, "Sede a dextris meis, donec
ponam inimicos tuos sub pedibus tuis" '? **45** Si ergo David vocat eum
dominum, quomodo filius eius est?"

## Luke 20:41–44

**41** Dixit autem ad illos, "Quomodo dicunt Christum filium David
esse? **42** Ipse enim David dicit in libro Psalmorum, 'Dixit Dominus
domino meo, "Sede a dextris meis, **43** donec ponam inimicos tuos
scabellum pedum tuorum." ' **44** David ergo dominum illum vocat, et
quomodo filius eius est?"

## Vocabulary

**Psalmi, -orum,** *m. pl.,* Psalms

**scabellum, -i,** *n.,* footstool

## Historical and Grammatical Notes

### Mark 12:35–37

35. **docens in Templo:** Jesus doesn't teach according to our modern notion. He asks a question whose answer he thinks should be clear. These verses give us an interesting look at how textual readings and analysis were probably conducted. **Quomodo dicunt scribae Christum filium esse David:** "How is it that scribes say that the Messiah is the son of David?" There is no independent, prior evidence that scribes, or the Pharisees, argued that the Messiah was to be a descendant of David.

36. **in Spiritu Sancto:** This is equivalent to saying that David was inspired by the Holy Spirit when he composed this psalm. Accordingly, the verse is God's own words, and therefore authoritative. **Dixit Dominus domino meo:** This is the paradox on which the passage turns. David writes that the Lord is saying something to David's lord. But how can a man's son also be the man's lord? So can it be right for the scribes to say that the Messiah is to be a son (descendant) of David? The answer seems to be no. A man cannot be both the son of someone and be his lord at the same time. This quite obviously is a problem for Christians, as the orthodox view is that Jesus was indeed a descendant of David as was required of the Messiah. The purpose of the elaborate genealogies that begin Matthew and Luke is to demonstrate Jesus's lineage from David. So what should we think of this passage in Mark, where Jesus needles the scribes for not seeing that the Messiah *cannot* be descended from David? A possible solution is that Jesus isn't advancing his own thought on the subject. He is simply silencing the scribes by giving them something to think about.

37. **et unde est filius eius:** "where is his son from?"

### Matthew 22:41–45

41. **Congregatis autem Pharisaeis:** Matthew has skipped over the lowly scribes and takes the conflict directly to the source.

42. **Dicunt:** The Pharisees are being put on the witness stand. The crowd is watching this cross-examination and probably enjoying it greatly. **David:** Again, there's no contemporary evidence that they thought this. Perhaps we should accept this passage as evidence that they did.

45. **quomodo filius eius est:** QED. The Messiah cannot be of the house of David.

# Mark 12:38–40

## *Beware Scribes*

Now Jesus takes aim at the scribes personally and denounces their haughty pride. He charges them with serving only their petty, worldly ambitions.

**38** Et dicebat in doctrinā suā, "Cavete a scribis, qui
volunt in stolis ambulare et salutari in foro, **39** et in
primis cathedris sedere in synagogis et primos discubitūs
in cenis, **40** qui devorant domos viduarum et ostentant
prolixas orationes.

### Matthew 23:1–7

**1** Tunc Iesus locutus est ad turbas et ad discipulos suos, **2** dicens,
"Super cathedram Moysis sederunt scribae et Pharisaei.

### Luke 20:46–47

**46** "Attendite a scribis, qui volunt ambulare in stolis et amant
salutationes in foro et primas cathedras in synagogis et primos
discubitūs in conviviis, **47** qui devorant domos viduarum et simulant
longam orationem.

## Vocabulary

**discubitus, -us,** *m.,* a reclining at a table
**forum, -i,** *n.,* marketplace
**ostento (1),** to show off; display
**prolixus, -a, -um,** extensive; comprehensive; wordy
**salutatio, -ionis,** *f.,* greetings
**stola, -ae,** *f.,* robe
**vidua, -ae,** *f.,* widow

## Historical and Grammatical Notes

### Mark 12:38–40

**38. in doctrinā suā:** Jesus is no longer interpreting Scripture; he's speaking his own mind. **a scribis, qui:** Is Jesus saying that all scribes behave in the way he describes or that some do and some don't? It's possible that he's not attacking all of the scribes, but only those who behave badly. The latter possibility has something to say for it since this pericope follows so closely on his warm praise of at least one scribe.

**39. primos discubitūs in cenis:** This is a mild zeugma (where the same word is followed by different dependent grammatical constructions). We can see zeugma in an English sentence like this: "I want to go to the movie with my friends, to get something to eat, and a hat." We can smooth this over by repeating "I want" before "a hat." Here *volunt* governs three infinitives, and then it takes an accusative direct object. To translate the Latin zeugma into idiomatic English, we can repeat the verb before *primos discubitūs*: "they want to walk about in robes, be greeted in the marketplace, sit in the first row in the synagogue, and [they want] honored seats at banquets."

**40. devorant domos viduarum:** It's not certain in what way the scribes would be devouring the houses of widows. It could be that as experts of the Law, they might settle estates, for which they'd charge very high fees. It could also be a proverbial way, going back to Isaiah 10:1–2, of accusing someone of being so greedy he'd steal even from a widow. **ostentant prolixas orationes:** "they make a show of their lengthy prayers."

### Matthew 23:1–7

**2. Super cathedram Moysis sederunt:** The Pharisees and scribes considered themselves to be authoritative interpreters of Mosaic law, so they could be said to sit on "Moses's chair." But there is reason to believe that this is more than a metaphor. Large stone chairs have been discovered in many excavated synagogues, where scribes and Pharisees may have sat while proclaiming the meaning of a law or a text.

### Luke 20:46–47

**46. amant:** Notice how Luke avoids the zeugma in Mark by inserting more finite verbs to govern the accusative objects.

# Mark 12:38–40 (cont.)

Hi accipient amplius iudicium."

## Matthew 23:1–7 (cont.)

**3** Omnia ergo, quaecumque dixerint vobis, facite et servate.
Secundum opera vero eorum, nolite facere. Dicunt enim et non
faciunt. **4** Alligant autem onera gravia et importabilia et imponunt in
umeros hominum, ipsi autem digito suo nolunt ea movere. **5** Omnia
vero opera sua faciunt, ut videantur ab hominibus. Dilatant enim
phylacteria sua et magnificant fimbrias. **6** Amant autem primum
recubitum in cenis et primas cathedras in synagogis **7** et salutationes
in foro et vocari ab hominibus 'Rabbi.' "

## Luke 20:46–47 (cont.)

Hi accipient damnationem maiorem."

## Vocabulary

**dilato (1),** to spread out
**importabilis, -e,** unbearable
**onus, -eris,** *n.,* burden
**phylacterium, -ii,** *n.,* amulet; phylactery
**umerus, -i,** *m.,* shoulder

## Historical and Grammatical Notes

### Matthew 23:1–7 (cont.)

**3. ergo:** Matthew is much more careful about distinguishing what they say from what they do. Because they have the authority to sit in Moses's chair, what they say is binding and must be obeyed, regardless of what we may think of them personally. **vero:** "but."

**4. Alligant autem onera gravia et importabilia:** The metaphor is that of a pack mule being loaded up.

**5. Dilatant enim phylacteria sua et magnificant fimbrias:** The *phylacteria* were, and still are, small wooden boxes containing Old Testament verses that Jews strap on to their foreheads and left arms when reciting prayers. The Pharisees and scribes make sure theirs are especially ornate and decorative.

# Mark 12:41–44

## *Gift from the Poor Widow*

Jesus praises a poor widow's gift of a few pennies to the Temple, saying it is greater than the handfuls of money rich people can offer.

**41** Et sedens contra gazophylacium aspiciebat
quomodo turba iactaret aes in gazophylacium, et multi
divites iactabant multa. **42** Et cum venisset una vidua
pauper, misit duo minuta, quod est quadrans. **43** Et
convocans discipulos suos ait illis, "Amen dico vobis,
vidua haec pauper plus omnibus misit, qui miserunt in
gazophylacium. **44** Omnes enim ex eo, quod abundabat
illis, miserunt. Haec vero de penuriā suā, omnia quae
habuit misit, totum victum suum."

### Luke 21:1–4

**1** Respiciens autem vidit eos, qui mittebant munera sua in
gazophylacium, divites. **2** Vidit autem quandam viduam
pauperculam mittentem illuc minuta duo **3** et dixit, "Vere dico
vobis, vidua haec pauper plus quam omnes misit. **4** Nam omnes hi
ex abundantiā suā miserunt in munera. Haec autem ex inopiā suā
omnem victum suum quem habebat misit."

# Vocabulary

**aes, aeris,** *n.,* bronze coin
**gazophylacium, -ii,** *n.,* coin box; treasury
**inopia, -ae,** *f.,* lack of resources; poverty
**minutum, -i,** *n.,* tiny coin
**penuria, -ae,** *f.,* poverty
**quadrans, -antis,** *m.,* a fourth part; one fourth of a penny
**victus, -us,** *m.,* means of living

# Historical and Grammatical Notes

### Mark 12:41–44

**41. contra gazophylacium:** A *gazophylacium* is an unstaffed, but locked, box of some sort, where people could drop in a donation. **divites:** "rich people." **multa:** adverbial: "a lot."

**42. quod est quadrans:** Mark helps his audience with the meaning of *minuta.* We're talking about pennies.

**43. plus omnibus . . . qui:** "more than all who . . ."

**44. ex eo, quod abundabat illis:** "from that which is abundant for them," or "from what they have a lot of." **totum victum suum:** appositional: "but this woman gives all she has from her poverty, [she gives] her entire means of living."

### Luke 21:1–4

Luke merely smooths over Mark's grammar and deletes the discussion of the value of the coins involved. For all intents and purposes, it's the identical narrative.

# Chapter 13

Chapter 13 is often called the "Little Apocalypse" or the "Olivet Discourse." Jesus departs from his normal practice of teaching in parables or responding to specific challenges and speaks at length about the vast, cosmic destruction that will mark the end times. Some of his pronouncements are cloaked in symbols and veiled references, but some are quite explicit.

# Mark 13:1–2

## *The Destruction of the Temple Predicted*

Impressed by the Temple compound, the disciples ask Jesus what he thinks of it. He replies that soon it will all be rubble.

**1** Et cum egrederetur de Templo, ait illi unus ex discipulis suis, "Magister, aspice quales lapides et quales structurae."
**2** Et Iesus ait illi, "Vides has magnas aedificationes? Hīc non relinquetur lapis super lapidem, qui non destruatur."

### Matthew 24:1–2

**1** Et egressus Iesus de Templo ibat, et accesserunt discipuli eius, ut ostenderent ei aedificationes Templi. **2** Ipse autem respondens dixit eis, "Non videtis haec omnia? Amen dico vobis, non relinquetur hīc lapis super lapidem, qui non destruetur."

### Luke 21:5–6

**5** Et quibusdam dicentibus de Templo, quod lapidibus bonis et donis ornatum esset, dixit, **6** "Haec quae videtis, venient dies in quibus non relinquetur lapis super lapidem, qui non destruatur."

## Vocabulary

**aedificatio, -ionis,** *f.*, construction
**destruo, -ere, -xi, -ctus,** to pull down; destroy
**orno (1),** to decorate; adorn

## Historical and Grammatical Notes

### Mark 13:1–2

1. **quales lapides et quales structurae:** Supply *sint* to complete the indirect question: "Do you see of what quality the rocks are? of what quality the construction is?" Jesus's apocalyptic narrative begins appropriately with the destruction of the Temple. This is the physical setting, after all, and admiring the Temple is something his disciples would be doing. All our ancient sources affirm that the Temple was one of the most splendid buildings in antiquity.
2. **qui non destruatur:** "which will be pulled down." The subjunctive probably shouldn't be inspected too closely. Vulgate Latin uses the indicative and subjunctive more loosely than allowed by the strict formulas of classical Latin. We've seen this in indirect statement where the two moods are interchangeable. The destruction will be so complete that no stone will be left on top of another.

### Synoptic Parallels

Both Matthew and Luke follow Mark closely with only minor editorial changes.

# Mark 13:3–13

## *The First Signs and Dangers for Jesus's Followers*

There will be signs, Jesus says, when the end of time is approaching. There will be false prophets, wars, geological convulsions, famine, persecution of the faithful, sedition, and murder even within families. Jesus reassures the disciples that God will give them words to speak when they are dragged before their oppressors.

**3** Et cum sederet in Montem Olivarum contra Templum, interrogabat eum separatim Petrus et Iacobus et Ioannes et Andreas, **4** "Dic nobis, quando ista erunt, et quod signum erit, quando haec omnia incipient consummari?"
**5** Iesus autem coepit dicere illis, "Videte, ne quis vos seducat. **6** Multi venient in nomine meo dicentes, 'Ego sum,' et multos seducent.

### Matthew 24:3–14

**3** Sedente autem eo super Montem Oliveti, accesserunt ad eum discipuli secreto, dicentes, "Dic nobis, quando haec erunt, et quod signum adventūs tui et consummationis saeculi?" **4** Et respondens Iesus dixit eis, "Videte, ne quis vos seducat. **5** Multi enim venient in nomine meo dicentes, 'Ego sum Christus,' et multos seducent.

### Luke 21:7–19

**7** Interrogaverunt autem illum, dicentes, "Praeceptor, quando ergo haec erunt, et quod signum, cum fieri incipient?" **8** Qui dixit, "Videte, ne seducamini. Multi enim venient in nomine meo dicentes, 'Ego sum,' et, 'Tempus appropinquavit.' Nolite ergo ire post illos.

## Vocabulary

**adventus, -us,** *m.*, approach; arrival
**consummatio, -ionis,** *f.*, fulfillment
**incipio, -cipere, -cepi, -ceptus,** to begin
**seduco, -ducere, -duxi, -ductus,** to lead astray
**separatim,** privately

## Historical and Grammatical Notes

### Mark 13:3–13

3. **contra Templum:** The entire Temple complex was visible from Mt. Olive. It would be said that he was sitting *contra Templum,* with the Temple on the other side of the Kidron Valley. **interrogabat:** This is the last prompt, and the balance of chapter 13 is a soliloquy by Jesus. Again we see Peter, James, and John singled out as three central disciples and the only ones privy to Jesus's predictions.

4. **ista:** It seems that they have more in mind than the destruction of the Temple. It looks like this verse originally belonged to some other narrative, or was perhaps free floating, and Mark inserted it here.

6. **Multi venient in nomine meo:** Jewish history is replete with self-proclaimed prophets and divine messengers, so Jesus's warning could just be a stock motif from apocalyptic literature. We are surely familiar in the modern age with people pretending to be able to predict the future, as well as those who claim that ancient biblical or other prophecies about the end of time are about to come true. *In nomine meo* may refer to specific men who claimed to be continuing Jesus's mission after his crucifixion.

### Matthew 24:3–14

3. **adventūs tui:** Mark doesn't explicitly equate the end of times with Jesus's return.

5. **Ego sum Christus:** This is merely a relocation of what Mark says in the next verses.

# Mark 13:3–13 (cont.)

**7** Cum audieritis autem bella et opiniones bellorum, ne
timueritis. Oportet fieri, sed nondum finis. **8** Exsurget
enim gens super gentem, et regnum super regnum, erunt
terrae motūs per loca, erunt fames. Initium dolorum haec.
**9** Videte autem vosmetipsos. Tradent vos conciliis, et in
synagogis vapulabitis, et ante praesides et reges stabitis
propter me in testimonium illis.

## Matthew 24:3–14 (cont.)

**6** Audituri enim estis proelia et opiniones proeliorum. Videte, ne
turbemini. Oportet enim fieri, sed nondum est finis. **7** Consurget
enim gens in gentem, et regnum in regnum, et erunt fames et terrae
motūs per loca. **8** Haec autem omnia initia sunt dolorum. **9** Tunc
tradent vos in tribulationem et occīdent vos, et eritis odio omnibus
gentibus propter nomen meum.

## Luke 21:7–19 (cont.)

**9** Cum autem audieritis proelia et seditiones, nolite terreri. Oportet
enim primum haec fieri, sed non statim finis." **10** Tunc dicebat
illis, "Surget gens contra gentem, et regnum adversus regnum.
**11** Et terrae motūs magni et per loca fames et pestilentiae erunt,
terroresque et de caelo signa magna erunt. **12** Sed ante haec omnia
inicient vobis manūs suas et persequentur tradentes in synagogas et
custodias, et trahemini ad reges et praesides propter nomen meum.

## Vocabulary

**concilium, -ii,** *n.*, council; assembly
**dolor, -is,** *m.*, pain; grief
**fames, -is,** *f.*, famine
**inicio, -icere, -ieci, -iectus,** to throw onto
**odium, -ii,** *n.*, hatred
**opinio, -ionis,** *f.*, opinion; rumor
**persequor, -qui, -cutus sum,** to persecute; hound
**pestilentia, -ae,** *f.*, plague; disease
**proelium, -i,** *n.*, battle
**seditio, -ionis,** *f.*, insurrection; disagreement
**terrae motus, -us,** *m.*, earthquake
**vapulo (1),** to be flogged

## Historical and Grammatical Notes

### Mark 13:3–13 (cont.)

**8. erunt terrae motūs per loca:** A standard element in an apocalypse narrative is that the end time is more than a social or political upheaval. It's a cosmic one, as well. In this context, moreover, Jesus might be referring to specific events. A famine is reported in Acts 11:28, and the Roman city of Pompeii and the Bay of Naples was rocked by earthquakes in 62 CE, a few years before the putative date of the composition of Mark. Much of the damage had not been repaired before the famed volcano of 79 CE. It might have seemed that the world was in fact in its final hours.

**9. Videte autem vosmetipsos:** "But look out for yourselves." The end times will be preceded by specific attacks on the first Christians. **in synagogis:** The Jewish authorities could carry out corporal punishment, which could be carried out in a synagogue. The important point is that Jesus predicted that Christians would be persecuted by Jews as much as by the Romans. Before he converted, Paul himself was an investigator for the Pharisees against the first Christians and was present at the stoning death of one of them, St. Stephen (Acts 22:20). **in testimonium illis:** *Illis* could be either "for them" or "for these things."

### Luke 21:7–19 (cont.)

**12. inicient vobis manūs suas:** *Manus* can mean a "gang" or "hand": "they will sic their gangs on you," or "they will lay hands on you." The Greek original, however, speaks of "hands."

# Mark 13:3–13 (cont.)

**10** Et in omnes gentes primum oportet praedicari
evangelium. **11** Et cum duxerint vos tradentes, nolite
praecogitare quid loquamini, sed, quod datum vobis fuerit
in illā horā, id loquimini. Non enim estis vos loquentes sed
Spiritus Sanctus. **12** Et tradet frater fratrem in mortem,
et pater filium. Et consurgent filii in parentes et morte
afficient eos. **13** Et eritis odio omnibus propter nomen
meum. Qui autem sustinuerit in finem, hĭc salvus erit.

## Matthew 24:3–14 (cont.)

**10** Et tunc scandalizabuntur multi et invicem tradent et odio
habebunt invicem. **11** Et multi pseudoprophetae surgent et seducent
multos. **12** Et, quoniam abundavit iniquitas, refrigescet caritas
multorum. **13** Qui autem permanserit usque in finem, hĭc salvus
erit. **14** Et praedicabitur hoc evangelium regni in universo orbe in
testimonium omnibus gentibus. Et tunc veniet consummatio."

## Luke 21:7–19 (cont.)

**13** Continget autem vobis in testimonium. **14** Ponite ergo in
cordibus vestris non praemeditari quemadmodum respondeatis. **15**
Ego enim dabo vobis os et sapientiam, cui non poterunt resistere
vel contradicere omnes adversarii vestri. **16** Trademini autem et a
parentibus et fratribus et cognatis et amicis, et morte afficient ex
vobis, **17** et eritis odio omnibus propter nomen meum. **18** Et capillus
de capite vestro non peribit. **19** In patientiā vestrā possidebitis
animas vestras."

## Vocabulary

**capillus, -i,** *m.,* hair
**caritas, -tatis,** *f.,* affection; love
**cognatus, -a, -um,** related; kindred
**contingo, -tingere, -tigi, -tactus,** to touch; happen to
**iniquitas, -tatis,** *f.,* injustice
**invicem,** in turn
**orbis, orbis,** *m.,* orb; world
**permaneo, -manere, -mansi, -mansus,** to remain to the end; endure
**praecogito (1),** to think ahead
**pseudopropheta, -ae,** *m.,* false prophet
**refrigesco, -frigescere, -frixi,** to grow cold

## Historical and Grammatical Notes

### Mark 13:3–13 (cont.)

**11. quod datum . . . loquimini:** = *loquimini id quod vobis datum fuerit in illā horā*: "say that which will have been given to you at that time." **loquentes:** substantive: "the ones speaking."

**12. Et tradet frater fratrem in mortem:** The list of catastrophes is not random. At the first there will be large-scale cataclysms in the world: earthquakes, famine, plague. These are the signs that the end is coming. The end itself starts with the persecution of Jesus's followers. They will be betrayed by their community and, worse, even by their own family. **odio omnibus:** This is the double dative: "you will be as an object of hatred to everyone." **morte afficient eos:** This surely means that they won't kill their parents themselves, but that they will have them put to death by the authorities.

**13. Qui autem sustinuerit in finem:** i.e., if he doesn't renounce his faith in Jesus.

### Matthew 24:3–14 (cont.)

**10. odio:** dative of specification: "they will hold you as an object of hatred."

### Luke 21:7–19 (cont.)

**13. Continget autem vobis in testimonium:** "It will provide you an opportunity for witnessing." God's purpose is expressed even in their persecution.

**15. cui:** singular, although there are arguably two antecedents: "to which all your adversaries will not be able to stand up or offer contradiction" = "which all your adversaries won't be able to resist or contradict."

**19. In patientiā vestrā possidebitis animas vestras:** "In your suffering you will retain your soul."

# Mark 13:14–23

## *How Quickly the Tribulations Will Arrive*

Jesus now widens the circle of destruction and tribulation from Jerusalem to the whole of Judea. There will be an explosion of false prophets and charlatans claiming to be Christ.

**14** "Cum autem videritis abominationem desolationis stantem ubi non debet—qui legit, intellegat—tunc, qui in Iudaeā sunt, fugiant in montes. **15** Qui autem super tectum, ne descendat nec introeat, ut tollat quid de domo suā. **16** Et, qui in agro erit, non revertatur retro tollere vestimentum suum. **17** Vae autem praegnantibus et nutrientibus in illis diebus! **18** Orate vero ut hieme non fiat.

### Matthew 24:15–28

**15** "Cum ergo videritis abominationem desolationis, quae dicta est a Daniele prophetā, stantem in loco sancto, qui legit, intellegat. **16** Tunc qui in Iudaeā sunt, fugiant ad montes. **17** Qui in tecto, non descendat tollere aliquid de domo suā. **18** Et, qui in agro, non revertatur tollere pallium suum. **19** Vae autem praegnantibus et nutrientibus in illis diebus! **20** Orate autem ut non fiat fuga vestra hieme vel Sabbato.

### Luke 21:20–24

**20** "Cum autem videritis circumdari ab exercitu Ierusalem, tunc scitote quia appropinquavit desolatio eius. **21** Tunc, qui in Iudaeā sunt, fugiant in montes; et, qui in medio eius, discedant. Et, qui in regionibus, non intrent in eam. **22** Quia dies ultionis hi sunt, ut impleantur omnia, quae scripta sunt. **23** Vae autem praegnantibus et nutrientibus in illis diebus!

## Vocabulary

**abominatio, -ionis,** *f.*, abomination
**desolatio, -ionis,** *f.*, desolation
**exercitus, -us,** *m.*, army
**fuga, -ae,** *f.*, flight; escape
**hiems, -is,** *f.*, winter
**nutriens, -ntis,** nursing
**praegnans, -ntis,** pregnant
**ultio, -ionis,** *f.*, revenge

## Historical and Grammatical Notes

### Mark 13:14–23

**14. abominationem desolationis stantem ubi non debet:** "the abomination of desolation standing where it shouldn't." This is a prediction from Daniel (9:26; 11:31, 12:11) that surely refers to the statue of Zeus erected in the Temple by a Syrian ruler in the third century BCE. What it could be referring to in this context is obscure. This could refer simply to the general Roman presence in the Temple and not to a specific event. The parenthetical remark *qui legit, intellegat* may be Mark's way of allowing this ambiguity to go unexplained to give him a degree of deniability. **qui in Iudaeā sunt, fugiant in montes:** Jesus is affirming the fact that when the end comes, God will not be protecting his city or Temple.

### Matthew 24:15–28

**20. vel Sabbato:** Only Matthew has this pious addition. Fleeing death and destruction on the Sabbath would be blasphemy.

### Luke 21:20–24

**20. scitote:** second person plural future imperative. There's nothing to be gained by trying to coax any significance out of the fact that the imperative is from a future form. It's just another form of the imperative. **desolatio eius:** This is all that's left of the reference to Daniel. Luke might have simplified the allusion because his audience would not have known who or what Daniel is, let alone have any idea of what would be meant by the "abomination of desolation." Contrary to Matthew and Mark, Luke never mentions Daniel by name.

# Mark 13:14–23 (cont.)

**19** Erunt enim dies illi tribulatio talis, qualis non fuit ab initio creaturae, quam condidit Deus, usque nunc, neque fiet. **20** Et nisi breviasset Dominus dies, non fuisset salva omnis caro. Sed propter electos, quos elegit, breviavit dies.

## Matthew 24:15–28 (cont.)

**21** Erit enim tunc tribulatio magna, qualis non fuit ab initio mundi usque modo neque fiet. **22** Et nisi breviati fuissent dies illi, non fieret salva omnis caro. Sed propter electos breviabuntur dies illi.

## Luke 21:20–24 (cont.)

Erit enim pressura magna super terram et ira populo huic, **24** et cadent in ore gladii et captivi ducentur in omnes gentes, et Ierusalem calcabitur a gentibus, donec impleantur tempora nationum."

## Vocabulary

**brevio (1),** to shorten
**calco (1),** to walk on; trample on
**captivus, -i,** *m.,* captive
**condo, -dere, -didi, -ditus,** to establish; found
**eligo, -ligere, -legi, -lectus,** to pick out; elect
**gladius, -ii,** *m.,* sword
**natio, -ionis,** *f.,* nation
**pressura, -ae,** *f.,* pressure; distress

## Historical and Grammatical Notes

### Mark 13:14–23 (cont.)

19. **Erunt enim dies illi tribulatio talis:** The sense is clear but the grammar is exceptionally compressed: "Those days will come when there will be such tribulation . . ." This verse is built on a quotation from Daniel 12:1: "For at that time there will be such affliction (oppression and tribulation) as has not been from the beginning of the creation that God created until this particular time—and positively never will be [again]."

20. **propter electos:** This is the first and only time in Mark we hear talk of an elect. It doesn't necessarily follow that God saves only his elect or that only those whom he elected will be saved. The elect may be simply the core of followers for whom God has a special purpose. There may be others who will be saved.

### Luke 21:20–24 (cont.)

24. **donec impleantur tempora nationum:** "until the times of the nations have been fulfilled." A clue to this mysterious verse may be in Paul's letter to the Romans 11:11–26. There he explains the purpose behind his own ministry to the Gentiles. He says that they will be offered a temporary path to salvation. When Jews see this happening, they will be tormented by jealously and convert to the belief that Jesus is the Messiah. Hence the time of the Gentiles might mean this expansion of the offer of salvation until the Jews see the error of their ways. This might have been a widely enough held understanding among the first Christians that Luke could allude to it without being explicit.

# Mark 13:14–23 (cont.)

**21** Et tunc, si quis vobis dixerit, 'Ecce: hīc est Christus!'
'Ecce: illic!' ne credideritis. **22** Exsurgent enim
pseudochristi et pseudoprophetae et dabunt signa et
portenta ad seducendos (si potest fieri) electos. **23** Vos
autem videte. Praedixi vobis omnia."

## Matthew 24:15–28 (cont.)

**23** Tunc si quis vobis dixerit, 'Ecce: hĭc Christus,' aut 'hĭc!' nolite
credere. **24** Surgent enim pseudochristi et pseudoprophetae et
dabunt signa magna et prodigia, ita ut in errorem inducantur (si
fieri potest) etiam electi. **25** Ecce: praedixi vobis. **26** Si ergo dixerint
vobis, 'Ecce: in deserto est!' nolite exire. 'Ecce: in penetralibus!'
nolite credere. **27** Sicut enim fulgur exit ab oriente et paret usque
in occĭdentem, ita erit adventus filii hominis. **28** Ubicumque fuerit
corpus, illuc congregabuntur aquilae."

## Luke 17:22–25

**22** Et ait ad discipulos, "Venient dies, quando desideretis videre
unum diem filii hominis et non videbitis. **23** Et dicent vobis, 'Ecce:
hīc!' 'Ecce: illic!' Nolite ire neque sectemini. **24** Nam sicut fulgur
coruscans de sub caelo in eā, quae sub caelo sunt, fulget, ita erit filius
hominis in die suā. **25** Primum autem oportet illum multa pati et
reprobari a generatione hac."

## Vocabulary

**aquila, -ae,** *f.,* eagle
**corusco (1),** to shake; flash
**desidero (1),** to wish; desire
**fulgeo, -gere, -si,** *or* **fulgo, -ere,** to flash
**fulgur, -uris,** *m.,* flash of lightning; splendor
**orior, -iri, ortus sum,** to arise
**pareo, -ere, -ui, -itum,** to appear; become visible
**penetralia, -orum,** *n. pl.,* inner chambers
**portentum, -i,** *n.,* portent; sign
**praedico, -dicere, -dixi, -dictus,** to predict
**prodigium, -ii,** *n.,* prodigy; portent
**pseudochristus, -i,** *m.,* false Messiah
**sector, -ari, -atus sum,** to follow eagerly; run after

## Historical and Grammatical Notes

### Mark 13:14–23 (cont.)

21. **hīc est Christus:** This isn't a mere repetition of verse 6. There the imposters will say only that they are prophets or deliverers of more information about the end times. When the final trials begin, however, there will be frauds who claim to be the Messiah himself.

22. **ad seducendos (si potest fieri) electos:** "lead astray the elect, if that is possible." Can any of the elect be led astray? It's not clear whether they can be from this verse, but these false prophets and Messiahs will try.

### Matthew 24:15–28 (cont.)

27. **Sicut enim fulgur:** There will be no doubt when this son of man arrives.

28. **aquilae:** This is often translated as "vultures," but both the Latin and Greek words mean "eagles." Since the eagle is the symbol of Roman military power, this may simply be a way of underscoring God's purpose in the destruction of the Temple.

### Luke 17:22–25 (cont.)

22. **Venient dies . . . non videbitis:** "There will come a time when you will want to see the son of man but you will not see him."

23. **neque sectemini:** "don't go running after him."

# Mark 13:24–27

## *The Cosmic Upheavals and the Arrival of the Son of Man*

The waves of destruction will eventually engulf the entire cosmos. This will be the final event before the Messiah is sent to earth with his angels to gather up the elect.

**24** "Sed in illis diebus post tribulationem illam sol
contenebrabitur, et luna non dabit splendorem suum, **25** et
erunt stellae de caelo decidentes, et virtutes, quae sunt in
caelis, movebuntur.

### Matthew 24:29–31

**29** "Statim autem post tribulationem dierum illorum, sol obscurabitur, et luna non dabit lumen suum, et stellae cadent de caelo, et virtutes caelorum commovebuntur.

### Luke 21:25–28

**25** "Et erunt signa in sole et lunā et stellis, et super terram pressura
gentium prae confusione sonitūs maris et fluctuum, **26** arescentibus
hominibus prae timore et exspectatione eorum, quae supervenient
orbi, nam virtutes caelorum movebuntur.

## Vocabulary

**aresco, -escere, -ui,** to become dry
**confusio, -ionis,** *f.*, confusion; perplexity
**contenebro (1),** to dim; grow dark
**decido, -dere, -di, -sus,** to fall down
**luna, -ae,** *f.*, moon
**obscuro (1),** to cover up; darken
**splendor, -oris,** *m.*, brightness
**stella, -ae,** *f.*, star

## Historical and Grammatical Notes

### Mark 13:24–27

**24. sol contenebrabitur:** There is no reason to suppose that Mark means this simply as a metaphor of earthly chaos. In their worldview, the cosmos was like a decorated house, certainly of immense size, but not infinitely large. The parallel between the destruction of the Temple and the potential collapse of the entire cosmos would not have seemed so astounding as it does to modern people whose concept of the universe is much vaster. **virtutes, quae sunt in caelis:** These are the other heavenly bodies whose function was to maintain the regular order of life on earth. It must be remembered that astrology was a widely accepted belief of the time. If these powers move from their regular positions, the consequences for the substellar realms are massive.

### Synoptic Parallels

Both Matthew and Luke follow Mark very closely with only minor stylistic or editorial changes. Luke does, however, discard the word "elect" and refers more generally to Jesus's followers as being the ones who will be saved.

# Mark 13:24–27 (cont.)

**26** Et tunc videbunt filium hominis venientem in nubibus cum virtute multā et gloriā. **27** Et tunc mittet angelos et congregabit electos suos a quattuor ventis, a summo terrae usque ad summum caeli."

## Matthew 24:29–31 (cont.)

**30** Et tunc parebit signum filii hominis in caelo, et tunc plangent omnes tribūs terrae et videbunt filium hominis venientem in nubibus caeli cum virtute et gloriā multā. **31** Et mittet angelos suos cum tubā magnā, et congregabunt electos eius a quattuor ventis, a summis caelorum usque ad terminos eorum."

## Luke 21:25–28 (cont.)

**27** Et tunc videbunt filium hominis venientem in nube cum potestate et gloriā magnā. **28** His autem fieri incipientibus, respicite et levate capita vestra, quoniam appropinquat redemptio vestra."

## Vocabulary

**nubis, -is,** *f.,* cloud

**tuba, -ae,** *f.,* horn

## Historical and Grammatical Notes

### Mark 13:24–27 (cont.)

**26. venientem in nubibus cum virtute multā et gloriā:** This is yet another reference to Daniel (7:13–14). This throws light on the expectation that Jesus is talking of, for in Daniel there is mention of an earthly kingdom over which the Messiah rules with his angels and selected assistants: "Next I saw the arrival of a man—or so he seemed to be—brought there on clouds from heaven. He approached the Ancient of Days [i.e., God] and was presented to him. He was given the ruling power and glory over all the nations of the world, so that all people of every language must obey him. His power is eternal—it will never end. His government shall never fall." It's worth remembering that the Kingdom of God was first conceived of as an earthly rule. God and his assistants were to take up residence in the Temple and rule the world from there. It's only after the passage of time and the annihilation of the Temple by the Romans in 70 CE that the Kingdom of God was understood as a spiritual or celestial rule.

**27. a quattuor ventis . . . summum caeli:** This is a typical way of covering all possible ground in ancient literature. This repetition gives the expression a sense of complete fulfillment. In this case, Jesus will gather his elect from wherever they are—left, right, back, forward, even up to the top of the heavens.

# Mark 13:28–37

## *No One Knows Exactly When the End Will Come*

No one, not even the son, knows on what day or at what hour the end will come. Jesus advises his disciples to keep watch.

**28** "A ficu autem discite parabolam. Cum iam ramus
eius tener fuerit et germinaverit folia, cognoscitis quia in
proximo sit aestas. **29** Sic et vos, cum videritis haec fieri,
scitote quod in proximo sit in ostiis. **30** Amen dico vobis,
non transiet generatio haec, donec omnia ista fiant.

## Matthew 24:32–36

**32** "Ab arbore autem fici discite parabolam. Cum iam ramus eius
tener fuerit, et folia nata, scitis quia prope est aestas. **33** Ita et vos,
cum videritis haec omnia, scitote quia prope est in ianuis. **34** Amen
dico vobis, non praeteribit haec generatio, donec omnia haec fiant.

## Luke 21:29–33

**29** Et dixit illis similitudinem. "Videte ficulneam et omnes arbores.
**30** Cum iam germinaverint, videntes vosmetipsi scitis quia iam
prope est aestas. **31** Ita et vos, cum videritis haec fieri, scitote
quoniam prope est regnum Dei. **32** Amen dico vobis, non praeteribit
generatio haec, donec omnia fiant.

## Vocabulary

**aestas, -tatis,** *f.*, summer
**ostium, -i,** *n.*, door; entrance
**prope,** nearby
**tener, -a, -um,** tender

## Historical and Grammatical Notes

### Mark 13:28–37

**28. ficu:** The fig tree put out leaves in the spring as a sign that summer and the harvest is on its way. This is different from most trees in Judea, which were mostly evergreens and didn't change their foliage or color with the seasons. **in proximo:** "near." **sit:** What is the subject? It could be either the son of man or the destruction of the Temple.

**30. donec omnia ista fiant:** This phrase caused great difficulties for the first Christians. All the things Jesus predicted had not come true within a generation, reckoned to be forty years. Only some of it did: the destruction of the Temple, famine, earthquakes, and the persecution of the first Christians. Either Jesus was in error or these lines are misunderstood somehow.

### Matthew 24:32–36

**32. folia nata:** Supply *fuerint*. **scitis quia prope est aestas:** Most trees in that part of the world are evergreen. The fig, as one of the few deciduous trees, would be an index plant for the coming of summer.

### Luke 21:29–33

**29. et omnes arbores:** Luke is writing for people outside of Judea and may not have been familiar with fig trees or might not have appreciated how they stand out from other trees in the Holy Land. They would have known other deciduous trees that are barren in the summer and produce fresh leaves in the spring. That's why Luke can make the same point by referring generally to trees and omit the specific reference to a fig tree.

**31. quoniam prope est regnum Dei:** This is how Luke interprets the subject of *sit* in Mark 13:29.

# Mark 13:28–37 (cont.)

**31** Caelum et terra transibunt, verba autem mea non
transibunt. **32** De die autem illo vel horā nemo scit, neque
angeli in caelo neque filius, nisi Pater. **33** Videte! Vigilate!
Nescitis enim, quando tempus sit. **34** Sicut homo, qui
peregre profectus reliquit domum suam et dedit servis
suis potestatem, unicuique opus suum, ianitori quoque
praecepit, ut vigilaret. **35** Vigilate ergo! Nescitis enim
quando dominus domūs veniat, sero an mediā nocte an
galli cantu an mane. **36** Ne, cum venerit repente, inveniat
vos dormientes. **37** Quod autem vobis dico, omnibus
dico, vigilate!"

## Matthew 24:32–36 (cont.)

**35** Caelum et terra transibunt, verba vero mea non praeteribunt. **36**
De die autem illā et horā nemo scit, neque angeli caelorum neque
filius, nisi Pater solus."

## Luke 21:29–33 (cont.)

**33** Caelum et terra transibunt, verba autem mea non transibunt."

## Vocabulary

**cantus, -us,** *m.,* singing
**gallus, -i,** *m.,* rooster
**ianitor, -oris,** *m.,* doorman
**repente,** suddenly
**unusquisque, unaquisque, unumquidque,** each one
**vigilo (1),** to be awake; be on guard; keep watch

## Historical and Grammatical Notes

### Mark 13:28–37 (cont.)

**32. neque filius:** another difficult expression for early Christians. According to the notion of the Trinity, Jesus and God are distinct but one in a mysterious way. Why wouldn't the Son know what the Father knows? These two words appear to subordinate the Son to the Father.

**34. Sicut homo . . .:** In this parable, Jesus is the lord of the house who has gone away and the disciples are his servants whom he instructs to watch over his house until he returns. **unicuique opus suum:** "to each one his own task." *Suum* doesn't refer to the lord of the house but to a servant: The master of the house divides up the chores and gives each one of his servants a specific duty.

**35. domūs:** genitive. **sero an mediā nocte an galli cantu an mane:** Jesus marks off the night in terms of the Roman system of three-hour watches, starting at sunset:

1. *sero* (6 to 9 p.m.);
2. *mediā nocte* (9 p.m. to midnight);
3. *galli cantu* (midnight to 3 a.m.);
4. *mane* (3 a.m. to 6 a.m.).

# Chapter 14

We are now in the heart of the narrative of Jesus's suffering and crucifixion. This is often called the "passion" narrative, from the Latin *patior,* "to suffer, endure." The conspiracy in Jerusalem against Jesus is gathering momentum. The authorities, with the help of Judas, will take him into custody outside of the city after the Passover feast. As if aware that Jesus will soon die, a woman anoints Jesus with very expensive perfume. They secure a place in the city for the celebratory Passover Feast. Jesus surprises his friends by telling them that the bread and wine of the meal are his flesh and blood. He proclaims over their protests that given the chance they will all abandon him. Jesus goes on a little ahead of the rest as they leave the city and privately grieves over his fate. He is arrested and his followers scatter. Only Peter follows him, but at a safe distance, as he's taken into custody. While the Jewish authorities interrogate him, Peter denies any knowledge of Jesus three times to a crowd that has gathered outside the tribunal hall.

# Mark 14:1–2

## *The Authorities Plot Against Jesus*

The authorities make their plans to move against Jesus, but only after the throngs of people in the city for the Passover meal have thinned out.

**1** Erat autem Pascha et Azyma post biduum. Et quaerebant summi sacerdotes et scribae, quomodo eum dolo tenerent et occīderent. **2** Dicebant enim, "Non in die festo, ne forte tumultus fieret populi."

## Matthew 26:3–5

**3** Tunc congregati sunt principes sacerdotum et seniores populi in aulam principis sacerdotum, qui dicebatur Caiphas, **4** et consilium fecerunt, ut Iesum dolo tenerent et occīderent. **5** Dicebant autem, "Non in die festo, ne tumultus fiat in populo."

## Luke 22:1–2

**1** Appropinquabat autem dies festus Azymorum, qui dicitur Pascha.
**2** Et quaerebant principes sacerdotum et scribae quomodo eum interficerent, timebant vero plebem.

## Vocabulary

**aula, -ae,** *f.*, court; hall; atrium
**Azymus, -a, -um,** unleavened
**biduum, -i,** *n.*, two days
**festus, -a, -um,** holiday
**Pascha, -atis,** *f.*, Passover

## Historical and Grammatical Notes

### Mark 14:1–2

1. **Pascha:** "Passover." The annual celebration of the Passover was commanded in Exodus 12 as a memorial to God's final plague on Egypt. The festival had two main parts: the Passover meal and the observation (the Azyma) of eating bread that had no yeast in it. On the first day of the festival, people would bring a lamb to be offered as a sacrifice at the Temple. They would be given a portion of the meat to take home to eat in the early evening as their Passover meal. **Azyma:** This commemorated how quickly the Hebrews had to leave Egypt after the final plague. They didn't even have time to let their bread rise. Leaven was sourdough, not the packaged yeast familiar in modern times.
2. **Non in die festo:** The authorities did not want to take Jesus into custody on the festival day, which would have been the day when the pilgrims were bringing their lambs to the Temple. The site would have been teeming with people, and they didn't want to stir them up by seizing one of their popular figures in front of their eyes. It would be much more prudent to wait until the people had dispersed.

### Matthew 26:3–5

3. **Seniores populi:** Matthew includes certain leaders of the people in the conspiracy.

### Luke 22:1–2

1. **Azymorum:** Supply *panium*: "of the Unleavened Loaves." **qui dicitur Pascha:** Luke may mean that the day of the Passover is the beginning of the Festival of the Unleavened Bread, not that they are the same. The prohibition against leavened bread continues for about a week after the Passover feast.

# Mark 14:3–9

## *Jesus Anointed with Expensive Perfume*

An unidentified woman puts expensive perfume on Jesus's head. Jesus's companions object that it could have been sold to benefit the poor. Jesus defends her, saying that she has prepared his body for the tomb.

**3** Et cum esset Bethaniae in domo Simonis leprosi et
recumberet, vēnit mulier habens alabastrum unguenti
nardi puri pretiosi. Fracto alabastro, effudit super caput
eius. **4** Erant autem quidam indigne ferentes intra
semetipsos, "Ut quid perditio ista unguenti facṭa est? **5**
Poterat enim unguentum istud veniri plus quam trecentis
denariis et dari pauperibus." Et fremebant in eam.

## Matthew 26:6–13

**6** Cum autem esset Iesus in Bethaniā, in domo Simonis leprosi,
**7** accessit ad eum mulier habens alabastrum unguenti pretiosi et
effudit super caput ipsius recumbentis. **8** Videntes autem discipuli,
indignati sunt, dicentes, "Ut quid perditio haec? **9** Potuit enim istud
venumdari multo et dari pauperibus."

## Luke 7:36–50

Luke places this event earlier, incorporating it into a dispute with the Pharisees. It does not presage Jesus's crucifixion. It is part of a narrative that illustrates a cluster of values: forgiveness, generosity, sincerity, and love.

**36** Rogabat autem illum quidam de Pharisaeis, ut manducaret cum
illo. Et ingressus domum Pharisaei discubuit. **37** Et ecce: mulier,
quae erat in civitate peccatrix, ut cognovit quod accubuit in domo
Pharisaei, attulit alabastrum unguenti. **38** Et stans retro secus pedes
eius flens lacrimis coepit rigare pedes eius et capillis capitis sui
tergebat, et osculabatur pedes eius et unguento ungebat. **39** Videns
autem Pharisaeus, qui vocaverat eum, ait intra se, dicens, "Hĭc si
esset propheta, sciret utique quae et qualis mulier, quae tangit eum,
quia peccatrix est."

## Vocabulary

**alabaster, -tri,** *m.*, perfume jar
**fremo, -ere, -ui, -itus,** to growl
**nardus, -a, -um,** of nard (perfume from a flower)
**osculor, -ari, -atus sum,** to kiss
**perditio, -ionis,** *f.*, waste
**pretiosus, -a, -um,** expensive
**rigo (1),** to moisten
**tergeo, -gere, -si, -sus** *or* **tergo, -ere,** to rub; wipe off
**trecenti,** three hundred
**unguentum, -i,** *n.*, perfume
**unguo, ung(u)ere, unxi, unctus,** to anoint
**veneo, -ire, -ii, -iturus,** to sell
**venumdo, -dăre, -dedi, -datus,** to give for sale

## Historical and Grammatical Notes

### Mark 14:3–9

3. **Bethaniae:** locative. **Simonis leprosi:** Nothing else is known of Simon the Leper. The fact that he's a leper may be enough to merit inclusion in the story because it again shows that Jesus associates with the most outcast members of the community. **mulier:** This creates a contrastive frame with the poor widow of 12:41–44, whose gift was all the more meaningful because of her poverty. The woman in this event is definitely not poor. She is not named in any of the Synoptics, but she is called Mary in John's Gospel (12:3). **nardi:** an exotic and very expensive perfume. The Greek word is "myrrh." **Fracto alabastro:** It was customary to rub some oil onto the hands, face, neck, and even the hair before a social occasion, and sometimes a few drops of perfume could be added. But breaking the bottle meant that the entire content was to be poured out.

4. **ut quid:** an intensive for *quid*: "for what reason did this waste of perfume happen."

5. **veniri:** not from the verb "to come," but from *veneo, -īre,* "to sell." **plus quam trecentis denariis:** "more than three hundred denarii." This is approximately one full year's wages for a laborer. We may estimate it at $20,000.

### Matthew 26:6–13

7. **recumbentis:** "while he was reclining at the table."

9. **multo:** "for a great amount."

### Luke 7:36–50

36. **quidam de Pharisaeis:** Luke completely repurposes Mark's narrative for a different point and places it in another spot in the narrative.

37. **in civitate peccatrix:** She was a prostitute.

38. **unguento ungebat:** She puts only ordinary oil on Jesus's feet. There is no implication in Luke that the woman recognized that Jesus was the Christ and anointed him with the finest perfume to symbolize his status.

39. **sciret utique quae . . . peccatrix est:** "he should know both who and what this woman who has touched him is: that she is a sinner."

# Mark 14:3–9 (cont.)

**6** Iesus autem dixit, "Sinite eam. Quid illi molesti estis?
Bonum opus operata est in me. **7** Semper enim pauperes
habetis vobiscum et, cum volueritis, potestis illis bene
facere. Me autem non semper habetis. **8** Quod habuit,
operata est. Praevēnit ungere corpus meum in sepulturam.
**9** Amen autem dico vobis, ubicumque praedicatum fuerit
evangelium in universum mundum, et quod fecit haec
narrabitur in memoriam eius."

## Matthew 26:6–13 (cont.)

**10** Sciens autem Iesus ait illis, "Quid molesti estis mulieri? Opus
enim bonum operata est in me. **11** Nam semper pauperes habetis
vobiscum. Me autem non semper habetis. **12** Mittens enim haec
unguentum hoc supra corpus meum, ad sepeliendum me fecit. **13**
Amen dico vobis, 'Ubicumque praedicatum fuerit hoc evangelium in
toto mundo, dicetur et quod haec fecit in memoriam eius.' "

## Luke 7:36–50 (cont.)

**40** Et respondens Iesus dixit ad illum, "Simon, habeo tibi aliquid
dicere." At ille ait, "Magister, dic." **41** "Duo debitores erant cuidam
feneratori: unus debebat denarios quingentos, alius quinquaginta.
**42** Non habentibus illis, unde redderent, donavit utrisque. Quis ergo
eorum plus diliget eum?" **43** Respondens Simon dixit, "Aestimo
quia is, cui plus donavit." At ille dixit ei, "Recte iudicasti." **44** Et
conversus ad mulierem, dixit Simoni, "Vides hanc mulierem? Intravi
in domum tuam. Aquam pedibus meis non dedisti. Haec autem
lacrimis rigavit pedes meos et capillis suis tersit. **45** Osculum mihi
non dedisti. Haec autem, ex quo intravi, non cessavit osculari pedes
meos. **46** Oleo caput meum non unxisti. Haec autem unguento unxit
pedes meos. **47** Propter quod dico tibi, 'Remissa sunt peccata eius
multa,' quoniam dilexit multum. Cui autem minus dimittitur, minus
diligit." **48** Dixit autem ad illam, "Remissa sunt peccata tua." **49** Et

coeperunt, qui simul accumbebant, dicere intra se, "Quis est hĭc, qui etiam peccata dimittit?" **50** Dixit autem ad mulierem, "Fides tua te salvam fecit. Vade in pace!"

## Vocabulary

**bene facio, -facere, -feci, -factus,** to do a good deed
**debitor, -is,** *m.,* debtor
**fenerator, -ris,** *m.,* moneylender
**molestus, -a, -um,** troublesome
**operor, -ari, -atus sum,** to perform
**quingenti, -ae, -a,** five hundred
**quinquaginta,** fifty
**sepultura, -ae,** *f.,* burial

## Historical and Grammatical Notes

### Mark 14:3–9 (cont.)

**6. illi:** dative complement after *molesti*: "why are you being harsh toward her?"

**8. Quod habuit, operata est:** "She has done what she could." **Praevēnit:** "She is the first to anoint my body for burial."

### Matthew 26:6–13 (cont.)

**12. ad sepeliendum:** "she made me [ready] for burying."

### Luke 7:36–50 (cont.)

**41. cuidam feneratori:** "[there were two men in debt] to some moneylender."

**42. Non habentibus illis, unde redderent, donavit utrisque:** The syntax is loose. Strictly speaking the participle *habentibus* is dative and agrees with *utrisque,* the indirect object of *donavit*: "he gave to each one [since] they didn't have (*habentibus illis*) the wherewithal (*unde*) to pay it back."

# Mark 14:10–11

## *Judas Conspires with the Authorities*

Judas offers to help the authorities arrest Jesus. They are delighted and promise to give him money.

**10** Et Iudas Iscarioth, unus de Duodecim, abiit ad summos
sacerdotes, ut proderet eum illis. **11** Qui audientes gavisi
sunt et promiserunt ei pecuniam se daturos. Et quaerebat
quomodo illum opportune traderet.

### Matthew 26:14–16

**14** Tunc abiit unus de Duodecim, qui dicebatur Iudas Iscariotes, ad
principes sacerdotum **15** et ait, "Quid vultis mihi dare, et ego vobis
eum tradam?" At illi constituerunt ei triginta argenteos. **16** Et exinde
quaerebat opportunitatem ut eum traderet.

### Luke 22:3–6

**3** Intravit autem Satanas in Iudam, qui cognominabatur Iscarioth,
unum de Duodecim. **4** Et abiit et locutus est cum principibus
sacerdotum et magistratibus, quemadmodum illum traderet eis.
**5** Et gavisi sunt et pacti sunt pecuniam illi dare. **6** Et spopondit et
quaerebat opportunitatem ut eis traderet illum sine turbā.

## Vocabulary

**argenteus, -a, -um,** of silver
**constituo, -uere, -ui, -utus,** to decide; to put upon; order
**magistratus, -us,** *m.,* official, magistrate
**opportune,** conveniently; easily
**paciscor, -isci, -tus sum,** to make a contract; agree
**prodo, -dere, -didi, -ditus,** to reveal; make known
**spondeo, spondere, spopondi, sponsus,** to pledge

## Historical and Grammatical Notes

### Mark 14:10–11

**10. proderet:** "to reveal," which is an accurate description of what Judas does. He doesn't have Jesus in his custody to hand him over to the authorities, but he knows where they can find him to make the arrest. We wish we were told more about his true motivation by the Synoptics. Judas is a minor, almost invisible figure among the Twelve and shows no signs of being less loyal to Jesus than any of the others. In Mark, money is part of the deal, but it's not what makes him betray Jesus. He comes to the authorities before he is offered anything. In Matthew, money is explicitly the cause of his betrayal. In Luke, he is corrupted by Satan and then he approaches the authorities. This cursory portrayal of Judas in the Synoptics is in sharp contrast to what we see in John, who goes out of his way to characterize him as corrupt from the beginning.

**11. daturos:** Supply *esse*: "they promised that they would give him money."

### Matthew 26:14–16

**15. vultis:** second person plural present indicative of *volo.* **argenteos:** "silver [pieces]." This is the famed thirty pieces of silver, which was the price of a slave in Exodus 21:32; Judas was bought by the authorities and made their slave.

### Luke 22:3–6

**6. sine turbā:** This is the key to the plot. The authorities know that they can't openly arrest Jesus, so they need information on where he would be apart from a crowd. Judas offers them that information.

# Mark 14:12–16

## *A Place Is Found for the Passover Meal*

Jesus sends two of his disciples into Jerusalem to secure a place for the Passover meal. He tells them that they will find a man carrying a pitcher of water and he will tell them where their dining hall will be.

**12** Et primo die Azymorum, quando Pascha immolabant,
dicunt ei discipuli eius, "Quo vis eamus et paremus,
ut manduces Pascha?" **13** Et mittit duos ex discipulis
suis et dicit eis, "Ite in civitatem, et occurret vobis
homo lagoenam aquae baiulans. Sequimini eum, **14** et,
quocumque introierit, dicite domino domūs,

## Matthew 26:17–19

**17** Primā autem Azymorum accesserunt discipuli ad Iesum,
dicentes, "Ubi vis paremus tibi comedere Pascha?" **18** Ille autem
dixit, "Ite in civitatem ad quendam et dicite ei,

## Luke 22:7–13

**7** Vēnit autem dies Azymorum, in quā necesse erat occīdi Pascha.
**8** Et misit Petrum et Ioannem, dicens, "Euntes parate nobis Pascha,
ut manducemus." **9** At illi dixerunt ei, "Ubi vis paremus?" **10** Et
dixit ad eos, "Ecce: introeuntibus vobis in civitatem, occurret vobis
homo amphoram aquae portans. Sequimini eum in domum, in quam
intrat. **11** Et dicetis patri familias domūs,

## Vocabulary

**amphora, -ae,** *f.*, large transport vase
**baiulo (1),** to carry
**immolo (1),** to roast; burn as part of a sacrifice
**lagoena, -ae,** *f.*, earthenware vessel; vase
**quo,** to what place; to where

## Historical and Grammatical Notes

### Mark 14:12–16

12. **Et primo die Azymorum, quando Pascha immolabant:** *Pascha* is used here to mean the lamb offering for the Passover, not the Passover itself. Jesus sends out his two disciples to find a place for the Passover meal, which would take place in the evening—therefore on the next day. By Jewish custom, a new day starts at sundown, not at midnight as it does in our way of defining a day. For the purposes of the celebration of the Passover, the entire city of Jerusalem was deemed sacred, and all Passover meals had to take place in a domestic setting within the walls of the city. Visitors, therefore, had to find someone who would allow them room at their table or grant them a room in their house for the meal. **Quo vis eamus et paremus:** Supply *ut* after *eamus* for the indirect command: "Where do you want us to go and make preparations." **Pascha:** Here it means the Passover meal.

13. **homo:** Carrying a water jug was a woman's task. Hence a man carrying water would have stood out. It appears that Jesus has allies living inside the city and that this is a prearranged meeting. These secretive measures were surely prudent, because it's clear from the narrative that Jesus was being targeted by the authorities. People associated with him could risk bringing down the suspicion of the authorities on themselves, even if all they were doing was being good Jews and welcoming guests into their homes on the Passover. **Sequimini:** imperative.

### Matthew 26:17–19

18. **ad quendam:** There's no prearrangement in Matthew. The disciples are merely to walk up to "somebody" and tell him that he is going to be having guests for the Passover meal. Again, this isn't as odd as it may seem, since residents of Jerusalem were probably used to drop-in guests from outside of the city for the Passover.

### Luke 22:7–13

7. **in quā necesse erat occīdi Pascha:** "on which the Passover had to be observed."

9. **vis paremus:** = *vis [ut] paremus.*

# Mark 14:12–16 (cont.)

'Magister dicit, "Ubi est refectio mea, ubi Pascha cum discipulis meis manducem?" ' **15** Et ipse vobis demonstrabit cenaculum grande stratum paratum. Et illic parate nobis." **16** Et abierunt discipuli et venerunt in civitatem et invenerunt, sicut dixerat illis, et paraverunt Pascha.

## Matthew 26:17–19 (cont.)

'Magister dicit, "Tempus meum prope est. Apud te facio Pascha cum discipulis meis." ' " **19** Et fecerunt discipuli, sicut constituit illis Iesus, et paraverunt Pascha.

## Luke 22:7–13 (cont.)

'Dicit tibi magister, "Ubi est deversorium, ubi Pascha cum discipulis meis manducem?" ' **12** Ipse vobis ostendet cenaculum magnum stratum. Ibi parate." **13** Euntes autem invenerunt, sicut dixit illis, et paraverunt Pascha.

## Vocabulary

**cenaculum, -i,** *n.,* dining room
**deversorium, -ii,** *n.,* living room
**grandis, -e,** large
**refectio, -ionis,** *f.,* dining room

## Historical and Grammatical Notes

### Mark 14:12–16 (cont.)

**15. cenaculum grande stratum paratum:** "a big, laid-out, prepared dining room." **stratum:** with rugs on the floor and linen on the table. It shouldn't be terribly surprising that the man would have a room all ready to go. Residents of Jerusalem were probably accustomed to receiving unexpected guests from outside of the city for the Passover meal. **Et illic parate nobis:** The meal would have been lamb, bitter herbs, wine, and unleavened bread.

# Mark 14:17–25

## *The Passover Feast*

It is now Thursday evening, which is equivalent to the beginning of Friday according to the Jewish way of reckoning days. Jesus and his twelve disciples have entered the man's house and are eating the Passover meal. Jesus says that one of them will betray him and offers them bread and wine that he says are his body and blood.

**17** Et vespere facto, vĕnit cum Duodecim. **18** Et
discumbentibus eis et manducantibus, ait Iesus, "Amen
dico vobis, unus ex vobis me tradet, qui manducat
mecum." **19** Coeperunt contristari et dicere ei singillatim,
"Numquid ego?" **20** Qui ait illis, "Unus ex Duodecim, qui
intingit mecum in catino. **21** Nam filius quidem hominis
vadit, sicut scriptum est de eo. Vae autem homini illi, per
quem filius hominis traditur! Bonum est ei, si non esset
natus homo ille."

### Matthew 26:20–29

**20** Vespere autem facto, discumbebat cum Duodecim. **21** Et
edentibus illis dixit, "Amen dico vobis, unus vestrum me traditurus
est." **22** Et contristati valde, coeperunt singuli dicere ei, "Numquid
ego sum, Domine?" **23** At ipse respondens ait, "Qui intingit mecum
manum in paropside, hĭc me tradet. **24** Filius quidem hominis vadit,
sicut scriptum est de illo. Vae autem homini illi, per quem filius
hominis traditur! Bonum erat ei, si natus non fuisset homo ille." **25**
Respondens autem Iudas, qui tradidit eum, dixit, "Numquid ego
sum, Rabbi?" Ait illi, "Tu dixisti."

### Luke 22:14–23

**14** Et cum facta esset hora, discubuit, et apostoli cum eo.

# Vocabulary

**catinus, -i,** *m.*, serving bowl
**intinguo, intingere, intinxi, intinctus,** to dip; soak
**paropsis, -idis,** *f.*, dish
**singillatim,** one at a time; individually
**singulus, -a, -um,** individual; one

# Historical and Grammatical Notes

## Mark 14:17–25

**17. vespere facto:** This would make it Preparation Day (the day before the Sabbath), since a new day begins at sunset, not at midnight.

**18. discumbentibus eis et manducantibus:** Jesus makes his accusation during the meal. The Passover feast observed a strict tradition of songs, prayers, and responses (Ex 7:1–23). It would surely have been startling for Jesus to make the accusation in this context, not just because of what he said, but because of the setting.

**20. qui intingit mecum in catino:** presumably one of those sitting close to him. Another interpretation is that Jesus means everyone at the table, since this was a common meal.

**21. scriptum est de eo:** The only Old Testament passage that comes close to fitting this proclamation is Daniel 7:21, which speaks generally of how the righteous must suffer. **Bonum est ei, si non esset natus homo ille:** Thus Jesus refutes the possible line of argument that the traitor is guiltless because he was acting in accordance with God's will. It's God's will *and* the traitor is guilty.

## Matthew 26:20–29

**25. Respondens autem Iudas:** We've already been told that each one of the Twelve protested that he would not betray Jesus, so it seems unnecessary for Matthew to have Judas speak out separately. It might be a way for Matthew to say that Jesus knew who it was going to be, and not that he knew only one of the Twelve would do it.

# Mark 14:17–25 (cont.)

**22** Et manducantibus illis, accepit panem et benedicens fregit et dedit eis et ait, "Sumite. Hoc est corpus meum."

## Matthew 26:20–29 (cont.)

**26** Cenantibus autem eis, accepit Iesus panem et benedixit ac fregit deditque discipulis et ait, "Accipite. Comedite. Hoc est corpus meum."

## Luke 22:14–23 (cont.)

**15** Et ait illis, "Desiderio desideravi hŏc Pascha manducare
vobiscum, antequam patiar. **16** Dico enim vobis, non manducabo
illud, donec impleatur in regno Dei." **17** Et accepto calice, gratias
egit et dixit, "Accipite hoc et dividite inter vos.

## Vocabulary

**antequam,** before

**desiderium, -ii,** *n.,* longing; desire

## Historical and Grammatical Notes

### Mark 14:17–25 (cont.)

**22. accepit panem:** Jesus offers the bread well into the meal, another departure from tradition, as the bread would have been passed around at the beginning of the meal. What were the disciples using to dip into the bowl of oil and herbs if not bread? **benedicens:** The Greek word is *eucharistēsas.* Hence the word "eucharist" is used to refer to this event and to the celebration of communion. **Sumite. Hoc est corpus meum:** These actions are such a familiar a part of Christian ritual that it is hard to imagine how shocking they must have been to the disciples. Stripped of their subsequent theological significance, the breaking of the bread as his body and the offering of the wine as his blood may not be an offer of grace so much as expressions of Jesus's dismay and anger with his disciples. This scene is framed by betrayal and abandonment. Consequently, Jesus may be saying something along these lines: "One of you here is going to betray me! Is that what you want? Here! Take this bread and eat it! Imagine it's my body! Go ahead. Eat me alive! And the wine? Think of it as my blood. Drink up!" There is clear evidence, however, that his earliest followers did not understand the scene this way. The ritual recreation of the Passover meal, together with the breaking of bread and the offering of the wine, was observed by the earliest Christians and continuously throughout the ages.

### Luke 22:14–23 (cont.)

**15. Desiderio desideravi:** "I desire with a desire." Though jarring in English, the repetition of cognate words isn't so odd in Latin or Greek. **hŏc Pascha:** *Pascha* can mean the Passover feast, the day of the Passover feast, or the meal eaten at the Passover feast. It means the latter here.

**16. donec impleatur in regno Dei:** Does this mean that Jesus didn't eat the meal with his disciples?

**19. Hoc est corpus:** Our word "hocus-pocus" may come from this. It was meant as a slur by Protestants against Catholic priests who could barely pronounce the Latin they repeated at Mass. Instead of distinctly intoning *hoc est corpus,* they could manage only to mumble something that sounded liked "hocus-pocus."

# Mark 14:17–25 (cont.)

**23** Et accepto calice, gratias agens dedit eis. Et biberunt
ex illo omnes. **24** Et ait illis, "Hĭc est sanguis meus novi
testamenti, qui pro multis effunditur. **25** Amen dico vobis,
iam non bibam de genimine vitis usque in diem illum,
cum illud bibam novum in regno Dei."

## Matthew 26:20–29 (cont.)

**27** Et accipiens calicem, gratias egit et dedit illis, dicens, "Bibite ex
hoc omnes. **28** Hĭc est enim sanguis meus novi testamenti, qui pro
multis effunditur in remissionem peccatorum. **29** Dico autem vobis,
non bibam amodo de hoc genimine vitis usque in diem illum, cum
illud bibam vobiscum novum in regno Patris mei."

## Luke 22:14–23 (cont.)

**18** Dico enim vobis, non bibam amodo de generatione vitis, donec
regnum Dei veniat." **19** Et accepto pane, gratias egit et fregit et dedit
eis, dicens, "Hoc est corpus meum, quod pro vobis datur. Hoc facite
in meam commemorationem." **20** Similiter et calicem, postquam
cenavit, dicens, "Hĭc calix novum testamentum est in sanguine
meo, qui pro vobis funditur. **21** Verumtamen ecce: manus tradentis
me mecum est in mensā, **22** et quidem filius hominis, secundum
quod definitum est, vadit. Verumtamen vae illi homini, per quem
traditur!" **23** Et ipsi coeperunt quaerere inter se quis esset ex eis, qui
hoc facturus esset.

## Vocabulary

**amodo,** from this time forward
**commemoratio, -ionis,** *f.*, commemoration
**definio, -ire, -ii** *or* **-ivi, -itus,** to determine
**genimen, geniminis,** *n.*, fruit
**verumtamen,** but truly
**vitis, -is,** *f.*, grapevine

## Historical and Grammatical Notes

### Mark 14:17–25 (cont.)

**23. biberunt ex illo omnes:** The disciples drink from the chalice before they are told its significance. Drinking the blood of a sacrificial victim was certainly not a Jewish custom. **Hĭc est sanguis meus novi testamenti:** All sacrifices were intended in part to affirm, restore, and recommence a relationship with the divine. The slaughter of the lamb and its blood reminded everyone of what God had done in the past, asked God for his forgiveness for their failures, and started another contract with him. That's what Jesus is modeling his comments after.

**25. non bibam de genimine vitis:** Jesus will be dead before the day is over. **illud bibam novum:** This probably means "until I drink wine again," instead of "until I drink that new [wine]."

### Matthew 26:20–29 (cont.)

**28. in remissionem peccatorum:** This is an essential purpose of sacrifice in many cultures. It is a way of offering the divine tangible evidence of regret and sorrow for transgressions.

**29. vobiscum:** The Kingdom of God is often depicted as a celestial feast (Mt 22:2) with seating at the table for special guests only. In Matthew, Jesus assures the disciples that, with the exception of Judas, they will have positions of authority in the future kingdom.

### Luke 22:14–23 (cont.)

**19. Hoc facite in meam commemorationem:** "Do this in remembrance of me." Only Luke records the formula that is so well known in Christian masses.

**21. me:** This is the object of the participle *tradentis*.

**23. qui:** relative clause of characteristic: "who of them would be such as to do this."

# Mark 14:26–31

## *Jesus Predicts That His Disciples Will Abandon Him*

After the Passover meal, Jesus turns on his disciples and predicts that their devotion to him will collapse when he is arrested. Peter tries to distinguish the depth of his commitment from that of the other disciples, but Jesus tells him that he'll turn down three chances to profess his faith.

**26** Et hymno dicto, exierunt in Montem Olivarum. **27**
Et ait eis Iesus, "Omnes scandalizabimini, quia scriptum
est, 'Percutiam pastorem, et dispergentur oves.' **28** Sed
posteaquam resurrexero, praecedam vos in Galilaeam."
**29** Petrus autem ait ei, "Et si omnes scandalizati fuerint,
sed non ego." **30** Et ait illi Iesus, "Amen dico tibi, tu
hodie, in nocte hāc, priusquam bis gallus vocem dederit,
ter me es negaturus." **31** At ille amplius loquebatur, "Et
si oportuerit me commori tibi, non te negabo." Similiter
autem et omnes dicebant.

### Matthew 26:30–35

**30** Et hymno dicto, exierunt in Montem Oliveti. **31** Tunc dicit
illis Iesus, "Omnes vos scandalum patiemini in me in istā nocte.
Scriptum est enim, 'Percutiam pastorem, et dispergentur oves
gregis.' **32** Postquam autem resurrexero, praecedam vos in
Galilaeam." **33** Respondens autem Petrus ait illi, "Et si omnes
scandalizati fuerint in te, ego numquam scandalizabor." **34** Ait illi
Iesus, "Amen dico tibi, in hāc nocte, antequam gallus cantet, ter me
negabis." **35** Ait illi Petrus, "Etiam si oportuerit me mori tecum, non
te negabo." Similiter et omnes discipuli dixerunt.

### Luke 22:33–34

**33** Qui [Petrus] dixit ei, "Domine, tecum paratus sum et in carcerem
et in mortem ire." **34** Et ille dixit, "Dico tibi, Petre, non cantabit
hodie gallus donec ter abneges nosse me."

## Vocabulary

**bis,** twice
**canto (1),** to sing; crow
**commorior, -mori -mortuus sum,** to die with
**dispergo, -gere, -si, -sus,** to scatter
**percutio, -tere, -ssi, -ssus,** to strike; beat
**posteaquam,** after
**priusquam,** before
**ter,** three times

## Historical and Grammatical Notes

### Mark 14:26–31

**26. hymno dicto:** The Passover meal traditionally ended with the chanting of a group of poems (Pss 113–18), which collectively made up the Hallel ("praise").

**27. Omnes scandalizabimini:** "You all will be shaken from your faith." **quia scriptum est:** Zechariah 13:7: "Strike down the shepherd and the sheep will scatter."

**28. praecedam vos in Galilaeam:** Jesus tells them just how quickly he will be resurrected. He will be in Galilee before they can get back.

**29. sed non ego:** Supply *scandalizabor*. Again we see Peter trying to exalt himself over the other disciples: "Maybe *they* will. But *I* won't." Jesus delivers a stern reproach: "You're going to be the most shameful!" Peter, at least, follows Jesus into the court where the trial takes place, while the other disciples run away. But that only makes his denial all the more manifest.

**30. Tu hodie, in nocte hāc:** that is, before the sun comes up on the morning of Preparation Day, the day before the Sabbath. **priusquam bis . . . ter:** This will be fulfilled in Mark 14:66–72. Contrary to common misconceptions, roosters don't wait until the sunrise to crow. They regularly crow anytime from midnight to dawn, and even throughout the day. They aren't at all a reliable way to keep time. It's likely that Jesus isn't referring to a living bird, but to the trumpet blasts that mark the passage from the third to the fourth nighttime watch at approximately 3 a.m. The trumpet blast was called the *gallicinium*, < *gallus* + *cano*.

### Matthew 26:30–35

**34. antequam gallus cantet:** Matthew drops the *bis*. When this prophecy is fulfilled in Matthew at 26:69–75, Peter denies Jesus three times and then the "rooster" crows for the one and only time.

### Luke 22:33–34

**34. nosse:** *novisse.*

# Mark 14:32–42

## *Jesus Grieves at Gethsemane While His Disciples Sleep*

After the Passover meal, Jesus and his disciples leave Jerusalem for their residence somewhere on Mt. Olive. When they arrive at Gethsemane along the way, Jesus takes Peter, James, and John with him while the others are told to wait behind. Up to this point, this appears only to be another instance where Jesus goes to pray at a defining moment of his mission. What follows, however, is a complete surprise. Jesus begins to be troubled and distressed to the point of begging God not to go through with his plan for him. While he is tormented by terror and doubt, the three disciples fall asleep, despite Jesus's repeated command that they stay awake and keep watch.

**32** Et veniunt in praedium, cui nomen Gethsemani, et ait
discipulis suis, "Sedete hīc, donec orem." **33** Et assumit
Petrum et Iacobum et Ioannem secum et coepit pavere
et taedere. **34** Et ait illis, "Tristis est anima mea usque ad
mortem. Sustinete hīc et vigilate."

## Matthew 26:36–45

**36** Tunc venit Iesus cum illis in praedium, quod dicitur Gethsemani.
Et dicit discipulis, "Sedete hīc, donec vadam illuc et orem." **37**
Et assumpto Petro et duobus filiis Zebedaei, coepit contristari et
maestus esse. **38** Tunc ait illis, "Tristis est anima mea usque ad
mortem. Sustinete hīc et vigilate mecum."

## Luke 22:39–46

**39** Et egressus ibat secundum consuetudinem in Montem Olivarum.
Secuti sunt autem illum et discipuli.

# Vocabulary

**maestus, -a, -um,** gloomy; despondent, depressed

**paveo, pavere, pavi,** to tremble with fear

**praedium, -i,** *n.,* farm; field

**taedeo, -ere,** to be tired; be stressed

# Historical and Grammatical Notes

### Mark 14:32–42

**32. Gethsemeni:** locative. The word means "oil press" in Aramaic. The location is not known, but Jesus and his disciples would have needed a rest stop as they went back and forth between Jerusalem and their residence somewhere on Mt. Olive.

**33. assumit Petrum et Iacobum et Ioannem:** Given Jesus's terror about what is going to happen to him, perhaps he asked the three to accompany him not for some theological reason but because he didn't want to be alone. The three might also have served as bodyguards, in case his arrest occurred when he was separated from the rest and before he was emotionally ready for the final sequence of events. **coepit pavere et taedere:** These words, and this scene, have precipitated many theological issues for Christians. How could Jesus be genuinely stricken by the suffering he's bound to endure by God's will?

**34. Sustinete hīc et vigilate:** There's a literary problem with the scene, or we might call it a problem with the setting. Until now, everything in Mark is set up in such as way that there are witnesses to everything recorded in the text. But here the only people who could have witnessed Jesus's anguish are either kept at a distance or are asleep. How could Jesus's prayers and torment have been recorded or remembered by anyone? Did Mark simply guess what Jesus would have said or might have said at this point? From what point of view, or from what evidence, do these prayers make their way into the Christian texts?

### Luke 22:39–46

**39. secundum consuetudinem:** "according to his usual practice." **et discipuli:** We're not told who was singled out to accompany him. Perhaps all the disciples went with him. It would solve the problem of the setting of Jesus's arrest in Mark and Matthew, which happens while he's speaking and in front of all the disciples.

# Mark 14:32–42 (cont.)

**35** Et cum processisset paululum, procidebat super
terram et orabat, ut, si fieri posset, transiret ab eo hora.
**36** Et dicebat, "Abba (Pater)! Omnia tibi possibilia sunt.
Transfer calicem hunc a me. Sed non quod ego volo, sed
quod tu." **37** Et vēnit et invēnit eos dormientes, et ait
Petro, "Simon, dormis? Non potuisti unā horā vigilare? **38**
Vigilate et orate, ut non intretis in tentationem. Spiritus
quidem promptus, caro vero infirma."

## Matthew 26:36–45 (cont.)

**39** Et progressus pusillum, procidit in faciem suam orans et, dicens,
"Pater mi, si possibile est, transeat a me calix iste. Verumtamen
non sicut ego volo, sed sicut tu." **40** Et vĕnit ad discipulos et invĕnit
eos dormientes, et dicit Petro, "Sic non potuistis unā horā vigilare
mecum? **41** Vigilate et orate, ut non intretis in tentationem. Spiritus
quidem promptus est, caro autem infirma."

## Luke 22:39–46 (cont.)

**40** Et cum pervenisset ad locum, dixit illis, "Orate, ne intretis in
tentationem." **41** Et ipse avulsus est ab eis, quantum iactus est
lapidis, et, positis genibus, orabat, **42** dicens, "Pater, si vis, transfer
calicem istum a me. Verumtamen non mea voluntas sed tua fiat."
**43** Apparuit autem illi angelus de caelo, confortans eum. Et factus
in agoniā prolixius orabat. **44** Et factus est sudor eius sicut guttae
sanguinis decurrentis in terram. **45** Et cum surrexisset ab oratione et
venisset ad discipulos, invēnit eos dormientes prae tristitiā, **46** et ait
illis, "Quid dormitis? Surgite. Orate, ne intretis in tentationem."

# Vocabulary

**Abba,** *indecl.,* father
**avello, -vellere, -velli** *or* **-vulsi** *or* **-volsi, -vulsus** *or* **-volsus,** to separate
**gutta, -ae,** *f.,* drop
**paululum,** a little
**promptus, -a, -um,** ready at hand; prepared
**sudor, -is,** *m.,* sweat
**tristitia, -ae,** *f.,* sorrow

# Historical and Grammatical Notes

## Mark 14:32–42 (cont.)

37. **Simon:** This is the only time in Mark that Jesus addresses anyone by name, and he uses Peter's real name and not the nickname he gave him. It suggests a genuine tenderness he has for Peter. Both Matthew and Luke delete it.

38. **ut non intretis in tentationem:** This seems to have no immediate application to the present scene. Jesus might have been speaking to a wider concern or to a wider audience. A constant theme in the "Little Apocalypse" of chapter 13 is that believers should be on guard for the signs of the end of time, but that's not temptation. It's not surprising at all that the three would have fallen asleep. It's late at night, or early in the morning, and they've just finished a large meal.

## Luke 22:39–46 (cont.)

41. **quantum iactus est lapidis:** Luke indicates that the disciples would have been able to see Jesus if they had a clear line of sight, perhaps addressing the issue of who heard Jesus's prayers. But would they have been able to hear him at such a distance? **positis genibus:** Jesus prays much less abjectly than in Mark and Matthew, where he throws himself face-first upon the ground. Jesus doesn't groan or cry out loud in terror or dread. His prayer to God is more measured, and he is even comforted by an angel, which presumably keeps him from the depths of the pain we see in Mark.

45. **prae tristitiā:** "because of their sorrow."

46. **Quid dormitis:** "why are you sleeping." Luke redoes the imperatives to make Jesus's comment sound more like a rebuke.

# Mark 14:32–42 (cont.)

**39** Et iterum abiens oravit, eundem sermonem dicens.
**40** Et veniens denuo invēnit eos dormientes. Erant enim
oculi illorum ingravati, et ignorabant quid responderent
ei. **41** Et vĕnit tertio et ait illis, "Dormite iam et requiescite.
Sufficit. Vēnit hora. Ecce: traditur filius hominis in manūs
peccatorum. **42** Surgite. Eamus. Ecce: qui me tradit,
prope est."

## Matthew 26:36–45 (cont.)

**42** Iterum secundo abiit et oravit, dicens, "Pater mi, si non potest
hoc transire, nisi bibam illud, fiat voluntas tua." **43** Et venit iterum
et invēnit eos dormientes. Erant enim oculi eorum gravati. **44** Et
relictis illis, iterum abiit et oravit tertio, eundem sermonem iterum
dicens. **45** Tunc vĕnit ad discipulos et dicit illis, "Dormite iam et
requiescite. Ecce: appropinquavit hora, et filius hominis traditur in
manūs peccatorum."

## Vocabulary

**denuo,** anew; once again

**ingravo (1),** to be heavy; weighed down

## Historical and Grammatical Notes

### MARK 14:32–42 (CONT.)

41. **Dormite iam et requiescite:** Jesus gives up trying to wake them and speaks somewhat tenderly as they sleep: "Sleep and rest."

### MATTHEW 26:36–45 (CONT.)

42. **secundo:** "for a second time."

44. **tertio:** "for a third time." **eundem sermonem iterum dicens:** It's always the same prayer. Jesus asks God to find another way, but if it's necessary that he suffer, then so be it.

# Mark 14:43–52

## *Jesus Is Arrested*

The Jewish leaders finally act against Jesus. With the help of Judas, they arrest him after a brief but violent confrontation with one of his followers. As predicted, his followers run away once it's clear that Jesus will not resist.

**43** Et confestim, adhuc eo loquente, vĕnit Iudas unus
ex Duodecim, et cum illo turba cum gladiis et lignis a
summis sacerdotibus et scribis et senioribus. **44** Dederat
autem traditor eius signum eis, dicens, "Quemcumque
osculatus fuero, ipse est. Tenete eum et ducite caute." **45**
Et cum venisset, statim accedens ad eum ait, "Rabbi," et
osculatus est eum. **46** At illi manūs iniecerunt in eum et
tenuerunt eum.

## Matthew 26:47–56

**47** Et adhuc ipso loquente, ecce: Iudas, unus de Duodecim, vēnit,
et cum eo turba multa cum gladiis et fustibus, missi a principibus
sacerdotum et senioribus populi. **48** Qui autem tradidit eum, dedit
illis signum, dicens, "Quemcumque osculatus fuero, ipse est. Tenete
eum." **49** Et confestim accedens ad Iesum dixit, "Ave, Rabbi!" et
osculatus est eum. **50** Iesus autem dixit illi, "Amice, ad quod venisti!"
Tunc accesserunt et manūs iniecerunt in Iesum et tenuerunt eum.

## Luke 22:47–53

**47** Adhuc eo loquente, ecce: turba. Et, qui vocabatur Iudas, unus de
Duodecim, antecedebat eos et appropinquavit Iesu, ut oscularetur
eum. **48** Iesus autem dixit ei, "Iuda, osculo filium hominis tradis?"

## Vocabulary

**antecedo, -cedere, -cessi, -cessus,** to go before; step forward
**caute,** carefully; under guard
**fustis, -is,** *m.,* club
**lignum, -i,** *n.,* wood; wooden club
**traditor, -is,** *m.,* traitor

## Historical and Grammatical Notes

### Mark 14:43–52

**43. confestim, adhuc eo loquente:** "immediately while he was still speaking." This doesn't quite fit with the previous passage. Jesus was alone with Peter, James, and John. Yet when he is arrested, Jesus is back with his disciples and at least one other person. How can we account for this? One possible explanation is that Mark is using two sources for the passion narrative and they didn't quite fit together at this point. **vĕnit Iudas:** He must have split off from the other disciples without being noticed.

**44. Dederat:** The pluperfect is quite logical. They agreed to this sign before Jesus was apprehended. It's not surprising that the gang sent by the authorities would need to have Jesus pointed out to them. Jesus was well known and would have been easily recognized by those whom he'd debated with, but not by the henchmen sent to arrest him.

**46. manūs:** accusative object of *inicerunt*: "they laid their hands on him." Jesus had never been touched by anyone before in Mark. He has touched others during cures and twice someone touched his garment, but this is the first time that Jesus's body is touched by someone who initiated the action. In this scene, Jesus is first kissed by Judas and then seized physically by his assailants. It's as if some barrier between Jesus and the world has been breached. It's fitting, therefore, that they initiate the sequence of events that lead to his death.

### Matthew 26:47–56

**50. ad quod venisti:** a statement: "This is what you've come for," not a question: "What have you come for?" It's clear that Jesus knew everything about the plot, including the signal that Judas had prearranged with the authorities.

# Mark 14:43–52 (cont.)

**47** Unus autem quidam de circumstantibus educens
gladium percussit servum summi sacerdotis et amputavit
illi auriculam. **48** Et respondens Iesus ait illis, "Tamquam
ad latronem existis cum gladiis et lignis comprehendere
me? **49** Cotidie eram apud vos in Templo docens, et
non me tenuistis? Sed adimpleantur Scripturae." **50** Et
relinquentes eum omnes fugerunt. **51** Et adulescens
quidam sequebatur eum amictus sindone super nudo, et
tenent eum. **52** At ille, reiectā sindone, nudus profugit.

## Matthew 26:47–56 (cont.)

**51** Et ecce: unus ex his, qui erant cum Iesu, extendens manum exemit
gladium suum et percutiens servum principis sacerdotum amputavit
auriculam eius. **52** Tunc ait illi Iesus, "Converte gladium tuum in
locum suum. Omnes enim, qui acceperint gladium, gladio peribunt.
**53** An putas quia non possum rogare Patrem meum, et exhibebit mihi
modo plus quam duodecim legiones angelorum? **54** Quomodo ergo
implebuntur scripturae quia sic oportet fieri." **55** In illā horā dixit
Iesus turbis, "Tamquam ad latronem existis cum gladiis et fustibus
comprehendere me? Cotidie apud vos sedebam docens in Templo,
et non me tenuistis? **56** Hoc autem totum factum est ut implerentur
scripturae prophetarum." Tunc discipuli omnes, relicto eo, fugerunt.

## Luke 22:47–53 (cont.)

**49** Videntes autem hi, qui circa ipsum erant, quod futurum erat,
dixerunt, "Domine, si percutimus in gladio?" **50** Et percussit unus
ex illis servum principis sacerdotum et amputavit auriculam eius
dextram. **51** Respondens autem Iesus ait, "Sinite usque huc!" Et cum
tetigisset auriculam eius, sanavit eum. **52** Dixit autem Iesus ad eos,
qui venerant ad se principes sacerdotum et magistratus Templi et
seniores, "Quasi ad latronem existis cum gladiis et fustibus? **53** Cum
cotidie vobiscum fuerim in Templo, non extendistis manūs in me.
Sed haec est hora vestra et potestas tenebrarum."

## Vocabulary

**adimpleo, -ere, -evi, -etus,** to complete
**amicio, -cire, -cui** *or* **-xi, -ctus,** to clothe
**circumstantes, -ium,** *m. pl.,* bystanders
**eximo, -imere, -emi, -emptus,** to take out, remove; release
**nudus, -a, -um,** naked
**reicio, -icere, -ieci, -iectus,** to throw down; discard
**sindon, -is,** *f.,* linen; sheet; covering of fine cloth
**tenebra, -ae,** *f.,* darkness; gloom

## Historical and Grammatical Notes

### Mark 14:43–52 (cont.)

**47. quidam de circumstantibus:** one of the disciples or someone else in Jesus's company? **illi:** dative of possession. The fact that he struck the servant's ear means that he was trying for his head and missed. He was trying to kill him.

**48. Tamquam ad latronem:** "like [to] a rebel." The word used here does not mean "thief," as it is often translated. It is the same word used for a revolutionary, a leader of a band of insurrectionists aiming at throwing off Roman rule and punishing their Jewish collaborators.

**49. Sed adimpleantur Scripturae:** This summarizes Jesus's general understanding of what is happening, not how it has happened. There's no Old Testament passage that specifies that the Messiah or the "suffering servant" would be arrested in this fashion. It's more of a sigh of submission: Let the Scriptures be fulfilled however they need to be.

**50. relinquentes eum:** Giving up any hope of resistance, the disciples and others who may have been present scatter, just as Jesus predicted.

**51. adulescens:** Only Mark mentions the young man dressed in linen. This is such a surprising and mysterious addition that many have speculated that the young man is none other than the author of this Gospel himself.

### Matthew 26:47–56 (cont.)

**54. quia sic oportet fieri:** "since it is supposed to happen this way."

### Luke 22:47–53 (cont.)

**51. Sinite usque huc:** literally: "Allow up to this!" = "That's enough!" or "No more of this!"

**53. Sed haec est hora vestra et potestas tenebrarum:** Jesus accuses them of being able to work their will only under the cover of darkness.

# Mark 14:53–65

## *Jesus before the Jewish Authorities*

Events move very quickly now. Jesus is brought before the Jewish authorities for a hearing of the charges. The case against Jesus begins to fall apart when the witnesses they've brought forth contradict one another. Finally the high priest demands to know whether Jesus thinks he is the Messiah. When Jesus says that he is, there is a great commotion and the assembly declares Jesus guilty of blasphemy. They physically abuse him.

**53** Et adduxerunt Iesum ad summum sacerdotem. Et
conveniunt omnes summi sacerdotes et seniores et scribae.
**54** Et Petrus a longe secutus est eum usque intro in atrium
summi sacerdotis et sedebat cum ministris et calefaciebat
se ad ignem.

### Matthew 26:57–68

**57** Illi autem tenentes Iesum duxerunt ad Caipham, principem
sacerdotum, ubi scribae et seniores convenerant. **58** Petrus autem
sequebatur eum a longe usque in aulam principis sacerdotum. Et
ingressus intro sedebat cum ministris, ut videret finem.

### Luke 22:54–71

**54** Comprehendentes autem eum, duxerunt et introduxerunt in
domum principis sacerdotum. Petrus vero sequebatur a longe. **55**
Accenso autem igni in medio atrio et circumsedentibus illis, sedebat
Petrus in medio eorum. [**56–65** *Luke inserts Peter's three denials at this point. They are deleted here and reproduced in this text as a parallel to Mark's account in the next periocope.*]

## Vocabulary

**calefacio, -facere, -feci, -factus,** to warm

**intro,** inside

## Historical and Grammatical Notes

### Mark 14:53–65

**53. conveniunt omnes:** This appears to be a formal hearing of a part of the Sanhedrin court. Whether it follows the customs or legal requirements of an official trial is immaterial to how Mark presents it. The fix is in and the hearing is only to give the appearance of a fair trial.

**54. usque intro in atrium:** "until the inside of the courtyard." It's thus possible that Peter heard the proceedings within.

# Mark 14:53–65 (cont.)

**55** Summi vero sacerdotes et omne concilium quaerebant
adversus Iesum testimonium, ut eum morte afficerent, nec
inveniebant. **56** Multi enim testimonium falsum dicebant
adversus eum, et convenientia testimonia non erant. **57** Et
quidam surgentes falsum testimonium ferebant adversus
eum dicentes, **58** "Nos audivimus eum dicentem, 'Ego
dissolvam Templum hoc manū factum, et intra triduum
aliud non manū factum aedificabo.' " **59** Et ne ita quidem
conveniens erat testimonium illorum.

## Matthew 26:57–68 (cont.)

**59** Principes autem sacerdotum et omne concilium quaerebant
falsum testimonium contra Iesum, ut eum morti traderent, **60** et non
invenerunt, cum multi falsi testes accessissent. Novissime autem
venientes duo **61** dixerunt, "Hĭc dixit, 'Possum destruere Templum
Dei et post triduum aedificare illud.' "

## Vocabulary

**conveniens, -ntis,** consistent; in agreement

**dissolvo, -vere, -vi, -utus,** to break down; destroy; take apart

**testis, -is,** *m./f.,* witness

## Historical and Grammatical Notes

### Mark 14:53–65 (cont.)

**55. ut eum morte afficerent:** "so that they could put him to death." There's an intense debate about whether the Sanhedrin had the authority under the terms of the Roman occupation to conduct a capital trial. It does appear in Mark that the authorities were acting only like a grand jury, as a prelude to the official arraignment before the Romans. But we can't press Mark's evidence very far. He's uninterested in the precise legal niceties. He may actually have been unaware of the distinction between a hearing and a trial, as many people today would be hard pressed to state the difference between a grand jury and a trial. He's a Gospel writer, not a scribe. **nec inveniebant:** They found reasons to be annoyed with him—his lax and contentious understanding of the law, for example—but they aren't finding crimes that would merit the death penalty.

**58. Ego dissolvam Templum:** The testimony here appears to be a mélange of things that Jesus did say. He did say that the Temple was going to be destroyed in the "Little Apocalypse" of chapter 13. He also talked about a resurrection in three days, though he didn't mean the resurrection of the Temple. It's also possible that Jesus did in fact say what he's accused of saying sometime during his mission and that it's not included for one reason or another in Mark's Gospel. This bit of evidence is singled out because it's a threat against the Temple itself, a blasphemy meriting a death sentence.

**59. ne ita quidem:** "Not even in this charge" was their evidence consistent.

### Matthew 26:57–68 (cont.)

**60. et non invenerunt:** They say that they were seeking *false* testimony and they couldn't even get their witnesses to tell the same stories!

# Mark 14:53–65 (cont.)

**60** Et exsurgens summus sacerdos in medium interrogavit
Iesum, dicens, "Non respondes quidquam ad ea, quae
isti testantur adversum te?" **61** Ille autem tacebat et nihil
respondit. Rursum summus sacerdos interrogabat eum et
dicit ei, "Tu es Christus, filius Benedicti?"

## Matthew 26:57–68 (cont.)

**62** Et surgens princeps sacerdotum ait illi, "Nihil respondes? Quid
isti adversum te testificantur?" **63** Iesus autem tacebat. Et princeps
sacerdotum ait illi, "Adiuro te per Deum vivum, ut dicas nobis, si tu
es Christus, filius Dei."

## Luke 22:54–71 (cont.)

**66** Et ut factus est dies, convenerunt seniores plebis et principes
sacerdotum et scribae et duxerunt illum in concilium suum, **67**
dicentes, "Si tu es Christus, dic nobis."

## Vocabulary

**rursum,** again

**testor, -ari, testatus sum,** to testify; bear witness

## Historical and Grammatical Notes

### Mark 14:53–65 (cont.)

**60. summus sacerdos:** He is probably irritated that the case they'd been preparing is falling apart. He interrupts the proceedings because they aren't leading anywhere and cuts to the real concern they have. It isn't about whether Jesus thinks this or that food or work prohibition is optional. Even the different factions in the Sanhedrin wouldn't agree on these questions. What they are hoping to find is blasphemy so serious that he can be executed. **ad ea, quae:** "to the things, which." Jesus's silence is perfectly understandable on its own terms without invoking any theological significance. The prosecution hasn't presented a coherent case yet, so what should he respond to?

### Matthew 26:57–68 (cont.)

**62. Quid:** "Why?" Matthew recognizes that the evidence doesn't make sense so it would be odd to ask Jesus to respond to it. He changes the question from why Jesus doesn't reply to the charge to why so many people are bringing charges against him.

### Luke 22:54–71 (cont.)

**66. ut factus est dies:** Until the Sanhedrin was assembled, Jesus was held at the house of the high priest. Interestingly, Luke changes the time of the trial from under the cover of darkness to daytime. The trial was more along the lines of recognized procedures and not a kangaroo court conducted under cover of darkness. The trial in Luke appears to have been more carefully and honestly conducted than it is in Mark or Matthew. He discards the false witnesses and doesn't openly accuse the authorities of bad motives.

# Mark 14:53–65 (cont.)

**62** Iesus autem dixit, "Ego sum, et videbitis filium hominis
a dextris sedentem virtutis et venientem cum nubibus
caeli." **63** Summus autem sacerdos scindens vestimenta
sua ait, "Quid adhuc necessarii sunt nobis testes? **64**
Audistis blasphemiam. Quid vobis videtur?" Qui omnes
condemnaverunt eum esse reum mortis. **65** Et coeperunt
quidam conspuere eum et velare faciem eius et colaphis
eum caedere et dicere ei, "Prophetiza!" Et ministri alapis
eum caedebant.

## Matthew 26:57–68 (cont.)

**64** Dicit illi Iesus, "Tu dixisti. Verumtamen dico vobis, 'Amodo
videbitis filium hominis sedentem a dextris Virtutis et venientem
in nubibus caeli.' " **65** Tunc princeps sacerdotum scidit vestimenta
sua, dicens, "Blasphemavit! Quid adhuc egemus testibus? Ecce:
nunc audistis blasphemiam. **66** Quid vobis videtur?" Illi autem
respondentes dixerunt, "Reus est mortis!" **67** Tunc exspuerunt in
faciem eius et colaphis eum ceciderunt. Alii autem palmas in faciem
ei dederunt, **68** dicentes, "Prophetiza nobis, Christe! Quis est, qui
te percussit?"

## Luke 22:54–71 (cont.)

Et ait illis, "Si vobis dixero, non credetis. **68** Si autem interrogavero,
non respondebitis mihi. **69** Ex hoc autem erit filius hominis sedens
a dextris virtutis Dei." **70** Dixerunt autem omnes, "Tu ergo es filius
Dei?" Qui ait ad illos, "Vos dicitis quia ego sum." **71** At illi dixerunt,
"Quid adhuc desideramus testimonium? Ipsi enim audivimus de
ore eius!"

## Vocabulary

**alapa, -ae,** *f.*, slap
**colaphus, -i,** *m.*, blow; punch
**palma, -ae,** *f.*, palm; opened hand
**scindo, scindere, scidi, scissus,** to cut; tear

## Historical and Grammatical Notes

### Mark 14:53–65 (cont.)

**62. Ego sum:** This is the critical moment in the Gospel. Jesus unambiguously reveals his true nature, fully aware that this is what they need to have him executed. There also may be some poignancy to the "I am." This is a standard translation of the Hebrew name for God (YHWH). Even pronouncing YHWH was grounds for stoning, let alone implying that one is YHWH. **virtutis:** This is a threat. Jesus says that he'll be back leading a heavenly army.

**63. scindens vestimenta sua:** This is the formal expression of outrage and grief at blasphemy.

**64. eum esse reum mortis:** "that he was guilty [of a crime worthy] of death."

**65. coeperunt quidam conspuere:** Only some of them abused Jesus. It appears to be a spontaneous expression of their personal disgust with Jesus more than an official way to conclude their business. **velare faciem eius:** They also put a hood over Jesus's head, beat him, and taunt him to guess who's hitting him.

### Matthew 26:57–68 (cont.)

**64. Tu dixisti:** Jesus continues with his riddling answers. This is a monumental change from Mark, where Jesus affirms that he is the Messiah without reservation. Caiaphas, the high priest, says that this is all the evidence he needs. He asks Jesus to answer a direct question and intensifies his question by an oath to God himself. A riddling reply from Jesus was an insult.

**66. Quid vobis videtur:** This is a formal call for their decision: "What seems right to you?"

**67. palmas in faciem ei dederunt:** "they covered his face with the palms [of their hands]." This is how Matthew renders *velare faciem*. In both, Jesus can't see what's going on. **Quis est, qui te percussit:** This is what Matthew thinks they asked: "Guess who's hitting you."

### Luke 22:54–71 (cont.)

**70. Tu ergo es filius Dei:** The court asks him twice. Once Jesus answers evasively: "You wouldn't believe me if I were to tell you." And "If I ask you, you will not answer *me*." (Some manuscripts add to this last remark "and let me go.")

# Mark 14:66–72

## *Peter Denies Knowing Jesus*

Peter trails behind as Jesus is led to his hearing before the members of the full Sanhedrin, the judicial and legislative body of the Jews. A servant woman charges Peter twice with being associated with Jesus and he denies it twice. Then others join in. He denies Jesus for a third time.

**66** Et cum esset Petrus in atrio deorsum, vĕnit una ex
ancillis summi sacerdotis, **67** et, cum vidisset Petrum
calefacientem se, aspiciens illum ait, "Et tu cum hoc
Nazareno, Iesu, eras!" **68** At ille negavit, dicens, "Neque
scio neque novi quid tu dicas!" Et exiit foras ante atrium,
et gallus cantavit. **69** Et ancilla, cum vidisset illum, rursus
coepit dicere circumstantibus, "Hĭc ex illis est!" **70** At
ille iterum negabat. Et post pusillum rursus, qui stabant,
dicebant Petro, "Vere ex illis es, nam et Galilaeus es."

### Matthew 26:69–75

**69** Petrus vero sedebat foris in atrio. Et accessit ad eum una ancilla,
dicens, "Et tu cum Iesu Galilaeo eras!" **70** At ille negavit coram
omnibus, dicens, "Nescio quid dicis!" **71** Exeunte autem illo ad
ianuam, vidit eum alia et ait his qui erant ibi, "Hĭc erat cum Iesu
Nazareno!" **72** Et iterum negavit cum iuramento, "Non novi
hominem!" **73** Post pusillum autem accesserunt qui stabant, et
dixerunt Petro, "Vere et tu ex illis es, nam et loquela tua manifestum
te facit."

### Luke 22:56–62

**56** Quem cum vidisset ancilla quaedam sedentem ad lumen et eum
fuisset intuita, dixit, **57** "Et hĭc cum illo erat!" At ille negavit eum,
dicens, **58** "Mulier, non novi illum!" Et post pusillum alius videns
eum dixit, "Et tu de illis es!" Petrus vero ait, "O homo, non sum!"
**59** Et intervallo facto quasi horae unius, alius quidam affirmabat,
dicens, "Vere et hĭc cum illo erat, nam et Galilaeus est!"

## Vocabulary

**ancilla, -ae,** *f.,* female servant; slave
**deorsum,** down from; downward
**intervallum, -i,** *n.,* space; interval
**loquela, -ae,** *f.,* language; speech

## Historical and Grammatical Notes

### Mark 14:66–72

**66. deorsum:** "from below." The Temple was on a promontory within the city.

**68. novi:** as a present tense: "I know."

**70. post pusillum:** "a little later." **qui stabant:** Peter is now confronting a crowd that accuses him of being with Jesus. **nam et Galilaeus es:** "for you're a Galilean, too."

### Matthew 26:69–75

**71. Exeunte autem illo ad ianuam:** This violates the strict separation of an ablative absolute from the grammar of the rest of the sentence that's observed in classical Latin: "While he was going out toward the door, another saw him . . ."

**73. manifestum te facit:** "makes you obvious" or "exposes you."

### Luke 22:56–62

**56. eum fuisset intuita:** "and had been looking him over." This is the pluperfect subjunctive of the deponent verb *intueor, -eri, intuitus sum.* We've seen before how the perfect of the verb *sum* can be used in place of the imperfect in compound tenses. This isn't a unique phenomenon of vulgate Latin but can be seen in classical Latin, too.

**59. Et intervallo facto quasi horae unius:** literally, "With there being a space of about one hour" or "After about an hour."

# Mark 14:66–72 (cont.)

**71** Ille autem coepit anathematizare et iurare, "Nescio
hominem istum, quem dicitis!" **72** Et statim iterum gallus
cantavit. Et recordatus est Petrus verbi, sicut dixerat ei
Iesus, "Priusquam gallus cantet bis, ter me negabis." Et
coepit flere.

## Matthew 26:69–75 (cont.)

**74** Tunc coepit detestari et iurare, "Non novi hominem!" Et
continuo gallus cantavit. **75** Et recordatus est Petrus verbi Iesu,
quod dixerat, "Priusquam gallus cantet, ter me negabis." Et
egressus foras ploravit amarē.

## Luke 22:56–62 (cont.)

**60** Et ait Petrus, "Homo, nescio quid dicis!" Et continuo adhuc illo
loquente cantavit gallus. **61** Et conversus Dominus respexit Petrum,
et recordatus est Petrus verbi Domini, sicut dixit ei, "Priusquam
gallus cantet hodie, ter me negabis." **62** Et egressus foras flevit amarē.

## Vocabulary

**amarus, -a, -um,** bitter
**anathematizo (1),** to curse
**detestor, -ari, detestatus sum,** to curse; renounce under oath

## Historical and Grammatical Notes

### Mark 14:66–72 (cont.)

72. **verbi:** a genitive after a verb of remembering is quite common.

### Matthew 26:69–75 (cont.)

75. **Iesu:** genitive. **Priusquam gallus cantet, ter me negabis:** In Matthew and Luke, the prediction was that he would deny Jesus three times before the "rooster" crows once.

### Luke 22:56–62 (cont.)

61. **Et conversus Dominus:** The room where the hearing is taking place must be close to the front hall where Peter is warming himself. Jesus overhears Peter's denials, and Peter can see Jesus glowering at him.

# Chapter 15

Early in the morning, Jesus is brought before the Roman governor, Pontius Pilate. Jesus is silent when asked whether he claims to be the "King of the Jews." Pilate allows the Jews to condemn Jesus to death by crucifixion. Jesus is led out of the city to Calvary—the place where criminals are crucified. Jesus is mocked and abused. To the surprise of many, he dies before the end of the day. His body is claimed by a wealthy Jew, Joseph from the city of Arimathea, who puts it in a tomb until it can be properly buried on the day after the Sabbath.

# Mark 15:1–15

## *Jesus Brought before Pilate*

At daybreak, Jesus is presented to Pontius Pilate, the Roman governor of Judea. Pilate asks Jesus not whether he is just a religious reformer, but whether he claims to be the "king" of the Jewish people, a title that would signal a potential insurrection against Rome. The crowd elects to have Pilate release Barabbas, an otherwise unknown political or religious agitator, over Jesus and insists that Jesus be crucified.

**1** Et confestim mane consilium facientes summi
sacerdotes cum senioribus et scribis, id est universum
concilium, vincientes Iesum duxerunt et tradiderunt
Pilato. **2** Et interrogavit eum Pilatus, "Tu es rex
Iudaeorum?" At ille respondens ait illi, "Tu dicis."

### Matthew 27:1–26

**1** Mane autem facto, consilium inierunt omnes principes
sacerdotum et seniores populi adversus Iesum, ut eum morti
traderent. **2** Et vinctum adduxerunt eum et tradiderunt Pilato
praesidi. [***3–10*** *Judas repents of what he's done and hangs himself.*]
**11** Iesus autem stetit ante praesidem, et interrogavit eum praeses,
dicens, "Tu es Rex Iudaeorum?" Dixit autem Iesus, "Tu dicis."

### Luke 22:66; 23:1–25

**66** Et ut factus est dies, convenerunt seniores plebis et principes
sacerdotum et scribae et duxerunt illum in concilium suum. [***67–71***
*This is where Luke inserts the trial before Jewish authorities. It is the
parallel for Mark's earlier pericope at 14:53–65 and was discussed
there.*] **23:1** Et surgens omnis multitudo eorum duxerunt illum
ad Pilatum. **2** Coeperunt autem accusare illum, dicentes, "Hunc
invēnimus subvertentem gentem nostram et prohibentem tributa
dare Caesari et dicentem se Christum regem esse." **3** Pilatus autem
interrogavit eum, dicens, "Tu es rex Iudaeorum?" At ille respondens
ait, "Tu dicis."

# Historical and Grammatical Notes

## Mark 15:1–15

**1. confestim mane:** It was not unusual for Roman trials to be held at dawn. **consilium facientes:** The first meeting with Jesus was only a hearing. Now the entire Sanhedrin meets and decides to refer the matter to the Roman procurator. **Pilato:** By most measures applicable for imperial rule, Pilate was a moderate and successful Roman procurator of a fractious land. His true feelings about Jesus are impossible to reconstruct, but it's probable that he had no opinion about Jesus. It's likely that he'd never heard of him until this moment. Pilate, like all governors, wanted order above all else, and if his Jewish allies told him that Jesus threatened the management of the people, then he wouldn't be disposed to second-guess them. This doesn't mean that he would pass up an opportunity to taunt them a little and make it hard for them to get what they want.

**2. rex:** Rome's interest in the matter would be only in the potential for revolution against its rule, which seems to have been the principal charge that the Jewish authorities brought before Pilate. The last time the Jews had a king was Herod the Great, who ruled 64–4 BCE. After his death the area was ruled directly by Rome, and there was unrest until the final and general insurrection in 66–70 CE. After Herod the Great, the district was carved up, probably as a hedge against a general uprising. Someone claiming that he was "King of Jews" would sound like another threat to throw off Roman rule.

## Luke 22:66; 23:1–25

**22:66. ut factus est dies:** In Mark and Matthew the hearing before Jewish authorities occurs before dawn and the trial before Pilate occurs at dawn. For Luke, the hearing before the Jewish authorities occurs at dawn and the trial before Pilate shortly thereafter.

**23:1. multitudo:** In the other two Synoptics, the crowd gathers *during* the process before Pilate. There is no crowd in the process before the Jewish authorities, as well there might not be, for it occurred before dawn. In Luke, the crowd has already assembled during the Jewish hearing that precedes the Roman trial. Indeed, Jesus is taken to Pilate *by* the crowd. Pilate, as we'll see, will send them off with Jesus to Herod Antipas on the pretext that since Jesus is from Galilee, it's a Galilean concern. Pilate will conduct an official trial only after he has heard from Herod.

**2. gentem nostram:** object of the participle *subvertentem*: "We found this man subverting our people." Luke's mob makes three charges, which could have been among the *in multis* in Mark 15:3. They all are forms of sedition.

# Mark 15:1–15 (cont.)

**3** Et accusabant eum summi sacerdotes in multis. **4** Pilatus
autem rursum interrogabat eum, dicens, "Non respondes
quidquam? Vide in quantis te accusant." **5** Iesus autem
amplius nihil respondit, ita ut miraretur Pilatus. **6** Per
diem autem festum dimittere solebat illis unum ex vinctis,
quem peterent.

## Matthew 27:1–26 (cont.)

**12** Et cum accusaretur a principibus sacerdotum et senioribus, nihil
respondit. **13** Tunc dicit illi Pilatus, "Non audis quanta adversum
te dicant testimonia?" **14** Et non respondit ei ad ullum verbum, ita
ut miraretur praeses vehementer. **15** Per diem autem sollemnem
consueverat praeses dimittere turbae unum vinctum, quem
voluissent.

## Luke 22:66; 23:1–25 (cont.)

**4** Ait autem Pilatus ad principes sacerdotum et turbas, "Nihil invenio
causae in hoc homine." **5** At illi invalescebant, dicentes, "Commovet
populum docens per universam Iudaeam et incipiens a Galilaeā
usque huc." [***23:6–12*** *Pilate judges this to be a matter for Herod
Antipas, the ruler over the area that includes Galilee, who happens to be
in Jerusalem for the Passover. Herod had been looking foward to meeting
with Jesus because of his reputation as a miracle worker and teacher, but
he is disappointed when Jesus doesn't respond to any of his questions.
He has Jesus abused and sends him back to Pilate.*] **13** Pilatus autem,
convocatis principibus sacerdotum et magistratibus et plebe, **14** dixit
ad illos, "Obtulistis mihi hunc hominem quasi avertentem populum,
et ecce: ego coram vobis interrogans nullam causam inveni in
homine isto ex his, in quibus eum accusatis, **15** sed neque Herodes.
Remisit enim illum ad nos. Et ecce: nihil dignum morte actum est ei.
**16** Emendatum ergo illum dimittam."

## Vocabulary

**emendo (1),** to correct; chastise
**invalesco, -escere, -ui,** to grow strong; prevail
**sollemnis, -is,** solemn; holy

## Historical and Grammatical Notes

### Mark 15:1–15 (cont.)

**5. ita ut miraretur Pilatus:** Jesus's silence is interpreted as a plea of *nolo contendere,* which is why Pilate breaks off the interrogation and begins to consider punishment.

**6. dimittere solebat:** A good translation strategy for *soleo* is to change it to an adverb, in this case "he *customarily* released," instead of the clumsy "he was in the habit of releasing." There's no independent evidence that Pilate or the Romans had a custom of granting amnesty to a criminal on a sacred day, but Pilate had the right to rule however he wished.

### Luke 22:66; 23:1–25 (cont.)

**13. convocatis . . . et plebe:** Luke returns to the setting that was interrupted by the trial before Herod. This is now an official proceeding.

**15. actum est ei:** *Ei* is the dative of agent: "nothing meriting capital punishment has been done by him." This is a feature of Greek grammar, not Latin, which gives the construction a formal tone that may suggest the exact wording of a principle of Roman law.

# Mark 15:1–15 (cont.)

**7** Erat autem qui dicebatur Barabbas, vinctus cum
seditiosis, qui in seditione fecerant homicidium. **8** Et
cum ascendisset turba, coepit rogare, sicut faciebat illis. **9**
Pilatus autem respondit eis et dixit, "Vultis dimittam vobis
regem Iudaeorum?" **10** Sciebat enim quod per invidiam
tradidissent eum summi sacerdotes.

## Matthew 27:1–26 (cont.)

**16** Habebant autem tunc vinctum insignem, qui dicebatur Barabbas.
**17** Congregatis ergo illis dixit Pilatus, "Quem vultis dimittam vobis,
Barabbam an Iesum, qui dicitur Christus?" **18** Sciebat enim quod
per invidiam tradidissent eum. **19** Sedente autem illo pro tribunali,
misit ad illum uxor eius, dicens, "Nihil tibi et iusto illi! Multa enim
passa sum hodie per visum propter eum."

## Luke 22:66; 23:1–25 (cont.)

**(17)** **18** Exclamavit autem universa turba, dicens, "Tolle hunc et
dimitte nobis Barabbam," **19** qui erat propter seditionem quandam
factam in civitate et homicidium missus in carcerem. **20** Iterum
autem Pilatus locutus est ad illos, volens dimittere Iesum, **21** at illi
succlamabant, dicentes, "Crucifige, crucifige illum!" **22** Ille autem
tertio dixit ad illos, "Quid enim mali fecit iste? Nullam causam
mortis invenio in eo. Corripiam ergo illum et dimittam."

# Vocabulary

**corripio, -ripere, -ripui, -reptus,** to arrest; punish
**insignis, -is,** distinguished; well-known
**invidia, -ae,** *f.,* ill will
**succlamo (1),** to cry out
**tribunal, -is,** *n.,* tribunal
**visus, -us,** *m.,* vision; dream

# Historical and Grammatical Notes

## MARK 15:1–15 (CONT.)

7. **Barabbas:** He's not otherwise known. His name means "Son-of-the-Father," and he is often given the complete name of "Jesus Barabbas." **qui in seditione fecerant homicidium:** The murder probably wasn't of a Roman soldier or official. Jewish insurrectionists and reformers more often killed other Jews whom they deemed insufficiently pure or complicit with Roman rule.

8. **sicut faciebat illis:** The sense of the imperfect is important here: "as he [usually] did for them."

9. **Vultis dimittam:** Supply *ut* before *dimittam* for the full volitive subjunctive construction: "You want that I release" or "You want me to release."

10. **Sciebat:** Pilate may be toying with the priests. He wants to torment them with the possibility that the people will choose Jesus. They scramble to incite the crowd to demand the release of Barabbas.

## MATTHEW 27:1–26 (CONT.)

16. **vinctum:** "a bound one," or "a prisoner."

19. **uxor:** Only Matthew reports this. It is not impossible that Pilate's wife was present during the trial and offered him her thoughts. The Romans were in fact notorious for being superstitious about dreams and portents. This has the effect of exonerating Pilate to some degree. He recognizes that this is an unjust sentence and only reluctantly yields to the crowd's demands. **Nihil tibi et iusto illi:** "Let there be nothing between you and this just man," or perhaps more colloquially: "Stay out of it." **Multa:** adverb: "much."

## LUKE 22:66; 23:1–25 (CONT.)

19. **homicidium:** governed by *propter* above. Barabbas was convicted of committing murder during an uprising in the city, most likely not against Rome directly, but against the local Jewish authorities.

20. **volens dimittere Iesum:** As in Matthew, Pilate is treated like an unwilling participant. He wants to release Jesus.

# Mark 15:1–15 (cont.)

**11** Pontifices autem concitaverunt turbam, ut magis
Barabbam dimitteret eis. **12** Pilatus autem iterum
respondens aiebat illis, "Quid ergo vultis faciam regi
Iudaeorum?" **13** At illi iterum clamaverunt, "Crucifige
eum!" **14** Pilatus vero dicebat eis, "Quid enim mali fecit?"
At illi magis clamaverunt, "Crucifige eum!" **15** Pilatus
autem, volens populo satisfacere, dimisit illis Barabbam et
tradidit Iesum flagellis caesum, ut crucifigeretur.

## Matthew 27:1–26 (cont.)

**20** Principes autem sacerdotum et seniores persuaserunt turbis, ut
peterent Barabbam, Iesum vero perderent. **21** Respondens autem
praeses ait illis, "Quem vultis vobis de duobus dimittam?" At illi
dixerunt, "Barabbam!" **22** Dicit illis Pilatus, "Quid igitur faciam de
Iesu, qui dicitur Christus?" Dicunt omnes, "Crucifigatur!" **23** Ait
autem, "Quid enim mali fecit?" At illi magis clamabant, dicentes,
"Crucifigatur!" **24** Videns autem Pilatus quia nihil proficeret, sed
magis tumultus fieret, acceptā aquā, lavit manūs coram turbā, dicens,
"Innocens ego sum a sanguine hoc. Vos videritis!" **25** Et respondens
universus populus dixit, "Sanguis eius super nos et super filios
nostros." **26** Tunc dimisit illis Barabbam. Iesum autem flagellatum
tradidit, ut crucifigeretur.

## Luke 22:66; 23:1–25 (cont.)

**23** At illi instabant vocibus magnis postulantes, ut crucifigeretur,
et invalescebant voces eorum. **24** Et Pilatus adiudicavit fieri
petitionem eorum. **25** Dimisit autem eum, qui propter seditionem et
homicidium missus fuerat in carcerem, quem petebant. Iesum vero
tradidit voluntati eorum.

## Vocabulary

**adiudico (1),** to grant
**concito (1),** to stir up
**flagellum, -ii,** *n.,* whip

## Historical and Grammatical Notes

### Mark 15:1–15 (cont.)

**11. ut magis:** "so that he would rather release Barabbas to them."

**12. vultis faciam:** *vultis [ut] faciam.*

**13. Crucifige eum:** The punishment was not a foregone conclusion. Barabbas was to be crucified for murder and incitement to revolt, but Jesus is charged only with saying outrageous things. Jesus might have annoyed the authorities, but that is hardly a capital offense.

**14. Quid enim mali fecit:** *Mali* is the complementary genitive after *quid*: "What evil has he done?" Pilate seems taken aback and asks the crowd to explain their demand.

**15. caesum:** supine showing purpose. **ut crucifigeretur:** According to Roman practice at the time, whipping preceded the actual crucifixion.

### Matthew 27:1–26 (cont.)

**20. perderent:** In Mark, the people decide on the punishment, but in Matthew, the Jewish authorities are explicitly behind the demand that Jesus be crucified.

**24. Vos videritis:** perfect subjunctive as the imperative: "Let *you* see it" or "Let *you* be witnesses."

**26. flagellatum:** supine of purpose.

### Luke 22:66; 23:1–25 (cont.)

**22. Corripiam:** Pilate even offers to arrest and punish Jesus before he sets him free. The mob isn't having any of it.

**23. illi instabant vocibus magnis postulantes:** "they press on, demanding in loud voices."

**24. adiudicavit fieri petitionem eorum:** "declares their request be granted."

# Mark 15:16–20

## *Jesus Mocked by Roman Soldiers*

Jesus is abused and ridiculed by the detachment of Roman soldiers who will lead him to his crucifixion. Appropriately, the scene is a parody of the obeisance they pay to their "king," Caesar.

**16** Milites autem duxerunt eum intro in atrium, quod
est praetorium, et convocant totam cohortem. **17** Et
induunt eum purpuram et imponunt ei plectentes
spineam coronam. **18** Et coeperunt salutare eum, "Ave,
rex Iudaeorum!" **19** Et percutiebant caput eius arundine
et conspuebant eum et ponentes genua adorabant eum.
**20** Et postquam illuserunt ei, exuerunt illum purpuram
et induerunt eum vestimentis suis. Et educunt illum, ut
crucifigerent eum.

## Matthew 27:27–31

**27** Tunc milites praesidis suscipientes Iesum in praetorio
congregaverunt ad eum universam cohortem. **28** Et exuentes eum,
clamydem coccineam circumdederunt ei, **29** et plectentes coronam
de spinis posuerunt super caput eius et arundinem in dexterā eius, et,
genu flexo ante eum, illudebant ei, dicentes, "Ave, rex Iudaeorum!"
**30** Et exspuentes in eum acceperunt arundinem et percutiebant
caput eius. **31** Et postquam illuserunt ei, exuerunt eum clamyde et
induerunt eum vestimentis eius et duxerunt eum, ut crucifigerent.

## Vocabulary

**arundo, -inis,** *f.*, cane; reed
**ave,** hail; greetings
**clamys, -dis,** *f.*, a general's cloak
**coccineus, -a, -um,** red; scarlet
**cohors, -tis,** *f.*, cohort
**corona, -ae,** *f.*, crown; garland
**exuo, -uere, -ui, -utus,** to take off; undress
**plecto, plectere, plexi, plectus,** to weave; braid
**praetorium, -ii,** *n.*, headquarters; governor's residence
**purpura, -ae,** *f.*, purple (cloak)
**spineus, -a, -um,** spiky; jagged

## Historical and Grammatical Notes

### Mark 15:16–20

**16. Milites:** These troops would have been levied from the non-Jewish population of Palestine and Syria, and, given where they are stationed, they probably had some notion of the implications of Jesus's claims. This explains why and how they ridicule him. **quod est praetorium:** This isn't Pilate's official residence, which was in Caesarea Maritima. The headquarters mentioned here would be where he set up his administration during his visits to the city. It's not surprising to see him in Jerusalem with a considerable military escort during the Passover, when large numbers of Jews were packed into the city. **totam cohortem:** A Roman cohort was one-tenth of a full legion, or somewhere between four hundred and six hundred men. It's hard to imagine that Pilate would dispatch all his troops to manage the affair with Jesus and lead him to his crucifixion. That would leave himself and other areas of the city undefended. A sizeable detachment would be advisable, nonetheless, given the potential for spontaneous trouble along the way.

**17. induunt eum purpuram:** a double accusative: "They put a purple cloak [on] him." Note below at verse 20 that the construction after *induo* uses an ablative of means. **spineam:** The Greek is *acanthos*, which is a leafy plant common in the Mediterranean area. Though the leaves do have sharp points and edges, the acanthus can't really be said to have thorns.

**20. exuerunt illum purpuram:** another double accusative: "They took the purple cloak [off] him."

### Matthew 27:27–31

**28. coccineam:** It's not necessary to suppose that Matthew means a different kind of military or political cloak. Purple has many shades.

**31. exuerunt eum clamyde et induerunt eum vestimentis:** Matthew evidently found the double accusatives in Mark to be clumsy and replaces them with an accusative and an ablative. *Clamyde* can be understood as an ablative of separation and *vestimentis* as an ablative of means.

# Mark 15:21–32

## *The Via Dolorosa; Jesus Crucified*

Jesus is paraded through the streets and out of Jerusalem to the place where crucifixions were conducted. His clothes are gambled over by the guards, and he is hung up on the cross with a placard above his head that explains his crime: "King of the Jews." He is further tormented by the priests and mocked by the two other criminals who are being crucified on either side of him.

**21** Et angariant praetereuntem quempiam Simonem Cyrenaeum venientem de villā, patrem Alexandri et Rufi, ut tolleret crucem eius. **22** Et perducunt illum in Golgothā locum, quod est interpretatum, "Calvariae locus." **23** Et dabant ei myrrhatum vinum. Ille autem non accepit. **24** Et crucifigunt eum et dividunt vestimenta eius, mittentes sortem super eis, quis quid tolleret. **25** Erat autem hora tertia, et crucifixerunt eum. **26** Et erat titulus causae eius inscriptus, "Rex Iudaeorum."

## Matthew 27:32–44

**32** Exeuntes autem invenerunt hominem Cyrenaeum nomine Simonem. Hunc angariaverunt, ut tolleret crucem eius. **33** Et venerunt in locum, qui dicitur Golgotha, quod est "Calvariae locus." **34** Et dederunt ei vinum bibere cum felle mixtum, et cum gustasset, noluit bibere. **35** Postquam autem crucifixerunt eum, diviserunt vestimenta eius, sortem mittentes **36** et sedentes servabant eum ibi. **37** Et imposuerunt super caput eius causam ipsius scriptam, "Hĭc est Iesus, Rex Iudaeorum."

## Luke 23:26–42

**26** Et cum abducerent eum, apprehenderunt Simonem quendam Cyrenensem venientem de villā et imposuerunt illi crucem portare post Iesum. [**27–31** *A large crowd of women follows Jesus. He tells them not to weep for him but for themselves and their children because of the disasters that are going to befall the Jews.*]

## Vocabulary

**angario (1),** to demand; require
**Cyreneus, -a, -um,** from Cyrene
**fellis, -is,** *f.*, bile
**myrrhatus, -a, -um,** spiced; spiced with myrrh
**quispiam, quidpiam,** a certain; some
**sors, sortis,** *f.*, lot; roll of the dice
**titulus, -i,** *m.*, title; plaque; sign

## Historical and Grammatical Notes

### Mark 15:21–32

**21. praetereuntem:** We will never know whether Simon was following Jesus out of devotion or whether he just happened to be passing by as Jesus was being led through the streets. **patrem Alexandri et Rufi:** Simon and his sons are not otherwise known, but they must have been devout Jews to have traveled so far from Libya for the Passover. Cyrene, in fact, became an early center for Christianity, perhaps because his two sons brought the word of Jesus back with them.

**22. Golgothā:** This is the Aramaic word for "skull." In English, the name is "Calvary." It could be named "skull" because the site was a large cliff or rock that resembled skull, or because this is where the crucifixions were held.

**23. myrrhatum vinum:** There's a lot of speculation about this "spiced wine." Did it have an analgesic effect that would help one suffer less, or was it yet another act of cruelty? There's no way to know.

**25. Erat autem hora tertia:** A day from sunrise and sunset was divided into twelve *horae*, starting at 6 a.m. and ending at 6 p.m. Hence the "third hour" is between 9 and 10 a.m.

### Matthew 27:32–44

**34. cum felle:** literally "with bile." Strictly speaking, bile is an odoriferous liquid stored in the gallbladder. It's unlikely that Jesus's tormenters would have bile ready at hand to put into the wine. But *cum felle* might mean defilement with any animal discharge that would be easier to come by, such as horse manure or dog feces. Matthew eliminates any possibility that this was an act of mercy.

**36. servabant eum:** "they kept watch over him."

# Mark 15:21–32 (cont.)

**27** Et cum eo crucifigunt duos latrones, unum a dextris
et alium a sinistris eius. (**28**) **29** Et praetereuntes
blasphemabant eum moventes capita sua et dicentes,
"Vah, qui destruit Templum et in tribus diebus aedificat,
**30** salvum fac temetipsum, descendens de cruce!" **31**
Similiter et summi sacerdotes ludentes ad alterutrum cum
scribis dicebant, "Alios salvos fecit, seipsum non potest
salvum facere. **32** Christus, rex Israel, descendat nunc
de cruce, ut videamus et credamus." Etiam qui cum eo
crucifixi erant, conviciabantur ei.

## Matthew 27:32–44 (cont.)

**38** Tunc crucifiguntur cum eo duo latrones, unus a dextris, et unus
a sinistris. **39** Praetereuntes autem blasphemabant eum, moventes
capita sua **40** et dicentes, "Qui destruis Templum et in triduo
illud reaedificas, salva temetipsum. Si filius Dei es, descende de
cruce!" **41** Similiter et principes sacerdotum illudentes cum scribis
et senioribus dicebant, **42** "Alios salvos fecit, seipsum non potest
salvum facere. Rex Israel est! Descendat nunc de cruce, et credemus
in eum. **43** Confidit in Deo! Liberet nunc, si vult eum. Dixit enim,
'Dei filius sum.' " **44** Idipsum autem et latrones, qui crucifixi erant
cum eo, improperabant ei.

## Luke 23:26–42 (cont.)

**32** Ducebantur autem et alii duo nequam cum eo, ut interficerentur.
**33** Et postquam venerunt in locum, qui vocatur Calvariae, ibi
crucifixerunt eum et latrones, unum a dextris et alterum a sinistris.
**34** Iesus autem dicebat, "Pater, dimitte illis, non enim sciunt quid
faciunt." Dividentes vero vestimenta eius miserunt sortes. **35**
Et stabat populus, exspectans. Et deridebant illum et principes,
dicentes, "Alios salvos fecit. Se salvum faciat, si hĭc est Christus
Dei electus!" **36** Illudebant autem ei et milites accedentes, acetum
offerentes illi **37** et, dicentes, "Si tu es rex Iudaeorum, salvum te fac!"

**38** Erat autem et superscriptio super illum: "Hĭc est rex Iudaeorum." [**39–42** *One of the two criminals being crucified alongside Jesus taunts him. The other criminal rebukes the first, because unlike them, he says, Jesus is innocent. He asks Jesus to remember him to his Father. Jesus replies that he will be with him in paradise on that very day.*]

## Vocabulary

**acetum, -i,** *n.,* bad wine; vinegar
**convicior, -ari, -atus sum,** to taunt
**impropero (1),** to assail
**inscribo, -bere, -psi, -ptus,** to write on; inscribe
**nequam,** *indecl. adjective,* useless; worthless
**reaedifico (1),** to rebuild
**superscriptio, -ionis,** *f.,* inscription

## Historical and Grammatical Notes

### Mark 15:21–32 (cont.)

**29. moventes capita sua:** This gesture of contempt is traditional and has Old Testament parallels (Lam 2:15, Ps 22:7, Ps 109:25). **Vah:** The insults of his tormentors indicated that they knew something of Jesus's preaching. The common people knew that he predicted the destruction of the Temple, and the priests knew that he healed people and claimed to be the Messiah.

**29–30. destruit . . . salvum fac:** The change of person from third to second is hard to account for. Perhaps "[As] one who destroys the Temple and rebuilds it in three days, save yourself . . ." Note that Matthew changes the third to the second person to make the verbs consistent, and Luke recasts the sentence.

**31. ad alterutrum:** Take this with *dicebant*: "they were saying to one another along with the scribes . . ." **fecit:** The crowd addresses Jesus, but the authorities address the crowd. They are still trying to whip them up against Jesus.

**32. Christus, rex Israel, descendat:** Take *rex Israel* as apposition: "Let the Christ, the king of Israel, come down."

### Matthew 27:32–44 (cont.)

**40. Qui destruis:** Matthew corrects the incongruity in Mark by changing the person of the verbs from third to second.

**42. Rex Israel est:** "He is the king of Israel, indeed!"

**43. Confidit in Deo:** "He trusts in God, does he? Well . . ."

### Luke 23:26–42 (cont.)

**35. Et stabat populus, exspectans:** In Luke, the people aren't as enthusiastic about the crucifixion as the authorities are. They are standing still, waiting to see what will happen. The authorities attack Jesus's former presumption in light of his current helplessness. They're trying to convince them that he was a fraud.

# Mark 15:33–41

## *The Death of Jesus*

Jesus is crucified at noon, and for three hours there is darkness over the land. By 3 p.m., Jesus cries out. Bystanders think that he is calling on Elijah to come take him down. They offer him a sponge filled with vinegar. Jesus dies, and a curtain in the Temple is simultaneously torn in two. A Roman centurion declares that Jesus surely was a son of God. Jesus's final moments are witnessed by a group of women who had been among his entourage in Galilee as well as other women who'd joined him in Jerusalem.

**33** Et factā horā sextā, tenebrae factae sunt per totam
terram usque in horam nonam. **34** Et horā nonā
exclamavit Iesus voce magnā, "Heloi, Heloi, lema
sabacthani?" quod est interpretatum, "Deus meus,
Deus meus, ut quid dereliquisti me?" **35** Et quidam de
circumstantibus audientes dicebant, "Ecce: Eliam vocat."

### Matthew 27:45–56

**45** A sextā autem horā tenebrae factae sunt super universam terram
usque ad horam nonam. **46** Et circa horam nonam clamavit Iesus
voce magnā, dicens, "Eli, Eli, lema sabacthani?" Hoc est, "Deus
meus, Deus meus, ut quid dereliquisti me?" **47** Quidam autem ex
illic stantibus audientes dicebant, "Eliam vocat iste."

### Luke 23:44–49

**44** Et erat iam fere hora sexta, et tenebrae factae sunt in universā
terrā usque in horam nonam, **45** et obscuratus est sol, et velum
Templi scissum est medium.

## Vocabulary

**derelinquo, -linquere, -liqui, -lictus,** to abandon; forsake

**nonus, -a, -um,** ninth

**velum, -i,** *n.,* curtain; covering

## Historical and Grammatical Notes

### Mark 15:33–41

**33. tenebrae factae sunt:** It's a commonplace in Jewish literature that the death of a king is accompanied by the darkening of the sun.

**34. ut quid dereliquisti me:** As we've seen before, the *ut* can be an intensive adverb for a question in vulgate Latin: "Why have you abandoned me?" The preservation of the original Aramaic, both here and in Matthew, taken together with the theological difficulty of the meaning of the words, both strongly suggest that these were Jesus's actual words. They are in the opening verse of Psalm 22, which begins with a complaint of God's apparent indifference to the suffering of innocents. The psalm ends with the vindication of God's purpose and ultimate justice. Should we take Jesus to be referring to the entire song, including the final reconciliation, or only to the cry of despair? At the very least, Jesus's cry is not merely one of physical torment, as one would expect, but is one of emotional and spiritual distance from God.

**35. quidam de circumstantibus audientes:** These bystanders can't be Jesus's disciples. The disciples have already scattered and only reappear in the disputed ending of the Gospel. But these people are versed well enough in Jewish literature to think that Jesus is calling out to Elijah when he says "*eloi, eloi.*"

# Mark 15:33–41 (cont.)

**36** Currens autem unus et implens spongiam aceto
circumponensque calamo potum dabat ei, dicens, "Sinite.
Videamus si veniat Elias ad deponendum eum." **37** Iesus
autem, emissā voce magnā, exspiravit.

## Matthew 27:45–56 (cont.)

**48** Et continuo currens unus ex eis acceptam spongiam implevit
aceto et imposuit arundini et dabat ei bibere. **49** Ceteri vero
dicebant, "Sine. Videamus an veniat Elias liberans eum." **50** Iesus
autem iterum clamans voce magnā emisit spiritum.

## Luke 23:44–49 (cont.)

**46** Et clamans voce magnā Iesus ait, "Pater, in manūs tuas
commendo spiritum meum." Et haec dicens exspiravit.

## Vocabulary

**calamus, -i,** *m.,* reed; pole
**circumpono, -ponere, -posui, -positus,** to place upon
**commendo (1),** to commit; hand over for protection; commend
**depono, -ponere, -posui, -positus,** to set down; take down
**emitto, -mittere, -misi, -missus,** to send out
**exspiro (1),** to expire; die
**spongia, -ae,** *f.,* sponge

## Historical and Grammatical Notes

### Mark 15:33–41 (cont.)

**36. potum:** a supine showing purpose. Jesus is offered strong wine again perhaps to revive him enough to permit him to continue calling out (as the bystanders suppose) to Elijah. The bystanders say that they are curious to see whether Elijah will really come down to rescue him. **Sinite:** "Let him [call to Elijah]."

### Matthew 27:45–56 (cont.)

**48. acceptam spongiam:** "a sponge [that he had] taken."

**49. Sine:** "[Go ahead and] let [him drink]."

### Luke 23:44–49 (cont.)

**46. Pater, in manūs tuas commendo spiritum meum:** In Luke's version, Jesus appears not to suffer physically or emotionally at all. Perhaps this is attributable to a growing consensus among the first Christians that Jesus was in some way God himself, and it would be theologically complicated to portray him as anguished and despairing at the end of his life. It might also be that Luke didn't pick up on how Psalm 22 is the interpretative key for Jesus's crucifixion and accordingly deleted Jesus's cries that the psalm prefigures.

# Mark 15:33–41 (cont.)

**38** Et velum Templi scissum est in duo, a sursum usque deorsum.

## Matthew 27:45–56 (cont.)

**51** Et ecce: velum Templi scissum est a summo usque deorsum
in duas partes, et terra mota est, et petrae scissae sunt. **52** Et
monumenta aperta sunt, et multa corpora sanctorum, qui
dormierant, surrexerunt, **53** et exeuntes de monumentis post
resurrectionem eius venerunt in sanctam civitatem et apparuerunt
multis.

## Vocabulary

**sursum**, upward

## Historical and Grammatical Notes

### MARK 15:33–41 (CONT.)

**38. velum Templi:** There were two curtains in the Temple in Jerusalem. They both concealed the central and most sacred building of the compound, where the "holy of holies" were kept. Only the high priest was allowed to enter and even then only once a year. (It was such as a sacrilege for any else to enter the inner sanctum that a rope was tied around the priest on the rare occasions that he was allowed in. This was so that no one would have go in to get his body if he should die while inside. The rope would make it possible for the body to be dragged out.) One curtain hung on the outer entrance of the sacred building and one hung just on the inside. Both of them were enormous, measuring approximately 9 meters (30') in width and 18 meters (60') in length. Having one torn in half from the bottom to the top would have been spectacular to say the least. We don't know which of the two Mark is referring to or even whether he means this literally or figuratively. It could be both. Jesus's death will eventually break down the separation between humankind and God that is symbolized by the curtains. It might also mean that God is no longer present in the Temple, portending its destruction. **a sursum usque deorsum:** "from the top to the bottom."

### MATTHEW 27:45–56 (CONT.)

**52. multa corpora sanctorum:** Only Matthew adds the dramatic event of the sleeping saints rising from their graves, not as ghosts, but in their physical bodies. They will walk into the city itself after Jesus's resurrection. The *sancti* aren't identified, but they were probably taken to be the Patriarchs and some of the prophets. **post resurrectionem eius:** Jesus would raid the underworld and release the *sancti* sleeping there. **apparuerunt multis:** again emphasizing that Matthew doesn't mean this metaphorically. The sleeping saints appear in bodily form to many people in the city.

# Mark 15:33–41 (cont.)

**39** Videns autem centurio, qui ex adverso stabat quia sic
clamans exspirasset, ait, "Vere homo hĭc filius Dei erat." **40**
Erant autem et mulieres de longe aspicientes, inter quas et
Maria Magdalene et Maria Iacobi minoris et Iosetis mater
et Salome, **41** quae, cum esset in Galilaeā, sequebantur
eum et ministrabant ei, et aliae multae, quae simul cum eo
ascenderant Hierosolymam.

## Matthew 27:45–56 (cont.)

**54** Centurio autem et, qui cum eo erant custodientes Iesum, viso
terrae motu et his, quae fiebant, timuerunt valde, dicentes, "Vere
Dei filius erat iste!" **55** Erant autem ibi mulieres multae a longe
aspicientes, quae secutae erant Iesum a Galilaeā ministrantes ei, **56**
inter quas erat Maria Magdalene et Maria Iacobi et Ioseph mater et
mater filiorum Zebedaei.

## Luke 23:44–49 (cont.)

**47** Videns autem centurio, quod factum fuerat, glorificavit Deum,
dicens, "Vere hĭc homo iustus erat!" **48** Et omnis turba eorum,
qui simul aderant ad spectaculum istud et videbant, quae fiebant,
percutientes pectora sua revertebantur. **49** Stabant autem omnes
noti eius a longe et mulieres, quae secutae erant eum a Galilaeā,
haec videntes.

# Vocabulary

**centurio, -ionis,** *m.,* centurion; captain
**notus, -a, -um,** known; familiar
**pectus, -oris,** *n.,* breast
**spectaculum, -i,** *n.,* event; scene

# Historical and Grammatical Notes

## Mark 15:33–41 (cont.)

**39. quia sic clamans exspirasset:** indirect statement dependent on *videns*: "that he had died crying out in this way." **Vere homo hĭc filius Dei erat:** Mark gives us no indication of what impressed the centurion so much that he said this. The idea that the world could be inhabited by "sons of god" would not have been entirely foreign to a Roman soldier. Julius Caesar and Augustus after him were declared to be "sons of gods," and it became quite ordinary for subsequent emperors to be hailed as a "son of god." Perhaps the centurion simply recognized the same kind of nobility in Jesus that he had come to expect from his own emperor.

**40–41. mulieres . . . multae:** None of the women named in this group are previously mentioned in Mark. Their presence here emphasizes the complete absence of Jesus's male disciples at his crucifixion.

## Matthew 27:45–56 (cont.)

**56. mater filiorum Zebedaei:** Matthew perhaps is not so sure that this woman is Salome, as she is named in Mark.

## Luke 23:44–49 (cont.)

**47. Vere hĭc homo iustus erat:** We again see Luke moving away from an important and potentially difficult comment in Mark. Though the centurion "praises God" with his observation, what he does say is hardly the same as "Truly, this man is the Son of God."

**48. spectaculum:** This is the ordinary word for a play or performance for entertainment. **percutientes pectora sua:** The crowd, which had previously been mocking Jesus, suddenly grieves. Or do they? It might be that beating one's breast was such a conventional gesture at a death or funeral that they perform it semiautomatically. Without any accompanying cries of sorrow or grief, these spectators might have been doing little more than applauding.

# Mark 15:42–47

## *Jesus's Tomb*

Jesus dies late on the equivalent of Friday afternoon—the day before the Sabbath. A heretofore unknown sympathizer of Jesus, Joseph from the city of Arimathea (often called "Joseph of Arimathea"), gets permission from Pilate to take Jesus's body to a tomb until it can be properly buried on the day after the Sabbath. (In modern terms, the Sabbath would be on Saturday. The soonest Jesus could be buried, therefore, would be Sunday morning.) Two of Jesus's female adherents see where his body is taken.

**42** Et cum iam sero esset factum, quia erat Parasceve,
quod est ante Sabbatum, **43** vēnit Ioseph ab Arimathaeā
nobilis decurio, qui et ipse erat exspectans regnum Dei, et
audacter introivit ad Pilatum et petiit corpus Iesu.

### Matthew 27:57–61

**57** Cum sero autem factum esset, vēnit homo dives ab Arimathaeā,
nomine Ioseph, qui et ipse discipulus erat Iesu. **58** Hĭc accessit ad
Pilatum et petiit corpus Iesu.

### Luke 23:50–56

**50** Et ecce: vir nomine Ioseph, qui erat decurio, vir bonus et iustus—
**51** hĭc non consenserat consilio et actibus eorum—ab Arimathaeā
civitate Iudaeorum, qui exspectabat regnum Dei. **52** Hĭc accessit ad
Pilatum et petiit corpus Iesu,

## Vocabulary

**audacter,** courageously
**consentio, -tire, -si, -sus,** to agree with
**decurio, -ionis,** *m.*, member of a council; commissioner
**Parasceve, -es,** *f.*, the Day of Preparation; the day before the Sabbath

## Historical and Grammatical Notes

### Mark 15:42–47

**42. quod est ante Sabbatum:** Mark's Jewish audience surely would have known the names of the days of the week. His purpose is to fix the exact chronology of events, not to explain how Jews name their days. Jesus dies right before the end of "Preparation Day" and just before the beginning of the Sabbath day. Unless Jesus's body is going to be allowed to hang in the open until the day after the Sabbath, it is going to have to be taken down soon. It can't be taken down on the following day, as that would violate the prohibition against work on the Sabbath. **Arimathaeā:** There is no record of a town named "Arimathea." It's possible that this is a transliteration of the Hebrew *ha-ramathaim,* which corresponds to Ramatha, a small town about five miles from Jerusalem.

**43. decurio:** It's possible, though not conclusive, that he was a member of the Sanhedrin. But if that's so, why didn't Mark use the word *concilium,* which he'd been using all along to refer to this body? He might have been an influential and well-known official in a local township. **audacter:** A crucified corpse would normally be allowed to decompose on the cross as a gruesome warning to other would-be criminals. It took some courage to request an exception for Jesus's body.

### Matthew 27:57–61

**57. discipulus:** This may only mean that he sympathized with Jesus and was impressed by his teachings. There is no evidence that Joseph of Arimathea was among Jesus's followers at any time.

### Luke 23:50–56

**51. hĭc non consenserat consilio et actibus eorum:** This accounts for why he could be called just and good. It doesn't necessarily mean that he was a member of the Sanhedrin.

# Mark 15:42–47 (cont.)

**44** Pilatus autem miratus est si iam obisset, et, accersito
centurione, interrogavit eum si iam mortuus esset. **45** Et,
cum cognovisset a centurione, donavit corpus Ioseph. **46**
Is autem mercatus sindonem et deponens eum involvit
sindone et posuit eum in monumento, quod erat excisum
de petrā, et advolvit lapidem ad ostium monumenti. **47**
Maria autem Magdalene et Maria Iosetis aspiciebant, ubi
positus esset.

## Matthew 27:57–61 (cont.)

Tunc Pilatus iussit reddi. **59** Et accepto corpore, Ioseph involvit illud
in sindone mundā, **60** et posuit illud in monumento suo novo, quod
exciderat in petrā, et advolvit saxum magnum ad ostium monumenti
et abiit. **61** Erat autem ibi Maria Magdalene et altera Maria sedentes
contra sepulcrum.

## Luke 23:50–56 (cont.)

**53** et depositum involvit sindone et posuit eum in monumento
exciso, in quo nondum quisquam positus fuerat. **54** Et dies erat
Parasceves, et Sabbatum illucescebat. **55** Subsecutae autem mulieres,
quae cum ipso venerant de Galilaeā, viderunt monumentum
et quemadmodum positum erat corpus eius. **56** Et revertentes
paraverunt aromata et unguenta. Et Sabbato quidem siluerunt
secundum mandatum.

## Vocabulary

**accerso, -ere, -ii** *or* **-ivi, -itus,** to call for; summon
**illucesco, -lucescere, -luxi,** to begin to shine
**mercor, -ari, -atus sum,** to buy
**mundus, -a, -um,** elegant
**sileo, -ere, -ui,** to be quiet; rest
**subsequor, -i, -secutus,** to follow from behind

## Historical and Grammatical Notes

### Mark 15:42–47 (cont.)

44. **si iam obisset:** "whether Jesus had already died." This is a perfectly natural question. Death by crucifixion would regularly take days. Jesus died after only a few hours.

46. **sindonem:** This is the source of the celebrated, or infamous, Shroud of Turin, a garment that many believe retains an image of Jesus.

47. **aspiciebant, ubi positus esset:** Mark, and the other two Synoptics after him, add editorial comments to remove any doubt that Jesus rose from the dead. Here Mark appears to be answering a charge that the two women mistook another tomb for the one Jesus was buried in. Consequently, when they came to prepare his body for burial on the day after the Sabbath, they went to the wrong tomb. That's why they found it empty. Mark insists that they made no such mistake because they saw where Jesus was placed.

### Matthew 27:57–61 (cont.)

58. **iussit reddi:** Joseph must have had some influence with Pilate. The request is granted without any special pleading. It also shows something about Pilate. He was willing to bend the rules of the standard practice of allowing a crucified body to decompose on the cross to accommodate the peculiar sensitivities of the officials of the people he was governing.

### Luke 23:50–56 (cont.)

53. **in quo nondum quisquam positus fuerat:** that is, there was no mistaking the fact that Jesus's body was gone on the morning after the Sabbath. A skeptic could argue that if there were more than one body in the tomb, the women might have been mistaken about which one was Jesus's.

54. **illucescebat:** The evening stars were beginning to emerge and the Sabbath was about to begin.

56. **secundum mandatum:** "according to the commandment."

# Chapter 16

There is almost unanimous agreement that Mark's Gospel ended after verse 8. Verses 9–20 are often called the longer ending of Mark. The consensus is that they were written by a Christian of the middle of the 2nd century CE who found the original, shorter ending of Mark unacceptably abrupt. He compiled bits and pieces of the other Gospels and Acts into a compressed summary of how Jesus appeared and what instructions he gave his disciples and others. In verses 1–8, the women who saw where Jesus was entombed on the day before the Sabbath arrive early in the morning at the tomb to tend to the body before its burial. They find the tomb open and Jesus's body missing. A young man dressed in white inside the tomb tells them that Jesus has risen. The terrified women run away and tell no one what they had seen.

# Mark 16:1–8

## *The Empty Tomb*

Three women come to where Jesus's body was placed for safe keeping until the morning after the Sabbath. They find the large rock that secured the tomb had been rolled away, and on the inside they find a young man in a white robe who tells them that Jesus has risen. He instructs them to tell the disciples that Jesus will meet them when they arrive back home in Galilee. The women are so terrified that they run away and say nothing to anyone.

**1** Et cum transisset Sabbatum, Maria Magdalene et Maria
Iacobi et Salome emerunt aromata, ut venientes ungerent
eum. **2** Et valde mane, primā Sabbatorum, veniunt ad
monumentum, orto iam sole. **3** Et dicebant ad invicem,
"Quis revolvet nobis lapidem ab ostio monumenti?" **4**
Et respicientes vident revolutum lapidem. Erat quippe
magnus valde. **5** Et introeuntes in monumentum viderunt
iuvenem sedentem in dextris, coopertum stolā candidā,
et obstupuerunt.

## Matthew 27:62–28:8

[***27:62–66*** *After sunset, which would be the beginning of the day after the Sabbath, Jewish leaders ask Pilate to put guards on the tomb. They tell him that if Jesus's body is stolen and the tomb is found to be empty, some might think that his prophecy that he would come back from the dead had come true. They warn Pilate that this would create a problem worse than the one that Jesus's crucifixion was supposed to solve.*] **28:1**
Sero autem post Sabbatum, cum illucesceret in primam Sabbati,
vēnit Maria Magdalene et altera Maria videre sepulcrum. **2** Et ecce:
terrae motus factus est magnus, angelus enim Domini descendit
de caelo et accedens revolvit lapidem et sedebat super eum. **3** Erat
autem aspectus eius sicut fulgur, et vestimentum eius candidum
sicut nix. **4** Prae timore autem eius exterriti sunt custodes et facti
sunt velut mortui.

## Luke 24:1–12

**1** Primā autem Sabbatorum, valde diluculo venerunt ad
monumentum portantes, quae paraverant, aromata. **2** Et invenerunt
lapidem revolutum a monumento. **3** Et ingressae non invenerunt
corpus Domini Iesu. **4** Et factum est, dum mente haesitarent de isto,
ecce: duo viri steterunt secus illas in veste fulgenti.

## Vocabulary

**cooperio, -ire, -ui, -tus,** to cover

**nix, nivis,** *f.*, snow

## Historical and Grammatical Notes

### Mark 16:1–8

**1. cum transisset Sabbatum:** This would be the evening of "Preparation Day," Friday afternoon in civil time.

**2. valde mane:** "early in the morning." **primā:** Supply *horā*. That is, approximately 6 a.m.

**4. revolutum lapidem:** Supply *esse*.

**5. iuvenem sedentem:** Is this the angel, or one of the angels, reported in the other two Synoptics? If it is, why didn't Mark refer to him as an angel? It could also be the young man at Mark 5:1–2, who fled when Jesus was arrested and left behind his robe. The women fled in terror and didn't find out who or what this young man was.

### Matthew 27:62–28:8

**27:62–66:** The claims of the early Christians that Jesus rose from the dead would have been met with understandable skepticism. One of the many objections surely would have been that Jesus's followers simply returned to the tomb at night and stole his body. Matthew's additional detail is designed to answer that charge. Pilate posted guards precisely to prevent that from happening.

**28:2. Terrae motus factus est magnus:** The women and the guards witness the dramatic arrival of an angel who rolls away the rock covering the entrance to the tomb and then sits on it. The guards are terrified into a stupor and the angel speaks to the women.

**4. dum mente haesitarent de isto:** literally, "while they are wavering in the mind about this."

### Luke 24:1–12

**1. Primā:** Supply *horā*.

# Mark 16:1–8 (cont.)

**6** Qui dicit illis, "Nolite expavescere! Iesum quaeritis
Nazarenum crucifixum. Surrexit. Non est hīc. Ecce:
locus, ubi posuerunt eum. **7** Sed ite. Dicite discipulis eius
et Petro, 'Praecedit vos in Galilaeam. Ibi eum videbitis,
sicut dixit vobis.' " **8** Et exeuntes fugerunt de monumento,
invaserat enim eas tremor et pavor. Et nemini quidquam
dixerunt, timebant enim.

## Matthew 27:62–28:8 (cont.)

**5** Respondens autem angelus dixit mulieribus, "Nolite timere vos!
Scio enim quod Iesum, qui crucifixus est, quaeritis. **6** Non est hīc,
surrexit enim, sicut dixit. Venite. Videte locum, ubi positus erat.
**7** Et cito euntes dicite discipulis eius, 'Surrexit a mortuis et ecce:
praecedit vos in Galilaeam. Ibi eum videbitis.' Ecce: dixi vobis."
**8** Et exeuntes cito de monumento cum timore et magno gaudio
cucurrerunt nuntiare discipulis eius.

## Luke 24:1–12 (cont.)

**5** Cum timerent autem et declinarent vultum in terram, dixerunt
ad illas, "Quid quaeritis viventem cum mortuis? **6** Non est hīc, sed
surrexit. Recordamini qualiter locutus est vobis, cum adhuc in
Galilaeā esset, **7** dicens, 'Oportet filium hominis tradi in manūs
hominum peccatorum et crucifigi et die tertiā resurgere.' " **8**
Et recordatae sunt verborum eius, **9** et regressae a monumento
nuntiaverunt haec omnia illis Undecim et ceteris omnibus. **10**
Erat autem Maria Magdalene et Ioanna et Maria Iacobi. Et ceterae
cum eis dicebant ad apostolos haec. **11** Et visa sunt ante illos sicut
deliramentum verba ista, et non credebant illis. **12** Petrus autem
surgens cucurrit ad monumentum et procumbens videt linteamina
sola. Et rediit ad sua mirans, quod factum fuerat.

## Vocabulary

**deliramentum, -i,** *n.,* nonsense
**expavesco, -escere, -i,** to be frightened
**invado, -dere, -si, -sus,** to enter upon; fall upon
**linteamen, -inis,** *n.,* a linen cloth
**tremor, -oris,** *m.,* trembling
**undecim,** eleven

## Historical and Grammatical Notes

### Mark 16:1–8 (cont.)

7. **sicut dixit vobis:** Even though Jesus doesn't say this anywhere in Mark, it doesn't mean that he couldn't have said something like this sometime in his ministry. Surely Jesus said and did more things than could have been recorded in Mark. **et Petro:** Why does the young man single out Peter from the other disciples? A possible explanation is that after his disgraceful denial of Jesus two days before, Peter might have separated himself from the others and would have needed to be sought out separately.

8. **nemini quidquam dixerunt:** Evidently the women said something to someone; otherwise this event wouldn't have been known. They were the only ones there. **timebant enim:** By near unanimous consent, Mark ends here. Some modern Bibles don't even have the next twelve verses.

### Matthew 27:62–28:8 (cont.)

8. **magno gaudio cucurrerunt nuntiare discipulis eius:** The women are terrified but also overjoyed. They run off to tell the disciples what the angel told them.

### Luke 24:1–12 (cont.)

7. **Oportet:** Luke might have been troubled that there was no textual evidence for what Jesus is reported to have said in Mark. He replaces it with something he is known to have said to them in Galilee.

10. **ceterae cum eis:** Luke multiplies the number of witnesses as well as the number of people whom they told what had happened.

11. **verba ista:** subject of *visa sunt*: "their words seemed in their eyes to be like nonsense."

12. **Petrus:** This is not in Mark. If we assume that Mark is a compilation of Peter's teachings, why would Peter not have mentioned the fact that he had returned to the tomb and confirmed much of what the women had seen? **ad sua mirans:** Some important manuscripts have *secum* instead. That makes better sense: "he was wondering deep inside himself."

# Mark 16:9–20

## *Jesus Appears to His Followers*

Jesus appears to Mary of Magdalene and at first his disciples don't believe her account of events. Then Jesus appears to two of the disciples, but in disguise. Again, the other disciples don't believe those who report seeing Jesus alive. Jesus then appears to all eleven disciples (i.e., the Twelve minus Judas) and chastises them for their doubts. He orders them to spread the word throughout the entire world and gives them powers to prove his authority. They will be able to speak in new languages, throw out demons, and heal the sick. They will also be immune from snake venom and poisonous drinks. Jesus is then taken up into heaven where he sits at the right hand of God. With God's help, the disciples go out to preach the Word and perform miracles.

**9** Surgens autem mane, primā Sabbati, apparuit primo
Mariae Magdalenae, de quā eiecerat septem daemonia. **10**
Illa vadens nuntiavit his, qui cum eo fuerant, lugentibus et
flentibus. **11** Et illi audientes quia viveret et visus esset ab
eā, non crediderunt.

### Matthew 28:9–20

**9** Et ecce: Iesus occurrit illis, dicens, "Avete." Illae autem accesserunt
et tenuerunt pedes eius et adoraverunt eum. **10** Tunc ait illis Iesus,
"Nolite timere. Ite! Nuntiate fratribus meis, ut eant in Galilaeam et
ibi me videbunt." **11** Quae cum abiissent, ecce: quidam de custodiā
venerunt in civitatem et nuntiaverunt principibus sacerdotum
omnia, quae facta fuerant. **12** Et congregati cum senioribus,
consilio accepto, pecuniam copiosam dederunt militibus, **13**
dicentes, "Dicite, 'Discipuli eius nocte venerunt et furati sunt eum,
nobis dormientibus.' **14** Et si hoc auditum fuerit a praeside, nos
suadebimus ei et securos vos faciemus." **15** At illi, acceptā pecuniā,
fecerunt, sicut erant docti. Et divulgatum est verbum istud apud
Iudaeos usque in hodiernum diem.

## Historical and Grammatical Notes

### Mark 16:9–20

**9. primā Sabbati:** *primā [horā] Sabbati*. That is, between 6 and 7 a.m. **apparuit:** This is inconsistent with the shorter ending, where the two women find only a young man dressed in a white robe in the tomb. Then they run away. **de quā eiecerat septem daemonia:** as related in Luke 8:2.

**10. nuntiavit his:** Supply *haec* or *hoc* as the object of *nuntiavit*. **eo:** Jesus.

### Matthew 28:9–20

**14. nos suadebimus:** This is another part of the effort to shore up the claim that Jesus was resurrected. Matthew adds the detail that there were guards positioned to watch over the tomb. This detail serves to counter the charge that the body was stolen by his followers.

**15. usque in hodiernum diem:** "even up to this day." We can well imagine the general and ongoing skepticism that greeted the claim that Jesus rose from the dead.

# Mark 16:9–20 (cont.)

**12** Post haec autem duobus ex eis ambulantibus ostensus
est in aliā effigie euntibus in villam. **13** Et illi euntes
nuntiaverunt ceteris, nec illis crediderunt.

## Luke 24:13–53

**13** Et ecce: duo ex illis ibant ipsa die in castellum, quod erat in
spatio stadiorum sexaginta ab Ierusalem, nomine Emmaus. **14** Et
ipsi loquebantur ad invicem de his omnibus, quae acciderant. **15**
Et factum est, dum fabularentur et secum quaererent, et ipse Iesus
appropinquans ibat cum illis. **16** Oculi autem illorum tenebantur,
ne eum agnoscerent. **17** Et ait ad illos, "Qui sunt hi sermones,
quos confertis ad invicem ambulantes?" Et steterunt tristes. **18** Et
respondens unus, cui nomen Cleopas, dixit ei, "Tu solus peregrinus
es in Ierusalem et non cognovisti, quae facta sunt in illā his diebus?"
**19** Quibus ille dixit, "Quae?" Et illi dixerunt ei, "De Iesu Nazareno,
qui fuit vir propheta, potens in opere et sermone coram Deo et
omni populo, **20** et quomodo eum tradiderunt summi sacerdotes
et principes nostri in damnationem mortis et crucifixerunt eum.
**21** Nos autem sperabamus, quia ipse esset redempturus Israel.
At nunc super haec omnia tertia dies hodie quod haec facta sunt.
**22** Sed et mulieres quaedam ex nostris terruerunt nos, quae ante
lucem fuerunt ad monumentum, **23** et, non invento corpore eius,
venerunt, dicentes se etiam visionem angelorum vidisse, qui dicunt
eum vivere. **24** Et abierunt quidam ex nostris ad monumentum et
ita invenerunt, sicut mulieres dixerunt. Ipsum vero non viderunt."
**25** Et ipse dixit ad eos, "O stulti et tardi corde ad credendum in
omnibus, quae locuti sunt Prophetae! **26** Nonne haec oportuit pati
Christum et intrare in gloriam suam?" **27** Et incipiens a Moyse et
omnibus Prophetis interpretabatur illis in omnibus Scripturis, quae
de ipso erant.

## Vocabulary

**agnosco, -noscere, -novi, -nitus,** to recognize
**effigies, -ei,** *f.,* form; imitation
**fabulor, -ari, -atus sum,** to talk
**interpretor, -ari, -atus sum,** to explain; translate
**peregrinus, -a, -um,** traveling; foreign
**tardus, -a, -um,** slow

## Historical and Grammatical Notes

### Mark 16:9–20 (cont.)

**12. in aliā effigie:** The two must have seen through his disguise because in the next verse they try to persuade others that they had seen Jesus and were not believed.

### Luke 24:13–53

**13. stadiorum sexaginta:** A stade was approximately two hundred meters, so sixty stades is a little more than ten kilometers (six miles).

**16. Oculi autem illorum tenebantur:** literally, "their eyes were held back" or "their eyes were kept from recognizing him." **Cleopas:** Jesus first appears to someone who is never mentioned anywhere else in the New Testament and his companion, who is not named at all. They were undoubtedly members of Jesus's larger circle of unnamed followers. The identity of Cleopas will be forever debated.

**21. tertia dies hodie quod haec facta sunt:** "today is the third day that (since) these things happened."

**27. incipiens a Moyse et omnibus Prophetis interpretabatur:** As the early Christians spread their claim that Jesus was indeed the Messiah, they would have been confronted with challenges to demonstrate how he had fulfilled sixty or so Old Testament prophecies about the Messiah. The effort, therefore, to provide documentary evidence of their claim would have started immediately.

# Mark 16:9–20 (cont.)

**14** Novissime recumbentibus illis Undecim apparuit, et
exprobravit incredulitatem illorum et duritiam cordis,
quia his, qui viderant eum resuscitatum, non crediderant.

## Matthew 28:9–20 (cont.)

**16** Undecim autem discipuli abierunt in Galilaeam, in montem ubi
constituerat illis Iesus, **17** et videntes eum adoraverunt. Quidam
autem dubitaverunt.

## Luke 24:13–53 (cont.)

**28** Et appropinquaverunt castello, quo ibant, et ipse se finxit longius
ire. **29** Et coegerunt illum, dicentes, "Mane nobiscum, quoniam
advesperascit, et inclinata est iam dies." Et intravit, ut maneret cum
illis. **30** Et factum est, dum recumberet cum illis, accepit panem et
benedixit ac fregit et porrigebat illis. **31** Et aperti sunt oculi eorum,
et cognoverunt eum. Et ipse evanuit ab eis. **32** Et dixerunt ad
invicem, "Nonne cor nostrum ardens erat in nobis, dum loqueretur
nobis in viā et aperiret nobis Scripturas?" **33** Et surgentes eādem
horā regressi sunt in Ierusalem et invenerunt congregatos Undecim
et eos, qui cum ipsis erant, **34** dicentes, "Surrexit Dominus vere et
apparuit Simoni." **35** Et ipsi narrabant, quae gesta erant in viā, et
quomodo cognoverunt eum in fractione panis. **36** Dum haec autem
loquuntur, ipse stetit in medio eorum et dicit eis, "Pax vobis!" **37**
Conturbati vero et conterriti existimabant se spiritum videre. **38**
Et dixit eis, "Quid turbati estis, et quare cogitationes ascendunt
in corda vestra? **39** Videte manūs meas et pedes meos, quia ipse
ego sum! Palpate me et videte, quia spiritus carnem et ossa non
habet, sicut me videtis habere." **40** Et cum hoc dixisset, ostendit eis
manūs et pedes. **41** Adhuc autem illis non credentibus prae gaudio
et mirantibus, dixit eis, "Habetis hīc aliquid, quod manducetur?"
**42** At illi obtulerunt ei partem piscis assi. **43** Et sumens, coram eis
manducavit. **44** Et dixit ad eos, "Haec sunt verba, quae locutus sum
ad vos, cum adhuc essem vobiscum, quoniam necesse est impleri
omnia, quae scripta sunt in Lege Moysis et Prophetis et Psalmis de
me." **45** Tunc aperuit illis sensum, ut intellegerent Scripturas. **46** Et

dixit eis, "Sic scriptum est, 'Christum pati et resurgere a mortuis die tertiā,' **47** et praedicari in nomine eius paenitentiam in remissionem peccatorum in omnes gentes, incipientibus ab Ierusalem. **48** Vos estis testes horum.

## Vocabulary

**advesperascit, -ascere, -avit,** to become dark; become evening
**assus, -a, -um,** broiled
**exprobo (1),** to chastise
**fingo, fingere, finxi, fictus,** to pretend
**fractio, -ionis,** *f.,* breaking
**inclino (1),** to fall
**ossum, -i,** *n.,* bone
**palpo (1),** to touch; pat
**porrigo, -rigere, -rexi, -rectus,** to extend; offer

## Historical and Grammatical Notes

### Matthew 28:9–20 (cont.)

**16. constituerat illis:** "had instructed them [to go]." The mountain is not named, but it is identified as Mt. Tabor, which is also the traditional site where the transfiguration of Jesus had occurred (Mark 9:2).

### Luke 24:13–53 (cont.)

**28. se finxit longius ire:** "he pretended that he was going on farther."

**31. Et aperti sunt oculi eorum:** because, presumably, they had been present at the Last Supper, where he broke the bread and blessed it.

**34. et apparuit Simoni:** A separate appearance to Peter isn't recorded in any of the other Gospel accounts. As Peter was presumably the source for Mark's Gospel, it's hard to imagine why the event is not in at least Mark as well.

**36. ipse stetit in medio eorum et dicit eis:** In Luke's account, Jesus appears to his disciples while they are still in Jerusalem, not, as in Matthew, on a mountain in Galilee.

**37. se spiritum videre:** a natural enough conjecture, and probably yet another objection to the claims by Christians that Jesus had been brought back from the dead. Skeptics could say that they only thought that they saw Jesus bodily resurrected. What follows is designed to prove that what they saw was no ghost, but a real, physical body.

**40. ostendit eis manūs et pedes:** presumably with the wounds from the crucifixion.

**47. incipientibus ab Ierusalem:** "starting with Jerusalem." The grammar of the participle is loose indeed, though the sense is clear enough.

# Mark 16:9–20 (cont.)

**15** Et dixit eis, "Euntes in mundum universum praedicate
evangelium omni creaturae. **16** Qui crediderit et
baptizatus fuerit, salvus erit. Qui vero non crediderit,
condemnabitur. **17** Signa autem eos, qui crediderint,
haec sequentur: in nomine meo daemonia eicient, linguis
loquentur novis, **18** serpentes tollent, et, si mortiferum
quid biberint, non eos nocebit, super aegrotos manūs
imponent, et bene habebunt." **19** Et Dominus quidem
Iesus, postquam locutus est eis, assumptus est in caelum
et sedit a dextris Dei. **20** Illi autem profecti praedicaverunt
ubique, Domino cooperante et sermonem confirmante,
sequentibus signis.

## Matthew 28:9–20 (cont.)

**18** Et accedens Iesus locutus est eis, dicens, "Data est mihi
omnis potestas in caelo et in terrā. **19** Euntes ergo docete
omnes gentes, baptizantes eos in nomine Patris et filii et Spiritus
Sancti, **20** docentes eos servare omnia, quaecumque mandavi
vobis. Et ecce: ego vobiscum sum omnibus diebus usque ad
consummationem saeculi."

## Luke 24:13–53 (cont.)

**49** Et ecce: ego mitto promissum Patris mei in vos. Vos autem
sedete in civitate, quoadusque induamini virtutem ex alto." **50**
Eduxit autem eos foras usque in Bethaniam et, elevatis manibus
suis, benedixit eis. **51** Et factum est, dum benediceret illis, recessit
ab eis et ferebatur in caelum. **52** Et ipsi adoraverunt eum et regressi
sunt in Ierusalem cum gaudio magno, **53** et erant semper in Templo
benedicentes Deum.

## Vocabulary

**cooperor, -ari, -atus sum,** to work with; cooperate

**mortiferus, -a, -um,** deadly

## Historical and Grammatical Notes

### Mark 16:9–20 (cont.)

17. **linguis loquentur novis:** In Acts 2:2–4, the disciples were granted the power to speak in languages they didn't know.

18. **serpentes:** presumably poisonous snakes. This immunity is declared, though perhaps only metaphorically, in Luke 10:19: *Ecce: dedi vobis potestatem calcandi* [of walking on] *supra serpentes et scorpiones et supra omnem virtutem inimici, et nihil vobis nocebit* "Behold, I gave you the power of treading on snakes and scorpions and on all the power of an enemy, and nothing will harm you." **mortiferum quid biberint:** This power is granted to them only in Mark.

### Luke 24:13–53 (cont.)

49. **quoadusque induamini virtutem ex alto:** This anticipates the book of Acts, also written by Luke, which begins with the disciples awaiting the bestowal of special powers upon them by the Holy Spirit.

# Sites Mentioned in the Synoptics

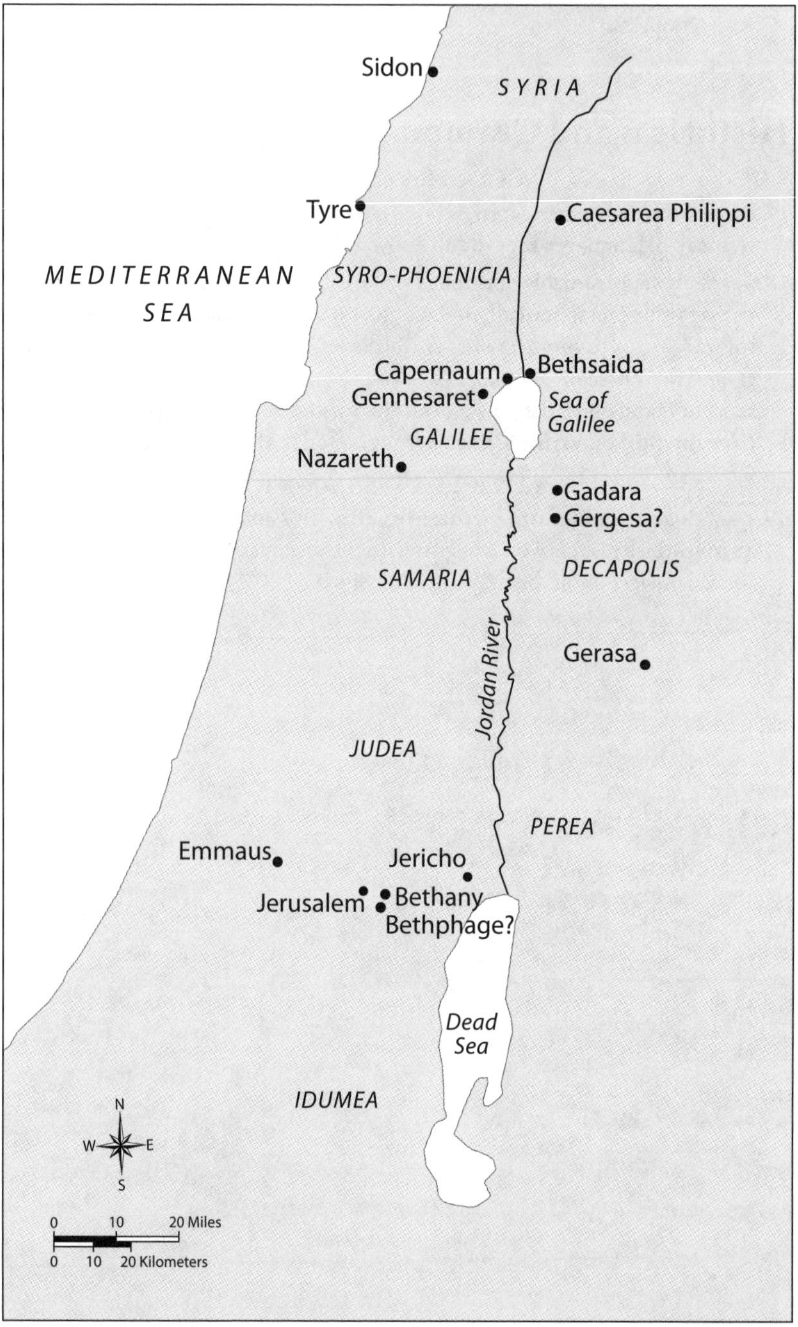

# Suggestions for Further Inquiry

## *Introduction to the Synoptic Gospels*

Stein, Robert H. *Studying the Synoptic Gospels: Origin and Interpretation.* 2nd ed. Grand Rapids, Michigan: Baker Academic, 2001.

Students unfamiliar with the arguments and evidence for the priority of Mark and its subsequent use by Matthew and Luke will benefit immensely from this very readable introduction to the Synoptic Problem.

## *Commentaries on the Gospel of Mark*

Card, Michael. *Mark: The Gospel of Passion.* Downers Grove, Illinois: IVP Books, 2012.

Card may be best known among evangelical Christians for his inspirational music CDs, but he has written a very lucid and moving personal commentary on Mark that students of all ages will find informative and enjoyable.

Healy, Mary. *The Gospel of Mark*. Catholic Commentary on Sacred Scripture. Grand Rapids, Michigan: Baker Academic, 2008.

Healy has written an excellent commentary on Mark that "focus[es] on the meaning of the text for faith and life" from the perspective of Roman Catholicism. Each section includes numerous cross-references to related biblical passages and helpful sidebars where historical and theological issues are discussed. Roman Catholic students and their teachers will appreciate the inclusion of brief catechism lessons.

Lane, William L. *The Gospel According to Mark*. Grand Rapids, Michigan: William B. Eerdman's Publishing Company, 1988. First published 1974.

William Lane is a towering figure in biblical studies, and he inspired a generation of New Testament scholars. His volume on Mark, though first published more than forty years ago, is still a central work that continues to reward careful study. Academic in tone and more demanding than the other two cited in this list, the book can be used profitably as a resource after the class discussion has spawned a search for more detailed historical and textual information.

## Vulgate Latin

Clackson, James, and Geoffrey Horrocks. *The Blackwell History of the Latin Language*. Malden, Massachusetts: Wiley-Blackwell, 2010.

Understandably, there is no single volume that quickly shows intermediate-level students how the classical Latin they're familiar with differs from the vulgate Latin of the fifth century. The two are so much alike that a complete book on the subject would hardly be justified. *The Blackwell History of the Latin Language* contains an excellent chapter on the subject: "Sub-Elite Latin in the Empire."

## Jerome's Translation

de Hamel, Christopher. *The Book: A History of the Bible*. London: Phaidon Press, 2001.

More than half of this magnificently illustrated volume covers St. Jerome's translation in the fifth century down to its publication as the first book printed by Gutenberg. The book is reasonably priced and has a place in the personal library of anyone interested in biblical studies.

## *Text of the New Testament Vulgate*

Kinney, Angela M., ed. *The New Testament*. Vol. 6 of *The Vulgate*. Dumbarton Oaks Medieval Library. Cambridge, Massachusetts: Harvard University Press, 2013.

This is the final volume of a six-volume edition of the entire Vulgate Bible, including the Old Testament. Each volume has a facing English translation. This library is elegantly produced, and at around thirty dollars per volume, it's very affordable.

Aland, Kurt, and Barbard Aland, eds. *Novum Testamentum Latine*. Stuttgart: Deutsche Bibelgesellschaft, 1991.

For a more compact volume (without English translation), the Nestle-Aland edition is an inexpensive choice. It has the additional virtue of including an apparatus criticus. This is an index at the bottom of each page listing significant manuscript variations.

# Complete Latin-to-English Glossary

A

**a(b)** + *ablative,* from, away from; by

**Abba,** *indecl.,* father

**abduco, -ducere, -duxi, -ductus,** to lead away; remove

**abeo, -ire, -ii** *or* **-ivi, -itus,** to depart; leave

**Abiathar,** *indecl., m.,* Abiathar

**abnego (1),** to refuse; deny

**abominatio, -ionis,** *f.,* abomination

**Abraham,** *indecl. proper name,* Abraham

**abscindo, -scindere, -scidi, -scissus,** to cut away; cut out

**absconditum, -i,** *n.,* cellar

**abscondo, -dere, -di** *or* **-didi, -ditus,** to hide; conceal

**absum, -esse, -fui, -futurus,** to be away from; be distant from

**abundo (1),** to overflow; be abundant

**abyssus, -i,** *f.,* abyss; bottomless pit

**ac,** and

**accedo, -cedere, -cessi, -cessus,** to draw near

**accendo, -dere, -di, -sus,** to kindle; set on fire

**accerso, -ere, -ii** *or* **-ivi, -itus,** to call for; summon

**accido, -cidere, -cidi,** to happen; fall upon

**accipio, -cipere, -cepi, -ceptus,** to get; acquire; take up

**accumbo, -cumbere, -cubui, -cubitus,** to recline at the dinner table

**accurro, -currere, -curri** *or* **-cucurri, -cursus,** to run to; approach; come to

**accuso (1),** to reproach
**acetum, -i,** *n.,* bad wine; vinegar
**acus, -us,** *f.,* needle
**ad** + *accusative,* to, toward; *with gerunds/gerundives to show purpose*
**ad invicem,** back and forth; in turn; one after another; to one another
**adaperio, -ire, -ui, -tus,** to open; reveal
**addo, -dere, -didi, -ditus,** to add to; join
**adduco, -ducere, -duxi, -ductus,** to lead to
**adeo, -ire, -ivi (-ii), -itus,** to come to
**adhaereo, -haerere, -haesi, -haesus,** to adhere to; cling to
**adhuc,** still
**adicio, -icere, -ieci, -iectus,** to throw to; put near
**adimpleo, -ere, -evi, -etus,** to complete
**adiudico (1),** to grant; pass judgment on
**adiuro (1),** to swear to; swear by
**adiuvo, -iuvare, -iuvi, -iutus,** to help
**admiror, -ari, -miratus sum,** to admire; be amazed
**admitto, -mittere, -misi, -missus,** to allow; permit; let in
**adoro (1),** to pray to; curse
**adsum, -esse, -fui, -futurus,** to be pressent; nearby
**adulescens, -entis,** *m.,* a young man
**adulterium, -ii,** *n.,* adultery
**adultero (1),** to commit adultery
**adulterus, -a, -um,** debauched; adulterous
**adventus, -us,** *m.,* approach; arrival
**advesperascit, -ascere, -avit,** to become dark; become evening
**adversus** + *accusative,* to; against
**advoco (1),** to summon
**advolvo, -vere, -vi, -utus,** to roll upon
**aedificatio, -ionis,** *f.,* construction
**aedifico (1),** to build
**aegrotus, -a, -um,** sick
**aequalis, -e,** + *dative,* equal
**aeramentum, -i,** *n.,* bronze vessel
**aerumna, -ae,** *f.,* hardship
**aes, aeris,** *n.,* bronze coin
**aestas, -tatis,** *f.,* summer
**aestimo (1),** to think
**aestuo (1),** to be hot; burn
**aeternus, -a, -um,** everlasting
**affero, -ferre, -tuli, -latus,** to bring to
**afficio, -ficere, -feci, -fectus,** to inflict upon; treat
**affirmo (1),** to affirm
**affligo, -gere, -xi, -ctus,** to brush up against
**ager, -gri,** *m.,* field; farm
**agnosco, -noscere, -novi, -nitus,** to recognize
**ago, -ere, egi, actus,** to make; perform; do
**agonia, -ae,** *f.,* pain; suffering
**agricola, -ae,** *m.,* farmer
**ait, aiunt,** he says/they say
**alabaster, -tri,** *m.,* perfume jar
**alapa, -ae,** *f.,* slap

**albus, -a, -um,** white
**Alexander, -ri,** *m.,* Alexander
**alibi,** elsewhere
**alioquin,** otherwise
**aliquis, aliquid,** someone; something
**alius, -a, -ud,** other; another; **alius . . . alius,** the one . . . the other
**allido, -dere, -si, -sus,** to strike
**alligo (1),** to bind; tie up
**Alphaeus, -i,** *m.,* Alphaeus
**alterus, -a, -um,** the other of two
**alteruter, alterautera** *or* **alterutera, alterumuterum** *or* **alteruterum,** one another
**altitudo, -inis,** *f.,* height; depth
**altus, -a, -um,** high; deep
**amarus, -a, -um,** bitter
**ambo, -ae, -o,** both
**ambulo (1),** to walk
**amen,** *Hebrew,* in truth; certainly
**amicio, -cire, -cui** *or* **-xi, -tus,** to clothe
**amicus, -i,** *m.,* friend; friendly to
**amo (1),** to love
**amodo,** from this time forward
**amphora, -ae,** *f.,* large transport vase
**amplius,** anymore; more; further
**amputo (1),** to cut off
**anathematizo (1),** to curse
**ancilla, -ae,** *f.,* female servant; slave
**Andreas, -ae,** *m.,* Andrew
**angario (1),** to demand; require
**angelus, -i,** *m.,* messenger
**angulus, -i,** *m.,* angle; corner
**anima, -ae,** *f.,* soul
**animaequus, -a, -um,** of good courage; of calm mind
**annuntio (1),** to announce
**annuo, -nuere, -nui, -nutus,** to nod to; signal to
**ante** + *accusative,* in front of; before; *as adv.,* previous; before
**antecedo, -cedere, -cessi, -cessus,** to go before; step forward
**antequam,** before
**antiquus, -a, -um,** old; ancient
**aperio, -ire, -ui, -tus,** to uncover; open
**apostolus, -i,** *m.,* apostle; *one who is sent out*
**appareo, -ere, -ui, -itum,** to appear
**applico (1),** to steer toward; put in at
**appono, -ponere, -posui, -positus,** + *dative,* to set before; serve
**apprehendo, -dere, -di, -sus,** to take hold of
**appropinquo (1)** + *dative,* to approach; arrive at
**apud** + *accusative,* nearby; in the house of
**aqua, -ae,** *f.,* water
**aquila, -ae,** *f.,* eagle
**arbor, -oris,** *m./f.,* tree
**archisynagogus, -i,** *m.,* a leader of a synagogue
**ardeo, -ere, arsi, arsurus,** to burn
**area, -ae,** *f.,* ground
**arefacio, -facere, -feci, -factus,** to make dry

**areo, -ere, arui,** to be dry
**aresco, -escere, -ui,** to become dry
**Arimathaea, -ae,** *f., city of* Arimathea
**argenteus, -a, -um,** of silver
**argentum, -i,** *n.,* silver
**aridus, -a, -um,** dry
**arma, -orum,** *n. pl.,* armament
**aroma, -atis,** *n.,* scent; perfume
**arripio, -ripere, -ripui, -reptus,** to lay hold of
**arundo, -inis,** *f.,* cane; reed
**ascendo, -ndere, -ndi, -nsus,** to rise up
**asina, -ae,** *f.,* female donkey
**asinarius, -a, -um,** of a mule
**aspectus, -us,** *m.,* look; appearance
**aspicio, -picere, -spexi, -spectus,** to look at; behold
**assimilo (1),** to compare to
**assumentum, -i,** *n.,* swath
**assumo, -ere, -psi, -ptus,** to take up as a companion; take aside
**assuo, -suere, -sui, -sutus,** to sew on
**assus, -a, -um,** broiled
**at,** but; and
**atrium, -i,** *n.,* central room
**attendo, -dere, -di, -tus,** to stretch to; pay attention to
**audacter,** courageously
**audio, -ire, -ivi** *or* **-ii, -itus,** to hear
**aufero, -ferre, abstuli, ablatus,** to take away
**aula, -ae,** *f.,* court; hall; atrium
**auricula, -ae,** *f.,* ear
**auris, -is,** *m.,* ear
**aurum, -i,** *n.,* gold
**aut,** or; **aut . . . aut,** either . . . or
**autem,** however, moreover
**avaritia, -ae,** *f.,* greed
**ave,** hail; greetings
**avello, -vellere, -velli** *or* **-vulsi** *or* **-volsi, -vulsus** *or* **-volsus,** to separate
**averto, -tere, -ti, -sus,** to turn away; remove
**avis, -is,** *f.,* bird
**Azymus, -a, -um,** unleavened; **Azyma, -orum,** *n.,* Feast of the Unleavened Bread

**B**

**baiulo (1),** to carry
**baptisma, -atis,** *n.,* washing
**baptismum, -i,** *n.,* baptism
**baptista, -ae,** *m.,* baptizer
**baptizo (1),** to baptize
**Barabbas, -ae,** *m.,* Barabbas
**Bariona,** Bar-Jona; son of Jonah
**Bartholomaeus, -i,** *m.,* Bartholomew
**Bartimaeus, -i,** *m.,* Bartimaeus
**beatus, -a, -um,** blessed; happy
**Beelzebul,** *indecl.,* Beelzebul; Satan
**bellum, -i,** *n.,* war
**bene,** well
**benedico, -cere, -xi, -ctus,** to bless
**benefacio, -facere, -feci, -factus,** to do a good deed
**bestia, -ae,** *f.,* wild animal
**Bethania, -ae,** *f.,* Bethany
**Bethfage,** *indecl.,* Bethfage
**Bethsaida, -ae,** *f.,* Bethsaida

**bibo, -ere, -ii,** to drink
**biduum, -i,** *n.,* two days
**bini, -ae, -a,** two by two; in pairs
**bis,** twice
**bivium, -i,** *n.,* crossroads; intersection
**blasphemo (1),** to blaspheme
**Boanerges,** *indecl.,* Sons of Thunder
**bonus, -a, -um,** good
**brevio (1),** to shorten

**C**

**cado, cadere, cecidi, casus,** to fall; fall on; attack
**caecitas, -tatis,** *f.,* blindness
**caecus, -a, -um,** blind
**caedo, caedere, cecidi, caesus,** to beat; come down on
**caelestis, -e,** heavenly
**caelum, -i,** *n.,* sky; heaven
**Caesar, -is,** *m.,* Caesar
**Caesarea Philippi, Caesareae Philippi,** *f., city of* Caesarea Philippi
**Caiphas, -ae,** *m.,* Caiphas
**calamus, -i,** *m.,* cane; reed; pole
**calceamentum, -i,** *n.,* shoe
**calceo (1),** to put on shoes; wear shoes
**calco (1),** to walk on; trample on
**calefacio, -facere, -feci, -factus,** to warm
**calix, -icis,** *m.,* cup
**calvaria, -ae,** *f.,* skull
**camelus, -i,** *m.,* camel
**candelabrum, -i,** *n.,* lampstand
**candidus, -a, -um,** bright
**canto (1),** to sing; crow
**cantus, -us,** *m.,* singing
**Capharnaum,** *indecl., city of* Capernaum
**capillus, -i,** *m.,* hair
**capio, -ere, cepi, captus,** to take; capture
**captivus, -i,** *m.,* captive
**captura, -ae,** *f.,* catch; take
**caput, -itis,** *n.,* head
**carcer, -eris,** *m.,* prison
**caritas, -tatis,** *f.,* affection; love
**caro, carnis,** *f.,* flesh
**castellum, -i,** *n.,* fort; village
**catellus, -i,** *m.,* puppy
**catena, -ae,** *f.,* chain
**cathedra, -ae,** *f.,* chair; cushioned seat
**catinus, -i,** *m.,* serving bowl
**causa, -ae,** *f.,* legal case; crime
**caute,** carefully; under guard
**caveo, cavere, cavi, cautus,** to beware of
**cena, -ae,** *f.,* meal
**cenaculum, -i,** *n.,* dining room
**ceno (1),** to dine; eat dinner
**census, -us,** *m.,* census
**centies,** a hundredfold
**centuplus, -a, -um,** a hundredfold
**centurio, -ionis,** *m.,* centurion; captain
**centum,** one hundred
**ceterus, -a, -um,** other
**cervical, -is,** *n.,* pillow
**cesso (1),** to cease
**Chananaeus, -a, -um,** of the land of Canaan; Canaanite
**Christus, -i,** *m.,* anointed one; Messiah
**cibum, -i,** *n.,* food

**circa** + *accusative,* around; for
**circuitus, -us,** *m.,* circle
**circumdo, -dăre, -dedi, -datus,** to envelop; surround
**circumeo, -ire, -ii** *or* **-ivi, -itus,** to go around
**circumfero, -ferre, -tuli, -latus,** to carry around; report; spread the word
**circumpono, -ponere, -posui, -positus,** to place upon
**circumsedeo, -sedere, -sedi, -sessus,** to sit around
**circumspicio, -spicere, -spexi, -spectus,** to look around; examine
**circumstantes, -ium,** *m. pl.,* bystanders
**cito,** quickly
**civitas, -atis,** *f.,* city
**clamo (1),** to cry out; shout
**clamys, -dis,** *f.,* a general's cloak
**clare,** clearly
**claudus, -a, -um,** limping
**clavis, -is,** *f.,* key
**Cleopas,** *indecl.,* Cleopas
**coago, -agere, -egi, -actus,** to force; order
**coccineus, -a, -um,** red; scarlet
**coepi, -isse, -tus,** to begin
**cogitatio, -ionis,** *f.,* thought
**cogito (1),** to think
**cognatio, -ionis,** *m.,* family; relations
**cognatus, -a, -um,** related; kindred
**cognomino (1),** to give as a second name; give as a nickname
**cohors, -tis,** *f.,* cohort
**coinquino (1),** to defile
**colaphus, -i,** *m.,* blow; punch; strike
**colloquor, -qui, -cutus sum,** to converse
**collum, -i,** *n.,* neck
**colo, colere, colui, cultus,** to worship; tend; devote oneself to
**colonus, -i,** *m.,* farmer; one who works in the soil
**columba, -ae,** *f.,* dove
**comedo, -edere** *or* **-esse, -edi, -esus,** to eat
**commemoratio, -ionis,** *f.,* commemoration
**commendo (1),** to commit; hand over for protection; commend
**comminor, -ari, -atus sum** + *dative,* to curse; threaten
**comminuo, -uere, -ui, -utus,** to weaken; make smaller; crumble to pieces
**commissura, -ae,** *f.,* seam; stitch
**commorior, -mori, -mortuus sum,** to die with
**commoveo, -movere, -movi, -motus,** to be in motion; aroused; stirred up
**communis, -e,** common; unwashed
**commutatio, -ionis,** *f.,* exchange
**compes, -edis,** *f.,* shackles
**complaceo, -cere, -cui, -citus,** to be pleasing to
**compleo, -ere, -evi, -etus,** to fill up
**complexo (1),** to embrace
**complures, -a,** very many

**compono, -ponere, -posui, -positus,** to collect together
**comprehendo, -dere, -di, -sus,** to arrest
**comprimo, -primere, -pressi, -pressus,** to press up against
**concedo, -cedere, -cessi, -cessus** + *dative,* to allow; grant to
**concido, -cidere, -cidi, -cisus,** to cut up
**concilium, -ii,** *n.,* council; assembly
**concito (1),** to stir up
**concludo, -dere, -si, -sus,** to encompass; close up on
**conculco (1),** to walk on; trample
**concupiscentia, -ae,** *f.,* lust
**concurro, -currere, -curri** *or* **-cucurri, -cursus,** to run together; assemble
**condemno (1),** to find guilty
**condio, -ire, -ii** *or* **-ivi, -itus,** to season; spice
**condo, -dere, -didi, -ditus,** to establish; found
**confestim,** immediately
**confido, -dere, -sus sum** + *dative,* to have faith; trust in
**confirmo (1),** to strengthen
**confiteor, -fiteri, -fessus sum,** to confess; admit
**conforto (1),** to strengthen
**confrico (1),** to rub together
**confringo, -fringere, -fregi, -fractus,** to break into pieces; shatter
**confundo, -fundere, -fudi, -fusus,** to blend together; bewilder
**confusio, -ionis,** *f.,* confusion; perplexity
**congrego (1),** to gather; assemble together
**coniungo, -gere, -xi, -ctus,** to join together
**conquasso (1),** to shake apart; break to pieces
**conquiro, -rere, -sivi** *or* **-sii, -situs,** to ask questions; wonder
**consentio, -tire, -si, -sus,** to agree with
**conservo (1),** to save
**considero (1),** to examine thoroughly
**consilium, -i,** *n.,* plan; advice
**conspuo, -ui, -utus,** to spit on
**consterno (1),** to perplex; overcome
**constituo, -uere, -ui, -utus,** to decide; to put upon; order
**consuesco, -escere, -evi, -etus,** to become accustomed
**consuetudo, -inis,** *f.,* habit; custom
**consummatio, -ionis,** *f.,* fulfillment
**consummo (1),** to bring about; accomplish; complete
**consummo, -ere, -psi, -ptus,** to use up; spend
**consurgo, -gere, -rexi, -rectus,** to rise up against
**contemno, -nere, -psi, -ptus,** to look down on; hold in contempt
**contenebro (1),** to dim; grow dark
**contentio, -ionis,** *f.,* conflict; argument

**contero, -terere, -trivi, -tritus,** to grind down
**conterreo, -ere, -terrui, -territus,** to frighten thorougly
**contingo, -tingere, -tigi, -tactus,** to touch; happen to
**continuo,** directly, immediately
**contra,** to the other side
**contradico, -dicere, -dixi, -dictus,** to speak against
**contrarius, -a, -um,** contrary; opposing
**contristatus, -a, -um,** sad
**contristo (1),** to make sad
**contubernium, -ii,** *n.,* dwelling place
**contumelia, -ae,** *f.,* insult; abuse
**conturbo (1),** to confuse; disturb
**conveniens, -ntis,** consistent; in agreement
**convenio, -venire, -vēni, -ventus,** to fit
**conversor, -ari, -atus sum,** to abide in; stay in
**converto, -tere, -ti, -sus,** to turn toward
**convicior, -ari, -atus sum,** to abuse; revile; taunt
**conviva, -ae,** *m.,* invited guest
**convivium, -i,** *n.,* party; feast
**convoco (1),** to call together; summon
**cooperio, -ire, -ui, -tus,** to cover
**cooperor, -ari, -atus sum,** to work with; cooperate
**cophinus, -i,** *m.,* basket
**copiosus, -a, -um,** well supplied
**cor, cordis,** *n.,* heart
**coram** + *ablative,* before; in front of
**Corban,** *indecl., Hebrew,* a gift offering to God
**corona, -ae,** *f.,* crown; garland
**corpus, -oris,** *n.,* body
**corrigia, -ae,** *f.,* lace
**corripio, -ripere, -ripui, -reptus,** to arrest; punish
**corruo, -ere, -i,** to fall; collapse
**corusco (1),** to shake; flash
**cotidie,** daily
**creatura, -ae,** *f.,* creature
**crebro,** frequently; in quick succession
**credo, -ere, -idi, -itus,** to believe; believe in
**creo (1),** to create; elect
**cresco, crescere, crevi, cretus,** to grow; increase
**crimen, -inis,** *n.,* crime
**crucifigo, -figere, -fixi, -fixus,** to crucify
**crux, crucis,** *f.,* cross
**cultor, -oris,** *m.,* farmer
**cum,** when; since; although
**cum** + *abl.,* with; *sometimes attached at the end of a personal pronoun,* **mecum, tecum, secum,** *etc.*
**cur,** why?
**curo (1),** to heal
**custodio, -ire, -ii** *or* **-ivi, -itus,** to guard; watch over
**Cyreneus, -a, -um,** from Cyrene

**D**

**daemon, -is,** *m.,* demon
**daemonium, -i,** *n.,* demon
**Dalmanutha,** *indecl., city of* Dalmanutha

**damno (1),** to convict
**Daniel, -is,** *m.,* Daniel
**David,** *indecl.,* David
**de** + *abl.,* from; about
**debeo, -ere, -ui, -itus,** to owe; ought
**debilis, -e,** crippled; lame
**debitor, -is,** *m.,* debtor
**Decapoli, -orum,** *m. pl.,* Decapolis
**decem,** ten
**decet, decuit,** *impers.,* it is fitting
**decido, -dere, -di, -sus,** to fall down
**decipio, -cipere, -cepi, -ceptus,** to mislead; deceive
**declino (1),** to fall; go down
**decollo (1),** to decapitate
**decumbo, -cumbere, -cubui,** to recline; be bedridden
**decurio, -ionis,** *m.,* member of a council; commissioner
**decurro, -currere, -curri** *or* **-cucurri, -cursus,** to run quickly; hasten
**deficio, -ficere, -feci, -fectus,** to fail; fall down; run out; collapse
**definio, -ire, -ii** *or* **-ivi, -itus,** to determine
**defungor, -i, -functus sum,** to be deceased; pass away; have done with
**deinde,** thereupon
**delictum, -i,** *n.,* crime
**deliramentum, -i,** *n.,* nonsense
**demergo, -gere, -si, -sus,** to sink; submerge
**demonstro (1),** to point out
**denarius, -ii,** *m.,* coin
**denego (1),** to deny
**dens, -ntis,** *m.,* tooth
**denuo,** anew; once again
**deorsum,** down from; downward
**depono, -ponere, -posui, -positus,** to set down; take down
**depreco (1),** to pray to
**deprecor, -ari, -atus sum,** to beg
**derelinquo, -linquere, -liqui, -lictus,** to abandon; forsake
**derideo, -dere, -si, -sus,** to laugh at
**descendo, -ndere, -ndi, -nsus,** to descend
**descensus, -us,** *m.,* descent
**desertum, -i,** *n.,* wilderness
**desiderium, -ii,** *n.,* longing; desire
**desidero (1),** to wish; desire
**desolatio, -ionis,** *f.,* desolation
**desolo (1),** to abandon; desert
**destruo, -ere, -xi, -ctus,** to pull down; destroy
**desum, -esse, -fui, -futurus,** + *dative,* to be lacking (to)
**deterior, -ius,** worse
**detestor, -ari, detestatus sum,** to curse; renounce under oath
**detineo, -tinere, -tinui, -tentus,** to restrain; impede
**detrimentum, -i,** *n.,* loss; damage
**deus, -i,** *m.,* God; god
**deversorium, -ii,** *n.,* living room
**devoro (1),** to eat up
**dexter, -tra, -trum,** right; on the right
**Diabolus, -i,** *m.,* the Devil
**dico, dicere, dixi, dictus,** to say; speak
**dictum, -i,** *n.,* a saying; something said

**dies, -ei,** *m./f.,* day
**diffamo (1),** to spread around
**difficilis, -e,** difficult
**digitum, -i,** *n.,* finger; *also* **digitus, -i,** *m.*
**dignus, -a, -um,** + *genitive or ablative, or + infinitive,* worthy; worthy of; worthy to
**diiudico (1),** to judge
**dilanio (1),** to tear to pieces
**dilato (1),** to spread out
**dilectus, -a, -um,** beloved
**diligo, -ligere, -lexi, -lectus,** to esteem highly; love
**diluculum, -i,** *n.,* dawn
**dimidium, -i,** *n.,* one half; half
**dimitto, -mittere, -misi, -missus,** to dismiss; forgive; divorce
**diripio, -ripere, -ripui, -reptus,** to steal; rob
**dirumpo, -rumpere, -rupi, -ruptus,** to burst
**discedo, -cedere, -cessi, -cessus,** to leave; get away
**discerpo, -ere, -si, -tus,** to tear apart; revile; rip into
**discipulus, -i,** *m.,* student
**disco, discere, didici,** to learn
**discubitus, -us,** *m.,* a reclining at a table
**discumbo, -cumbere, -cubui, -cubitus,** to recline at the dinner table
**discus, -i,** *m.,* plate
**dispergo, -gere, -si, -sus,** to scatter
**dispertio, -ire, -ii** *or* **-ivi, -itus,** to apportion out; divide
**disputo (1),** to explain; dispute
**dissero, -ere, -ui, -tus,** to discuss
**dissipo (1),** to disperse; scatter
**dissolvo, -vere, -vi, -utus,** to break down; destroy; take apart
**disto, -stare, -steti, -status,** to be away from
**distribuo, -uere, -ui, -utus,** to distribute
**dives, divitis,** rich
**divido, -videre, -visi, -visus,** to divvy up
**divitiae, -arum,** *f. pl.,* wealth
**divulgo (1),** to spread around; divulge; publish
**do, dăre, dedi, datus,** to give
**doceo, -ere, -ui, -tus,** to teach; preach
**doctor, -oris,** *m.,* teacher
**doctrina, -ae,** *f.,* teaching
**dolor, -is,** *m.,* pain; grief
**dolus, -i,** *m.,* deceit; trick
**domicilium, -ii,** *n.,* home
**dominor, -ari, -atus sum,** + *ablative or genitive,* to rule over
**dominus, -i,** *m.,* lord; Lord God
**domo (1),** to subdue, tame
**donec,** while; until
**dono (1),** to give as a gift
**donum, -i,** *n.,* gift
**dormio, -ire, -ii** *or* **-ivi, -itus,** to sleep
**dubito (1),** to hesitate; doubt
**duco, ducere, duxi, ductus,** to lead; think; marry
**dum,** while; + *subjunctive,* until
**duo, duae, duo,** two
**duodecim,** twelve
**duritia, -ae,** *f.,* hardness; stubbornness

## E

**e(x)** + *ablative,* out of
**ecce,** behold
**ecclesia, -ae,** *f.,* church
**edissero, -ere, -ui, -tus,** to explain
**edo, -ere** *or* **esse, edi, essus,** to eat
**educo, -ducere, -duxi, -ductus,** to draw out
**effetha,** *Hebrew imperative,* be open
**efficio, -ficere, -feci, -fectus,** to produce; end up; come about
**effigies, -ei,** *f.,* form; imitation
**effundo, -fundere, -fudi, -fusus,** to pour out
**egeo, -ere, -ui,** + *ablative,* to need
**egredior, -gredi, -gressus sum,** to go out; depart
**eicio, -icere, -ieci, -iectus,** to throw out; expel
**eiulo (1),** to wail
**elevo (1),** to lift up
**Eli,** *Hebrew exclamation,* my God (cf. **Eloi**)
**elido, -dere, -si, -sus,** to break to pieces
**eligo, -ligere, -legi, -lectus,** to pick out; elect
**emendo (1),** to correct; chastise
**emitto, -mittere, -misi, -missus,** to send out
**Emmaus,** *indecl., city of* Emmaus
**emo, emere, emi, emptus,** to buy
**emundatio, -ionis,** *f.,* healing; cure
**enavigo (1),** to sail out
**enim,** for; truly
**eo, ire, ii** *or* **ivi, itus,** to go
**ergo,** therefore
**erogo (1),** to spend
**erro (1),** to go astray; make a mistake
**erubesco, -escere, -ui,** to blush; be ashamed of
**eruo, -ere, -i, -tus,** to dig out; tear out
**esca, -ae,** *f.,* food
**esurio, -ire, —, -tus,** to be hungry
**et,** and; even; **et . . . et,** both . . . and
**etiam,** even still; be that as it may
**evanesco, -escere, -ui,** to disappear
**evangelium, -ii,** *n.,* good news; good report
**evangelizo (1),** to preach; spread the word about
**evenio, -venire, -vēni, -ventus,** to occur; happen to
**evigilo (1),** to wake up
**exaestuo (1),** to grow hot; be scorched
**exaresco, -escere, -ui,** to dry up
**excelsus, -a, -um,** high
**excido, -dere, -di, -sus,** to cut out
**excipio, -cipere, -cepi, -ceptus,** to take out; exclude
**excito (1),** to rouse; awaken
**exclamo (1),** to shout out
**excutio, -cutere, -cussi, -cussus,** to shake off
**exeo, -ire, -ii** *or* **-ivi, -itus,** to go out; leave
**exerceo, -ere, -ui, -itus,** to exercise; wield; employ
**exercitus, -us,** *m.,* army
**exhibeo, -ere, -ui, -itus,** to hold forth; deliver; offer

**eximo, -imere, -emi, -emptus,** to take out, remove; release
**exinde,** next; thereupon
**existimo (1),** to wonder
**exodus, -i,** *f.,* way out; death
**exorior, -iri, -tus sum,** to rise up
**expavesco, -escere, -i,** to be frightened
**expedio, -ire, -ii** *or* **-ivi, -itus,** to be ready; be at hand
**expello, -pellere, -puli, -pulsus,** to expel; throw out
**exprobo (1),** to chastise
**exsilio, -ire, -ui,** to spring forth; spring up; jump up
**exspecto (1),** to wait for
**exspiro (1),** to expire; die
**exspuo** *or* **expuo, -uere, -ui, -utus,** to spit
**exstinguo, -guere, -xi, -ctus,** to put out
**exsurgo, -gere, -rexi,** to rise up
**extendo, -dere, -di, -tus** *or* **-sus,** to extend; reach out
**exterreo, -ere, -ui, -itus,** to frighten
**extra** + *accusative,* besides; out of; not including
**extremum, -i,** *n.,* last; **in extremis,** in the final moments of life; extreme suffering
**extrinsecus,** from the outside
**exuo, -uere, -ui, -utus,** to take off; undress

**F**

**faber, fabri,** *m.,* craftsman
**fabulor, -ari, -atus sum,** to talk
**facies, -ei,** *f.,* face; presence
**facilis, -e,** easy
**facio, facere, feci, factus,** to do; make
**fallacia, -ae,** *f.,* deceit
**falsus, -a, -um,** untrue; false
**falx, falcis,** *f.,* sickle
**fama, -ae,** *f.,* report; rumor; word
**fames, -is,** *f.,* famine
**favus, -i,** *m.,* honeycomb
**febricito (1),** to have a fever
**febris, -is,** *f.,* fever
**fellis, -is,** *f.,* bile
**femina, -ae,** *f.,* woman
**fenerator, -ris,** *m.,* moneylender; money exchanger
**fenum, -i,** *n.,* hay
**fere,** almost; nearly
**fermentum, -i,** *n.,* yeast
**fero, ferre, tuli, ablatus,** to bear; carry
**festinatio, -ionis,** *f.,* haste
**festus, -a, -um,** holiday
**ficulnea, -ae,** *f.,* a fig tree
**ficus, -i,** *f.,* fig tree; a fig
**fides, -ei,** *f.,* faith
**fiducia, -ae,** *f.,* trustworthiness
**filia, -ae,** *f.,* daughter
**filiola, -ae,** *f.,* little daughter
**filiolus, -i,** *m.,* little son
**filius, -i,** *m.,* son
**fimbria, -ae,** *f.,* border; tassel; edge
**fines, -ium,** *f. pl.,* borders; land
**fingo, fingere, finxi, fictus,** to pretend
**finis, -is,** *m.,* end
**fio, fieri, factus est,** to be made; to happen
**flagello (1),** to whip; scourge
**flagellum, -ii,** *n.,* whip

**flecto, -ctere, -xi, -ctus,** to bend
**fleo, -ere, -evi, -etus,** to cry
**fluctus, -us,** *m.,* flood; wave
**flumen, -inis,** *n.,* river
**fluxus, -us,** *m.,* flow
**fodio, fodere, fodi, fossus,** to dig
**folium, -ii,** *n.,* a leaf
**fons, -ntis,** *m.,* source; origin
**foramen, -inis,** *n.,* small opening; eye
**foras,** outside
**foris,** outside
**fornicatio, -ionis,** *f.,* adultery
**forsitan,** perhaps
**forte,** by chance; perhaps
**fortis, -e,** strong; powerful
**fortitudo, -inis,** *f.,* strength; courage
**forum, -i,** *n.,* marketplace
**fovea, -ae,** *f.,* ditch
**fractio, -ionis,** *f.,* breaking
**fragmentum, -i,** *n.,* crumb
**frango, frangere, fregi, fractus,** to break
**frater, -tris,** *m.,* brother
**fraus, fraudis,** *f.,* lie; false dealing
**fremo, -ere, -ui, -itus,** to growl
**frequenter,** frequently; often
**fretum, -i,** *n.,* strait; body of water
**frons, frondis,** *f.,* a leafy branch
**fructifico (1),** to produce fruit
**fructus, -us,** *m.,* fruit
**frumentum, -i,** *n.,* fruit; produce; crop
**fuga, -ae,** *f.,* flight; escape
**fugio, fugere, fugi, fugiturus,** to flee
**fulgeo, -gere, -si,** *or* **fulgo, -ere,** to flash
**fulgur, -uris,** *m.,* flash of lightning; splendor
**fullo, -onis,** *m.,* fuller
**fundo, -ere, fudi, fusus,** to pour out
**furor, -ari, -atus sum,** to steal
**furor, -oris,** *m.,* madness; rage
**furtum, -i,** *n.,* theft
**fustis, -is,** *m.,* club
**futurus, -a, -um,** future; about to be

**G**

**Gadareni, -orum,** *m. pl.,* Gadarene
**Galilaea, -ae,** *f.,* Galilee
**gallus, -i,** *m.,* rooster
**gaudeo, gaudere, gavisus sum,** to rejoice; be pleased
**gazophylacium, -ii,** *n.,* coin box; treasury
**gehenna, -ae,** *f.,* hell; a dump heap
**generatio, -ionis,** *f.,* generation; nation
**genimen, geniminis,** *n.,* fruit
**Gennesaret,** *indecl.,* Gennesaret
**gens, -ntis,** *f.,* nation; non-Jewish people
**genu, -us,** *n.,* knee
**Geraseni, -orum,** *m. pl.,* Gerasa
**germino (1),** to bud; germinate
**gero, -ere, gessi, gestus,** to carry on; conduct; manage; wage
**gladius, -ii,** *m.,* sword
**gloria, -ae,** *f.,* glory
**glorifico (1),** to glorify
**Golgotha, -ae,** *f., Aramaic,* skull
**Gomorraei, -orum,** *m. pl., city of* Gomorrah

**grabatum, -i,** *n.,* stretcher
**Graecus, -a, -um,** Greek
**grandis, -e,** large
**granum, -i,** *n.,* grain
**gratis,** freely
**gravo (1),** to burden; weigh down
**grex, gregis,** *m.,* flock; herd
**gusto (1),** to taste
**gutta, -ae,** *f.,* drop

**H**

**habeo, -ere, -ui, -itus,** to have; consider
**habito (1),** to inhabit
**haesito (1),** to hesitate; doubt
**Heloi,** *Hebrew,* my God!
**herba, -ae,** *f.,* plant
**heres, heredis,** *m./f.,* heir
**heritas, -tatis,** *f.,* inheritance
**Herodes, -is,** *m.,* Herod
**Herodianus, -i,** *m.,* a Herodian
**Herodias, -adis,** *f.,* Herodias
**hīc,** here
**hic, haec, hoc,** this/these
**hiems, -is,** *f.,* winter
**Hierosolyma, -ae,** *f.,* Jerusalem
**Hierosolymitas, -ae,** *m.,* resident of Jerusalem
**hodie,** today
**hodiernus, -a, -um,** of this day; today's
**holocaustoma, -atis,** *n.,* burnt offering
**holus, -eris,** *n.,* vegetable plant
**homicidium, -ii,** *n.,* homicide; murder
**homo, -inis,** *m.,* human being; man
**honorifico (1),** to honor; glorify
**honoro (1),** to honor
**hora, -ae,** *f.,* time; hour
**hortus, -i,** *m.,* garden
**Hosanna,** *Hebrew imperative,* Help; Save
**huc,** to this place; hither
**huiusmodi,** of this kind
**humilio (1),** to humble
**hymnus, -i,** *m.,* song; poem
**hypocrita, -ae,** *m.,* hypocrite; dissembler

**I**

**iaceo, -ere, -cui, -itum,** to be lying down
**Iacobus, -i,** *m.,* Jacob = James
**iacto (1),** to buffet; shake; brandish
**Iairus, -i,** *m.,* Jairus
**iam,** already; straightaway
**ianitor, -oris,** *m.,* doorman
**ianua, -ae,** *f.,* door; gate
**ibique,** there; in that place
**ideo,** on this account; therefore
**Idumaea, -ae,** *f.,* Idumea
**ieiuno (1),** to fast
**ieiunus, -a, -um,** fasting; hungry
**Ieremias, -ae,** *m.,* Jeremiah
**Iericho,** *indecl.,* Jericho
**Ierusalem,** *indecl.,* Jerusalem
**Iesus, -us** (*dat.* **-u,** *acc.* **-um,** *abl.* **-u**), *m.,* Jesus
**igitur,** therefore
**ignis, -is,** *m.,* fire
**ignoro (1),** not to know; be ignorant of
**ille, illa, illud,** that/those
**illic,** there; in that place

**illucesco, -lucescere, -luxi,** to begin to shine; become dawn
**illudo, -dere, -si, -sus,** to laugh at; mock
**imago, -inis,** *f.,* image
**immitto, -mittere, -misi, -missus,** to insert
**immolo (1),** to roast; burn as part of a sacrifice
**immundus, -a, -um,** unclean
**impero (1)** + *dative,* to command
**impetus, -us,** *m.,* rush
**impleo, -ere, -evi, -etus,** to fill up; fulfill
**impono, -ponere, -posui, -positus,** to place on
**importabilis, -e,** unbearable
**impossibilis, -e,** impossible
**impropero (1),** to assail
**imprudens, -ntis,** foolish
**impudicitia, -ae,** *f.,* shamelessness
**in** + *ablative,* in; on; + *accusative,* into
**inanis, -e,** empty; void
**incipio, -cipere, -cepi, -ceptus,** to begin
**inclino (1),** to fall
**incredulitas, -tatis,** *f.,* disbelief
**incredulus, -a, -um,** not believing; incredulous
**increpo (1),** to scold; grumble at
**incresco, -escere, -evi,** to increase; grow
**inde,** thereupon
**indico (1),** to explain
**indigeo, -ere, -ui** + *ablative,* to be in need of
**indigne,** indignantly; with great displeasure
**indignor, -ari, -atus sum,** to deem unworthy; be angry with
**induco, -ducere, -duxi, -ductus,** to lead in
**induo, -uere, -ui, -utus,** to put on; clothe
**ineo, -ire, -ii** *or* **-ivi, -itum,** to enter into; collude in
**inexstinguibilis, -e,** unable to be put out; inextinguishable
**infans, -ntis,** *m.,* child; infant
**inferum, -i,** *n.,* the lower place; the underworld
**infidelis, -e,** disloyal; untrustworthy
**infirmus, -a, -um,** weak; sick
**infremo, -ere, -ui,** to growl at; roar, rage
**ingemisco, -ere, -ui,** to sigh; groan
**ingemo, -ere, -ui,** to groan
**ingravo (1),** to be heavy; weighed down
**ingredior, -gredi, -gressus sum,** to enter into
**inicio, -icere, -ieci, -iectus,** to lay upon; throw onto
**inimicus, -i,** *m.,* enemy
**iniquitas, -tatis,** *f.,* injustice
**initium, -i,** *n.,* beginning
**innocens, -ntis,** innocent
**inopero (1),** to work; to perform
**inopia, -ae,** *f.,* lack of resources; poverty
**inquit, inquunt,** he/she/it says; they say
**inscribo, -bere, -psi, -ptus,** to write on; inscribe

**inscriptio, -ionis,** *f.,* inscription; title
**insidiator, -oris,** *m.,* conspirator; someone who sets an ambush; spy
**insidio (1),** + *dative,* to plot against
**insignis, -is,** distinguished; well-known
**insipientia, -ae,** *f.,* stupidity; ignorance
**insto, -stare, -stiti,** to stand near *or* upon; be imminent; threaten
**insulsus, -a, -um,** unsalted; tasteless
**intellectus, -us,** *m.,* understanding
**intellego, -gere, -xi, -ctus,** to understand
**inter** + *accusative,* among; between
**interficio, -ficere, -feci, -fectus,** to kill
**interpretatus, -a, -um,** translated
**interpretor, -ari, -atus sum,** to explain; translate
**interrogo (1),** to ask questions of; interrogate
**intervallum, -i,** *n.,* space; interval
**intinguo, intingere, intinxi, intinctus,** to dip; soak
**intro (1),** to enter into
**intro,** inside
**introduco, -ducere, -duxi, -ductus,** to lead into
**introeo, -ire, -ii** *or* **-ivi, -itus,** to enter
**intueor, -eri, -itus sum,** to look carefully upon
**invado, -dere, -si, -sus,** to enter upon; fall upon
**invalesco, -escere, -ui,** to grow strong; prevail
**invenio, -ire, -vēni, -ventus,** to find
**invicem,** in turn
**invidia, -ae,** *f.,* ill will
**involvo, -vere, -vi, -utus,** to wrap up; roll
**Ioannes, -is,** *m.,* John
**Ionas, -ae,** *m.,* Jonah
**Iordanes, -is,** *m.,* the Jordan River
**Ioseph,** *indecl.,* Joseph
**ipse, ipsa, ipsum,** the very; self
**ira, -ae,** *f.,* anger
**irrideo, -dere, -si, -sus,** to laugh at
**irritus, -a, -um,** invalid; useless
**irruo, -ere, -rui, -rutus,** to rush toward
**is, ea, id,** he/she/it; this
**Isaac,** *indecl.,* Isaac
**Isaias, -ae,** *m.,* Isaiah
**Iscariotes,** *indecl.,* Iscariot
**Iscarioth,** *indecl.,* Iscariot
**Israel,** *indecl.,* Israel
**iste, ista, istud,** that/this; these/those
**ita,** thus; so
**itaque,** and so; also
**iterum,** again
**iubeo, -bere, -ssi, -ssus,** to command; order
**Iudaea, -ae,** *f.,* Judea
**iudex, -icis,** *m.,* judge
**iudicium, -ii,** *n.,* judgment
**iudico (1),** to judge
**iunior, -ius,** younger
**iuramentum, -i,** *n.,* oath
**iuro (1),** to swear an oath

**iusiurandum, iurisiurandi,** *n.,* oath
**iustitia, -ae,** *f.,* divine will; justice
**iustus, -a, -um,** righteous
**iuventus, -tutis,** *f.,* youth
**iuxta** + *accusative,* close to; in accordance with

**L**

**labia, -ae,** *f.,* lip
**laboro (1),** to struggle
**lacrima, -ae,** *f.,* tear
**lacus, -us,** *m.,* pond
**lagoena, -ae,** *f.,* earthenware vessel; vase
**languidus, -a, -um,** sick
**languor, -is,** *m.,* disease; ailment
**lapido (1),** to stone
**lapis, -idis,** *m.,* stone
**lateo, -ere, -ui,** to be concealed; hidden
**latro, -onis,** *m.,* outlaw; rebel
**laudo (1),** to praise
**laus, laudis,** *f.,* praise
**lavo, -are, -avi, lavatus** *or* **lotus,** to wash
**laxo (1),** to spread out
**lectulum, -i,** *n., diminutive of* **lectus,** little bed
**lectus, -i,** *m.,* couch
**legio, -ionis,** *f.,* legion
**lego, legere, legi, lectus,** to pick; read
**lema,** *Hebrew,* why?
**lepra, -ae,** *f.,* leprosy
**leprosus, -a, -um,** afflicted with leprosy; a leper
**Levi, -is,** *m.,* Levi
**levo (1),** to lift up
**Lex, Legis,** *f.,* the Laws; the Pentateuch
**libellus, -i,** *m.,* little book; writ
**libenter,** freely; willingly; with pleasure
**liber, -bri,** *m.,* book
**libero (1),** to set free
**licet, licere, licuit** + *dative and infinitive,* it is permitted
**lignum, -i,** *n.,* wood; wooden club
**ligo (1),** to tie; bind
**lingua, -ae,** *f.,* tongue
**linteamen, -inis,** *n.,* a linen cloth
**litus, -oris,** *n.,* shore
**loco (1),** to place; contract out to someone
**locusta, -ae,** *f.,* locust; grasshopper
**longe,** far from
**loquela, -ae,** *f.,* language; speech
**loquor, loqui, locutus sum,** to speak
**luceo, -cere, -xi,** to shine
**lucerna, -ae,** *f.,* lamp
**lucidus, -a, -um,** full of light
**lucro (1),** to gain
**ludo, -dere, -si, -sus,** to play; mock
**lugeo, -gere, -xi, -ctus,** to lament
**lumbus, -i,** *m.,* loin
**lumen, -inis,** *n.,* light
**luna, -ae,** *f.,* moon
**lunaticus, -a, -um,** mad; insane
**luscus, -a, -um,** with one eye closed
**lux, lucis,** *m.,* light; dawn

**M**

**maereo, -ere,** to be sad
**maestus, -a, -um,** gloomy; despondent, depressed
**Magadan,** *indecl.,* Magadan

**Magdalene, -ae,** *f.,* the Magdalene; of Magdala
**magis,** more; even more; greater
**magister, -tri,** *m.,* teacher; master
**magistratus, -us,** *m.,* official, magistrate
**magnifico (1),** to fuss over; make a big deal of
**magnitudo, -inis,** *f.,* size
**maiestas, -tatis,** *f.,* majesty; grandeur
**maior, maius,** greater
**male,** badly
**maledico, -dicere, -dixi, -dictus** + *dative,* to curse
**mandatum, -i,** *n.,* command
**mando (1),** to entrust; commit; order
**manduco (1),** to eat
**mane,** in the morning; at dawn
**maneo, -ere, -si, -sus,** to remain
**manifesto (1),** to make clear; reveal; expose
**manifesto,** openly
**mansuesco, -escere, -evi, -etus,** to tame
**manus, -us,** *f.,* hand
**mare, -is,** *n.,* sea
**Maria, -ae,** *f.,* Mary; Mariam
**masculus, -a, -um,** male
**mater, -tris,** *f.,* mother
**Matthaeus, -i,** *m.,* Matthew
**mecum,** *see* **cum**
**medicus, -i,** *m.,* doctor
**medius, -a, -um,** midst; middle
**mel, mellis,** *n.,* honey
**melior, -ius,** *comparative of* **bonus, -a, -um,** better
**memoria, -ae,** *f.,* memory
**mendico (1),** to beg
**mens, -ntis,** *f.,* mind
**mensa, -ae,** *f.,* table
**mensura, -ae,** *f.,* measure
**mercennarius, -i,** *m.,* employee; hired man
**merces, -cedis,** *f.,* reward; payment
**mercor, -ari, -atus sum,** to buy
**mergo, -gere, -si, -sus,** to cause to sink
**messis, -is,** *f.,* harvest
**metior, -iri, mensus sum,** to measure out; reckon; judge
**metuo, -uere, -ui, -utus,** to fear; respect
**mica, -ae,** *f.,* crumb
**migro (1),** to depart
**milia, -ium,** *n. pl.,* + *genitive,* thousands
**miles, -itis,** *m.,* soldier
**minimus, -a, -um,** least; smallest
**minister, -tri,** *m.,* servant
**ministro (1)** + *dative,* to take care of; tend to
**minus,** *comparative adv. of* **parvus, -a, -um,** less
**minutum, -i,** *n.,* tiny coin
**mirabilis, -e,** wonderful; miraculous
**miror, -ari, -atus sum,** to be astonished
**misceo, -ere, -ui, -xtus,** to mix
**misereor, -eri, -rtus sum** + *genitive,* to feel sorry for; take pity on
**misericordia, -ae,** *f.,* pity; sympathy; mercy
**mitto, -ere, misi, missus,** to send

**modium, -ii,** *n.,* basket
**modo,** just now; recently
**moechor, -ari, moechatus sum,** to commit adultery
**mola, -ae,** *f.,* millstone
**molaris, -is,** belonging to a millstone
**molestus, -a, -um,** troublesome
**mons, -ntis,** *m.,* mountain
**monumentum, -i,** *n.,* grave; tomb
**morior, -i, mortuus sum,** to die
**mors, mortis,** *f.,* death
**mortiferus, -a, -um,** deadly
**moveo, -ere, movi, motus,** to move
**Moyses, -is,** *m.,* Moses
**mulier, -is,** *f.,* woman; wife
**multitudo, -inis,** *f.,* crowd of people
**multum,** greatly; much
**mundo (1),** to heal; make whole
**mundus, -a, -um,** elegant
**munus, -eris,** *n.,* gift; offering
**murmuro (1),** to whisper; murmur
**mutus, -a, -um,** mute; dumb
**myrrhatus, -a, -um,** spiced; spiced with myrrh
**mysterium, -i,** *n.,* mystery; secret rite; secret

**N**

**nam,** for
**nardus, -a, -um,** of nard (perfume from a flower)
**narro (1),** to tell; narrate
**nascor, -i, natus sum,** to be born
**natalis, -e,** birth; birthday
**natio, -ionis,** *f.,* nation
**navicula, -ae,** *f.,* small boat; skiff
**navigo (1),** to sail; navigate
**navis, -is,** *f.,* boat
**Nazarenus, -a, -um,** Nazarene; of Nazareth
**Nazareth** *(indecl.),* Nazareth
**ne,** lest; not
**nec,** nor; **ne . . . ne,** neither . . . nor
**necdum,** not yet
**necessarius, -a, -um,** necessary
**necesse,** necessary
**necessitas, -atis,** *f.,* necessity
**nego (1),** to deny
**nemo, -inis,** *m./f.,* no one
**nequam,** *indecl. adjective,* useless; worthless
**neque,** and not; **neque . . . neque,** neither . . . nor
**nequitia, -ae,** *f.,* evildoing
**nescio, -ire, -ii** *or* **-ivi, -itus,** not to know
**nihil,** nothing
**nimis,** excessively; very
**nisi,** unless; if not
**nix, nivis,** *f.,* snow
**nobilis, -e,** well born; noble; worthy
**nobiscum,** *see* **cum**
**noceo, -ere, -ui, -itum,** to harm
**nolo, nolle, nolui,** not to want
**nomen, -inis,** *n.,* name
**nomino (1),** to name; call
**nomisma, -atis,** *n.,* coin
**non,** not
**nondum,** not yet
**nonne,** No? Right? Is it not?
**nonus, -a, -um,** ninth
**nos, nostri/nostrum, nobis, nos, nobis,** we, of us, etc.

**nosco, noscere, novi, notus,** to come to know; recognize
**noster, -tra, -trum,** our; ours
**notus, -a, -um,** known; familiar
**novellus, -a, -um,** new
**novissime,** at last; finally
**novissimus, -a, -um,** newest; the very last
**novus, -a, -um,** new
**nox, noctis,** *f.,* night
**nubis, -is,** *f.,* cloud
**nubo, nubere, nupsi, nuptum** + *dative,* to wed; cover; veil; be married
**nudo (1),** to strip bare; uncover
**nudus, -a, -um,** naked
**nullus, -a, -um,** no; none; not any
**numerus, -i,** *m.,* number
**nummularius, -i,** *m.,* a money changer
**numquam,** never
**numquid,** *interrogative to begin a question,* what
**nunc,** now
**nuntio (1),** to announce; proclaim
**nuptiae, -arum,** *f. pl.,* wedding festivities
**nutriens, -ntis,** nursing
**nutrio, -ire, -ii** *or* **-ivi, -itus,** to raise; bring up

**O**

**O,** O
**ob** + *accusative,* on account of
**obcaecatus, -a, -um,** blinded
**obdormio, -ire, -ivi** *or* **-ii, -itus,** to fall asleep
**obeo, -ire, -ii** *or* **-ivi, itus,** to go meet; perish
**obliviscor, -i, oblitus sum,** + *infinitive or genitive,* to forget
**obmutesco, -escere, -ui,** to grow silent
**oboedio, -ivi, -itus** + *dative,* to be obedient to
**obscuro (1),** to cover up; darken
**obsecratio, -ionis,** *f.,* supplication; prayer
**obsecro (1),** to implore; beg
**observo (1),** to look upon; observe
**obstupesco, -escere, -pui,** to be astonished
**obumbro (1),** to cast a shadow on
**obviam** + *dative,* up to
**occido, -cidere, -cidi, -casum,** to fall, sink
**occīdo, -cīdere, -cidi, -cisus,** to kill
**occurro, -currere, -curri** *or* **-cucurri, -cursum,** + *dative* to meet; encounter
**occultus, -a, -um,** hidden
**octo,** eight
**oculus, -i,** *m.,* eye
**odium, -ii,** *n.,* hatred
**offero, -ferre, obtuli, oblatus,** to bring before; offer; exhibit
**oleum, -i,** *n.,* oil
**oliva, -ae,** *f.,* olive
**omnis, omne,** all; each; every
**onus, -eris,** *n.,* burden
**operarius, -ii,** *m.,* laborer
**operio, -ire, -ui, -tus,** to cover over
**operor, -ari, -atus sum,** to perform
**opinio, -ionis,** *f.,* opinion; rumor
**oportet, -uit,** to be necessary; appropriate

**opportune,** conveniently; easily
**opportunus, -a, -um,** opportune; suitable
**optimus, -a, -um,** *superlative of* **bonus, -a, -um,** best
**opus, -eris,** *n.,* + *dative,* work; task; duty; a need for
**oratio, -ionis,** *f.,* prayer
**orbis, orbis,** *m.,* orb; world
**orior, -iri, ortus sum,** to arise
**orno (1),** to decorate; adorn
**oro (1),** to pray
**os, oris,** *n.,* mouth; speech
**osculor, -ari, -atus sum,** to kiss
**ossum, -i,** *n.,* bone
**ostendo, -dere, -ndi, -tus** *or* **-sus,** to show
**ostento (1),** to show off; display
**ostium, -i,** *n.,* door; entrance
**ovis, -is,** *f.,* sheep

**P**

**paciscor, -isci, -tus sum,** to make a contract; agree
**paenitentia, -ae,** *f.,* repentance
**paeniteor, -eri,** to repent
**palam,** openly; **in palam,** in the open
**pallium, -i,** *n.,* a cover
**palma, -ae,** *f.,* palm; opened hand
**palpo (1),** to touch; pat
**panis, -is,** *m.,* bread; loaf
**pannus, -i,** *m.,* piece of cloth
**parabola, -ae,** *f.,* parable; riddle; metaphor; allegory
**paralyticus, -i,** *m.,* paralytic
**Paraseve, -es,** *f.,* the Day of Preparation; the day before the Sabbath
**parens, -ntis,** *m./f.,* parent
**pareo, -ere, -ui, -itum,** to appear; become visible
**pariter,** equally; alongside
**paro (1),** to make ready; prepare
**paropsis, -idis,** *f.,* small plate for desserts *or* side dishes
**pars, partis,** *f.,* part; area
**parvulus, -i,** *m.,* child
**Pascha, -atis,** *f.,* Passover
**pasco, pascere, pavi, pastus,** to feed; pasture; *in the passive voice,* to graze
**pastino (1),** to till and make furrows in the ground; prepare the land
**pastor, -oris,** *m.,* shepherd
**pater, -tris,** *m.,* father
**paterfamilias, patrisfamiliae,** *m.,* head of the household
**patientia, -ae,** *f.,* suffering; patience
**patior, -i, passus sum,** to suffer; endure
**patria, -ae,** *f.,* fatherland
**pauci, -ae, -a,** few
**paululum,** a little
**pauper, -eris,** poor
**pauperculus, -a, -um,** *diminutive of* **pauper, -eris,** poor (little)
**paveo, pavere, pavi,** to tremble with fear
**pavor, -oris,** *m.,* fear; dread
**pax, pacis,** *f.,* peace
**peccator, -oris,** *m.,* a sinner
**peccatrix, -cis,** *f.,* sinful; a sinful woman
**peccatum, -i,** *n.,* sin; fault
**pectus, -oris,** *n.,* breast

**pecunia, -ae,** *f.,* money
**pedester, -tris, -tre,** on foot
**peior, peius,** worse
**pelliceus, -a, -um,** leather; made of animal skin
**pendeo, pendere, pependi,** to depend
**penetralia, -orum,** *n. pl.,* inner chambers
**penuria, -ae,** *f.,* poverty
**per** + *accusative,* through; by means of
**pera, -ae,** *f.,* pouch; bag
**peragro (1),** to walk through; traverse
**perambulo (1),** to spread out; get around
**percipio, -cipere, -cepi, -ceptus,** to take possession of; seize
**percurro, -currere, -curri** *or* **-cucurri, -cursus,** to run through
**percutio, -tere, -ssi, -ssus,** to strike; beat
**perditio, -ionis,** *f.,* waste
**perdo, -dere, -didi, -ditus,** to destroy
**peregre,** abroad; away from home
**peregrinus, -a, -um,** traveling; foreign
**pereo, -ire, -ii** *or* **-ivi, -itus,** to die, perish; be destroyed
**perficio, -ficere, -feci, -fectus,** to make perfect
**perfodio, -odere, -odi, -ossus,** to dig through
**periclito (1),** to be in danger
**peritus, -a, -um,** experienced; skilled
**permaneo, -manere, -mansi, -mansus,** to remain to the end; endure
**permitto, -mittere, -misi, -missus,** + *dative,* to allow
**pernocto (1),** to spend the night
**perpetior, -peti, -pessus sum,** to endure
**persecutio, -ionis,** *f.,* persecution; pursuit
**persequor, -qui, -secutus sum,** to follow after; look for; persecute; hound
**persevero (1),** to adhere to; persevere
**persona, -ae,** *f.,* actor; mask; personality
**persuadeo, -dere, -si, -sum,** to persuade + *dative*
**pertineo, -ere, -ui,** to reach; extend
**pervenio, -venire, -vēni, -ventus,** to arrive
**perversus, -a, -um,** evil; wrong
**pes, pedis,** *m.,* foot
**pestilentia, -ae,** *f.,* plague; disease
**peto, -ere, -ii** *or* **-ivi, -itus,** to seek; ask for
**petra, -ae,** *f.,* rock
**petrosus, -a, -um,** rocky
**Petrus, -i,** *m.,* Peter
**phantasma, -atis,** *n.,* ghost
**Pharisaeus, -i,** *m.,* a Pharisee
**Philippus, -i,** *m.,* Philip
**phylacterium, -ii,** *n.,* amulet; phylactery
**Pilatus, -i,** *m.,* Pontius Pilate
**pilus, -i,** *m.,* hair
**piscator, -oris,** *m.,* fisherman

**pisciculus, -i,** *m.,* little fish
**piscis, -is,** *m.,* fish
**placeo, -ere, -ui, -itum,** to be pleasing to + *dative*
**plaga, -ae,** *f.,* wound; ailment
**plango, -gere, -xi, -ctus,** to strike; wail in grief
**planto (1),** to set in place; plant
**platea, -ae,** *f.,* broad street; major road
**plebs, -is,** *f.,* the people; crowd
**plecto, plectere, plexi, plectus,** to weave; braid
**plenus, -a, -um** + *ablative or genitive,* filled by; full of
**ploro (1),** to cry
**plurimus, -a, -um,** *superlative of* **magnus, -a, -um,** very many; very much
**plus, pluris,** *comparative of* **magnus, -a, -um,** more
**polliceor, -eri, -itus sum,** to promise
**pono, ponere, posui, positus,** to put; place
**pontifex, -icis,** *m.,* priest
**populus, -i,** *m.,* people; the common people
**porcus, -i,** *m.,* pig
**porrigo, -rigere, -rexi, -rectus,** to extend; offer
**porro,** at a distance; furthermore
**porta, -ae,** *f.,* gate
**portentum, -i,** *n.,* portent; sign
**porto (1),** to bring; carry
**possessio, -ionis,** *f.,* possession
**possibilis, -e,** doable; possible
**possideo, -sidere, -sedi, -sessus,** to own
**possum, posse, potui,** to be able
**post** + *accusative,* after; behind; *as an adv.,* after
**postea,** afterward
**posteaquam,** after
**postquam,** after
**postulo (1),** to ask for
**potens, -ntis,** powerful
**potestas, -tatis,** *f.,* power; authority
**potius,** rather
**poto, potare, potatus** *or* **potus,** to drink
**potus, -us,** *m.,* a drink
**prae** + *ablative,* before; in front of; *as an adv.,* before; previously
**praecedo, -cedere, -cessi, -cessus,** to go on before; to lead the way
**praeceps, -cipitis,** *n.,* teaching
**praeceptor, -oris,** *m.,* teacher
**praeceptum, -i,** *n.,* commandment; order; precept; teaching
**praecessor, -oris,** *m.,* superior; *literally,* one who walks in front
**praecipio, -cipere, -cepi, -ceptus** + *dative,* to instruct; order
**praecogito (1),** to think ahead
**praedico (1),** to preach
**praedico, -dicere, -dixi, -dictus,** to predict
**praedium, -i,** *n.,* farm; field
**praeeo, -ire, -ii** *or* **-ivi, -itus,** to go before; go in front of
**praeficio, -ficere, -feci, -factus,** to accomplish
**praegnans, -ntis,** pregnant
**praegredior, -gredi, -gressus sum,** to go before; precede
**praemeditor, -ari, -atus sum,** to plan beforehand

**praemoneo, -ere, -ui, -itus,** to forewarn
**praeparo (1),** to make ready; equip
**praeses, -idis,** *m.,* governor; ruler of a district
**praesto,** *indecl.,* available; at hand
**praeter** + *accusative,* besides; except for
**praeterea,** therefore
**praetereo, -ire, -ii** *or* **-ivi, -itus,** to pass by
**praetorium, -ii,** *n.,* headquarters; governor's residence
**praevaleo, -ere, -ui,** to prevail; succeed; be victorious
**praevenio, -venire, -vēni, -ventus,** to come before; anticipate
**pressura, -ae,** *f.,* pressure; distress
**pretiosus, -a, -um,** expensive
**primus, -a, -um,** *superlative of* **prae**, first
**princeps, -cipis,** *m.,* leader
**principatus, -us,** *m.,* imperial authority
**principor, -ari,** to rule
**prior, prius,** earlier
**priusquam,** before
**pro** + *ablative,* before; on behalf of; *as an adv.,* before
**procedo, -cedere, -cessi, -cessus,** to go forth
**procella, -ae,** *f.,* storm
**procido, -cidere, -cidi,** to fall before; fall forward
**procumbo, -cumbere, -cubui, -cubitus,** to lean down; fall forward
**prodigium, -ii,** *n.,* prodigy; portent
**proditor, -oris,** *m.,* traitor
**prodo, -dere, -didi, -ditus,** to reveal; make known
**produco, -ducere, -duxi, -ductus,** to lead forth
**proelium, -i,** *n.,* battle
**profecto,** certainly
**proficio, -ficere, -feci, -fectum,** to work; succeed
**proficiscor, -i, -fectus sum,** to set out
**profluvium, -ii,** *n.,* flow
**profugio, -fugere, -fugi, -fugiturus,** to flee; escape
**profundum, -i,** *n.,* deep
**progredior, -gredi, -gressus sum,** to come forth; advance
**prohibeo, -ere, -ui, -itus,** to prevent; hold back
**proicio, -icere, -ieci, -iectus,** to cast out in front of
**prolixus, -a, -um,** extensive; comprehensive; wordy
**promissus, -us,** *m.,* a promise
**promitto, -mittere, -misi, -missus,** to put forth; promise
**promptus, -a, -um,** ready at hand; prepared
**prope,** nearby
**propero (1),** to rush; hurry
**propheta, -ae,** *m.,* prophet
**propheto (1),** to prophesy
**propono, -ponere, -posui, -positus,** to place before; prefer
**propositio, -ionis,** *f.,* presentation; conception
**propter** + *accusative,* on account of

**propterea,** for that reason
**prosum, prodesse, profui,** to be helpful to; be useful to
**protinus,** straightaway
**prout,** insofar as
**provolvo, -vere, -vi, -utus,** to roll forth; bow down
**proximus, -a, -um,** nearby
**proximus, -i,** *m.,* a neighbor
**Psalmi, -orum,** *m. pl.,* Psalms
**pseudochristus, -i,** *m.,* false Messiah
**pseudopropheta, -ae,** *m.,* false prophet
**publicanus, -i,** *m.,* tax collector; public contractor
**puella, -ae,** *f.,* girl
**puer, -i,** *m.,* boy
**pugillo,** carefully
**pullus, -i,** *m.,* young animal; colt
**pulvis, -eris,** *m.,* dust
**puppis, -is,** *f.,* stern
**purgo (1),** to clean; cleanse
**purpura, -ae,** *f.,* purple (cloak)
**purus, -a, -um,** clean; pure
**pusillum,** a little
**pusillus, -a, -um,** small; insignificant
**puto (1),** to think

## Q

**quā,** *place* where
**quadraginta,** forty
**quadrans, -antis,** *m.,* a fourth part; one fourth of a penny
**quaero, -rere, -sivi, -situs,** to look for; ask about
**qualis, -e,** what sort; such a sort
**qualiter,** just as
**quam,** how; than
**quamdiu,** how long; so long as
**quando,** when; *after* **ne,** ever; in any way
**quantus, -a, -um,** how many; as many
**quare,** for what/which reason; why
**quartus, -a, -um,** fourth
**quasi,** as if; like
**quattuor,** four
**quemadmodum,** just as; how
**qui, quae, quod,** who, which
**quia,** because; since; that
**quicumque, quaecumque, quodcumque,** whosoever; whatsoever
**quid,** why? what?
**quidam, quaedam, quod[d]am,** a certain; some
**quidem,** indeed; in fact
**quidnam,** what?, whatsover?
**quingenti, -ae, -a,** five hundred
**quinquageni, -ae, -a,** fifty; fifty each
**quinquaginta,** fifty
**quinque,** five
**quippe,** surely; obviously
**quis, quid,** who, what?
**quisnam, quidnam,** whoever, whatever
**quispiam, quidpiam,** a certain; some
**quisquam, quaequam, quicquam** *or* **quidquam,** anyone; anything
**quisquis, quidquid,** whosoever, whatsoever
**qum,** *Hebrew,* Arise!

**quo,** to what place; to where
**quoadusque,** up until what point?
**quocumque,** to wheresoever
**quod,** because; that
**quomodo,** how
**quoniam,** since; that
**quoque,** and also
**quot,** how many
**quotquot,** as many as
**quousque,** until when

**R**

**Rabbi,** *indecl.,* Rabbi; Teacher
**Rabboni,** *indecl.,* Rabbi; Teacher
**radix, -cis,** *f.,* root
**ramus, -i,** *m.,* branch
**rapio, -ere, -ui, -tus,** to carry off by force; steal
**reaedifico (1),** to rebuild
**recedo, -cedere, -cessi, -cessum,** to withdraw
**recipio, -cipere, -cepi, -ceptus,** to take back; recover
**recordor, -ari, -atus sum,** to remember
**recte,** correctly; properly
**rectus, -a, -um,** straight
**recumbo, -cumbere, -cubui,** to lay down; recline at a table
**reddo, -dere, -didi, -ditus,** to give back; render
**redemptio, -ionis,** *f.,* redemption; a buying back
**redeo, -ire, -ii** *or* **-ivi, -itus,** to go back; return
**redimo, -ere, -emi, -emptus,** to buy back; redeem
**reduco, -ducere, -duxi, -ductus,** to lead back; accompany
**refectio, -ionis,** *f.,* dining room
**refero, -ferre, rettuli, relatus,** to bear back; report
**reficio, -ficere, -feci, -fectus,** to repair
**refrigesco, -frigescere, -frixi,** to grow cold
**refulgeo, -gere, -si,** to shine back
**regeneratio, -ionis,** *f.,* rebirth
**regio, -ionis,** *f.,* area; region
**regnum, -i,** *n.,* kingdom
**regredior, -gredi, -gressus sum,** to withdraw from
**reicio, -icere, -ieci, -iectus,** to throw down; discard
**relinquo, -liqui, -lectus,** to leave behind
**reliquiae, -arum,** *f. pl.,* leavings
**reliquus, -a, -um,** left over; left behind; the remaining
**remetior, -iri, -mensus sum,** to measure out again
**remigo (1),** to row
**remissio, -ionis,** *f.,* forgiveness; remission
**remitto, -mittere, -misi, -missus,** to send back
**renuntio (1),** to bring word; report back
**repente,** suddenly
**repleo, -ere, -evi, -etus,** to fill up
**reprehendo, -dere, -i, -sus,** to hold back; catch
**reprobo (1),** to disapprove of; condemn; reject
**repudium, -ii,** *n.,* repudiation; divorce
**requiesco, -escere, -evi, -etus,** to rest

**requiro, -quirere, -quisivi** *or* **-quisii, -quisitus,** to look for; ask after
**rescindo, -scindere, -scidi, -scissus,** to rescind; repeal
**resideo, -sidere, -sedi,** to sit down
**respicio, -spicere, -spexi, -spectus,** to have thought for; consider
**respicio, -spicere, -spexi, -spectus,** to look around; look back
**resplendeo, -ere,** to shine
**respondeo, -ere, -di, -sus,** to answer
**responsum, -i,** *n.,* answer
**restituo, -tuere, -tui, -tutus,** to restore; make whole
**resurgo, -gere, -rexi, -rectum,** to rise up again
**resurrectio, -ionis,** *f.,* resurrection
**resuscito (1),** to revive; renew
**rete, -is,** *n.,* net
**retineo, -tinere, -tinui, -tentus,** to hold back; keep
**retro,** behind
**reus, -a, -um,** accused; guilty of
**revelo (1),** to reveal
**revereor, -eri, -itus sum,** to respect; revere
**revertor, -verti, -versus sum,** to turn back; go away
**revolvo, -vere, -vi, -utus,** to roll back; reveal
**rex, regis,** *m.,* king
**rigo (1),** to moisten
**rogo (1),** to ask
**rubicundus, -a, -um,** red
**rubus, -i,** *m.,* bush
**rudis, -e,** rough; raw
**Rufus, -i,** *m.,* Rufus
**rumor, -oris,** *m.,* reputation
**rumpo, rumpere, rupi, ruptus,** to burst
**ruo, -ere, -i, -tus,** to fall into ruin
**rursum, rursus,** again
**rutilo (1),** to grow red

**S**

**sabacthani,** *Hebrew,* you have forsaken me
**Sabbatum, -i,** *n.,* the Sabbath
**sacerdos, -otis,** *m.,* priest
**sacrificium, -i,** *n.,* sacrifice
**Sadduces, -ei,** *m.,* a Sadducee
**saeculum, -i,** *n.,* generation; age; the people of an age
**saepe,** often
**saepes, -is,** *f.,* fence; hedge
**saevus, -a, -um,** savage; wild
**sal, -is,** *n.,* salt
**salio, -ire, -ivi, -itus,** to salt
**Salome,** *indecl.,* Salome
**salto (1),** to dance
**salutatio, -ionis,** *f.,* greetings
**saluto (1),** to greet; bless
**salvus, -a, -um,** safe; saved
**Samaritani, -orum,** *m. pl.,* of Samaria; Samaritans
**sanctus, -a, -um,** holy
**sandalium, -ii,** *n.,* sandals
**sanguis, -inis,** *m.,* blood
**sano (1),** to heal
**sanus, -a, -um,** healthy; whole
**sapienter,** wisely
**sapientia, -ae,** *f.,* wisdom
**sapio, -ere, -ivi** *or* **-ii,** to know; be wise about

**sata, -orum,** *n. pl.,* grain; crops
**Satanas, -ae,** *m.,* Satan
**satisfacio, -facere, -feci, -factus,** to fulfill; satisfy
**saturo (1),** to fill up; satisfy
**saxum, -i,** *n.,* rock
**scabellum, -i,** *n.,* footstool
**scandalizo (1),** to cause to stumble
**scandalum, -i,** *n.,* impediment; stumbling block
**scindo, scindere, scidi, scissus,** to cut; tear
**scio, -ire, -ii** *or* **-ivi, -itus,** to know
**scissura, -ae,** *f.,* rip; tear
**scriba, -ae,** *m.,* a scribe
**scribo, -ere, scripsi, scriptus,** to write
**scriptura, -ae,** *f.,* writing; Scripture
**secedo, -cedere, -cessi, -cessus,** to go away
**secessus, -us,** *m.,* departure
**secreto,** in secret
**sector, -ari, -atus sum,** to follow eagerly; run after
**secum,** *see* **cum**
**secundum** + *accusative,* according to; along
**secundus, -a, -um,** following; second; favorable
**securus, -a, -um,** without worries; secure
**secus** + *accusative,* along; nearby
**sed,** but
**sedeo, sedere, sedi, sessus,** to sit
**sedes, -is,** *f.,* seat; chair; throne
**seditio, -ionis,** *f.,* insurrection; disagreement
**seditiosus, -a, -um,** seditious; plotting; conniving
**seduco, -ducere, -duxi, -ductus,** to lead astray
**semen, -inis,** *n.,* seed
**semens, -ntis,** *f.,* the act of sowing; seeding
**semetipsum,** *compound intensive pronoun from* **se + met + ipsum,** his/her/their very self/selves. *Note also forms such as* **temetipsum, vosmetipsos,** *etc.*
**semino (1),** to sow seeds
**semita, -ae,** *f.,* path
**semper,** always
**sempiternus, -a, -um,** everlasting
**seniores, -ium,** *m. pl.,* elders
**sensus, -us,** *m.,* a perceiving; observation
**sentio, -tire, -si, -sus,** to feel; perceive
**seorsum,** apart; separately
**separatim,** privately
**separo (1),** to separate
**sepelio, sepelire, sepelii** *or* **sepelivi, sepultus,** to bury; give the funeral rites
**septem,** seven
**septimus, -a, -um,** seventh
**sepulcrum, -i,** *n.,* tomb
**sepultura, -ae,** *f.,* burial
**sequor, sequi, secutus sum,** to follow; come next
**serenus, -a, -um,** calm
**sermo, -onis,** *m.,* talk; speech
**sero,** late at night
**serpens, -ntis,** *m./f.,* serpent; snake
**servo (1),** to save
**servus, -i,** *m.,* slave; servant

**sex,** six
**sexagesimus, -a, -um,** sixtieth
**sexaginta,** sixty
**sextus, -a, -um,** six
**si,** if
**sic,** thus; so
**sicco (1),** to dry out
**sicut,** thus; as
**Sidon, -onis,** *f.,* city of Sidon
**signum, -i,** *n.,* sign; evidence
**silentium, -ii,** *n.,* silence
**sileo, -ere, -ui,** to be quiet; rest
**silvester, -tris, -tre,** of the woods; wild
**similis, -e,** like; similar to
**similiter,** in the same way; similarly
**similitudo, -inis,** *f.,* likeness; comparison; parable; riddle
**Simon, -is,** *m.,* Simon
**simplex, -icis,** simple; straightforward; good
**simul,** at the same time
**simulo (1),** to imitate; make a pretense of
**sinapis, -is,** *n.,* mustard plant
**sindon, -is,** *f.,* linen; sheet; covering of fine cloth
**sine** + *ablative,* without
**singillatim,** one at a time; individually
**singularis, -e,** alone
**singulis,** one at a time, individually
**singulus, -a, -um,** individual; one
**sinister, -tra, -trum,** left; on the left
**sino, sinere, sivi, situs,** to allow, permit
**Sion,** *indecl.,* Zion
**siquidem,** since indeed
**socius, -i,** *m.,* friend
**socrus, -us,** *m./f.,* father or motherinlaw
**Sodomi, -orum,** *m. pl.,* city of Sodom
**sol, -is,** *m.,* sun
**soleo, -ere, solitus sum,** to be accustomed to
**solitudo, -inis,** *f.,* solitude; wilderness
**sollemnis, -is,** solemn; holy
**sollicitudo, -inis,** *f.,* care; anxiety
**solus, -a, -um,** alone; sole
**solvo, -vere, -ui** *or* **-ii, -utus,** to set free; untie
**somnus, -i,** *m.,* sleep
**sonitus, -us,** *m.,* sound
**soror, -oris,** *f.,* sister
**sors, sortis,** *f.,* lot; roll of the dice
**spargo, -gere, -si, -sus,** to scatter
**spatium, -ii,** *n.,* space; time
**species, -ei,** *f.,* appearance
**spelunca, -ae,** *f.,* cave
**spectaculum, -i,** *n.,* event; scene
**spero (1),** to hope
**spica, -ae,** *f.,* ear of grain
**spiculator, -oris,** *m.,* scout; spy; explorer
**spina, -ae,** *f.,* thorn
**spineus, -a, -um,** spiky; jagged
**spiritus, -us,** *m.,* spirit
**splendentius, -a, -um,** radiant
**splendor, -oris,** *m.,* brightness
**spolia, -orum,** *n. pl.,* goods; spoils
**spondeo, spondere, spopondi, sponsus,** to pledge
**spongia, -ae,** *f.,* sponge

**sponsus, -i,** *m.,* groom
**sporta, -ae,** *f.,* basket
**spumo (1),** to foam; froth
**stadium, -ii,** *n.,* a stade (a distance of about two hundred yards)
**stagnum, -i,** *n.,* lake
**statim,** immediately
**statuo, -uere, -ui, -utus,** to set up
**stella, -ae,** *f.,* star
**sterno, sternere, stravi, stratus,** to spread; cover
**sterquilinium, -ii,** *n.,* dung pit
**sto, -are, steti, status,** to stop; stand
**stola, -ae,** *f.,* robe
**strideo, -ere, -i** *or* **strido, -ere, -i,** to hiss; shriek
**structura, -ae,** *f.,* a building; construction
**stultitia, -ae,** *f.,* foolishness; stupidity
**stultus, -a, -um,** foolish; stupid
**stupefacio, -facere, -feci, -factus,** to strike dumb; stun
**stupeo, -ere, -ui,** to be astonished
**stupor, -oris,** *m.,* astonishment
**suadeo, -dere, -si, -sus,** to persuade
**sub** + *ablative,* under
**subduco, -ducere, -duxi, -ductus,** to bring up; dock
**subito,** immediately
**subiugalis, -e,** used to the yoke; broken
**subsequor, -i, -secutus,** to follow from behind
**substantia, -ae,** *f.,* resource; wealth
**substerno, -sternere, -stravi, -stratus,** to scatter below
**subtus,** beneath
**subverto, -tere, -ti, -sus,** to subvert; cause to rebel
**succlamo (1),** to cry out
**sudor, -is,** *m.,* sweat
**suffero, -ferre, sustuli, sublatus,** to endure; suffer
**sufficio, -ficere, -feci, -fectus,** to suffice; be enough
**suffoco (1),** to choke out; suffocate
**sui, sibi, se, se,** *3rd person reflexive pronoun*
**sum, esse, fui, futurus,** to be
**summitto, -mittere, -misi, -missus,** to send underneath; pass through; lower down
**summus, -a, -um,** highest; high
**sumo, sumere, sumpsi, sumptus,** to take up
**super** + *accusative or ablative,* upon; on; concerning
**superbia, -ae,** *f.,* pride
**supero (1),** to overcome
**superscriptio, -ionis,** *f.,* inscription
**supersum, -esse, -fui,** to be left over
**supervenio, -venire, -vēni, -ventus,** to fall upon; attack
**supplementum, -i,** *n.,* patch
**supra,** above; + *accusative,* about
**suprascriptio, -ionis,** *f.,* inscription
**surdus, -a, -um,** deaf
**surgo, -gere, -rexi, -rectus,** to get up; rise up

**sursum,** upward
**suscipio, -cipere, -cepi, -ceptus,** to undertake
**suscito (1),** to lift up; revive
**suspendo, -dere, -di, -sus,** to hang on; fix on
**suspicio, -spicere, -spexi, -spectus,** to look up to; honor
**sustineo, -tinere, -tinui,** to hold up; stop; support; endure
**suus, -a, -um,** his/her/its own
**synagoga, -ae,** *f.,* synagogue
**Syrophoenissa, -ae,** *f.,* Syrophoenician woman

**T**

**tabernaculum, -i,** *n.,* tent
**taceo, -ere, -ui, -itus,** to be silent
**taedeo, -ere,** to be tired; be stressed
**talis, -e,** such; so great a(n)
**Talitha,** *indecl., Aramaic,* little girl
**tam,** so, thus
**tamen,** nevertheless
**tamquam,** as; like
**tango, tangere, tetigi, tactus,** to touch
**tantum,** only
**tantummodo,** just; only
**tantus, -a, -um,** such; so great
**tardus, -a, -um,** slow
**tectum, -i,** *n.,* dwelling; roof
**tecum,** *see* **cum**
**tegula, -ae,** *f.,* rafter
**teloneum, -i,** *n.,* tollbooth; tax table
**temetipsum,** *see* **semetipsum**
**tempestas, -atis,** *f.,* storm; weather
**Templum, -i,** *n.,* the Temple in Jerusalem
**temporalis, -e,** temporary
**tempus, -oris,** *n.,* time
**tenebra, -ae,** *f.,* darkness; gloom
**tenebrosus, -a, -um,** dark; full of shadows
**teneo, -ere, -ui, -ntus,** to hold
**tener, -a, -um,** tender
**tentatio, -ionis,** *f.,* temptation
**tento (1),** to tempt; taunt
**ter,** three times
**tergeo, -gere, -si, -sus** *or* **tergo, -ere,** to rub; wipe off
**terminus, -i,** *m.,* boundary line
**terra, -ae,** *f.,* land; earth
**terrae motus, -us,** *m.,* earthquake
**terreo, -ere, -ui, -itus,** to frighten
**terror, -oris,** *m.,* terror; fear
**tertius, -a, -um,** third
**testamentum, -i,** *n.,* testament
**testificor, -ari, -atus sum,** to bear witness; attest
**testimonium, -i,** *n.,* witness; evidence
**testis, -is,** *m./f.,* witness
**testor, -ari, testatus sum,** to testify; bear witness
**tetrarcha, -ae,** *m.,* tetrarch
**Thaddaeus, -i,** *m.,* Thaddeus
**thesaurus, -i,** *m.,* treasure
**Thomas, -ae,** *m.,* Thomas
**thronus, -i,** *m.,* throne
**tibicen, -inis,** *m.,* flute player
**Timaeus, -i,** *m.,* Timaeus
**timeo, -ere, -ui,** to fear; be afraid
**timidus, -a, -um,** timid
**timor, -oris,** *m.,* fear
**titulus, -i,** *m.,* title; plaque; sign

**tolerabilis, -e,** tolerable
**tollo, tollere, sustuli, sublatus,** to lift up; destroy
**tonitruum, -i,** *n.,* thunder
**torcular, -is,** *n.,* wine cellar
**torqueo, -quere, -si, -tus,** to torture
**totus, -a, -um,** whole; entire
**tracto (1),** to treat; consider
**traditio, -ionis,** *f.,* a handing over; surrender
**traditor, -is,** *m.,* traitor
**trado, -dere, -didi, -ditus,** to hand over; betray
**traho, -here, -xi, -ctus,** to draw; drag
**tranquillitas, -atis,** *f.,* calm; peacefulness
**trans** + *accusative,* across; through
**transcendo, -dere, -di, -sus,** to pass over
**transeo, -ire, -ii** *or* **-ivi, -itus,** to pass through
**transfero, -ferre, -tuli, -latus,** to carry across; transport
**transfiguro (1),** to change shape; change image
**transfreto (1),** to transport back; cross over
**transgredior, -gredi, -gressus sum,** to pass through; pass over
**trecenti,** three hundred
**tremo, -ere, -ui,** to tremble
**tremor, -oris,** *m.,* trembling
**tres, tria,** three
**tribulatio, -ionis,** *f.,* tribulation
**tribunal, -is,** *n.,* tribunal
**tribunus, -i,** *m.,* tribune; politician
**tribus, -us,** *m.,* tribe
**tributum, -i,** *n.,* tax
**tricesimus, -a, -um,** thirtieth
**triduum, -i,** *n.,* a three-day period; three days
**triginta,** thirty
**tristis, -e,** sad; gloomy
**tristitia, -ae,** *f.,* sorrow
**tu, tui, tibi, te, te,** you (sg.), of you, etc.
**tuba, -ae,** *f.,* horn
**tumultuor, -ari, -atus sum,** to make a disturbance
**tumultus, -us,** *m.,* uproar
**tunc,** then; thereupon
**tunica, -ae,** *f.,* tunic; shirt
**turba, -ae,** *f.,* crowd
**turbo (1),** to stir up; disturb
**turris, -is,** *f.,* tower
**tuus, -a, -um,** your (sg.); yours
**Tyrus** *or* **Tyros, -i,** *m.,* Tyre

**U**

**ubi,** where; when
**ubicumque,** everywhere; wherever
**ubique,** everywhere
**ullus, -a, -um,** any; anyone, anything
**ultio, -ionis,** *f.,* revenge
**ultra** + *accusative,* beyond
**ultra,** any longer, anymore
**ultro,** on its own; without being asked
**umbra, -ae,** *f.,* shade
**umerus, -i,** *m.,* shoulder
**umor, -oris,** *m.,* moisture
**umquam,** even
**unā,** + **cum,** together with
**unde,** when

**undecim,** eleven
**undique,** from everywhere
**ungo, -ere, unxi, unctus,** to put oil on; oil
**unguentum, -i,** *n.,* perfume
**unguo, ung(u)ere, unxi, unctus,** to anoint
**unicus, -a, -um,** sole; only
**universus, -a, -um,** all; entire
**unoculus, -a, -um,** one-eyed
**unus, -a, -um,** one
**unusquisque, unaquisque, unumquidque,** each one
**urceus, -i,** *m.,* pitcher
**usque,** from everywhere; up until
**usquequo,** until what point?
**ut,** + *indic.,* when; since; + *subjunc.,* that, so that
**uter, utris,** *m.,* leather bag; skin for wine
**utilis, -e,** useful
**utique,** most assuredly
**uxor, -oris,** *f.,* wife

## V

**vacuus, -a, -um,** empty; empty-handed
**vado,** to go; walk
**vae,** woe
**vah,** alas
**valde,** really; very much
**valeo, -ere, -ui, valiturus,** to be healthy; prevail
**validus, -a, -um,** powerful
**vanus, -a, -um,** vain
**vapulo (1),** to be flogged
**varius, -a, -um,** diverse; differing
**vas, vasis,** *n.,* vessel; dish; utensil
**vasum, -i,** *n.,* vase
**vehementer,** violently
**vel,** or; either; perhaps
**vello, vellere, velli** *or* **vulsi** *or* **volsi, vulsus** *or* **volsus,** to pick
**velo (1),** to cover up; veil
**velum, -i,** *n.,* curtain; covering
**velut,** like
**vendo, -ere, -idi, -itus,** to sell
**veneo, -ire, -ii, -iturus,** to sell
**venio, -ire, veni, ventum,** to come
**venter, -tris,** *m.,* stomach
**ventus, -i,** *m.,* wind; a windstorm
**venumdo, -dăre, -dedi, -datus,** to give for sale
**verax, -acis,** truthful
**verbum, -i,** *n.,* word; speech
**vere,** truly
**vereor, -eri, -itus sum,** to fear
**veritas, -atis,** *f.,* truth
**vermis, -is,** *m.,* worm
**vero,** truly; but
**versus,** facing; toward
**versutia, -ae,** *f.,* craftiness; slyness
**verto, -ere, -i, versus,** to turn to; go
**verumtamen,** but truly
**vesper, -eris** *or* **-eri,** *m.,* evening; evening star
**vester, -tra, -trum,** you (pl.); yours
**vestimentum, -i,** *n.,* clothing
**vestio, -ire, -ii** *or* **-ivi, -itus,** to dress
**vestis, -is,** *f.,* clothing; attire
**vestitus, -a, -um,** dressed
**veto (1),** to prevent; deny
**vetus, -eris,** old
**vexo (1),** to disturb; make ill; torment

**via, -ae,** *f.,* way; road
**victus, -us,** *m.,* means of living
**vicus, -i,** *m.,* village
**video, -ere, vidi, visus,** to see
**vidua, -ae,** *f.,* widow
**vigilia, -ae,** *f.,* watch
**vigilo (1),** to be awake; be on guard; keep watch
**villa, -ae,** *f.,* villa; country house; farm
**vincio, -cire, -xi, -ctus,** to bind
**vinco, vincere, vici, victus,** to overcome; vanquish
**vinculum, -i,** *n.,* chain
**vinea, -ae,** *f.,* vineyard
**vinum, -i,** *n.,* wine
**violo (1),** to injure; dishonor
**vir, viri,** *m.,* man
**virga, -ae,** *f.,* walking stick
**viridis, -e,** green
**virtus, -tutis,** *f.,* power
**vis, vi** *(dat. and abl.),* **vim** *(acc.),* power; violence; **vires, -ium** *(pl.), f.,* strength
**visio, -ionis,** *f.,* vision
**visus, -us,** *m.,* vision; dream
**vita, -ae,** *f.,* life
**vitis, -is,** *f.,* grapevine
**vivo, vivere, vixi, victus,** to live
**vix,** scarcely
**vobiscum,** *see* **cum**
**voco (1),** to call
**volo, velle, volui, voliturus,** to wish; want
**volucris, -is,** *f.,* bird
**voluntas, -tatis,** *f.,* will
**voluptas, -tatis,** *f.,* pleasure
**volutor, -ari, volutus sum,** to roll about
**vos, vestri/vestrum/vobis, vos, vobis,** you (pl.), of you, *etc.*
**vosmetipsos, vosmetipsi,** *see* **semetipsum**
**vox, -cis,** *f.,* voice
**vulnero (1),** to wound
**vultus, -us,** *m.,* face

**Z**

**Zebedaeus, -i,** *m.,* Zebedee
**Zelotes, -ae,** *m.,* the eager one; zealous one
**zona, -ae,** *f.,* belt